THE MIND AND ART OF
COVENTRY PATMORE

Coventry Patmore

The Mind and Art of
COVENTRY
PATMORE

by

J. C. REID

The Macmillan Company

NEW YORK

Copyright 1957
by Routledge & Kegan Paul Ltd

TO MY WIFE

*Made and Printed in Great Britain
by William Clowes and Sons, Limited
London and Beccles*

Foreword

THIS WORK BEGAN as an attempt to assess the particular quality of Coventry Patmore's poetry, as seen by a mid-twentieth-century reader, and to do some homage to a personality who seems to me to have been particularly striking even in an age of strong personalities. But I soon found that Patmore's poetry could hardly be estimated in its depth and breadth without a fairly detailed study of his reading and especially of his sources, and that this, in turn, led inevitably to his prose writings, both matters which have been neglected by previous critics. In tracing the development of Patmore's ideas, I became convinced not only that the generally accepted estimate of his work is less than just to his real achievement but also that such an estimate is based upon an imperfect knowledge of his whole production and of the man himself.

The need for some such re-appraisal as I have attempted is underlined by a passing comment by that usually perceptive writer Martin Turnell which chanced to catch my eye as I was completing this study. In an article in *The Commonweal*, May 13, 1955, Mr. Turnell glancingly said, 'In Patmore we find a highly personal and decidedly Freudian sexuality masquerading as Divine Love.' It is because I believe that such a view misrepresents the nature of Patmore's poetry as completely as it ignores the sources of his inspiration that what began as a small study of Patmore's poetry has broadened out into an attempt to see Patmore whole, in his prose as well as in his poetry, and to present as complete an exegesis of his thought as possible.

I am indebted for the opportunities to gather material for this book to the United States Educational Foundation in New Zealand, which provided me with a travel grant, and to the University of Wisconsin, which granted funds to enable me to work there, and to the Institute of International Education, for a travel and study grant to enable me to work in the libraries of the Eastern United States. It is almost impossible to complete such a project as this in

Foreword

New Zealand, where library facilities are limited, and where access to documents must be indirect and unsatisfactory. Without the generous help of these American educational institutions this book would never have been completed.

I owe a particular debt of gratitude to Dr. Helen C. White, of the University of Wisconsin, that fine scholar whose advice and encouragement meant so much to me in the early stages of my research. While I must take responsibility for the final form of the work, Miss White's scholarly example has been one of the most important factors in its making. To my colleagues in the English Department of Auckland University College, Professor S. Musgrove, Mr. M. K. Joseph and Dr. W. Pearson, I offer sincere thanks for continued encouragement and help.

I must record, too, my indebtedness to the writings of Mr. Frederick Page, the foremost living Patmore scholar. His deep love for the poet first stimulated my own interest in Patmore; the fact that Mr. Page's name occurs so often in the pages that follow is an indication of my high respect for his work, even when I have found myself compelled to disagree with some of his conclusions.

I have also many other helps and courtesies to acknowledge, especially from librarians. Among those to whom I would particularly extend my thanks for special facilities, generously given, and for permission to examine, and quote from, papers are Rev. Father Terence L. Connolly, S.J., Librarian of the Boston College Library; Alexander P. Clark, Curator of Manuscripts, Princeton University Library; and Gilbert H. Doane, Librarian of the University of Wisconsin. Also of great assistance were the staffs of the New York Public Library and of the Boston Public Library. To the Council of my own University College, for granting me a year's special leave to engage in this research, and to Mr. Arthur Sandall, Auckland University College Librarian, and his staff, for their diligence and patience in seeking out-of-the-way material for me, my best thanks.

Above all, perhaps, I am indebted to my wife for untiring patience, encouragement and practical assistance, including that of typing the final draft of the book.

The deficiencies of the work, I need hardly add, are wholly my own.

J. C. REID

Auckland University College,
New Zealand.

Contents

Contents

PART ONE

INTRODUCTION

I

The Fate of a Reputation

OR ABOUT A QUARTER OF A CENTURY, Coventry Patmore was one of the most popular of Victorian poets. In parts, and as a whole, his 'domestic epic', *The Angel in the House*, was not only a critical success, but went into five editions in nine years. It has been estimated that, without counting a popular edition of 1887, a quarter of a million copies were sold between its first appearance in 1854 and the poet's death in 1896. Yet his later work, *The Unknown Eros*, aroused little interest in the critics and less in the public; and in the late 'seventies, Patmore's reputation speedily declined. Towards the end of his life, there was something of a minor revival of his work, and his poems were reprinted five times between 1885 and 1897.

At the same time, his early popularity was a stigma in the eyes of a new generation of critics who found occasion only for derision in the 'goody-goody dribble' of *The Angel in the House*.[1] This work never regained the favour it enjoyed in the 'sixties; it is impossible that it will ever recover it. Yet the poet's reputation stands in a curious position today; he has inspired passionate attachment in some critics, active hostility or indifference in others and almost equal proportions of respect and disdain in the majority. It may be

[1] Frederic Harrison, *The Choice of Books and other Literary Pieces* (Macmillan & Co., 1886), p. 74.

fairly said that not only has Patmore not been accorded his just position in English poetry, but he has not been accorded any position at all.

Patmore's first book, *Poems*, published when he was twenty-one, met with a somewhat mixed reception; but the opinions of Browning, Bulwer-Lytton and Rossetti and his fellows at the Royal Academy were most favourable. *Tamerton Church-Tower*, which followed in 1853, added little to his reputation. It was with *The Betrothal* (1854) and *The Espousals* (1856), the two parts of *The Angel in the House*, that Patmore established himself as a poet of note. The plan of this poem called for six parts. After the first two, Patmore completed only two more, originally called *Faithful For Ever* (1860) and *The Victories of Love* (1863), and later grouped together under the latter title. While Ruskin thought this poem at least the equal of *The Angel*, Rossetti felt that Patmore was drawing the whole thing out inordinately, and, parodying Tennyson, asked: '"Of love which never finds its published close, what sequel!" And how many?'[1]

Despite this conflict of opinion, both poems continued to be bought in increasing numbers by the public, a large proportion of their readers being people who normally did not read poetry at all. Patmore had succeeded in writing a phenomenally popular work which was also respected by the majority of contemporary critics.

In 1864, the poet became a Catholic and married his second wife, Marianne Byles. It is highly probable that both of these events affected his poetic reputation. A public which had been charmed by the placid Anglican atmosphere of *The Angel in the House* must have felt betrayed by the author's 'perversion', while others who had been entranced by the picture of an ideal marriage and of enduring love may have been disturbed by the apparent inconsistency of the poet's remarriage. Patmore's conversion and his moving from London to Sussex cut him off from several old friends and literary acquaintances, and removed him from literary circles. His popularity, in any case, began to wane.

The privately-printed volume of nine odes with which he resumed poetry in 1868 was so different in spirit and ostensibly in subject from his earlier poems that it met with almost complete indifference. Patmore made no secret of his disappointment at the reception of this book, and of the two increasingly enlarged editions of *The Unknown Eros* in 1877 and 1878. Yet, gradually, *The Unknown Eros* came to be more carefully appraised by critics, including

[1] Basil Champneys, *Memoirs and Correspondence of Coventry Patmore*, two vols. (George Bell & Sons, 1900), Vol. II, p. 310.

several who had contemned *The Angel* because of its popularity. Edmund Gosse, Francis Thompson and Robert Bridges became respectful admirers. In the main, however, the praise of Patmore's fellow-writers was reserved for *The Unknown Eros*, irking the poet, who looked upon his poetic writing as a unit. After 1879, he virtually gave up the writing of verse, although other editions of his collected poems appeared, and were carefully revised by him.

The rise of the new poetry of the 'nineties and the growing influence of the Aesthetics helped to make Patmore's poetry appear exceptionally *vieux jeu*. Swinburne parodied *The Angel*, and the occasional references to Patmore at this time were mainly either derisive or patronizing. He had written complex and eccentric odes, which some claimed to have poetic value; but he had also been a 'popular poet', tickling bourgeois taste with interminable 'epics' of domesticity; this was enough to damn him in modish literary circles.

In 1900, four years after Patmore's death, Basil Champneys, an architect-friend, published his two massive volumes, *Memoirs and Correspondence of Coventry Patmore*, a solid piece of old-style biography which will always be a source-book for students of the poet, both for its fine collection of documents and for its fair and balanced judgments on the man and his work. This memorial, impressive, if in many ways over-elaborate, was received by the public with respect, but with little enthusiasm. It was followed in 1905 by Gosse's briefer book,[1] which filled out some of the gaps in Champneys', but was sketchy on Patmore's early years and deficient in understanding of his personality, his philosophy and religious beliefs.

For the first two decades of this century, however, Patmore seems to have been, to critics and public alike, only one name among the many minor Victorian poets, and to have been regarded as the poet of a Roman Catholic coterie. The latter charge was not unreasonable. Most of those who discussed his poetry at this time, Francis Thompson, Alice Meynell and Lionel Johnson, for instance, were fellow-Catholics concerned chiefly with its doctrinal and 'mystical' content, and given to somewhat uncritical adulation. Still, for most Catholics, and, indeed, for most non-Catholics, the lush melodies of Francis Thompson had a fascination far stronger than that of Patmore's more austere poetry; and the older poet was seen only in relation to Thompson, as the model which, it was believed, the disciple had outdone.

Apart from such devotees as Percy Lubbock, John Freeman and Osbert Burdett, who kept Patmore's name alive, most Patmore

[1] *Coventry Patmore* (Hodder & Stoughton, 1905).

criticism before 1920 was of the 'appreciative' kind—general appraisals, reminiscences and the like. The main exception was the work of Frederick Page, beginning about 1912 with several scholarly and perceptive pieces and culminating in the best book yet written on the poet, *Patmore—A Study in Poetry* (1933). In the nineteen-twenties, Page's voice was one of the very few to proclaim the poet's high quality. A writer who seemed to have nothing to offer save, on the one hand, a sentimental uxoriousness, and, on the other, erotic mysticism, or, as one critic put it, 'the angelico-domestic' and 'the incognito-erotic',[1] could hardly be expected to appeal to the post-war generation. Nevertheless, in 1921, Osbert Burdett, in *The Idea of Coventry Patmore*, endeavoured to present Patmore as a powerful and original philosopher of love and marriage. His analysis of the plan of *The Angel* and his claims for this poem and its sequel as a 'domestic epic' did much to cut a path through the 'appreciations'; but his attempt to construct a rounded and fully consistent system out of the ideas of the poetry gives the book, most valuable though it is, a rather lop-sided character.

During those years when many minor Victorians were being revalued by scholars, Patmore was almost completely ignored, remaining damned by Richard Garnett's comment in the *Dictionary of National Biography*: 'He had no perception of the sublime in other men's writings or of the ridiculous in his own.'[2] In 1932, Clifford Bax could refer to him as 'the most neglected of our notable poets'.[3] But, almost immediately afterwards, interest in Patmore deepened. Page's book, Derek Patmore's *Portrait of My Family* (1935), which drew on Champneys and Gosse to present the poet's personality to a new generation, and several articles were indications of a more serious assessment of his quality.

Old clichés of evaluation still persisted in the text-books. George Sampson in the *Concise Cambridge History of English Literature* makes the conventional clear-cut division between the earlier and later poems and adds: 'Patmore, often for reasons not poetical, has been over-praised; but he is original enough to survive.'[4] Grierson and Smith call him 'an arrogant, uxorious mystic', say that 'his realism, unsafeguarded by humour, makes him ridiculous when he means to be sprightly', describe *The Unknown Eros* as 'a strange

[1] Percy H. Osmond, *The Mystical Poets of the English Church* (S.P.C.K., 1919), p. 334.
[2] *Supplement to the D.N.B.*, Vol. XXII (Oxford University Press, 1901), pp. 121–124.
[3] Letter to the *Times Literary Supplement*, May 12, 1932.
[4] *Concise Cambridge History of English Literature* (Cambridge University Press, 1946), p. 733.

medley', dominated by 'erotic, anthropomorphic mysticism', and end with the grudging: 'When all deductions are made, Patmore remains a classic, if a minor classic, of the Mid-Victorian age.'[1]

Despite this, Patmore's stature has slowly but certainly grown in the past twenty-five years. In France, Paul Claudel, Charles du Bos and Valéry Larbaud; in Italy, Mario Praz and Augusto Guidi; in America, George N. Shuster, Terence L. Connolly and Eleanor Downing, among others, have accepted him as a major poet. C. C. Abbott's 1938 edition of the Hopkins-Patmore letters and Frederick Page's Oxford University Press edition of the collected poems (1949) renewed interest in the man and his works. If Patmore's best poetry is still not generally accorded the place Sir Herbert Read claims for it beside Dante, Donne, Lucretius and Crashaw, at least signs that it will take a far higher place than it has yet done are seen in Sherard Vines' brief but balanced assessment in *100 Years of English Literature*,[2] W. H. Gardner's careful appreciation in *The Month*,[3] and especially the account of Patmore in *The Darkling Plain*, in which John Heath-Stubbs writes: 'It is usual to speak of Tennyson and Browning as the "great" Victorian poets, yet if any poet, between the time of Keats and that of Hopkins, merits that title, I believe that in spite of his manifest eccentricities, it is Coventry Patmore.'[4]

Why has Patmore's reputation fluctuated so much? In his own day, most of his readers were attracted to *The Angel in the House* by its more superficial qualities—its placid love-story, its lyrics, its prettiness—and were unaware of the transcendental philosophy it embodied. But *The Unknown Eros* was neglected for similarly superficial reasons—Patmore's Tory politics, his contempt for popular notions of 'progress', his esoteric sources, his individual tone of voice. The idea that he was two poets, too, caused those who could not see the essential unity of his work to fall between two stools of appreciation. And it is also relevant that, on the surface, Patmore was an uncomfortable union of contradictions—first a conventionally Anglican poet of domestic joys and of the deanery; then a Catholic squire, three times married, and writing odes expressing rapturous religio-erotic experience, a decidedly un-English type. He was a patriotic Little-Englander, and at the same time a Catholic mystic. He was, in other words, a perplexing and inconsistent

---

1 *A Critical History of English Poetry* (Chatto & Windus, 1944), pp. 453–455.
2 (Gerald Duckworth & Co., 1950), pp. 48–49.
3 "The Achievement of Coventry Patmore", I and II, *The Month*, Vol. 7, No. 2, Feb. 1952; Vol. 7, No. 4, April 1952.
4 *The Darkling Plain* (Eyre & Spottiswoode, 1950), p. 130.

Introduction

person. Behind much criticism of Patmore (and indeed of Newman) lies a strong sense of unease before an uncompromising personality; so that, while some critics have praised him for reasons not connected with poetry, others have denigrated him for the same reasons. Another reason for the neglect of his poetry must surely be the breakdown of the traditional Christian view of monogamy and the spread of divorce. Patmore's views on love and marriage, while more profound and more metaphysical than those of his mid-Victorian contemporaries, were essentially those of orthodox Christianity. His exaltation of the bonds of matrimony was later found difficult of acceptance by a generation reacting against such bonds, and quite often, in fiction at least, equating 'love' with adultery. Similarly, Patmore's attitude towards women and their rights, and his apparent Pasha-like sense of feminine 'inferiority', which seem to reflect some of the least desirable of Victorian attitudes, are uncongenial to an age of female emancipation.

Yet, on the whole, the climate of opinion has altered, more recently, in a direction less unfavourable to Patmore. Writers turning from undisciplined experiments to a new sense of form find much to admire in Patmore's metrical skill and the 'controlled freedom' of *The Unknown Eros*. The elements of traditional Christian theology and mysticism assimilated by Charles Williams, T. S. Eliot, Ronald Duncan, Christopher Fry and others have familiarized modern readers with concepts which were highly exotic to his contemporaries. Renewed interest in, and revaluation of, Victorian writers gives Patmore's work perhaps its best opportunity for many years. And a certain revulsion against relaxed sexual standards makes his ideas of love and marriage rather less out-of-date than once they seemed.

Patmore remains a challenging figure, unsusceptible to neat cataloguing either as a man or as a poet. Yet the amount of serious critical writing on his work is exceptionally small. The very superfluity of occasional appreciative articles is a hindrance to full understanding of his achievements. Page's study is alone in English as an attempt to explore the particular nature of his poetic vision. Many areas of his personality, of his thought and his sensibility remain to be charted. Despite Page and Burdett, the notions persist that he is an exceedingly narrow poet, that he wrote in two quite distinct manners on two different aspects of the same subject, and that his poetry reflects all the literary vices of his age, and none of its virtues.

If Patmore's verse has rarely been submitted to close scrutiny, his writings on aesthetics, literary principles, metrics, architecture, politics and theology have been almost completely ignored save for the purpose of illuminating an aspect of the poetry. Yet it is possible to regard Patmore's prose as a substantial contribution to nineteenth-century thought on a variety of topics. These essays reveal the breadth of his reading and interests and throw intriguing sidelights on his mind and personality. Likewise, only the most cursory attention has been given to Patmore's sources and the traditional roots of his philosophical and poetic concepts, leading most often to charges of wilful eccentricity. This writer, who on the surface appeared to some a prattling innocent, laid under tribute such diverse writers as Emerson, Coleridge, Aquinas, Plato, St. Augustine, Swedenborg and St. John of the Cross, assimilated ideas from them into an individual philosophy of love and constructed round it an imaginative poetic world far removed from the Victorian gardens and deaneries which apparently constituted its limits. Patmore is, above all, an 'intellectual' poet; his affinities are not with those contemporaries he began by imitating, but with the seventeenth-century 'metaphysicals'. His poetry is supported by a close-knit intellectual structure, as is that of Donne and Lord Herbert of Cherbury. In the following pages I have tried to show the degree to which Patmore's thought, while deriving in great part from the philosophers and mystics in whom he read, is original and represents the vehicle of a deeply-felt personal experience.

Here, then, is no freakish 'minor', no laughable eccentric, no sentimental rhymster to be accorded a pitying footnote, but a vital and living poet with astonishing bursts of inspired lyricism, a writer with a tremendous amount to say and a most individual way of saying it. The present work is a contribution towards an assessment of the totality of Patmore's writing. No detailed biography is given. The main focus is directed towards his thought and poetry, and pays only incidental attention to those aspects of his personality and life which have been already amply documented. Because I am convinced that the lack of a close scrutiny of Patmore's sources is the main reason why the depths of his verse are too seldom recognized, and the conventional dichotomy between the Patmore of *The Angel* and the Patmore of *The Unknown Eros* still exists, the first part of this study details such influences and shows how they provided fuel for the burning heart of his idea of love.

My reading of the prose writings, including the many uncollected periodical articles, convinces me that some discussion of them is indispensable, not only to an understanding of Patmore's poetic development and of his ideas, but also to the filling out of the map of his curious and many-faceted mind. I have also, in the final section, taken a fresh look at the poetry, on which the bulk of past criticism has centred. Here some of the unpublished letters of Patmore, especially those to Sutton, have thrown some fresh light on Patmore's poetic intention. I feel that, great though the debt of students of Patmore must always be to Frederick Page, he displays excessive partisanship with regard to the poetry, rarely admitting the possibility of defects. This is a not unnatural reaction against those who would have it that Patmore is no poet. I have, with Mr. Page, come to love Patmore's poetry, and to see much of what appears at first sight as blemishes as integral parts of his particular vision, but I do not feel that any service is done to the poet by ignoring his weaknesses. On the poetry above all, Patmore's claim to serious consideration chiefly rests, and consequently, although the ground has been fairly well-trodden already, I hope that, in considering afresh the plans of his major works and their relationship both to his thought and to his particular sensibility, I have made his verse more poetically meaningful.

In what follows, I have tried to acknowledge my debts to all those to whose writings on the poet I am indebted for special insights. My intention has been mainly to examine those aspects of his work and personality which have been thus far conspicuously neglected, as well as to re-assess the more deliberated aspects; in sum, by giving a rounded picture of his work, to establish a case for Coventry Patmore as one of the most original and significant poets of the past century. I would be far from claiming that I have examined every aspect of this man's work, or that my study has not been without its bias, but I have at least tried to broaden the basis of appreciation of a remarkable writer and to bring to light neglected aspects in the hope that others may turn with renewed interest to his passionate pages.

PART TWO

INFLUENCES ON PATMORE
AND HIS THOUGHT

I

Personal Influences

HE PERSONAL INFLUENCES which helped to mould the personality of Coventry Patmore, and to determine the direction of his thinking as well as the nature of his inspiration, go back to his childhood. Many of his idiosyncrasies can be traced to his early environment and his unusual education. His talented but erratic father, Peter George Patmore, had preferred a literary career to joining his own father in his jewellery business. As editor of the *New Monthly Magazine* from 1841 to 1853, as contributor to most of the important reviews of the day, as versifier, novelist and dramatic critic, P. G. Patmore became a figure of some note in the literary life of London. He numbered among his friends and acquaintances Thomas Campbell, Leigh Hunt, Lady Blessington and Plumer Ward, Hazlitt and Lamb, most of whom the boy Coventry met in their homes or at the salons of the Basil Montagus and the Bryan Waller Procters, where his father often took him. Quite early, then, he had become accustomed to literary conversation and to the atmosphere of literary society.

Peter George indulged his favourite son, did everything in his power to encourage the various talents of which he gave early evidence, and made him, in effect, his literary pupil. He introduced him to the classic and the great English poets, and stimulated his interest in poetic form. It was on his father's recommendation, too, that the boy studied the Greek philosophers, notably Plato, who was to be a major formative influence on his thought. From his father Coventry derived his life-long affection for Wordsworth, recognizing affinities between his own youthful experiences of nature and 'intimations of immortality' and those expressed by the Romantic poet. In his 'autobiography', Patmore writes with gratitude of his father's encouraging of his liking for literature, and praises his taste, which, he said, 'was so severely good that, at fifteen, I cared little for any but the classics of English literature.'[1] P. G. Patmore, while professing disbelief in any spiritual existence, had a reverence for the forms and ideas of Christianity, and strong positive virtues, some of them in logical contradiction to his unbelief.[2] A letter written by Peter George to Coventry while the boy was studying in Paris reveals the exceptionally close sympathy between father and son, and the sensitive understanding which Peter George had of Coventry's tastes and interests. One sentence is of particular significance in view of the later emergence of the young man's literary philosophy:

> 'Nothing gives me more pleasure than what you feel about Miller and his book—and consequently what you feel about those simplicities of Nature of which his book is so pleasing a transcript. While you preserve these two loves—the love of Nature and the love of Books—you may contrive (if needful) to dispense with all *other* loves, and to set at defiance all that is the opposite of love.'[3]

In addition to fostering Coventry's talents for art, exhibiting his mathematical gifts by posing problems for him to solve mentally before friends, and taking him to the theatre while pursuing his own calling as a dramatic critic, Peter George equipped a small scientific laboratory for his son, and encouraged him to experiment in it. Coventry recorded:

> 'I did not stop at repeating the experiments of others, but carried on original investigations, not altogether without results, among which was the discovery of a new chloride of Bromine.'[4]

On this claim Gosse drily comments, 'That new chloride of bromine was an impressive ornament of conversation in Patmore's later years, and was always received, of course, in respectful silence. But one would like to have had Faraday's opinion.'[5] Patmore's note-book recording these youthful experiments, which is preserved

---

[1] Champneys, *Memoirs and Correspondence*, Vol. II, p. 43.
[2] *Ibid.*, Vol. II, p. 41.   [3] *Ibid.*, Vol. I, p. 39.
[4] *Ibid.*, Vol. II, p. 42.   [5] *Coventry Patmore*, p. 9.

in the Library of Boston College, gives some grounds for Gosse's implied scepticism. It bears on the front cover: 'Poetry together with Original Notes on Scientific Subjects', and on the inside cover the motto: 'Poetry is the flower of science'. No verses remain in the book, and as several pages have been torn out, it is reasonable to suppose that these contained the first drafts of the 1844 *Poems*. Fifty-five pages of notes on chemical experiments remain, and the much talked-of experiment on the chloride of bromine is recorded under the date Nov. 14, 1840. Most of the experiments appear to have been of a rather elementary and conventional nature, but some of the comments show evidence of fairly wide, if unco-ordinated, reading. Typical Patmorean touches, however, are revealed even at this tender age, in such comments as: 'Considering with Galvani the brain to be a Voltaic pile—I have traced an analogy, which perhaps has hitherto escaped observation, namely that both it (the brain) and the pile are by being discharged . . . rendered for a time inert.' The youthful chemical experimenter appears, at any rate, not to have lacked confidence.

In 1838, Coventry Patmore was awarded the silver palette of the Society of Arts for a copy of one of Landseer's pictures, and for a short while toyed with the idea of becoming an artist, but this was abandoned for the career of a poet, when the publication of his first volume of poems in 1844 showed him the path he was to follow. The River and The Woodman's Daughter, both written between 1839 and 1841, were circulated in manuscript by the proud father and drew high praise from his literary friends. Inspired by the publication of Tennyson's collected poems in 1842, and urged on by his father, Coventry quickly composed Lilian, Sir Hubert and some smaller pieces, and these, added to the earlier compositions, made up the 1844 volume which P. G. Patmore had published by Moxon, the publisher of Keats and Wordsworth. Later Coventry was to speak of these youthful efforts as 'rubbish' (although he published revised versions of them in all his collected editions), and lament to H. S. Sutton of his 'foolish haste to publish before my taste was matured'.[1] At the same time, the publication of this early book, however premature, was decisive in freeing him from the indecisions of his adolescence.

In 1844 P. G. Patmore, who had lived beyond his means for some time, speculated rashly in railway shares. He found himself heavily in debt, and, unable to meet his obligations, fled to France in 1845 to evade his creditors. Both Coventry and his brother George were thrown on their own resources. and, unprepared for

[1] *Memoirs*, Vol. II, p. 152.

any other kind of work, Coventry Patmore made a precarious living by free-lance journalism until in 1846 he received a position in the British Museum Library through the kindness of Monckton Milnes.

Patmore owed very little to the published writings of his father,[1] but in other directions P. G. Patmore's influence on his son was deep and lasting. It is almost certain that his father's proud exhibition of Coventry's many talents, and his eager encouragement of the youth's precocious interest in science and the arts helped to develop the qualities of hauteur and arrogance in the older Coventry. In another direction, however, P. G. Patmore influenced his son's habits of thinking. Gosse points out that the elder Patmore had a habit of marking in pencil what he considered the best passages in books, and that by commending these alone to the boy, he developed in Coventry a preference for a collection of specimens to a general system of knowledge.[2] This habit of culling and marking continued throughout his entire life. When he was courting Emily Augusta Andrews, he sent her a copy of Emerson's *Essays*, asking her to mark her favourite passages, and was delighted to find that they were almost identical with his own. His copies of the works of his most favoured authors, Swedenborg, Coleridge, St. Augustine, St. Thomas Aquinas, St. Bernard, St. Catherine of Genoa, Maine de Biran, Ford, and others, are heavily scored and annotated. This habit is connected with the fact that, throughout his prose, Patmore has a tendency to repeat isolated phrases from Goethe, Aristotle, Aeschylus and Wordsworth in essay after essay. Similarly, his selective emphasis on those portions of the writings of Augustine and Aquinas which especially appealed to him suggests that the habit of picking out isolated ideas rather than absorbing the entire content of a writer was his normal way of study. This eclecticism, which is related to his preference for aphoristic books, and his own delight in writing in epigrams, accounts for certain weaknesses and contradictions in his thought. As his distaste for systematic philosophies reveals, Patmore's mind was one which gathered selected ideas in accordance with intuitions rather than one which approached philosophy and theology with the intent of grasping the whole direction of a system.

In less fundamental ways, Patmore continued to feel the impact

---

1 Alice Meynell points out that Coventry Patmore's ode, 'St. Valentine's Day', is indebted more than a little to the essay on February in P. G. Patmore's *The Mirror of the Months*. See 'A Hundred Years Ago', *The Second Person Singular and Other Essays* (Oxford University Press, 1922), pp. 68–74.

2 *Coventry Patmore*, p. 11.

of his father's personality. In 1854, a year before he died, Peter George Patmore published in England, to which he had earlier returned, three volumes entitled *My Friends and Acquaintances*. This work, containing much that is lively, amusing, and useful to the literary historian, was bitterly attacked by the critics, largely because it contained some pieces of tactless gossip. Most of the critics took occasion to recall P. G. Patmore's association with the duel of 1821 in which John Scott, editor of *The London Magazine*, for whom Patmore acted as second, was shot by a Mr. Christie, representing J. G. Lockhart, editor of *Blackwood's Magazine*. *Blackwood's* had already expressed its opinion of the poetry of the son of P. G. Patmore in a review of the 1844 *Poems*, which is a classic piece of critical vituperation.[1] The appearance of *My Friends and Acquaintances* just as Coventry Patmore was about to publish *The Betrothal* caused the poet to withhold his name from the title-page lest he should once more share in the abuse which was being poured on the name of Patmore. In at least one case, P. G. Patmore's activities affected his son's literary criticism. As the intimate friend of William Hazlitt, the elder Patmore was the recipient of the letters which Hazlitt poured out about his infatuation for Sarah Walker, and he encouraged Hazlitt to publish them as *Liber Amoris* in 1823, earning much critical buffeting for his part in this unfortunate business. Coventry Patmore was ashamed of his father's association with *Liber Amoris*. Years afterwards, he found among his father's papers some unpublished letters from Hazlitt about Sarah Walker, and sent them to Hazlitt's son to destroy. He was furiously angry when he found that they had been sold and published, and wrote to *The Times*, expressing his disgust. The fastidiousness which caused Patmore to find the *Liber Amoris* distasteful is brought out, too, by a comparison between this book and *The Angel in the House*. Hazlitt's uncensored expression of his infatuation is in contrast to Patmore's poem, in which, although it draws much of its strength from his love for his first wife, the autobiographical touches are of the slightest, the whole work is 'distanced', and the subject of love itself is treated with delicacy. It is no wonder, then, that Patmore the essayist had little time for Hazlitt. He hardly ever refers to the critic in his prose writings; when he does so it is with a note of disdain.

It is safe to assume, then, that, although Coventry was wise enough not to try to live up to the idealized picture of himself as

---

[1] *Blackwood's Edinburgh Magazine*, Vol. LVI, No. CCCXLVII, Sept. 1844, pp. 331–342.

the boy-poet painted by P. G. Patmore in his novel *Chatsworth*,[1] the indulgent attitude of his father to the favourite and gifted son helped incalculably to mould his temperament, his ambitions and his philosophy, and left distinct traces in details of his work. Peter George Patmore appears to have been a man of slight but genuine talent, which he was content to exercise lightly, somewhat irresponsible and rather a poseur, with a broad streak of vulgarity, from which his son was not wholly free. Yet he had a genuine sensibility, and a real affection for literature; he respected the achievements of others and he was at pains to cultivate his own taste in the arts. The poet was always loyal to the memory of his father, aware that he owed his literary and his philosophical interests, and his beginnings as a poet, to him.

In marked contrast, Eliza Patmore, the boy's mother, seems to have had little direct influence on him. Very few impressions of her survive. But from what Champneys and Gosse record of her, as well as from the absence of references to her by Patmore himself, she appears to have been cold, stern and authoritative, with little interest in her son's or her husband's literary pursuits and so impatient in her dealings with her children that they were concerned to evade her. Gosse, in fact, attributes something of Patmore's priggishness as a child to his revolt against the sternness of his mother.[2]

J. M. Cohen suggests that: 'There is a very clear connection between her undemonstrative, and possibly cold nature, and the poet's impassioned craving for love, his three marriages, and, indeed, the whole character of his religious approach.'[3] It is possible to accept such a connection without regarding Mrs. Patmore's coldness as the hidden centre of a huge rationalization. The happiness of Patmore's marriages, his celebration of the joys of family life, the complexity of his religious philosophy and the sense of delight and fulfilment in his poetry indicate that, even with a normal mother's love, his temperament would have prompted him to explore quite as thoroughly the field of wedded love. But it is certainly probable that his mother's apparent indifference played an important part in developing in the boy a precocious interest in the philosophy of love and in the man a genius for husbandhood.

---

[1] *Chatsworth, or The Romance of a Week*, edited by the author of 'Tremaine', 'De Vere', etc.: in three vols. (London: Henry Colburn, 1844), Chap. XIV, 'The Boy Poet', pp. 78–85.

[2] *Coventry Patmore*, p. 5.

[3] 'Prophet Without Responsibility', *Essays in Criticism*, Vol. I, No. 3, July 1951, p. 285.

In another sense, it is possible that his mother contributed something to his personality. Not only did Coventry detect inconsistency in Peter George's attitude towards religion, but the contrast between the almost pagan outlook of his father and the Puritanism of his mother must have helped to shape the individuality of his own later religious beliefs. His unswerving adherence to Catholic dogma and his intense spirituality existed side by side with a refusal to believe that the Catholic Church had a monopoly of goodness, and his reserving to himself the right to make up his mind on all matters on which the Church had not authoritatively spoken. Patmore's Catholicism in some senses combines the differing religious attitudes of both his parents.

The major emotional experience of Patmore's youth, which set him writing poetry, was his falling in love at the age of sixteen with the eighteen-year-old daughter of Mrs. Charles Gore, the novelist and friend of his father. While in Paris in 1839, the youth spent some time at the home of the Gores. It seems that Miss Gore did not take the shy, awkward boy's infatuation seriously. In any case, she soon afterwards married Lord Edward Thynne. Nevertheless, this youthful love-affair made a lasting impression on the poet, and he always regarded it as the most precious of the intuitions into truth that he captured as an adolescent. Champneys, in an admirable phrase, described it as 'his matriculation in the school of love', which 'initiated him in the mysteries of emotion and feeling which were the foundation of his later poetry.'[1]

The immediate effect of Patmore's love for Miss Gore was to set him to work on his first two long poems, The River and The Woodman's Daughter. And his rejection is mirrored in the subjects of these early poems—stories of frustrated and disillusioned love, of fickleness and treachery; such subjects, as much as Patmore's handling of detail, made the young Pre-Raphaelites elect him as their representative poet. However, the poems written a year or so later to pad out the 1844 volume, namely, Lilian, Sir Hubert and especially a sonnet beginning: 'At nine years old I was Love's willing page', show that Patmore was not content merely to brood over disappointment, but that he had hope in future love and its regenerative power. Such signs of adult feeling, together with a remarkable sensitivity to nature expressed in other poems, prevent this first volume from being just the poetic record of adolescent frustration; Patmore's philosophy of love and marriage is already beginning to flower.

[1] *Memoirs*, Vol. I, p. 42.

However, the most fruitful and most lasting personal influence on Coventry Patmore was his ideally happy first marriage. He married Emily Augusta Andrews in 1847. Their love was based upon a remarkable harmony of outlook and temperament. Emily, a woman of strong personality and deep religious convictions, was gifted with almost all the qualities that go to make an outstanding wife and mother, and with her, Patmore entered into the fullness of married love. She became for him 'Love's self, so Love's interpreter', who not only possessed womanly tenderness, but had the ability to make this real and intelligible to her husband. Even if Patmore himself had not so often and so directly paid tribute to her qualities as a wife, or if the letters between them had not revealed such a delicate intimacy, the joyous celebration of marriage in *The Angel in the House* would have provided evidence in plenty of the part Emily played in releasing the flood of poetry in him and in inspiring him to develop his philosophy of love.

Emily's portrait was painted by Millais and Brett, Browning, Ruskin, Carlyle paid warm tributes to her beauty and character, and Richard Garnett enthusiastically praised her domestic virtues.[1] Her good sense and lack of sentimentality made a powerful appeal to the young husband, and helped to accentuate the same native qualities in him. From his youthful experiences and meditations Patmore had already formed a conception of marriage as a sacrament. In his first marriage he received actual confirmation of this. Emily re-awakened in him the urge to devote himself to poetry, and this time his impulse was to write, not scattered lyrics, but a great work of art, a long poem in six parts, which would embody the whole nature of love. 'I have been meditating a poem for you; but I am determined not to give you anything I write unless it is the best thing I have ever written. O, how much the best it ought to be, if it would do justice to its subject,'[2] he wrote to her. The daily companionship with Emily, which did not stale, but only deepened, their mutual affection, gave Patmore a profound understanding of womanhood, and provided the greatest emotional experience of his life, the stuff out of which his poetry is made.

'The relationship of the soul to Christ *as his betrothed wife* is the key to the feeling with which prayer and love and honour should be offered to Him. In this relation is a mine of undiscovered joy and power. *She* showed me what that relationship involves of heavenly submission and spotless, passionate loyalty.'[3]

---

[1] 'Recollections of Coventry Patmore', *The Saturday Review*, Vol. 82, No. 2145, Dec. 5, 1896, p. 583.
[2] Champneys, *Memoirs*, Vol. I, p. 135.   [3] *Ibid.*, Vol. I, p. 146.

After Emily's death, Patmore regarded her as a saint, and, to the end of his life, even during his subsequent marriages, he kept the anniversary of her death as a day of seclusion and prayer. *The Angel in the House* was dedicated 'To the Memory of her by whom and for whom I became a poet'; and the last part of *The Angel, The Victories of Love*, published in 1863, the year after her death, contains the postscript:

> 'The Plan of the Poem, or series of Poems, of which this volume is the conclusion, involved, as it was schemed more than fourteen years ago, a final section on the subject of the hope which remains for individual love in death. It is well, perhaps, for the interest of poetry in this great and hitherto unapproached theme, that my weak voice has been hushed. I no longer have, at every step, the needful encouragement of an approval which was all that my heart valued of fame.'

Such a statement, written out of grief, was not to prevent Patmore's completion of *The Unknown Eros*, but it unequivocally indicates the extent to which *The Angel in the House* reflected his own experience of marriage.

Although the personality of Emily permeates *The Angel*, Alice Meynell pointed out that 'the angel' was not Emily herself, as sentimental readers had thought, but Love.[1] Woman, for Patmore, is not Scott's 'ministering angel', but the 'Angel' of Love, in the sense that she is the 'messenger' of the Divine. The framework of the poet Vaughan and his wife was designed to place the poem at one remove from Patmore's personal life, and Emily in person enters only in the descriptive lines, brief enough—

> her Norman face;
> Her large sweet eyes, clear lakes of love.
> (*A.H.*, I, i)

In a diary of Patmore's written after Emily's death, Champneys found the heading: 'Passages of "The Angel in the House" which more particularly describe or apply to her', with a very modest space following, and that left blank.[2] In sum, although Patmore goes to some trouble to objectify his study of love and marriage, and very largely succeeds, the whole mood of nuptial tenderness, the purity of feeling, and the realistic depth of the whole poem are clearly the products not only of poetic inspiration, but of the experience of the love of an exceptional woman.

Amelia, which Patmore wrote nearly fifteen years after Emily's death, is much more filled with the direct presence of Emily than is

[1] Introduction to the *Catalogue of Coventry Patmore's Library*, p. 3.
[2] *Memoirs*, Vol. I, pp. 117–118.

The Angel, despite the fact that its fable of a middle-aged man taking his young fiancée on their first unchaperoned walk to visit the grave of his former fiancée, would seem to arise more directly out of the circumstances of his second marriage. However, not only does the title of the poem echo her name, but, as Emily Honoria, Patmore's eldest daughter, pointed out in her charming memoir of her mother, the lines

> How changed, in shape no slender Grace,
> But Venus, milder than the dove;

refer to Emily Augusta. Patmore proposed marriage to Emily on a walk across the fields at Hampstead, and the lovely evocative walk in *Amelia* is clearly based upon a poetic recollection of the joy of that significant moment.

Again, Patmore often used to speak with rapture of his first sight of the sea as a little boy while driving to Hastings with his parents. The memory of that childhood revelation, which played its part in determining him to live at Hastings in later life, lies behind the opening lines of *Amelia*:

> Whene'er mine eyes do my Amelia greet
> It is with such emotion
> As when, in childhood, turning a dim street,
> I first beheld the ocean.

But this recollection is blended with another memory. Gosse relates:

> 'Patmore told me that his wife and he spent their honeymoon at Hastings, and that an exclamation of hers, on descending the beach for the first time, inspired, long afterwards, the beautiful lines with which "Amelia" opens.'[1]

The fusion of these two recollections, Patmore's own and Emily's, shows how much he treasured a loving recognition of identity of response.

Patmore regarded *Amelia* as his best poem, therefore, not only because of his satisfaction with what is possibly his finest piece of poetic craftsmanship and a fusion of his ideas of love and woman with a remarkable realism of setting, but also because his love for his first wife 'recollected in tranquillity' found here its most devoted expression.

A personal note much more direct than any in *The Angel in the House* makes itself felt in *The Victories of Love*. The fatal illness of Emily and Patmore's passionate grief at the time are reflected in

[1] 'The History of a Poem', *North American Review*, No. CCCLXXXIV, March 1897, p. 285.

the sickness and death of the heroically uncomplaining Jane. Jane's letters to Frederick, written to be read after her death, which form sections VII and VIII of *The Victories of Love*, and which constitute one of the most heart-rending moments in Patmore's poetry, echo Emily Patmore's will. In 1860, after she had almost died during a long illness, Patmore found her will in a desk, and this read, in part:

> 'I leave my wedding-ring to your second wife with my love and blessing ... also, I leave you my grateful acknowledgement of your goodness and love to me, my last prayer that God may bless and console you, my first, last, and only love. If in a year or two, you are able to marry again, do so happily, feeling that if my spirit can watch you, it will love her who makes you happy, and not envy her the reward of a part of your love, the best years of which I have had.'[1]

Jane's words to Frederick are almost a direct paraphrase of this passage:

> The only bond I hold you to
> Is that which nothing can undo.
> A man is not a young man twice;
> And if, of his young years, he lies
> A faithful score in one wife's breast,
> She need not mind who has the rest.
> In this do what you will, dear Love,
> And feel quite sure that I approve.
> And should it chance as it may be,
> Give her my wedding-ring from me;
> And never dream that you can err
> T'wards me by being good to her;

Despite the fact that the change in temper between *The Angel in the House* and *The Victories of Love* is part of Patmore's plan of showing the different aspects of married life, the suffering and the pathos of the latter poem are, though artistically distanced, projections of Patmore's own emotions. And when Emily died, Patmore's grief wrung from him some of the most naked expressions of sorrow in English verse. The years immediately after her death were those in which he wrote his best poetry. The odes, 'The Azalea', 'Departure', 'The Day After Tomorrow', 'Farewell', 'Tristitia' and 'Tired Memory' are the products of this time, while 'If I were Dead' is conceivably based upon a remark of Emily's during her her last illness.

It is on the matter of religious belief that the relationship between Patmore and Emily is perhaps most interesting, especially in view of the intimations of Catholic doctrine in *The Angel*, his increasing

[1] *Memoirs*, Vol. I, p. 133.

interest in Catholic theology during his years at the British Museum, and his conversion to Catholicism after her death. Emily Augusta Andrews, the daughter of a Congregationalist minister, was a Protestant of a somewhat Puritanical type, while Patmore, at the time of his first marriage, was something like a 'High Anglican'. On the basis of some remarks of Patmore in his autobiography about that difference, some critics, for instance, Vincent T. Eaton,[1] have attempted to establish that Emily so strongly disapproved of her husband's Rome-wards leanings that she not only deliberately retarded his movement towards Catholicism but caused him considerably to modify the doctrinal content of *The Angel in the House*. From his vantage point of twenty-six years later, Patmore wrote in his 'autobiography':

> 'I believe that, when I reached the age of thirty-five, what mainly held me back was the steady repugnance of my wife to the faith which I was gradually approaching. Her natural judgment was so good and her goodness so perfect that her opposition was in itself a very weighty argument. She had been terrified from her cradle with the hideous phantom which Protestantism conjures up when the Catholic religion is named. . . . Only a few days before she died, she said to me with tears, "When I am gone, they (the Catholics) will get you; and then I shall see you no more!"' [2]

After his conversion, he was anxious to establish that he had been a Catholic in inclination and philosophy long before he actually became one. In view of other errors of fact and emphasis in the 'autobiography', it is more than likely that, although the above account is in the main accurate, the details have been modified by hindsight. On the one hand, the religious differences between Patmore and his wife are over-emphasized and on the other, the pre-conversion 'Catholicism' of the poet is exaggerated. Champneys, whose authority not only as an intimate friend but as a thoroughly conscientious biographer gives his words particular weight, wrote:

> 'It is necessary to assert positively on the strength of convincing evidence, that Emily Patmore was, during the greater part of her married life, in complete harmony with her husband, not merely on subordinate matters of opinion, but on the higher ground of religious thought. . . . I am convinced that in the retrospect taken after his change of creed the leaning towards Rome seemed to him to have been stronger and the variance from his wife's position greater than it actually was.' [3]

[1] 'The First Mrs. Patmore', *The Catholic World*, Vol. 164, October 1946, p. 54.
[2] *Memoirs*, Vol. II, p. 53.   [3] *Ibid.*, Vol. I, pp. 123-125.

In the published correspondence between Emily and Coventry there are no indications whatever of any specific Catholic leanings in the poet. His early essays contain only one or two references to Catholicism, and these are anything but friendly. He wrote in a study of Sir Kenelm Digby, on the matter of Digby's conversion to Catholicism: 'Digby's mind which was "As wide as Asia, and as weak" was precisely of the nature to acknowledge the plausible pretensions of the Roman Church, and to deliver up his intellect to her service with delight.'[1] So, too, W. M. Rossetti notes in his edition of the *Pre-Raphaelite Diaries and Letters* that 'Patmore, who became a fervent Roman Catholic towards 1863, was in 1849 a strict and indeed prejudiced Protestant.'[2]

It cannot be questioned that in the late eighteen-fifties, Patmore was moving, almost certainly unconsciously, towards the Catholic Church; but this did not lead to a breach with his wife, nor was it sufficiently marked to move Emily either to tamper with his poetry or in any other direct way to impede his development. In any case, Patmore himself was certain that it was Emily's influence, and no other, which elevated him for months after her death to a region of high spirituality. 'It was not,' he wrote, 'that of supernatural grace in me, but the natural love of the beauty of supernatural grace as I recalled it in her; and, at the end of a year, I found myself greatly advanced indeed towards that inviolable fidelity to God which He requires, but still unmistakably short of its attainment.'[3] Emily Augusta was the realization of his highest ideals of love and marriage; she remained with him as a constant standard of virtue, womanliness and wifehood, even during his two future happy marriages; and both her life and her death tapped deep springs of poetry in him.

The discernible effects of Patmore's second and third wives on his verse are much less profound. Marianne Caroline Byles's money enabled him to retire from the British Museum Library, to buy his Sussex estate, Heron's Ghyll, and to live the rest of his life in comfort as a country squire, with leisure to prosecute his reading in mysticism and theology. It is likely that this sudden accession of wealth, a contrast to the earlier financial worries, especially while supporting an invalid wife and six children on his slender Library income, helped to accentuate the proud side of his character. His

[1] 'Sir Kenelme Digby, His Character and Writings', *The Gentleman's Magazine*, May 1848, p. 481.
[2] *Pre-Raphaelite Diaries and Letters*, edited by W. M. Rossetti (London: Hurst & Blackett, 1900), p. 233, n.
[3] *Memoirs*, Vol. II, pp. 53–54.

conversion and virtual retirement to Sussex, which meant a break with many former friends, may have further fostered his idiosyncrasies. In any case, Patmore made a second happy marriage, during which he composed the bulk of *The Unknown Eros*, and had plenty of opportunity to develop his practical talents as a man of business. He proved himself a most successful administrator and improver of a large estate, which he later sold to the Duke of Norfolk, making a substantial profit on the deal.

Patmore met Marianne Caroline Byles while on a visit to Rome in 1864, with his friend, Aubrey de Vere. She had been friendly with Manning, and a year or so after Manning's conversion, she followed him into the Catholic Church, and embraced her new faith with ardour. The piety and goodness of this young woman made a deep impression on Patmore. However, it cannot be claimed that Patmore became a Catholic in order to marry her. He had been delighted with the cultured Catholic society into which de Vere had introduced him; its manners and its ideas appealed deeply to him; and he had already been taking religious instructions, although he could not yet bring himself to the point of submission. When he proposed marriage to Miss Byles, she at first refused him, because she had made some kind of religious promise not to marry. Then, Patmore records in the 'autobiography', he continued on his previous line of meditation, until one night he suddenly decided that nothing less than submission would satisfy his conscience. He at once made his submission, and 'From that time—now twenty years ago—to this no shadow of religious doubt has ever crossed my understanding or my conscience.'[1] Beneath Patmore's brief and rather detached account of his conversion, it is possible to see that, given his temperament, the act of surrender to the authority of the Church involved a decision of great difficulty. It seems that his new passion for Marianne Byles provided, not necessarily the cause, but the occasion, for his decision, the final prod he needed. There is nothing in Patmore's account, however, nor in the biographical records, to justify Derek Patmore's suggestion: 'One cannot help feeling that Miss Byles held out his different faith as a barrier to their marriage.'[2]

Marianne Patmore made a conscientious and beloved stepmother to Patmore's children. She was somewhat 'old-maidish', self-effacing and reserved in temper. Yet she had a most active mind. She shared her husband's political convictions, and took a prominent part in local Conservative politics; she translated St.

[1] *Memoirs*, Vol. II, p. 55.
[2] *Life and Times of Coventry Patmore* (Constable, 1949), p. 134.

Bernard's *On the Love of God*, which Patmore completed after her death. There is no room for doubt that Patmore loved her dearly, and that he was able to accommodate his devotion to Emily with the feeling he had for Marianne. In 1867, three years after their marriage, he wrote to her:

'Believe me, I could not love you more had I never loved another. My dear, I may say

"I could not love thee, dear, so *much*
Loved I not 'Honor' more." '

As Coventry Patmore's children grew older Mary Patmore (as her friends called her), a devout Catholic, ordered her life as a religious might do, assigning special parts of the day to meditation, prayers and good works. Her health was never robust, and after some years of invalidism, she died in 1880. It is puzzling to find L. Wheaton asserting that 'the second Mrs. Patmore lived in conformity with her vow'[1] (presumably of chastity) unless he has misunderstood Champneys's words—'As the family grew older, some settling elsewhere, and those who remained at home becoming less dependent on her, she reverted to her former intention, and so far as circumstances allowed, laid out her life as a "religious" might do',[2] the practice already alluded to above. Before her marriage to Patmore, Marianne had contemplated taking the veil; all that Champneys's words convey is that, so far as was compatible with married life, she combined with it as much of the devout practices of a religious as she could. It is possible that, in view of her invalidism, normal marriage relations might have been suspended, and that in this state of enforced celibacy, the second Mrs. Patmore reverted to the kind of religious practices she had carried out in the days of her spinsterhood. It is inconceivable, at any rate, that such an un-Catholic idea as a 'virgin marriage' would have been contemplated by two such devout Catholics as Mary and Coventry, and especially by a man like Coventry.

However, the not improbable circumstances of a suspension of marriage relations being imposed by the later chronic invalidism of his wife may have had some effect upon the nature of the 'Psyche' odes. Perhaps Patmore's struggle in these poems, not always with success, to achieve a sublimation of the sensual in the spiritual, owes something to the tensions of this time. But this is a different

[1] 'Psyche and the Prophet', *The Catholic World*, Vol. CXVIII, No. 705, Dec. 1925, p. 356.
[2] *Memoirs*, Vol. I, p. 216.

thing from suggesting that Marianne Patmore entered marriage to live the life of a nun, and Coventry that of a monk. In the letter already quoted, he recalls their honeymoon, and writes:

> 'Dear Wife,
>
> Here is a snowdrop from the garden where I walked and sat, two years and a half ago, with my bride of a day.
>
> I know your dear heart would glow with pleasure if you could see how mine has glowed with the thought of the happiness I have had and have in you.'

These are not the words of a Patmore living a life of celibate dedication. The progress of Patmore in developing his conception of the mystical inwardness of marriage indicates that, if Marianne was not another Emily, at least she made him very happy, and gave additional confirmation to his intuitions of married love.

Patmore married his third wife, Harriet Robson, in 1881. She had been a slightly older school-fellow of his daughter, Emily Honoria, and had become governess to the Patmore children during the illness of Marianne. Derek Patmore somewhat unconvincingly depicts her as a calculating, Becky-Sharp-like person, who, by charm and flattery, insinuated herself into the affections of the ageing poet.[1] Patmore's letters to her are among the most intimate which have been preserved, and show no diminution in his genius for married love. The birth of a son to Harriet, called Francis Epiphanius, gave Patmore intense joy.

With her husband, Harriet joined the Third Order of St. Francis; this, the tone of their correspondence, and the devotion with which she preserved Patmore's papers, show an identity of religious views and of emotional response, and a closer intimacy than Derek Patmore would allow. Among Harriet Patmore's papers was this fragment, probably accompanying some anniversary gift: 'To my dearest, with renewal of the vows of entire love and fidelity, which have never been broken for a moment'; and after twelve years of married life, he wrote to her, in 1893: 'You have been for twelve years a thoroughly good and sweet little wife, and your trouble, during the past few months—although it has greatly troubled me—makes me love you the more, since it shows how much you love me.' However, Harriet Robson came too late in his life, and lacked sufficient intellectual stature to provide any real influence on his thought. Her chief function was that of the tactful, loving and accommodating wife of a celebrated poet.

[1] *Life and Times*, p. 178.

The really potent influence, after the death of his daughter, was that of Alice Meynell. Here there has been a good deal of conflict in assessing the real nature of the personal relationship between the two writers. Patmore had admired Alice Meynell's poems for some time before he became intimate with Wilfrid and Alice Meynell in 1892. She, on her side, had written a sensitive appreciation of *The Unknown Eros*.[1] After they met, Patmore was captivated by Mrs. Meynell's charm and intelligence. When the Laureateship fell vacant at Tennyson's death, he wrote to *The Saturday Review*, proposing Mrs. Meynell for the post. She wrote several essays and reviews on Patmore's work; and, in 1895, she edited a selection of his poems, *Poetry of Pathos and Delight*. The Meynells often visited Patmore at his home in The Lodge, Lymington; and he stayed with them in London, on occasion helping them with their multifarious journalistic pursuits. Through them, too, he met Francis Thompson, Wilfrid Meynell's protégé, with whom Patmore shared so much of his secret self during his last four years.

There can be little doubt that Patmore, who was almost seventy when he met Alice Meynell, developed a passionate attachment to her. The difficulty lies in ascertaining the precise nature of his feeling. A complex and subtle personality like Coventry Patmore might be expected to experience a type of emotion not easy to classify under any of the ordinary headings. Champneys did little more than record the fact that Patmore became friendly with the Meynells, and accordingly Derek Patmore accuses Champneys of deliberately suppressing all details concerning the poet's 'passionate friendship' with Mrs. Meynell for fear of offending the last Mrs. Patmore.[2] After Patmore's death Mrs. Meynell burnt nearly all the poet's letters to her; but one or two have been preserved, as have some little poems he wrote to her. She also published anonymously, for his eyes especially, in the *Pall Mall Gazette* in 1895, the following lines, which Patmore, without acknowledging the reference to himself, reprinted in his essay, Mrs. Meynell's New Essays:

> Why wilt thou chide,
> Who hast attained to be denied?
> Oh learn, above
> All price is my refusal, Love.
> My sacred Nay
> Was never cheapened by the way.
> Thy single sorrow crowns thee lord
> Of an unpurchasable word.

[1] *National Observer*, July 25, 1891.   [2] *Life and Times*, p. 1.

Oh strong, oh pure!
As Yea makes happier loves secure,
I vow thee this
Unique rejection of a kiss.
I guard for thee
This jealous sad monopoly.
I seal this honour thine; none dare
Hope for a part in thy despair.

From such evidence, Derek Patmore in his two books about Coventry Patmore has deduced that the ageing poet experienced a grand physical passion for Mrs. Meynell which she rejected. Nevertheless, his treatment of the matter is singularly ambiguous. Although Harriet, he writes, was jealous of Patmore's London friends, these momentary doubts were compensated for by the depth of his love, 'for his infidelities were only spiritual or intellectual'[1]—surely an extraordinary kind of qualification. Later, he says: 'Through all his adoration of Mrs. Meynell, he still loved his wife.'[2] And, again, 'By 1894, this great friendship reached its zenith. . . . Although all former biographers have been extremely reticent concerning the whole friendship, there is no doubt that Coventry Patmore had fallen physically in love with her.'[3] Apart from the contradictory nature of these statements, it is difficult to associate any kind of guilty passion with Patmore, not only because of the evidence of his life and principles, but also because of the closeness of his friendship with Wilfrid Meynell, his frank and friendly letters to him, which rule out any idea of an 'intrigue', and his sharing with Harriet of his friendship with the Meynells.

When Alice Meynell turned to George Meredith as her chief literary intimate, Patmore turned to Francis Thompson to share his sorrow:

'*Dieu et Ma Dame*, is the legend of us both. But at present Ma Dame is too much for the balance, peace and purity of my religion. There is too much heartache in it.'[4]

Yet even this need not be read as implying a senile infatuation. Derek Patmore appears too ready to interpret as merely physical passion a fervent attachment of a kind uniquely Patmore's own. Patmore had a vast capacity for many different kinds of love; in his devotion to Alice Meynell can be seen not only the effect of that kind of fascination she seemed to exercise over many literary men, but also admiration for her talents as wife and mother, mixed with

1 *Life and Times*, p. 206.   2 *Ibid.*, p. 231.
3 *Ibid.*, p. 233.   4 *Ibid.*, p. 235.

an idealized love which represented a later stage of that kind of neo-Platonic love which played a considerable part in Patmore's development.

Patmore's critics have interpreted the relationship in various ways. In her study of Mrs. Meynell, Anne Kimball Tuell speaks of 'the noble poetic friendship of two poets' and of the 'quickening of spirit' which Patmore's influence caused in Alice Meynell's work.[1] J. M. Cohen puts the matter thus:

> 'Physically the ageing poet was deeply bound to her (Harriet), though, mentally unsatisfied, he sought for a companion who would be his intellectual equal, as Emily Patmore had been. This, I think, is the cause of his late and unhappy love for Alice Meynell.'[2]

Perhaps the most authoritative pronouncement comes from Viola Meynell, one of Alice Meynell's daughters, who, in discussing her mother's friendship with Patmore, had the advantage of access to intimate family papers, and her own childish recollections, as well as the opinions of her father, to draw on. In a memoir of her mother, published in 1929, she gives an important clue to a possible reason for the replacement of Coventry Patmore by George Meredith as 'special friend', when she writes:

> 'It is to be feared that in this friendship, and in others, my mother did fail to some extent to make her love felt. . . . Probably some explanation is simply that she was so provided with love within her family, so satisfied with her happy occupation of writing, that she did not make those who loved her feel her need of them. There is perhaps always inequality in the love that two people exchange—undiscovered or tolerable inequality. But the inequality where one has need of a beloved friend and the other has not, discovers itself and cannot be borne.'[3]

In a more recent book, however, Viola Meynell goes further, to provide the most satisfying summing-up of the affair, putting the whole relationship in a clearer perspective, and superseding the speculations of Derek Patmore.

> 'What Patmore sought from her in this last distraught grief of his life is undefined,' Miss Meynell writes. 'He may have thought that in her marriage there could not be full communion with what was to him her rare genius. It was not unnatural to think of her separately from those close about her. She was distinct, as a person of creative genius must

---

[1] *Mrs. Meynell and Her Literary Generation* (New York: E. P. Dutton & Co., 1925), pp. 215–217.

[2] 'Prophet Without Responsibility', p. 296.

[3] *Alice Meynell: A Memoir* (Jonathan Cape, 1929), pp. 121–122.

be. . . . Patmore was at the same time the last person to wish to ignore or injure a marriage-tie, but somewhere, beside her marriage and above all else in her life, he thought a place was his. Her exceeding love of his poetry made it seem certain. But this conception of his may have been one not quite realizable in any human relation; it was not realizable with her.'[1]

Such a view is the only one which accords with the facts; with Alice Meynell Patmore was striving for some kind of intimate spiritual relationship incapable of fulfilment, but of a type essentially different from the 'physical falling in love' of Derek Patmore. It is certain that his disappointment in this relationship helped to make his last two years difficult ones. His son, Francis J. Patmore, tells how he used to accompany his father in his last years on long night-time country walks:

'During these walks he would often exclaim aloud; "My God, how cold, how cold!" One hot July night, as I was sweating under his weight, I ventured to protest that he could not possibly be cold, especially as he always wore at night a heavy ulster. He said, "Oh, it is a spiritual cold I feel." And in this internal spiritual life, his last years were far from happy and his soul longed, I think, for death and to see his God face to face.'[2]

The spiritual stress in Patmore which this incident and others illustrate is related to his curious mixture of innocence and experience, of passionate sensuality and restraint. One of the reasons why *Amelia* is such a typically Patmorean poem is that to make a success of a piece in which a middle-aged lover takes his young fiancée to the grave of her predecessor requires unusual purity and innocence of spirit. Patmore had that innocence; but it existed side by side with a deeply sensual impulse which it was one of his life's aims to conquer by means of religion and will-power and to sublimate through the legitimate pleasures of marriage.

The struggle of Patmore to reconcile his physical experience of love in marriage and the demands of his nature with his spiritual conception, to find in married intimacy a reality as truly sacramental as it was in theory, is evident in his poetry. Most of the poems in the 1844 volume, notably The River, reveal the same awareness of the dangers of sexual feeling as does his 'autobiography' when, for instance, he says that among his youthful intuitions was a discerning of the difference between the 'tangible

1 *Francis Thompson and Wilfrid Meynell* (Hollis & Carter, 1952), p. 106.
2 'Coventry Patmore—A Son's Recollections', *The English Review*, Vol. LIV, February 1932, p. 140.

blackness' of sexual impurity and the 'bliss' of virginal purity.[1]
Yet, even in such an early work as The River, he looked forward to
the consecration of sexual love and the stilling of the passions in
marriage when he ended the poem:

> And the river, through the ivied bridge,
> Flows calm as household love.

The purgation of purely sensual desire is a major theme in *Tamerton
Church-Tower*. Patmore told Sutton that its purpose was 'to shew
the right nature—or rather the wrong nature, and through that the
right—of love for a woman.'[2] After the poet-narrator's wife, Blanche,
is drowned, he experiences a deep sense of guilt in that he has not
brought his love into line with religion, that, in fact, he has really
had no understanding of the true significance of love. His mature
idealism, too, is contrasted with his friend Frank's purely physical
way of looking at love.

Even in the happy domesticity of *The Angel in the House*, there
is much piercing analysis of the psychology of love, of the doubts
and perplexities which arise in the lover's mind, which shows
Patmore's awareness of the clash in his spirit between desire and
idealization. And, besides the many reminders of the trials of
marriage in *The Victories of Love*, there is the important indication
that

> ... what we have to gain
> Is, not one battle, but a weary life's campaign.
> (*U.E.*, 'Faint Yet Pursuing')

From this point of view *The Unknown Eros* is one result of
Patmore's attempt to fuse his sensuality with his religion, or rather
to pass beyond the sensual impulse to the transfiguration of that
impulse, to reconcile the natural with the supernatural. On the
whole he succeeds, but some of the erotic imagery in the "Psyche"
odes shows that the reconciliation was not achieved without a
struggle against himself. *The Rod, the Root and the Flower* was
clearly many years in the making[3]; yet, despite the signs of various
earlier stages of Patmore's thinking, all trace of the sensual is purged
out, and only the pure peace and calm of spiritual identification, of
'all passion spent' remains. Francis Thompson's intimacy with
Patmore made him privy to some of the old man's most secret

---

[1] Champneys, *Memoirs*, Vol. II, p. 45.   [2] *Ibid.*, Vol. II, p. 159.
[3] 'Seeing how short it was, I asked him how long it had taken him to write.
"All my life", he replied.'—Francis J. Patmore, 'Coventry Patmore—A Son's
Recollections', *The English Review*, p. 139.

confidences. In the poem which Thompson wrote after Patmore's death, *A Captain of Song*, there is a passage which can hardly refer to anything else but the spiritual struggles which the poet waged successfully against his sensuality:

> Ye shall mark well
> The mighty cruelties which arm and mar
> That countenance of control,
> With minatory warnings of a soul
> That hath to its own selfhood been most fell,
> And is not weak to spare:
> And lo! that hair
> Is blanchèd with the travel-heats of hell.

The personal influence, which, after that of Emily, most significantly affected Coventry Patmore and helped to lead him beyond passion to a reconciliation of the religious and the erotic was that of his remarkable daughter, Emily Honoria. The eldest daughter and the third child of Emily and Coventry, she was born in 1853. Intelligent, high-spirited, yet somewhat introspective, Emily Honoria became a Catholic with the other children following upon her father's conversion, and very early revealed a bent towards the religious life. But when at sixteen Emily Honoria wanted to enter a convent both Coventry and her step-mother felt that she was too young to know her own mind, and so in 1869 they sent her to a convent school.

As her wish remained unchanged, Patmore then took her on a round of London social life, which made no appeal to her. Consequently, on the feast of the Epiphany, 1873, Emily Honoria entered a recently founded teaching order, the Society of the Holy Child Jesus; when she took her vows, in 1875, she adopted the name 'in religion' of Sister Mary Christina. Her short life was full of self-denial, pious living and development of the contemplative life, and her dedicated personality made a strong impression on all who knew her.[1] Her vocation, in fact, fulfilled in detail Patmore's ideal of the mystic. Emily Honoria's inherited delicacy of constitution, her convent activities and her own austerities cut her life short in 1882, with a death which, even making allowances for some pious

[1] Emily Honoria's life is set out in *A Daughter of Coventry Patmore*, by A Religious of the Society (London: Longmans, Green & Co., 1924). Articles on her life and poetry include two by L. Wheaton: 'Emily Honoria Patmore', *Dublin Review*, Vol. 163, No. 327, Oct.–Dec. 1918, and 'Psyche and the Prophet', *The Catholic World*, Vol. CXVII, No. 705, Dec. 1925; and 'A Daughter of Coventry Patmore', by Audrey Gwynn, *Studies*, Dublin, Vol. XIII, No. LI, Sept. 1924.

embroidery on the part of her biographer, a fellow-religious, was undoubtedly a source of edification to the other nuns.

Among the complex of influences which helped to shape Patmore's later philosophy, that of Sister Mary Christina is one of the most potent. There was an unusual sympathy between the two. Emily Honoria's verse, which her father never saw, echoes his vocabulary, his metres and his thought. Patmore sent the *Unknown Eros* odes to her as he composed them, and her comments show not only how fully she understood her father's vision, but the extent to which he was prepared to rely upon her advice.

That the mystical experiences of Coventry Patmore and those of his daughter were connected can hardly be doubted. Many of the letters between them have disappeared—in any case, as she was in a convent near Hastings, they saw each other often enough not to need to correspond much—but it is of the deepest significance that as Sister Mary Christina, so close to her father's heart, was advancing in the ways of contemplation and dedication, the Psyche odes were written, and that, after her death in 1882, Patmore wrote no more poetry.

It is clear from *The Unknown Eros* and from *The Rod, the Root and the Flower* that Emily's life as a 'bride of Christ', and her dedication to Divine Love assisted Patmore in his struggle to submit himself to God as woman to man; and that her consecrated virginity made him see more deeply into the spiritual nature of virginity. Technical virginity is treated very coldly in his early poems, and even a virginity dedicated to a life of prayer and good works is regarded as a second best. For instance, in Letter XI of *The Victories of Love*, Mary Churchill, Honoria's unmarried sister, writes to her father, the Dean, regretting her state; and in The Pearl, originally one of the Preludes to Idyll VI of *The Espousals*, but omitted in later editions, he said:

> Say, Muse, who warblest at mine ear
>   That Prothalamium jubilant
> Which I, in meekness and in fear,
>   Repeat and of its glory scant,
> Say, what of those who are not wives,
>   Nor have them; tell what fate they prove
> Who keep the pearl which happier lives
>   Cast in the costly cup of Love?
> I answer (for the sacred Muse
>   Is dumb) 'Ill chance is not for aye;
> But who with erring preference choose
>   The sad and solitary way,

And think peculiar praise to get
  In heaven, where error is not known,
They have the separate coronet
  They sought, but miss a worthier crown.
Virgins are they before the Lord,
  Whose hearts are pure; the vestal fire
Is not, as some misread the Word,
  By marriage quenched, but flames the higher.'

Strikingly different is the warmth and sympathy of his treatment of virginity in 'Deliciae Sapientiae de Amore', in which the force of the example of both the Virgin Mary and of the cloistered religious as a love-way is felt:

'Hail Virgin in Virginity a Spouse!'
Heard first below
Within the little house
At Nazareth;
Heard yet in many a cell where brides of Christ
Lie hid, emparadised,
And where, although
By the hour 'tis night,
There's light,
The Day still lingering in the lap of snow.

In Patmore's progress beyond and through the sanctified analogy of married love to a wider acceptance of love in which, mystically, the body is made holy through rejection of the pleasures of the body, and in which, while married love is still accepted as a great and holy love, a foreshadowing of the union with God, dedicated celibacy is a love of at least equal and perhaps higher virtue, Sister Mary Christina's example was paramount.

A final non-literary influence on Patmore's thought and vision, one which blends with and completes that of his daughter, was the effect of his deeper knowledge of Catholic teaching on the Blessed Virgin Mary. Both before and after his conversion, he wrote in his 'autobiography', he found himself out of harmony with Catholic practice concerning the Blessed Virgin, including the Rosary and other Marian devotions. However, in 1877, against his natural inclination and without any sensible devotion, but to make an external profession of the Church's mind, he made a pilgrimage to Lourdes.

'Accordingly', he says, 'on the 14th of October, 1877, I knelt at the shrine by the River Gave, and rose without any emotion or enthusiasm or unusual sense of devotion, but with a tranquil sense that the prayers of thirty-five years had been granted. I paid two visits of thanksgiving

36

to Lourdes in the two succeeding Octobers, for the gift which was then received, and which has never since been for a single hour withdrawn.'[1]

At the beginning of 1876,[2] he was contemplating a great poem on the marriage of the Blessed Virgin. It is likely that his uncertainty as to whether, in view of his attitude towards the Blessed Virgin, he was really fitted to embark on a poem in her honour, played some part in determining him to make a journey to Lourdes. From his own words it is plain that the pilgrimage was the occasion of a deep religious experience; it provided him with the tranquillity of spirit he was seeking, and gave him, too, the final symbol which made all his previous glimpses intelligible, as the last lines of 'The Child's Purchase' show. For many reasons, including the death of his daughter, Patmore abandoned the poem after completing only the introduction.

Frederick Page has analysed the copious notes which Patmore made for this unwritten poem, and these, taken in conjunction with 'The Child's Purchase' itself, show that the work was to be, in Patmore's words, 'the most "concrete", simply vivid, and unabstract of poems'[3] and that in it was to be celebrated a mystical reconciliation of marriage and virginity. The Virgin Birth was to be the core of the poem; in words which recall his ode, 'The Contract', Patmore notes:

'The birth of our Lord was the natural result of the virgin marriage in its perfection, and Jesus would probably have been born of Eve had she and Adam persevered—for the Incarnation was necessary, and independent of the idea of Redemption, and there would have been no reason for four thousand years' delay, but for the sin of Adam and Eve.'[4]

Another note shows that he had now, through the example of his daughter and by a deeper understanding of the place of the Blessed Virgin in Catholic theology, come to accept a high place for virginity, while still retaining his exalted view of marriage:

'Be careful to shew the essential purity of marriage alongside with that of virginity, and explain the prohibitions of the church as defences not denials of that purity.'[5]

[1] Champneys, *Memoirs*, Vol. II, p. 56.
[2] In a letter of February 1876, Sister Mary Christina refers to her thinking of her father's 'intention' on the Feast of the Espousals of the Blessed Virgin (Champneys, *Memoirs*, Vol. I, p. 276).
[3] *Patmore, A Study in Poetry*, by Frederick Page (Oxford University Press, 1933), p. 135.
[4] *Ibid.*, p. 133.   [5] *Ibid.*, p. 142.

With the exception of his father, then, the chief personal influences on Coventry Patmore were feminine. He was a man who delighted in female society; he had a genius for making women happy; and the five women with whom his life was most closely bound up all produced different kinds of responses in him, the effects of which can be seen in his work. His friendships with men were firm and intimate, but the influence that Tennyson and Hopkins, for example, had on him was literary, and not emotional or philosophical. The poet who exalted woman and found in man's relations with her a key to the mysteries of the universe learned in life what he expressed in his poetry.

II
Early Influences on Patmore's Thought

FROM EARLY YOUTH, as we have seen, Patmore was an avid reader, interested at first in aesthetics, poetry, philosophy and criticism, and later turning to theology and mysticism. Books gave him both confirmations of his earlier intuitions and ideas he was to confirm in his own living. Most of his later reading, in particular, was devoted to seeking not so much new illuminations as more evidence of what he had already come to regard as the very heart of truth. Because he blended the language and viewpoints of several writers with his own outlook, on such a topic as Nature, for instance, it is almost impossible to assign any definite source for many of his ideas. Swedenborg owed something of his philosophy to traditional Catholic sources, and, as Patmore studied Swedenborg side by side with Aquinas, the precise extent of his debt to each writer for ideas they have in common cannot be disentangled from his own formulation of those ideas. It is only when Patmore elaborates salient features of Swedenborg's teaching or of that of Coleridge, for example, using terms uniquely those of a particular writer, and acknowledging his debt to him, that we can, in most instances, see direct indebtedness. For a writer who read as much as Patmore did, the question of sources must be a complicated one. Nevertheless, there is enough evidence to show who were the writers to whom he owed most, and also to indicate what he owed to each of them.

Among the earliest influences on Patmore's mind were Plato, Aristotle and Emerson. That he read Plato while yet a boy is plain from his father's words in *Chatsworth*: 'He looked upon Plato as the nearest to a poet of any human being that ever lived.'[1] Champneys did not think that Patmore was much given to reading Plato in later life, and felt that he had so thoroughly assimilated the philosopher's ideas and even phrasing that those passages in his prose which recall Plato were written without consciousness of the debt.[2]

A letter written by Patmore to Emily Augusta in 1848 clearly shows this earlier interest: 'The desire of mind to mind is never satiated but rather continually increased by inter-communion: when this desire of soul for soul is true, all other desire follows, and, as far as possible, keeps pace; and receives glory from its happy symbolization of the spiritual yearning.'[3] And the final paragraph of an essay written over forty years later bears out Champneys's point that Plato's influence was an enduring, if unconscious, one:

> 'There comes a time to those who follow perfection, in which all possible forms of beauty are, as it were, discerned at once; it is not beautiful things, but Beauty itself which is perceived; and in the light of this faint aurora of the great and unspeakable vision, all particular forms of beauty, such as quicken the tongue of Art, fail to arrest interest and attention and to excite the desire of communicating them to others. A sculptor who could see, at one moment, all the possible forms of beauty which might be wrought from his block of marble would be quite unanxious and unable to develop any one of them.'[4]

Whether or not Patmore understood a great deal of Plato's teaching is another matter. He does appear to have found the philosopher difficult and obscure; although full of suggestion and illuminations. In *The Rod, the Root and the Flower*, he wrote: 'A man may read Plato without clearly comprehending much of what he means. He cannot read him without becoming, in some degree, a changed man.'[5] Yet he looked upon Plato as a 'great psychologist' and as such coupled him with St. Paul and Hegel.[6] His imagination was enkindled by the metaphor of the Cave of Shadows; and, although he did not accept the theory of knowledge implied in Plato's image, he wrote in *The Rod, the Root and the Flower*: 'Plato's cave of shadows is the most profound and simple statement of the relation of the natural to the spiritual life ever made.'[7] At least one echo of the same image is to be found in his poetry:

---

[1] *Chatsworth*, p. 84. [2] Champneys, *Memoirs*, Vol. II, p. 5.
[3] *Ibid.*, Vol. I, p. 135.
[4] 'A People of a Stammering Tongue', *Religio Poetae*, p. 50.
[5] *Rod, Root and Flower*, p. 86.
[6] 'Swedenborg' (*St. James's Gazette*, April 16, 1886), *Courage in Politics*, p. 102.
[7] *Rod, Root and Flower*, p. 76.

> For all delights of earthly love
> Are shadows of the heavens, and move
> As other shadows do.
>   (*V.L.*, "*Wedding Sermon*")

Although Patmore read the *Phaedo*, the *Phaedrus*, the *Republic* and the *Symposium*, it was the latter work alone which seems to have left a permanent impression. The title-page of the fourth edition of *The Angel in the House* (1866) quotes from Shelley's translation of the *Symposium*: 'Is it not strange that there are innumerable hymns and poems composed for other Gods, but not one of the many poets who spring up in the world has ever composed a verse in honour of Love, who is such and so great a God?', which looks forward to *The Unknown Eros*. In Socrates's report of his conversation with Diotima in the *Symposium* are various concepts similar to those which later dominated Patmore's mind, modified by his own thinking and the reading of Coleridge and Swedenborg. For Diotima, love is one of the links between the sensible and the eternal world; for Patmore, it became *the* link. Plato's Eros is an intermediary between gods and men but for Patmore, the 'Unknown Eros' is God Himself. And Patmore never accepted Plato's idea that physical procreation is the lowest of the forms of love. The whole tenor of his work is towards a glorification of the body, as well as of the soul; and, accepting the Christian dogma of the Incarnation with all that it implies in ordinary human life, he came to look upon man not as a duality with soul contending with, or 'riding' the body, but as a fusion of both, with the soul as the 'form' of the body. While Plato emphasized physical beauty, there is probably not another poet in English who has written so much of love yet who devotes so little space to the celebration of the beauty of the beloved as Patmore does. And the homosexuality of Plato's love, however 'spiritualized', was certainly distasteful to Patmore. 'Do you think that Plato and Socrates would have fallen into sensualities, which one does not even utter, had they known Christ, the Son of God, crucified?'[1] he wrote on one occasion to H. S. Sutton.

The *Symposium* is the earliest source in which Patmore is likely to have come across the idea of sexual duality as a basic principle in the universe. His notion of 'Homo', the male and female constituents of 'man', owed much to Swedenborg, but it almost certainly had its spring in the myth which Plato put into the mouth of Aristophanes in the *Symposium*. Here the story is told of the original three sexes, the third of which, partaking of the nature of both of the others,

---

[1] *Memoirs*, Vol. II, p. 145.

was cut into two by Zeus, so that the severed halves of Man's original body yearn to reunite and grow together again. In one of the passages in which Patmore expounds his concept of 'Homo', in relation to the nature of the Trinity, he refers directly to this portion of the *Symposium*, coupling Plato now with corroborations from his other reading:

> 'Nothing whatever exists in a single entity but in virtue of its being thesis, antithesis, and synthesis, and in humanity and natural life this takes the form of sex, the masculine, the feminine, and the neuter, or third, forgotten sex spoken of by Plato, which is not the absence of the life of sex, but its fulfilment and power, as the electric fire is the fulfilment and power of positive and negative in their "embrace".'[1]

Although Patmore is often regarded as having taken a poor view of woman's spiritual capacities by comparison with those of man, his attitude towards women, and especially towards woman as mother, contrasts sharply with Plato's despising of physical parenthood, and his claim that, with rare exceptions, men alone attain spiritual parenthood. If Patmore did not favour the kind of social and intellectual equality between the sexes which has come to be largely taken for granted today, at least his attitude gives more dignity to woman than Plato's does: 'Woman is the sum and complex of all nature, and is the *visible* glory of God.'[2]

As Patmore began to advance in the knowledge of love he came to look upon Plato's concepts as unrealistic. He always maintained an idealistic attitude towards love, but the transcendence of the body through an adoration of the beauty found in and through the body did not appeal to him. Likewise, as Gosse puts it, he 'loathed and rejected the scholastic theory, that marriage is nothing but a *remedium amoris*, a compromise with frailty, a best way of getting out of a bad business.'[3] He came finally to express his awareness of the inadequacy of Platonic love, succinctly, but unequivocally, in The Kites:

> I saw three Cupids (so I dream'd)
> Who made three kites, on which were drawn
> In letters that like roses gleam'd,
> 'Plato', 'Anacreon' and 'Vaughan'.
> The boy who held by Plato tried
> His airy venture first; all sail,
> It heav'nward rush'd till scarce descried,
> Then pitch'd and dropp'd, for want of tail.

[1] 'The Bow Set in the Cloud', *Religio Poetae*, pp. 53–54.
[2] *The Rod, the Root and the Flower*, p. 113.
[3] *Coventry Patmore*, p. 99.

Anacreon's Love, with shouts of mirth
That pride of spirit thus should fall,
To his kite link'd a lump of earth,
And, lo, it would not soar at all.
Last, my disciple freighted his
With a long streamer made of flowers,
The children of the sod, and this
Rose in the sun, and flew for hours.

(*A.H.*, II, i)

Here both the idealism of Plato and the 'earthiness' of Anacreon are rejected in favour of a love which exists on the realistic and idealistic levels at once.

Aristotle, too, played his part in Patmore's formative years, chiefly in interesting him in aesthetics and critical principles. Patmore himself was always to emphasize the importance of laws and rules in criticism, and often to bemoan the evidence of their absence in Victorian literature. 'We seek in vain', he wrote, ' . . . for any consistent and considerate estimate of the vocation of the Muses, or for anything more full and satisfactory upon the subject, than various assertions of certain "exalting", "purifying", "expanding" and other influences, which they are said to exert upon the soul.'[1] Much of his respect for literary 'laws' he owed to his reading of Aristotle in youth. He studied the *Rhetoric*, the *Ethics* and the *Poetics*, and his copy of the latter, in particular, he extensively pencil-marked.[2] His estimate of Aristotle as a philosopher was exceptionally high; and this opinion was probably reinforced in later life through his devotion to Aquinas, from whom he could hardly help deriving an increased respect for the Greek. In a letter to Alice Meynell occurs this statement: 'Aristotle, who is worth fifty Platos, says that "after exceeding ill, a little good is the essence of pathos".'[3] This, one of his three favourite quotations from Aristotle, forms the starting-point of his essay on 'Pathos' in *Principle in Art*. It also, as Patmore himself pointed out in the same letter, appears in disguised form in his ode 'Eurydice':

And tears come free and quick
And more and more abound
For piteous passion keen at having found,
After exceeding ill, a little good.

[1] 'Tennyson's Poems—"The Princess" ', *North British Review*, May 1848, p. 47.
[2] *Catalogue of the Library of Coventry Patmore.*
[3] *Mystical Poems of Nuptial Love by Coventry Patmore*, edited by Terence L. Connolly, S.J., Ph.D. (Boston: Bruce Humphries, 1938), p. 172.

The other two phrases which Patmore most often quotes from Aristotle indicate the nature of his indebtedness to the philosopher. Again and again, he defines the language of poetry as having a 'slight but continual novelty'.[1] and he speaks as often of things that are 'unintelligible to man in proportion as they are simple'.[2]

Coleridge was to be the chief shaper of Patmore's critical instincts, yet the early study of the Greek made Patmore aware of the need for control in art, and convinced that the 'laws' of literature should be enunciated and widely understood. Insistence upon a body of laws underlying creative writing, but not rigidly binding the artist, is a feature of Patmore's literary criticism, just as the same insistence on universally applicable law is both the strength and the weakness of his architectural criticism.

The two essays which show the most direct effects of his study of Aristotle are 'The Ethics of Art' (1849) and 'Pathos' (1887). In the former, he argues that

> 'art must have for one of its conditions, a *tendency* to elevate. . . . All really great artists have perceived the comparative worthlessness of literal verisimilitude. . . . Direct representation, if it is artistical, is always *ideal*. . . . '[3]

He accepts, in short, the Aristotelian idea of 'imitation' in the genuine sense—not as the literal transcript of the world of reality, but as an 'imitation' of the ideal. Later, in the same essay, Patmore writes, 'True poetry, as Aristotle says, is the most philosophical of all writing', which appears to be an individual interpretation of Aristotle's 'Poetry, therefore, is a more philosophical and a higher thing than history: for poetry tends to express the universal, history the particular.'[4]

While Plato found reality only in the world of ideas, Aristotle found the primary reality in the concrete thing, and saw in fine art a rational faculty which divines nature's unfulfilled intention and reveals her ideal to sense. So, for Patmore,

> 'The artistic confines itself . . . to phenomena and to the First Cause, and takes note of no relationships between the former and the latter, but such as are immediate and direct. The artist does not regard

---

[1] " 'Legends and Lyrics' and 'The Wanderer' ' ", *North British Review*, Vol. XXX, No. LX, May 1859, p. 408.

[2] 'Love and Poetry', *Religio Poetae*, p. 141; also 'Thoughts on Knowledge, Opinion and Inequality', *Religio Poetae*, p. 126.

[3] 'The Ethics of Art', *British Quarterly Review*, Vol. X, No. XX, Nov. 1849, pp. 442–444.

[4] S. H. Butcher, *Aristotle's Theory of Poetry and Fine Art, with critical text and translation of the Poetics* (Macmillan, 1923), IX, 3, p. 35.

phenomena as unreal but rather as the only realities, apart from his soul and from God.'[1]

On the matter of beauty in art, too, Patmore is closer to Aristotle than he is to Plato or Plotinus. Aristotle makes beauty a regulative principle of art, but does not regard the manifestation of the beautiful as the end of art. Patmore put it like this: 'Beauty is one among the *many* realities which Art now grasps. The artist reveals reality whenever he exhibits or suggests the true relation of any object to the rest of the universe.'[2]

The essay 'Pathos', written thirty-eight years after 'The Ethics of Art', owes much less to Aristotle directly, but at least finds its inspiration in the Greek philosopher's description of the nature of pity or compassion. Patmore begins: 'Aristotle has described in his *Rhetoric*, with the greatest acuteness and sensibility, the conditions and modes of exciting pity. But pity includes much that is excluded by pathos'[3]; and goes on to define the difference between pity and pathos by saying that the latter is simply emotional, and reaches no higher than the sensitive nature, while pity is helpful and is not repelled by circumstances which disgust the simply sensitive nature. In the course of this he refers to Aristotle again: 'The author of the *Rhetoric* shows his usual incomparable subtilty of observation when he notes that a little good coming upon or in the midst of extremity of evil is a source of the sharpest pathos'; and comes finally to a piquant and typically Patmorean conclusion: 'Pathos is the luxury of grief; and when it ceases to be other than a keen-edged pleasure it ceases to be pathos.'

There is little in Patmore's work to suggest a really close study of Aristotle. It is not unlikely, in view of his movement away from Plato, that his reading of Aristotle, however, not only made him aware of the limitations of Plato's philosophy, but also prepared him for his more intensive study of Aquinas. It was for his sensitivity to critical principles, for a 'classic' sense of law and form in poetry, and for one or two basic ideas about the nature of art that he was indebted to Aristotle. For the rest, that he was as eclectic in his approach to the philosopher as he was to other writers is indicated by his words: 'The writings of Aristotle and St. Augustine alone contain more wise and pithy sentences on points which concern all men than are to be found in the entire sum of proverbial literature.'[4]

---

[1] 'The Ethics of Art', p. 445.   [2] *Ibid.*, p. 447.
[3] 'Pathos', *Principle in Art*, p. 37.
[4] 'Proverbs and Bon-Mots', *St. James's Gazette*, Oct. 7, 1886; *Courage in Politics*, p. 32.

The same impulse which carried Patmore to Plato took him also to Emerson. His first reaction to the American's works was one of undiluted enthusiasm. In the early 1840's, when Emerson's works were fast gaining admirers in Britain, Patmore became acquainted with his *Essays*, and his instinctive youthful idealism responded warmly to the American's philosophical idealism. In one of his earliest articles, he reviewed Emerson's *Essays: Second Series*, in terms of almost unqualified praise, showing himself enraptured even by Emerson's obscurity.[1] And in the same essay we find one source of Patmore's life-long conception of the poet as the *seer* who perceives with the intuition of genius truths which the philosopher must fumble for and the scientist miss altogether: 'That Emerson is, in a high degree, possessed of the faculty and vision of the *seer*, none can doubt who will earnestly and with a kind and reverential spirit peruse these nine essays.'[2] He quotes generously from 'The Poet' and 'Nature', wherein Emerson sets forth this concept of the poet as 'the only teller of news' and 'beholder of ideas'; and his conclusion is:

'Emerson and other philosophers do not write to save thinking, but to suggest it. They write to stimulate the active powers of the soul, and do not intend to trot round the intellect they seek to instruct, in a ready-made ring of ideas.'[3]

However, on February 15, 1847, in a letter to H. S. Sutton, Patmore reveals that he has already developed serious reservations about Emerson, reservations which were to grow stronger with the years:

'I am a lover of "Ralph Emerson".... Loving him so much, I am quite enraged with him that he will not let me love him more. He is very inconsistent, which a *very* great man never is: I think he lacks the quality of reverence.... I dislike much of his language, for I think that it shows a want of profound and practical sincerity. I don't think he understands true Christian humility or repentance: the peace of God which passeth all understanding is not, I fear, an abiding guest with him.'[4]

In subsequent letters to Sutton, Patmore continued the attack on Emersonian religion, making it clear that, much as he at the time admired some aspects of Emerson's writing, the American's attitude towards religion and especially towards Christ, annoyed Patmore, who had by now come to accept the main tenets of orthodox Christianity.

[1] 'Essays, Second Series by R. W. Emerson', *Douglas Jerrold's Shilling Magazine*, Vol. I, No. II, Feb. 1845, p. 184.

[2] *Ibid.*, p. 185.   [3] *Ibid.*   [4] Princeton University Library.

In 1847–1848, when Emerson was visiting England, Patmore was introduced to the writer by Sutton, and saw a good deal of him. Emerson was one of those who did most to start *The Angel in the House* on its way to overwhelming popularity in America.

Yet, despite these personal contacts, or perhaps partly because of them, Patmore's reaction against Emerson continued to grow. His maturing mind became dissatisfied with the vague romanticism and the often wordy idealism of Emerson, and when the first enthusiasm died, he found in Coleridge a more inspiring guide. After the essays just quoted, Patmore did not mention Emerson for some years; when he turned to him again, it was to write a very critical article on his life and works,[1] which shows that his later attitude towards the American contained a mixture of attraction and repulsion which he is not alone in having felt. He attacks Emerson on the basis that he preached 'absolute nonconformity with everything' and that he enjoined men to look upon their individual insight as the one infallible guide, 'though it may bid us go one way today and the opposite tomorrow', and he offers a basic criticism of Emerson's personality:

'Emerson, though a good man—that is, one who lived up to his lights
—had little or no conscience. He admired good, but did not love it;
he denounced evil, but did not hate it, and did not even maintain that
it was hateful, but only held that it was greatly inexpedient.'

Above all this, Emerson is, in his view, totally deficient in reverence and in religious sense, and that is enough, for all his good points, to damn him. The essay is not always accurate, by no means fair, and more than a little perverse. Some of Patmore's points are perceptive, yet the slightly off-centre view suggests that he had, in fact, not read Emerson for thirty or forty years.

For all his disclaimers, and for all his later rejection of Emerson, it was to the American writer that he owed his first glimpses of some of the ideas which were to become permanent parts of his thought. These words from 'The Ethics of Art':

'Now the artist, or the man of genius, is capable not only of perceiving
realities with much greater vividness than other men, but also of
perceiving realities of a higher kind than are seen by other men, save
those in whom God's spirit more especially dwells.'[2]

say much the same as Emerson does in 'The Poet':

'The signs and credentials of the poet are that he announces that which
no man foretold. He is the true and only doctor; he knows and tells;

[1] 'Emerson', *St. James's Gazette*, Nov. 1886; *Principle in Art*, pp. 113–121.
[2] 'The Ethics of Art', p. 448.

he is the only teller of news, for he was present and privy to the appearance which he describes.'[1]

In the same essay, Emerson wrote of the poet: 'Nature offers all her creatures to him as a picture-language. . . . Things admit of being used as symbols because nature is a symbol, in the whole, and in every part'[2]; while Patmore puts the identical thought thus: 'Simple nature is full of endless significance and symbolism; meaning within meaning . . . the great difficulty in art is not to infuse nature with significance; but to apprehend and express the significance of nature.'[3] 'The Poet' lays great stress on the ability of the writer, by an 'interior intellectual perception' to give a new power to symbols, and on his significance as a Namer and a Language-maker. In terms similar to those used by Emerson, Patmore writes:

'The poet is doing his noblest work in resuscitating moral truths from the inert condition of truisms and conferring upon them a perennial bloom and power. . . . The poet more than justifies his adoption of truisms and stale legends by his mode of dealing with them; he shows that, in such things, acknowledged and spoken of by all men, there are more and deeper meanings than may be fully expressed or comprehended by any man.'[4]

Again, what Patmore has to say about the superior value of 'intuitions' as against mere opinions, in, for instance, 'Thoughts on Knowledge, Opinion and Inequality', is, in both idea and phrasing, much like Emerson's assertion, in his essay 'Intellect' of the greater value of the 'spontaneous or intuitive faculty' over the 'arithmetical or logical'. Patmore's insistence, likewise, in the same essay, upon individuality and the right of the honest man of genius to be true to his 'knowledge' as against the 'opinion' of the world seems to owe a good deal to Emerson's description of 'real character' found in the man who 'sees that the event is ancillary; it must follow *him*'.[5]

One of the major differences, however, between Patmore's and Emerson's conceptions of 'orginality' of character is that, while Emerson never clearly defines the limitations of individuality, even though he believes the gifted individual will find himself in touch with certain vaguely described 'laws', Patmore's hold on Christian

---

1 'The Poet', *Essays* by Ralph Waldo Emerson, Second Series (Boston and New York: Houghton Mifflin Co., 1903), p. 8.
2 *Ibid.*, p. 13.
3 'American Poetry', *North British Review*, Aug. 1852, p. 418.
4 'New Poets', *Edinburgh Review*, Vol. CIV, No. 212, Oct. 1856, p. 339.
5 *Essays, Second Series*, pp. 96–97.

dogma, both before and after his conversion, made him temper his conception of 'originality' with the demands of the moral law and Christian ethics. His essay 'The Limitations of Genius' can be read as a corrective of the idea implied, if not stated by Emerson, that the man of genius can become so God-like that he is, to a great extent, above the codes which control ordinary men. 'There are many that can discern Genius on his starry track, though the mob is incapable,' wrote Emerson; and Patmore:

'Unless "originality" . . . works in submission to and harmony with general law, it loses its nature. In morals it becomes sin or insanity, in manners and art oddity and eccentricity, which are in reality the extreme opposites and travesties of originality.'[1]

At the same time, we can see the extent to which Patmore owed to Emerson his notion of the superiority of the intuitive faculty to the scientific and of the importance of the insight which leaps to truth ahead of scientific elaboration by comparing two passages, the first from Emerson's 'Nature', the second from Patmore's 'Seers, Thinkers and Talkers''. Emerson wrote:

'Every known fact in natural science was divined by the presentiment of somebody, before it was actually verified. A man does not tie his shoe without recognizing laws which bind the farthest regions of nature; moon, plant, gas, crystal, are concrete geometry and numbers. Common sense knows its own, and recognizes the fact at first sight in chemical experiment. The common sense of Franklin, Dalton, Davy, and Black is the same common sense which made the arrangements it now discovers.'[2]

Patmore has it:

'What is called "common sense" is much more nearly allied to genius, or true intellect, either than talent, which is the outcome of the discursive reason, or than learning, which is that of memory. . . . Science is generally considered to be the outcome solely of the observation of facts and the discursive reason; but in men like Kepler, Newton and Faraday there is no lack of "the vision and the faculty divine". The discovery of gravitation by the fall of an apple was pure vision; and it is doubtful whether there was ever a Smith's Prizeman who had not a touch of a higher faculty than that which gropes step by step from premises to conclusions.'[3]

In writing these lines, Patmore may not consciously have been recalling Emerson, but the tone of them, and of much else in the

---

[1] 'Limitations of Genius', *Religio Poetae*, p. 109.
[2] 'Nature', *Essays, Second Series*, pp. 183–184.
[3] 'Seers, Thinkers and Talkers', *Religio Poetae*, p. 89.

same essay suggests that Emerson remained, even as late as 1886, when the essay was written, a layer of influence in Patmore's mind.

In one important, but indirect way, Emerson may have had an enduring effect on Patmore—by helping to guide him to Swedenborg. The many references to Swedenborg in the *Essays* and the outline of the philosopher's science of love and marriage in *Representative Men* must surely have attracted Patmore's attention. 'Emerson, he confessed, had led him to Swedenborg',[1] states Frank Harris of Patmore, but Harris is notoriously unreliable, especially as a reporter of conversations. It is interesting that Patmore never refers to Emerson in connection with Swedenborg; but on several occasions quotes Coleridge's description of the philosopher as 'the man of ten centuries', which indicates that it was Coleridge rather than Emerson who first awakened his interest in Swedenborg.

Because of the powerful impact of Coleridge on Patmore, and because, owing as they do some of their ideas to the same sources, a certain amount of Coleridge's thinking is not dissimilar to that of Emerson, it is almost impossible to disentangle one influence from the other. Some of Patmore's views on genius, character, imagination and intuition which appear Emersonian in origin are more probably Coleridgean. His instinct for law and principle early carried him, as has been seen, to a reaction against characteristic Emersonian doctrines—his pantheism, his transcendental idealism and his distaste for dogma. In turning from the vagueness of Emerson to the logic of Coleridge he was following a natural instinct.

He records in his 'autobiography' that, in his youthful reading, Coleridge's *Aids to Reflection* occupied a high place. Whether or not this was the first prose work of Coleridge he read it is difficult to say; yet it is certain that he knew well all of Coleridge's prose that was available during Patmore's life-time. His copies of *Aids to Reflection* and *Table-Talk*, which are preserved in the Boston College Library, show that he read these books, at least, thoroughly. Notes in his handwriting have at one time almost covered the entire margin of every page; several of these have subsequently been erased. The reason for these deletions may be deduced from a comment, dated 1886, on the Dedication-page to *Table-Talk*: 'The Pencil-notes in this book were mostly made when I was quite a boy —about 16.' Some of the annotations in the *Aids to Reflection* throw light on the part this book played in leading Patmore towards Christianity. Facing the title-page is a note:

---

[1] 'Coventry Patmore', *Contemporary Portraits, Third Series*, by Frank Harris (New York: published by the Author, 1920), p. 198.

'"That which we find within ourselves which is more than ourselves". (See page 15.) It is more than ourselves only when it is not
practical. This passage suggests an overthrow to such as hope that
they are safe because this divinity stirs within them. "*But it is not
themselves. My reason* is *God. I* am my *will.*" Dec. 1843.'

And under the author's address to the reader, Patmore has written:
'I have read this book through—a great many times—but the first
reading did all this, and more. Coventry K. Patmore, Dec./1843.'
Many important passages are heavily underscored and annotated.
References to parallel passages or similar statements in Butler's
Analogy are pencilled in here and there. Among the characteristic
marginal comments in *Table-Talk* are these:

'Unless Christianity be viewed and felt in a high and comprehensive
way, how large a portion of our intelligence and moral nature does it
leave without object or action' (page 279).

'Half the infidels in the world are so because of the limited Christianity
of Christians' (page 279).

Significantly, he has heavily underlined Coleridge's words on page
47: 'The man's desire is for the woman; but the woman's desire is
rarely other than for the desire of the man.'
Patmore's attitude towards Coleridge the man and the writer
comes out clearly in the four essays he wrote on the poet in 1886
and 1887. 'To him', he states in the first of these, 'more than to any
other Englishman of the present century, we are indebted for such
"sweetness and light" as our present culture possesses.'[1] His review
of Hall Caine's *Life of Coleridge* is especially interesting for the fact
that, contrary to the most widely-held opinion at the time, he
refused to regard Coleridge as a man who idled away his years,
dissipated his talents and energies in futile and uncompleted projects, and led a 'wasted life'. He outlines the effects of his work in
poetry, criticism, politics, and religion; and, summing up, finds
Coleridge's life 'one of singular innocence, humility, integrity and
laboriousness'.[2] A review of Brandl's *Samuel Taylor Coleridge and the
Romantic School* develops this theme, and goes further in saying:

'Coleridge's philosophical services did not consist in the origination of
new ideas and systems; but in a special power of realizing and applying
to modern use that fundamental wisdom which is found in the earliest
dawn of literature ... and his services in this way have been all the
greater because he followed the example of all the wisest in adopting

[1] 'Great Talkers. 1. Coleridge', *St. James's Gazette*, March 13, 1886; *Courage
in Politics*, p. 70.
[2] 'Coleridge', *St. James's Gazette*, March 16, 1887; *Courage in Politics*, p. 86.

an aphoristic instead of a systematic mode of teaching. Coleridge, in a haphazard but most effectual way, has seen and re-uttered with singular clearness all that is most vital in all philosophies; and it is most fortunate for the effect of his teaching that he never attained the ambition he seems always to have had before him, to systematize and reconcile that which our present powers appear to be incapable of systematizing or reconciling.'[1]

Such a comment is typically Patmorean, in its implied justification and defence of his own methods.

Patmore's devotion to Coleridge as a man as well as a thinker comes out clearly in his discussion of Coleridge's unhappy marriage in a review of *Memorials of Coleorton*. Here he, the constant singer of the joys of marriage as the highest kind of human union, defends Coleridge's separation from his wife on the grounds that: 'The marriage of a most tender heart and meteoric spirit with a creature of frost could have but one ending; and the fault was not in separating, but in having come together.'[2] As a Catholic, Patmore rejected what he called the 'vulgar solution' of divorce; his treatment of the 'hard case' of Coleridge's marriage is in line with Catholic teaching, in that it justifies separation, without remarriage. But his whole analysis of Coleridge's marriage is both more sensible and more charitable than that of most of his contemporaries.

Patmore's own prose shows traces of the Coleridgean rhetoric, just as something of Coleridge's poetic manner can be noted in his early verse. The relationship between the prose styles of the two writers is somewhat difficult to illustrate; but it is no less real despite this difficulty. Thoughts similar to those of Coleridge or 'corollaries' to his thinking, expressed in a manner similar to Coleridge's own, abound in Patmore's prose. And this is a result, not of deliberate imitation, but of identification, as can be seen in passages from *Anima Poetae*, published shortly before Patmore's death, and consisting of extracts from Coleridge's note-books, which Patmore could not have seen, and which yet in many cases might have been written by Patmore rather than by Coleridge. For instance, aphorisms like these have the real Patmorean ring: 'Love, a myrtle wand, is transformed by the Aaron touch of jealousy into a serpent so vast as to swallow up every other stinging woe, and make us mourn the exchange.'[3] 'Love transforms the soul into a conformity with the

1 'Coleridge', *St. James's Gazette*, June 13, 1887; *Courage in Politics*, pp. 91–92.

2 'Memorials of Coleorton', *St. James's Gazette*, Dec. 6, 1887; *Courage in Politics*, p. 95.

3 *Anima Poetae*, from the unpublished note-books of S. T. Coleridge, edited by Ernest Hartley Coleridge (London: Heinemann, 1895), pp. 1–2.

object loved.'[1] 'Human happiness, like the aloe, is a flower of slow growth.'[2]

Coleridge's 'I am persuaded that we love what is above us more than what is under us'[3] may be compared with Patmore's 'Love is sure to be something less than human if it is not something more.'[4] There is a long passage in *Anima Poetae*[5] which discloses a sense of the richness of married love so like that of Patmore that it might almost be taken as a paraphrase of the Prologue and Epilogue of *The Angel*: and in view of the use Patmore was later to make of the *Song of Songs*, the following lines of Coleridge must be quoted:

> '*Solomon's Song*. There was a time when I thought scorn of this charming Idyll . . . in being more than an epithalamium on Solomon's marriage with a Princess of Egypt. But the more extensive my acquaintance has become with the Persian poets, and the more attentively I have studied verse by verse the Song itself . . . the more disposed I find myself to adopt the contrary judgment. The analogous passages in several of the Prophets . . . demonstrate what indeed Paul's writings seem to me already to prove, that the Spiritual Conception of the Messiah, and of his Communion with the Soul, was entertained by some at least of the Doctors between the Return from the Captivity and the Birth of our Lord. In fact the lovely allegory of Cupid and Psyche shews that the Idea was spread among the Gentiles.'[6]

Even Patmore's concept of 'Homo', of the essential part each sex plays in completing the other, is hinted at in Coleridge's manuscript note: 'Each sex is necessary to even the *special* Virtues of the other. Man (whether male or female) was not made to live alone.'[7] It is, of course, possible that the source of some of these ideas is, in both cases, Swedenborg; but the tone of Patmore's statement is, in most instances, closer to Coleridge than to Swedenborg, suggesting that his use of Swedenborg often paralleled Coleridge's own use of the philosopher.

It would be hard to over-estimate the amount Patmore owed for his religious development to Coleridge's *Aids to Reflection*. He confided to Sutton that his early religious outlook had been derived chiefly from the Bible, as interpreted by the method he had learned from Coleridge. One of the passages in *Aids to Reflection* so fully sums up Patmore's sacramental view of marriage and of its symbolical character that it could almost be, save for its argument

[1] *Ibid.*, p. 2. [2] *Ibid.*, p. 3. [3] *Ibid.*, p. 253.
[4] 'Love and Poetry', *Religio Poetae*, p. 144. [5] *Anima Poetae*, p. 216.
[6] *Inquiring Spirit: A New Presentation of Coleridge*, edited by Kathleen Coburn (London: Routledge & Kegan Paul, 1951), p. 150.
[7] *Ibid.*, p. 303. The note is a MS. note on Henry More's 'Observations upon Anthroposophia Theomagica by Alagonamastix Philalthes'.

against the Sacrament in the Church's sense, a 'manifesto' written by Patmore himself, and makes less surprising the correspondences between Patmore's writings and Coleridge's note-books:

> 'It might be a means of preventing many unhappy Marriages if the youth of both sexes had it early impressed on their minds that Marriage contracted between Christians is a true and perfect Symbol or Mystery; that is, the actualizing Faith being supposed to exist in the Receivers, it is an outward Sign co-essential with that which it signifies, or a living Part of that, the whole of which it represents. Marriage, therefore, in the Christian sense (Ephesians v, 22–33) as symbolical of the union of the Soul with Christ the Mediator, and with God through Christ, is perfectly a *sacramental* ordinance, and is not retained by the Reformed Churches as one of *The* Sacraments, for two reasons; first, that the Sign is not *distinctive* of the church of Christ, and the Ordinance not peculiar nor owing its origin to the Gospel Dispensation; secondly, it is not of universal obligation, not a means of Grace enjoined on all Christians. In other and plainer words, Marriage does not contain in itself an open Profession of Christ, and it is not a Sacrament of the Church, but only of certain Individual Members of the Church. It is evident, however, that neither of these Reasons affect or diminish the *religious* nature and dedicative force of the marriage Vow, or detract from the solemnity of the Apostolic Declaration: *This Is a Great Mystery.*'[1]

Years afterwards, Patmore quoted the early portion of this passage in one of his essays: 'If it be other than a symbol, that is as Coleridge defines a symbol to be, a part taken to represent the whole, then love, which the heart of every lover knows to be the supreme sanity, must be condemned by the intellect as the supreme insanity.'[2]

In several other places, Patmore directly acknowledges particular debts to Coleridge. The name of his last collection of essays, *Religio Poetae*, was borrowed from the older poet, who at one time proposed to write his own 'Religio Poetae', and the essay on 'The Point of Rest in Art', one of Patmore's best critical statements, in which he insists on the importance of classical calm as opposed to the turbulence of contemporary romantic art, is based on a single passage from Coleridge. There are innumerable other parallels. In a passage which may be one of Patmore's sources for his conception of universal duality, Coleridge writes:

---

[1] *Aids to Reflection*, edited by Thomas Fenby (London: George Routledge & Sons, n.d.), note to pp. 35–36. In Patmore's own copy of this book, this passage, which occurs on p. 27, is heavily underlined and ticked in the margin. At the bottom of the page is this comment: 'All mysteries are symbols, though all symbols are not mysteries.'

[2] 'The Precursor', *Religio Poetae*, p. 16.

'God, the absolute Will or Identity=Prothesis. The Father=Thesis. The Son=Antithesis. The Spirit=Synthesis.'[1]

Patmore, extending the concept into the realm of sex, puts it:

'Nothing whatever exists in a single entity but in virtue of its being thesis, antithesis and synthesis, and in humanity and natural life, this takes the form of sex, the masculine, the feminine and the neuter, or third, forgotten sex spoken of by Plato.'[2]

Again, Coleridge writes: 'The man's desire is for the woman; but the woman's desire is rarely other than for the desire of the man'[3]; while Patmore has it: 'She only really loves and desires to become what he loves and desires her to be.'[4] Patmore's insistence on the basic importance of the fact of the Incarnation is anticipated in Coleridge's: 'The Trinity is the idea; the Incarnation, which implies the Fall, is the fact; the Redemption is the mesothesis of the two— that is—the religion '[5]; a hint of that revealing analysis of masculine and feminine elements in literature which Patmore used, notably with reference to Keats, is given in Coleridge's: 'Of all the men I ever knew, Wordsworth has the least femineity in his mind. He is *all* man. He is a man of whom it might have been said "It is good for him to be alone"',[6] and even a suggestion of Patmore's symbolical interpretation of architecture and his insistence on the religious significance of Gothic as giving it superiority over other styles is found in Coleridge's: 'The principle of the Gothic architecture is infinity made imaginable. It is, no doubt, a sublimer effort of genius than the Greek style; but then it depends much more on execution for its effect.'[7]

In the early part of his life, at least, Patmore thought of himself not as a 'philosopher' or 'mystic' but as a 'psychologist of love'—a poetic psychologist, to be sure. The subtle analysis of the moods of a man in love in the 'Preludes' of *The Angel in the House* is one characteristic which distinguishes his poem from most other love-poems of the time. This psychological approach depends in Patmore, as it does in Coleridge, on the poet's keen sense of the experiencing self, and of the complexity of the human personality. There are passages in the works of both writers in which both Freud and the Existentialists are anticipated. In his essay 'Attention', Patmore seems completely aware of what Coleridge often referred to as 'below consciousness'. This psychological acuteness remained with

---

[1] *Table-Talk*, p. 51. This passage is marked in Patmore's copy, and the words '& Mesothesis' written in after 'Synthesis'. A further note reads 'See "Aids" '.
[2] 'The Bow Set in the Cloud', *Religio Poetae*, p. 54.   [3] *Table-Talk*, p. 56.
[4] 'The Weaker Vessel', *Religio Poetae*, pp. 154–155.   [5] *Table-Talk*, p. 263.
[6] *Ibid.*, p. 339.   [7] *Ibid.*, p. 231.

him long after he went beyond 'psychology' into metaphysics, and had given allegiance to mystical writers whom Coleridge had not read.

To some degree, too, Patmore's critical principles show the effect of his reading of Coleridge. As Sir Herbert Read has pointed out, Coleridge owes his distinction as a critic largely to his adoption of the psychological method.[1] Patmore tended to follow him in this; but he lacked the unusual critical acumen of Coleridge, and, while he is stimulating on principles, his application of these tends to be erratic. At the same time, he is just as concerned as Coleridge is with *law* and its relation to critical practice, and all his criticism, like Coleridge's, was based upon results derived from his own practice. There was much in which Patmore could not follow Coleridge—in his dislike of Roman Catholicism, in many of his literary judgments, and in his analytical logic. Also, although Patmore read Schopenhauer and Hegel, he never acquired Coleridge's deep knowledge of German philosophy. Coleridge's mind was more 'academic' than Patmore's, more widely-ranging and more profoundly original. Yet it is surprising in how much they are alike—in their particular spiritual sensitivity, in their apprehension of the symbolical character of nature and the sacramental character of marriage, in their trust in the revelatory character of intuitions, in their psychological approach to love and life, in their awareness of the central importance of Christian dogmas, in their description of the nature of childhood and its relation to genius, in their combination of good sense and spiritual idealism.

Wordsworth's influence, if neither so deep nor so extensive as that of Coleridge, was as lasting. The main ideas which Patmore either derived from Wordsworth or found confirmed in the earlier poet were his trust in the precious nature of childhood insights, the belief that the eye of the poet could transform the details of common life, and a transcendental sense of the 'inwardness' of Nature. In his celebration of the pure vision of the child, Patmore belongs to the line of Vaughan and Wordsworth. For him two basic intuitions offer man a glimpse of the Divine; these are love and the way in which a child looks at Nature. The two are related in one of the 'preludes' to *The Angel in the House*:

The Revelation

An idle poet, here and there,
    Looks round him; but, for all the rest,
The world, unfathomably fair,
    Is duller than a witling's jest.

---

[1] *Coleridge as a Critic*, by Herbert Read (Faber & Faber, 1949).

Love wakes men, once a lifetime each;
    They lift their heavy lids, and look;
And, lo, what one sweet page can teach,
    They read with joy, then shut the book.
And some give thanks, and some blaspheme,
    And most forget; but, either way,
That and the Child's unheeded dream
    Is all the light of all their day.

                     (*A.H.*, I, viii)

In retrospect, Patmore viewed his childhood much as Wordsworth did his and felt that he had drawn the same lessons from it. In his 'autobiography', he wrote:

'Angels spoke from time to time to me, as they do to all, and I frequently saw, as others do in youth, the things of earth lighted up with light which was not of the earth.'[1]

in which there is a hint of Swedenborg, as well as the mark of Wordsworth. In other places, Patmore links his own awareness with his favourite quotation from Wordsworth:

'With children it is far otherwise. They have the open spiritual eye; the "light which lighteth all men" has not been quenched by vices, selfishness and sordid thoughts; they have still the "grace divine", by which, as Wordsworth says, "O Nature, we are thine"; and they are capable of those primary perceptions which are knowledge indeed— knowledge which the heart never forgets though it may possibly fade altogether from the external memory.'[2]

He never ceased to admire the 'Immortality' Ode, and his own 'Auras of Delight' rings with memories of Wordsworth's poem.

The transcendental experience of Nature plays a greater part in Patmore's verse than is realized by those who look upon him only as the poet of wedded love. Apart from the exquisite symbolizing of Nature in the four 'seasonal' odes, and the sense of creation's glories elsewhere in the *Unknown Eros*, *The Angel in the House* is full of sensitive response to the inner heart of Nature. Patmore is, in simple fact, one of the most purely Wordsworthian of Victorian poets. Not only is his 'innocent sensuality' like that of Wordsworth, however, but verbal reminiscences of the great Romantic poet are scattered through *The Angel in the House*; for instance, in the preludes 'The Rainbow' and 'Love and Duty'. Patmore saw beyond the apparent pantheism of the essentially religious Wordsworth,

---

1 *Memoirs*, Vol. II, p. 45.
2 'A Safe Charity', *St. James's Gazette*, Aug. 27, 1887; *Courage in Politics*, pp. 48–49.

whose roots were in eighteenth-century Christianity, and who claimed that his *Ecclesiastical Sonnets* had anticipated the Oxford Movement by many years. It is surely more than coincidence that in 'The Child's Purchase', writing of the Immaculate Conception, Patmore should have echoed in his line:

> The world's sad aspirations' one Success,

Wordsworth's sonnet on the Blessed Virgin:

> Our tainted nature's solitary boast.

That sacramental view of Nature which informs the poetry of Wordsworth and Coleridge also informs that of Patmore, part of whose originality lay in transferring the sacramental sense and the insights of Wordsworth to the married state. As Wordsworth had found occasions of joy in external Nature which poets had not recorded before, so Patmore found similar occasions in marriage. For Wordsworth, since Nature was an inexhaustible revelation of beauty and wisdom, it must be a reflection of God Himself; for Patmore, the natural relationship of marriage is a source of so much delight that it must be a foretaste, as well as a symbol, of the union of the soul with God.

Finally, both poets treat man and Nature realistically. One of the major differences between Patmore's early poetry and his later work is that the earlier is much more manifestly Wordsworthian, the later more Spenserian, Biblical and Miltonic. But on the earlier poetry, Frederick Page has written:

> 'What is questionable in *The Angel in the House*, as in the *Lyrical Ballads*, is the artistic theory. In both it was a theory of realism, which Wordsworth and Patmore held to override "the conventional decorums of verse". There, and not in the characters of the authors, is the target of criticism.'[1]

Like Wordsworth, Patmore was not always able to transmute the details, and this results in an occasional flatness and banality. However, inspired by Wordsworth's example, he tried to give to the most homely details of living a radiant significance, so that they would both be the external signs of a sacramental universe of love, and harmonize with that universe.

> 'The one true subject (of poetry)', he wrote, 'is the divine spirit of love and light, which, pouring through the inspired imagination, is reflected by everything, and asks chiefly not to be interfered with by foreign interests in the reflecting medium. The things which supply

[1] *Patmore, A Study in Poetry*, p. 87.

the true poet with his best subjects are such as would be no subjects in the hands of anyone else. The event which has occurred a thousand times, the moral truism, the scene in which *we* can see little or nothing, because we have seen it so often—these are the themes which delight us most, and most justly, when, by the poet's help, we behold them as he, in his inspired moments, beholds them.'[1]

There are some other writers whose effect on Patmore should be mentioned at this stage—writers to whom he refers from time to time, and who supplied him with corroboration of his critical ideas, or who helped strengthen his conviction of the truth of Christianity. One such was Hegel, traces of whose aesthetic theories may be found in Patmore's essays. He wrote one article on Hegel, which does not show a very close acquaintance with the major philosophical writings of the German, but rather suggests that, although he knew Hegel's writings on aesthetics at first hand, his knowledge of Hegel's more comprehensive philosophy was confined to what he learnt from Coleridge. The chief work discussed in this essay is Hegel's *The Philosophy of Art*, whose aesthetic principles Patmore admired greatly.

> 'The very purpose of art (which Hegel discloses, in words that ought to be written in letters of gold, is "to bring the highest interests of the spirit into consciousness") is only obscurely recognized by our four or five best writers on the subject."[2]

he writes, and devotes most of the remainder of the paper to a discussion of his own idea of 'health' in art, a concept which owes something to Hegel and something to Coleridge. Hegel's dialectical philosophy—the thesis, antithesis and synthesis at the basis of all being—is in accord with Patmore's idea of the sexual duality of nature and the significance of the fusion of the two elements; but he had already adopted the dialectical notion from Coleridge before he came across Hegel. Since he refers to Hegel only rarely, apart from the essay, and then either as an aesthetician or in the most general contexts, it is safe to assume that, although he read some of Hegel's works, his mind was by this time so nourished on the writings of Catholic theologians and mystics that Hegel served him merely to provide him with one or two marginal ideas.

Much the same may be said of Schopenhauer. Edmund Gosse claims that Patmore 'was drawn with a vehement attraction to the dark philosophy of Schopenhauer, of whom he was one of the earliest students in this country.'[3] Nevertheless, Patmore never refers to, nor

1 'William Barnes. The Dorsetshire Poet', *Macmillan's Magazine*, p. 156.
2 'Hegel', *St. James's Gazette*, March 22, 1886; *Courage in Politics*, p. 107.
3 *Coventry Patmore*, p. 193.

quotes from, Schopenhauer, and nothing that is characteristic of the German's pessimistic philosophy colours his work. The most that can be said is that, as Gosse observes, he recognized that Schopenhauer, for all his apparent atheism, was still dominated by Christian formulas. Patmore's interest in Schopenhauer may be taken, then, as an indication of his breadth of sympathies rather than as a recognition of any fundamental connection between his ideas and those of the German.

Another, and somewhat unexpected, minor influence on Patmore's thought or, rather, a handy source-book for quotations and illustrations, was Hooker's *Laws of Ecclesiastical Polity*. In his 'autobiography', Patmore testified that, during his youth, he read incessantly on the subject of religion, his favourite works being the *Analogy*, the *Ecclesiastical Polity*, the *Divine Legation* and others of a kind not intended to regulate devotion.[1] Later, in the 'autobiography', almost as if to show that he had not forgotten Hooker, he quotes a sentence from him to the effect that 'Such perfect friends are truth and love that neither lives where both are not.'[2] In an 1856 essay he also quotes from the same source[3] and in L'Allegro, the lines:

> And judging outer strangers by
> Those gentle and unsanction'd lines
> To which remorse of equity
> Of old hath moved the School divines,

were, as Patmore told Hopkins, taken 'nearly verbatim from Hooker's *Ecclesiastical Polity*'.[4] Hooker's views on the relationship between man and woman and on marriage were in tune with Patmore's own, and, on the occasions when he does quote Hooker, it is not on matters of ecclesiastical law or Christian doctrine, but as a 'psychologist' of love.[5]

As with Hooker, so with Bishop Butler. Butler's *Analogy*, like the *Ecclesiastical Polity*, helped to convince Patmore of the reasonableness of Christianity; a close study of it removed once and for all for him all possibility of intellectual doubt on matters of religious truth. It was, in fact, the only Protestant work which he put on the same level as Catholic books of devotion which gave him 'a simple sense of reality'; and he felt that it had played a major part

[1] *Memoirs*, Vol. II, p. 47.   [2] *Ibid.*, Vol. II, p. 52.
[3] 'New Poets', *Edinburgh Review*, Oct. 1856, p. 339.
[4] *Further Letters of Gerard Manley Hopkins* (Oxford University Press, 1938), p. 177.
[5] E.g. 'Thoughts on Knowledge, Opinion and Inequality', *Religio Poetae*, p. 134.

in leading him towards Catholicism.[1] Even allowing for a certain amount of rationalization and 'hindsight' here, it is obvious that Butler's arguments deeply impressed Patmore, and may even have been the source of some of the religious 'intuitions' of which he became so certain later. And this is borne out by his remarks in a letter to Sutton, written closer to the actual time of his study of the *Analogy*. Speaking of the stage just before he actually entertained Christianity seriously, Patmore says that when he had been able to reach nothing but strong probability in favour of Christianity, it was Butler who, in showing that probability is the foundation of belief, had, in fact, enabled him to attain an unshakeable faith.[2] Although Patmore passed beyond Butler to Aquinas and Augustine, he never lost his regard for this work which had so early indicated to him the direction in which his religious instincts would find their fulfilment, for in his last prose work, *The Rod, The Root and the Flower*, he remembers Butler and calls him 'the most prudent of theologians'.[3]

Finally, one curious and obscure work played some part in helping to develop his insight into the psychology of the lover. This is John Norris's translation of Robert Waring's *Effigies Amoris* (1649), under the title of *The Picture of Love Unveil'd* (1682). Frederick Page points out that in one of Patmore's note-books is the entry: 'Eff. Am. 112.c.62', which is the press-mark of the British Museum copy of Norris's translation.[4] Furthermore, Patmore appended the following note to the 1856 edition of *The Espousals*:

'The writer of the *Angel in the House* is indebted, for some appropriate thoughts, chiefly embodied in lines 23–40 of "The Paradox" to the prose essay, by Robert Waring, called *Effigies Amoris*.'

The passage alluded to, from a 'prelude' retitled Love's Perversity in later editions, is as follows:

> She looks too happy and content
> For whose least pleasure he would die.
> Oh, cruelty, she cannot care
> For one to whom she's always kind!
> He says he's nought, but oh, despair,
> If he's not Jove to her fond mind!
> He's jealous if she pets a dove,
> She must be his with all her soul;
> Yet 'tis a postulate in love
> That part is greater than the whole,

[1] Champneys, *Memoirs*, Vol. II, pp. 49–50.   [2] *Ibid.*, Vol. II, pp. 146–147.
[3] *Rod, Root and Flower*, 'Homo', XXV, p. 130.
[4] Patmore, *A Study in Poetry*, p. 120.

And all his apprehension's stress,
    When he's with her, regards her hair,
Her hand, a ribbon of her dress,
    As if his life were only there;
Because she's constant, he will change
    And kindest glances coldly meet,
And all the time he seems so strange,
    His soul is fawning at her feet.

Not only these, but preceding lines in the same poem:

He makes his sorrow, when there's none;
    His fancy blows both cold and hot;
Next to the wish that she'll be won,
    His first hope is that she may not,

echo a passage from *Effigies Amoris*, which runs in part:

'Indeed every Lover is a Riddle and a blind problem to himself. He lives *Amphibiously*, and is made up of contradictory Passions. . . . Is it so that there is so much Madness and *Maliciousness* in the Desires of *Lovers*, as to wish them miserable who are most dear to them, only that they may have an Opportunity to relieve their Misfortune? . . . For 'tis expedient that the Person *Lov'd*, as well as the *Lover*, be blind. How also does the feverish and Love-sick Breast labour under the alternate Paroxisms of Heat and Cold. Neither is there any *Love* without a mixture of Indignation.'[1]

Waring's philosophy is Platonic, and deals not only with the love of man and woman, but also with the Platonic friendship between man and man. Although Patmore, having rejected Platonism, must have been out of sympathy with the underlying doctrine of Waring's work, the *Effigies Amoris* in its delineation of the effects of love and in its understanding of the contradictions of the passion appears to have provided him with useful 'corollaries'. He seems to have been struck by the psychological truth of Waring's often quaintly expressed observations, and to have carried over some of the details of the work, not only into other parts of *The Angel*, but into *The Unknown Eros* as well. For instance, Waring's notion of the civilizing power of love, which he calls the 'Passion which composes all other Commotions of the Mind, which Civilizes Men, Brutes and Philosophers',[2] is much like the idea which Patmore expresses in the

---

[1] *The Picture of Love Unveil'd*, edited by Terence L. Connolly (printed for private circulation: Boston College, 1936), pp. 5–6.
[2] *Ibid.*, p. 8.

preludes 'The Nursling of Civility' and 'Unthrift', where woman's 'priceless gift' is described as that

> Which, spent with due, respective thrift,
> Had made brutes men, and men divine.

Waring's words:

> '*Love* has not as other things any End or Satiety, neither is it like Hunger and Thirst to be allay'd by its Aliment. It is never glutted with its Gratifications but is still whetted on with fresh Delights; and as if the Object were always new, the *Lover* enjoys a daily *Epicurism* on his admired Face.'[1]

have their parallel in the prelude The Amaranth which ends:

> Whate'er the up-looking soul admires,
>   Whate'er the senses' banquet be,
> Fatigues at last with vain desires,
>   Or sickens by satiety;
> But truly my delight was more
>   In her to whom I'm bound for aye
> Yesterday than the day before,
>   And more to-day than yesterday.

There are several other resemblances between this work and *The Angel*, such as between Waring's:

> 'But O what a profitable Bill of Exchange has this *Cupid* the *Usurper* of Hearts! Whence the same Plastick view of Cementing Souls which out of many makes one, diffuses also one into many! So 'tis the same Unit which, incapable by itself of Computation, is yet the Principle of Number. So Multiplication and Addition belong to the same Art.'[2]

and Patmore's A Demonstration:

> Nature, with endless being rife,
>   Parts each thing into 'him' and 'her',
> And, in the arithmetic of life,
>   The smallest unit is a pair.

And, more strikingly still, Waring's comment:

> 'With this lovely envy while the Steel is drawn with Admiration of the Load-stone, and by and by with mutual Breathings and Nuptial Embraces exhales his precious Soul, as if 'twere now it self become a Loadstone, exercises Charms of its own, and draws other things as 'tis drawn it self . . .'[3]

[1] *Ibid.*, p. 12.   [2] *Ibid.*, p. 15.   [3] *Ibid.*, p. 30.

may have given Patmore the image in his prelude Venus Victrix:

> Fatal in force, yet gentle in will,
>> Defeats, from her, are tender pacts,
> For, like the kindly lodestone, still
>> She's drawn herself by what she attracts.

The Unknown Eros shows that Waring remained in Patmore's mind. Page is of the opinion that the title was suggested to Patmore by Waring's words:

> 'But, O *Cupid*, the least of Gods, and greatest of Deities, I should think it less than your Deserts (if yet there could be anything greater) that you are Deifi'd by those bold Philosophers the Poets. You have this Property of a God, to be unknown, and to receive Homage from Men.'[1]

While this passage may have had something to do with the framing of the title, it is much more likely that Patmore, whose knowledge of the Bible was exceptionally close, had in mind that part of the Acts of the Apostles in which St. Paul, preaching to the Athenians, described the altar he found inscribed *To the Unknown God* (Acts xvii, 23). Yet Patmore could hardly have helped gaining confirmation of his desire to celebrate the 'Unknown Eros' in the language of human love from Waring's words:

> 'Well, henceforth, let it be permitted to *Lovers*, to compliment one another with Metaphors fetch'd from Heaven, to court in the Sordid *Dialect* of Religion.'[2]

There are, also, interesting correspondences between individual Odes and Waring's views. Both The Day After Tomorrow and Tired Memory might have been written on texts supplied by passages of Waring's work.[3]

The ode 'To the Unknown Eros' which opens Book II of *The Unknown Eros* is now and again reminiscent of Waring, as in the lines:

> Thou art not Amor; or, if so, yon pyre,
> That waits the willing victim, flames with vestal fire,

which recall Waring's:

> 'Nor do I think any one can Envy at the Divinity of so mild a God, whose Anger may be appeased without Slaughter, who does not, like other Gods, require Beasts, but only cheerful Votaries for Sacrifice,

[1] *The Picture of Love Unveil'd*, edited by Terence L. Connolly, p. 57. See *Patmore, A Study in Poetry*, p. 120.
[2] *Love Unveil'd*, p. 58.   [3] See *Ibid.*, p. 34 and p. 11.

and that he may not want Temples, Erects Flaming Altars in Human Breasts. . . . Then as to the Properties of the Etherial Fire, it Burns and Refreshes . . . it is Inviolable . . . equalling the Virgin-excellency of the Vestal Flames.'[1]

However, despite these and other similarities to the *Effigies Amoris*, in no case is there a simple poeticizing of Waring's thought or words. What Patmore took from Waring, he reshaped in accordance with his own philosophy and vision and made an integral part of his own poetry. Discarding the Platonism and passing over the many extravagances of Waring's celebration of love, he assimilated what he felt to be valuable human intuitions, testing them by his own experience and making them part of himself.

[1] *Ibid.*, pp. 58–59. This resemblance is pointed out by Frederick Page, *op. cit.*, p. 122.

III

Patmore and Swedenborg

OF ALL THE PHILOSOPHICAL INFLUENCES on Coventry Patmore that of Swedenborg, if not the most profound, is possibly the most extensive. In fact, Caroline Spurgeon has said of Patmore that he is 'the English writer most saturated with Swedenborg's thought'.[1] Certainly, apart from William Blake, no other English poet absorbed so many typically Swedenborgian concepts into his own vision. It is an indication of the different ways in which the two poets regarded Swedenborg that Patmore disliked most of Blake's poetry, in particular that which is most Swedenborgian in nature, which he said was almost all 'mere drivel'.[2] Patmore approached Swedenborg as a source of poetic ideas, images and psychological insights; Blake as one visionary inflamed by another. In many instances where definite resemblances can be found between Patmore and either Coleridge or Wordsworth, to say that Patmore is directly indebted to either is to risk postulating 'influences' where the ideas in question are not always original with Coleridge or Wordsworth. But, in the case of Swedenborg and Patmore, the parallels in idea, phraseology and emphasis are so many and so close that it is certain that many concepts which give a flavour of originality to Patmore's poetry are Swedenborgian in origin, although they were, in many cases, modified by Thomist ideas.

Apart from Emerson's and Coleridge's admiration, many other things combined to lead Patmore to Swedenborg. Elizabeth Barrett

---

[1] *Mysticism in English Literature*, by Caroline F. E. Spurgeon (Cambridge University Press, 1913), pp. 31–32. [2] 'Blake', *Principle in Art*, p. 92.

Browning, with whom the poet was friendly, was also a student of the philosopher. During the time when Patmore was intimate with Tennyson, the older poet himself was interested in Swedenborg; his brother, Frederick Tennyson, was a former disciple and devoted interpreter of the seer. In the 1840's Patmore became acquainted with H. S. Sutton, a student of Swedenborg, who published commentaries on his philosophy. In the correspondence between Patmore and Sutton the topics discussed are mainly Emerson and the former's poetry, but one of Patmore's last letters to Sutton, written in the year of his death, thanks him for a presentation copy of his *Five Essays for Students of the Divine Philosophy of Swedenborg*.[1] The poet also corresponded with another Swedenborgian, J. J. Garth Wilkinson, on the subject of the seer's philosophy. He reviewed Wilkinson's *Life of Swedenborg* (1847), together with two other books on the philosopher in the *National Review*, April 1858; and Frederick Page has pointed out that Wilkinson's words in this book describing Swedenborg's imperturbability: 'The ether can only be moved by the ether, or by something still more movingly tranquil', are echoed in the final lines of Patmore's 'Winter':

> the sphere
> Of ether, moved by ether only, or
> By something still more tranquil.[2]

Patmore had read Swedenborg before 1852, for in that year he quotes from *Heaven and Hell*, in an essay on 'American Poetry', the philosopher's description of what poetical language should be.[3] In his 'autobiography', he refers to the middle years of his life with Emily in words which show not only that he had come to know Swedenborg thoroughly by that time, but also that he had passed beyond him in most respects to what he believed to be a truer expression of fundamental truths, namely, Catholic doctrine:

'I also discovered at this time that the transcendently subtle, and to me attractive psychology of Swedenborg had been drawn from the great Catholic doctrines with which he seems to have been well acquainted, and that, indeed, his whole system, his doctrines of "Correspondence", the "Grand Man", the symbolism of events and language in Scripture, the sacred nature and significance of marriage, etc., etc., were to be found as clearly, though much less diffusely, enumerated

1 Champneys, *Memoirs*, Vol. II, pp. 164–165. Letter of March 30, 1896.
2 Abbott, *Further Letters of G. H. Hopkins*, p. 193.
3 'American Poetry', *North British Review*, Vol. XVII, No. XXXIV, Aug. 1852, p. 419.

in the writings of Catholic saints and doctors, and in the services of the Church.'[1]

Patmore's admiration for Swedenborg is often revealed in his letters. He tells one correspondent that he never tires of reading him; 'he is unfathomably profound and yet simple'[2]; and to another says: 'Ninety-nine hundredths of what Swedenborg writes about is in perfect harmony with the Catholic Faith, or rather, it is the Catholic Faith.'[3] That, despite the modification of his views by a knowledge of Catholic theology, his respect for Swedenborg lasted to the end of his life is seen from the reference to him in *The Rod, The Root and the Flower*: 'We have had only one psychologist and human physiologist—at least, only one who has published his knowledge—for at least a thousand years, namely Swedenborg.'[4]

However, Patmore's attitude to Swedenborg was never that of an uncritical disciple, nor did he look upon the philosopher as an inspired religious teacher. In his three essays on Swedenborg, his published judgments temper with adverse criticism the enthusiastic recommendations of Swedenborg's books in letters to friends, and show, not only that, like many readers since him, he found much of Swedenborg dull, repetitive and even naive, but that, as he learned more about Catholic dogma, he tested the philosopher's utterances critically against the demands of that dogma.

In the essay of 1857, he bewails the fact that Swedenborg is relatively little known, although Wordsworth, Coleridge, Flaxman and Blake acknowledge his influence; but, at the same time, he repudiates any connection with the New Church, which he calls 'one of those narrow sects which are the strength-wasting imposthumes of great individual reputations.'

'"We" are no "Swedenborgians",' he continues. 'We give up all the *peculiar* theology of our philosopher, for the very sufficient reason that it *is* peculiar; his visions we do not object to regard as hallucinations of the senses. What, then, some will ask, do we learn of him to be admired and believed in? *The greatest psychological observer that the world has yet produced.*'[5]

In the following year, reviewing several of Swedenborg's books, including *Heaven and Hell* and *Conjugial Love*, he compares

---

[1] Champneys, *Memoirs*, Vol. II, pp. 52–53.   [2] *Ibid.*, Vol. II, pp. 84–85.
[3] *Ibid.*, Vol. II, p. 85.
[4] *Rod, Root and Flower*, 'Knowledge and Science', XXXVI, p. 99.
[5] 'Emanuel Swedenborg', *Fraser's Magazine*, Vol. LV, No. CCCXXVI, Feb. 1857, p. 174.

Swedenborg with Dante in 'his great and unquestionable intellectual claims'. The *Arcana Coelestia*, wherein is set out the symbolical interpretation of Scripture which was so greatly to influence his own conception of symbol, he finds 'an unreadable performance' and the interpretations themselves 'far-fetched'; but he praises *Conjugial Love* and *Heaven and Hell*, saying significantly (since he was in fact to turn several of Swedenborg's ideas into poetry): 'Some of the "memorable relations" in this volume (*Heaven and Hell*) require nothing but the garb of verse in order to render them poems of almost unrivalled beauty and significance.'[1]

At no time, of course, was Patmore a Swedenborgian in the sectarian sense. A modern Swedenborgian minister writes: 'Genuine students of Swedenborg, recognizing in their author the divinely appointed herald of a New Church, are not likely to acclaim Coventry Patmore as a brother in the Faith.'[2] On the other hand, George Trobridge, in an essay on Patmore's debt to Swedenborg, ignores all other philosophical influences on the poet, and, by so doing, endeavours to attribute the entire body of his thought on sex and marriage to the Swedish philosopher.[3]

Without going as far as Trobridge, it is possible to show not only that Patmore was indebted to Swedenborg for certain basic concepts of love and marriage, which he acknowledged, but that Swedenborg played his part in directing Patmore towards the Catholic Church. Always conscious of the inadequacies of the Swedish thinker as a religious guide, he regarded the 'visions' as the undisciplined rovings of a mind which had a powerful intuition of important truths, but which lacked the discipline of authority and dogma; his most pithy and revealing assessment of Swedenborg as a religious teacher is given in a jotting printed by Champneys:

> 'Swedenborg, the Anti-Christ, whose doctrine would deceive the very elect but for the special grace of God, i.e. deceive them by giving the whole doctrine of the Church and denying the *life* of the Church, i.e. its authority.'[4]

The notes written by Patmore in his own copies of the *Arcana Coelestia* and *The True Christian Religion* point to those aspects of Swedenborg's philosophy that most appealed to him. That he indeed found the vast *Arcana Coelestia* 'an unreadable performance'

1 'Swedenborgiana', *National Review*, April 1858, p. 350.
2 'An Appreciation of Coventry Patmore', *Arthur Edgar Beilby, His Book*, ed. by Charles A. Hall (London: New Church Press, 1936), p. 148.
3 'Coventry Patmore and Swedenborg', *Westminster Review*, Vol. CLXV, No. 1, Jan. 1906, pp. 76–90.
4 Champneys, *Memoirs*, Vol. II, p. 72.

is clear from the fact that, whereas the first two volumes are anno-tated, nearly all the rest are unmarked, and show signs (some pages remaining uncut) of having been merely dipped into. However, the two volumes of the massive 'Index' to the *Arcana Coelestia*, in which Swedenborg gives the symbolic significance of his most frequently used terms, and sets out the main lines of his teaching in brief articles under various headings, obviously provided Pat-more with a wealth of material. Page after page is marked and annotated, many sentences are underlined, and the presence of many dates in the margins shows that the book, for a time at least, provided him with daily reading, and that, in later life, he returned to it many times.[1]

So deeply did Swedenborg's teachings colour Patmore's thought and so often is the philosopher mentioned by him that the clearest way to set out the relationship between the main concepts of the two is to deal with these ideas under separate headings.

Vision

Patmore's conception of illumination, seerdom and perception obtained much confirmation from Swedenborg. He praises him for his preservation of the insights of childhood and writes, for instance:

'The homeliness and simplicity . . . of all the "spiritual" works of Swedenborg can scarcely be described. It is as if an infant of a higher race were speaking. They are full of childlike intuitions of moral and spiritual truths.'[2]

But the special quality of *seer* is possessed by Swedenborg in Patmore's view, not because he has 'memorable relations' and 'visions' but because of his instinct for seeing reality. And by 'seeing reality' Patmore meant the ability, by means of the inner eye, to discern spiritual causes beyond material effects. This is Coleridgean; it is also Swedenborgian. Patmore claims:

'Attention to realities, rather than the fear of God, is "the beginning of wisdom"; but it seems to be the last effort of which the minds, even of cultivated people, are at present capable. No good and excellent thing requiring the least act of sustained attention to reality has any chance of recognition among us; original insight is dead, and men can see only the things which others . . . have seen before them, and even these they can scarcely be said to see with their own eyes.'[3]

[1] These volumes are to be found in the Francis Thompson Room of the Boston College Library. See Appendix A for an analysis of Patmore's annota-tions.

[2] 'Swedenborgiana', *National Review*, April 1858, p. 342.

[3] 'Attention', *Religio Poetae*, p. 31.

And Swedenborg describes the spiritual blindness of men who disdain to face up to realities, in these terms:

'Those who have turned themselves away from thinking of the Divine, and have thereby become corporeal-sensual, do not consider that the sight of the eye is so gross and material that it sees many small insects as one obscure object. . . . Since the sight of the eye is so gross that many insects, with the unnumerable parts of each, appear to it as a small, obscure thing, and yet sensual men think and conclude from that sight, it is manifest how very gross their mind is, and thence in what darkness they are with respect to spiritual things.'[1]

Correspondences

One of the basic doctrines of Swedenborg was that of 'correspondences'—that all visible things have a spiritual meaning, and that every natural object corresponds to a spiritual object. Just as the deeds and works of man reveal his inward character, so, too, God's works set forth His wisdom and goodness, not just in the general sense, but in a particular fashion in which everything that is is the embodiment of some aspect of Divinity. This concept, which was common in medieval times and plays a part in Renaissance thinking, is taken much further by Swedenborg, who asserts that all things in man correspond with all things of the spiritual universe. In other words, there is a chain of symbols, or more directly 'identities', between all aspects of creation, or, as he put it:

'The whole natural world corresponds to the spiritual world, not only the natural world in general, but also in particular. Whatever, therefore, in the natural world exists from the spiritual, is said to be its correspondent.'[2]

Convinced that in his theory of correspondences lay the key to the mystical interpretation of the Bible, Swedenborg wrote:

'That the Word of the Old Testament includes arcana of heaven, and that all its contents, to every particular, regard the Lord, his heaven, the church, faith, and the things relating to faith, no man can conceive who only views it from the letter . . . that all and every part of its contents, even to the most minute, not excepting the smallest jot and tittle, signify and involve spiritual and celestial things, is a truth to this day deeply hidden from the Christian world.'[3]

[1] *The True Christian Religion*, No. 12. As different English translations of Swedenborg's works have been consulted, and as different translations vary only slightly, all quotations from Swedenborg are identified by his own paragraph numbers, which are given in all translations, and not by page numbers.
[2] *Heaven and Hell*, No. 89.   [3] *Arcana Coelestia*, No. 1.

The immense *Arcana Coelestia* is an attempt to present the 'inner' meaning of the books of Genesis, and two books on the Apocalypse do the same for Revelation. Deeply impressed by this aspect of Swedenborg's teaching, Blake began a poem in the manner of the *Arcana Coelestia*, and his work *The Ghost of Abel* is an endeavour, following Swedenborg, to interpret the Biblical story of Cain and Abel in terms of its correspondences.

Direct evidence of Patmore's interest in the doctrine of correspondences is provided by several of his notes in the 'Index' to the *Arcana Coelestia*. On page 84 of Volume I, beside the passage headed *Comparison* and reading:

> 'Comparisons taken from nature are also representatives. . . . Natural objects serve for comparisons according to their signification. . . . All comparisons used in the Word are made by significatives. . . . They are real correspondences, and not mere metaphors of language . . . '

Patmore remarks: 'So with nearly all poetical "similes". They are the *real* words, and are not likenesses, but symbols.' Later, on page 98, he also notes, beside Swedenborg's: 'The science of correspondences, though it is now antiquated and lost, far excels all other sciences', 'Poetry is the modern representative of this science.' Volume II contains this memorandum on page 855: 'It would be worth while to try Swedenborg's system of correspondences in the interpretation of Egyptian hieroglyphics.'

Here is the source of his idea, set out most fully in 'The Precursor' and 'The Language of Religion', that the Bible and the writings of the mystics, the liturgy of the Church and the ancient mythologies contain a body of esoteric doctrine which can be penetrated only by those versed in an understanding of the language of symbols in the sense of Swedenborg's correspondences. 'The Precursor', in fact, is a thoroughly Swedenborgian interpretation of the significance of St. John the Baptist, the precursor of Christ, as symbolizing the natural love which prepares the way for Divine love. St. Bernard and St. Paul are invoked, but it is Swedenborg who dominates the piece, and who is quoted directly, without being named, as authority for parts of the interpretation, which are, in the final analysis, Patmore's own:

> '"Honey", writes one of the most deeply learned in this vocabulary, "signifies natural good." "Locusts", says the same writer, "signify nutriment in the extreme natural" and camel's hair and a leathern girdle "denote what is natural", skin and hair being those things which are most external.'[1]

[1] 'The Precursor', *Religio Poetae*, p. 12.

In 'The Language of Religion', Patmore quotes Swedenborg again :

'The teaching of every great religion, the Jewish and the Christian perhaps above all, when it once leaves the preparatory stage of natural religion and formal dogma, becomes mainly enigmatical and mythical. ... It is at this point that *real* religion, *which is self-evident*, begins and at this point occurs that great change in the mode of the soul's progress which is well known to Catholic psychologists. Up to this point the progression is from truth to good; afterwards from good to truth, its rule then becoming "prove all things; hold fast (not "that which is true" but) "that which is good"; the substance becomes the guide to the form, whereas, before, the form was the guide to the substance.'[1]

However, the influence of Swedenborgian correspondences and symbolic language is not confined to these two essays. Elsewhere Patmore has it: 'Parables and symbols are the only possible means of expressing realities which are clear to perception though dark to the understanding',[2] and many passages in *The Rod, the Root and the Flower* present essentially the same idea.

Patmore found confirmation of Swedenborg's notion of an 'arcane' philosophy underlying religious writings in his reading of Catholic theology and mysticism. His enthusiasm for this concept infected Francis Thompson, who wrote to the older poet in 1895 to disclaim plagiarism on his part in the 'Orient Ode'. This led to a correspondence in which the two poets exchanged ideas as to the symbolical significance of the points of the compass, and similar matters. In the course of this, Patmore said :

'I wish I could see and talk to you on the subject of the symbolism you speak of. The Bible and all the theologies are full of it, but it is too deep and significant to get itself uttered in writing. ... Meanwhile I will only hint that the North represents the simple Divine virility, the South the Divine womanhood, the East their synthesis in the Holy Spirit, and the West the pure natural womanhood "full of grace".'[3]

Although Patmore's derivations from the point of the compass are characteristically his own, it is significant that for Swedenborg the points of the compass are mystically very important, and according to his interpretation, they represent particular leanings of the soul, according to which the angels are disposed.[4]

---

1 'The Language of Religion', *Religio Poetae*, pp. 18–19. Cf. *Conjugial Love*, Nos. 60–61.
2 'Love and Poetry', *Religio Poetae*, p. 141.
3 Quoted in *Francis Thompson and Wilfred Meynell*, pp. 109–110.
4 *Heaven and Hell*, No. 150.

The New Dispensation

Patmore did not accept Swedenborg's declaration that he had been given a special Divine mission to lead men to eternal truth, any more than he believed that Swedenborg himself intended to found a new church. Therefore he regarded Swedenborg primarily as 'a great psychologist', as a fount of poetic imagery, as a gifted perceiver of hidden truths, and later as a stimulating expresser of Catholic doctrines. But he seems, unconsciously perhaps, to have been impressed by Swedenborg's idea that Christianity needs to be rediscovered; that a new 'church' would in time emerge, not a congregation, but a new understanding of old religious truths on the part of men of all creeds. There is considerable dispute as to whether or not Swedenborg saw the 'new church' as a new body; the most generally accepted view, not shared by the sectarian Swedenborgians, however, is that the Swedish philosopher propounded the idea of a new illumination which would unite men in an invisible 'church', which would not spoil the vision by externalizing it. The concluding section of the essay 'Religio Poetae' is perhaps the clearest expression among the several in Patmore's works of this Swedenborgian sense of 'the New Dispensation'. The phrase itself is Swedenborg's own, and Patmore's use of it in a passage unmistakably Swedenborgian in sentiment indicates the extent of his indebtedness:

> 'I think that it must be manifest to fitly qualified observers that religion . . . is actually, both by tendency from within and compulsion from without . . . in the initial stage of a new development, of which the note will be *real apprehension*, whereby Christianity will acquire such a power of appeal to the "pure among the Gentiles", i.e. our natural feelings and instincts, as will cause it to appear almost like a New Dispensation, though it will truly be no more than the fulfilment of the express promises of Christ and His Apostles to the world. . . . Or would it be too vast a hope that such a development may truly assume the proportions and character of a New Dispensation, the Dispensation of the Holy Spirit, the Spirit of Life and perceived Reality, continuing and fulfilling the Dispensation of Christ, as His did that of the Father . . . '[1]

Patmore was unquestionably a faithful, practising son of the Catholic Church. Yet his attitude to religion in general and to his own in particular indicates a distrust of externals. He seems not to have been interested in any kind of rapprochement or reunion of the Churches, and on points of dogma he would concede nothing to other communions; yet he felt a strong kinship towards, and

---

[1] 'Religio Poetae', *Religio Poetae*, p. 8.

charity for, other Christians; and he interpreted in the sense
intended, and not in the sectarian sense, the teaching, 'No salvation
outside the Catholic Church.' St. Augustine's 'Love is above the
Sacraments' was constantly on his lips. As for the future, Patmore
said, 'I believe in Christianity as it will be ten thousand years
hence.'[1]

He appears, then, to have managed to assimilate a good deal of
Swedenborg's apocalyptic teaching into his Catholicism without
strain, or without the surrender of fundamental Catholic dogma.
Behind this teaching, he felt, there lay truths for which the mass of
humanity was not yet ready; he believed in the emergence of new
aspects of dogma, foreseen by saints and by seers. This is, at bottom,
very like Swedenborg's concept of a 'New Dispensation'. Although
Coventry Patmore passed from Swedenborg to Aquinas, he never
really cast the Swedish philosopher from his consciousness.

Married Love and the Relationship of the Sexes

'Conjugial love' and the relationship of the sexes form a most
important element in Swedenborg's philosophy. For him, there is a
sexual duality at the basis of all being; the two fundamental principles of life are male and female, which are separate and contrary,
but all the time moving towards unity. Sex is not just a physical
distinction, but a spiritual one as well. In the married state is to be
found the fundamental love of all loves, because the sexual act in
marriage is the natural correspondence of the Divine impulse
towards union, order, conjunction:

> 'Considered in itself, love is nothing else than a desire and thence an
> effort after conjunction; and conjugial love for conjunction into one.
> For the male human being and the female human being have been so
> created, that from two they may become as one human being or one
> flesh; and when they become one, then, taken together, they are the
> human being in his fulness; but without this conjunction they are
> two, and each like a divided or half a human being.'[2]

Patmore's conception of 'Homo' goes beyond Swedenborg,
especially in finding in both man and woman, a male-female
duality which the Swedish philosopher denied. For Patmore,
marriage in heaven is not the literal spiritual marriage of man to
woman that it is in Swedenborg, but the union of the soul with God,
to whom every soul, whether of a man or of a woman, is in the
spiritual sense female.

However, so far as the basic principle of sexual duality in the

---

[1] *Memoirs*, Vol. II, p. 29.   [2] *Conjugial Love*, No. 37.

universe is concerned, Patmore owes much to Swedenborg, and the fact that it played an increasingly significant part in his thought may be attributed to the effect of his continual reading of the philosopher. In a pencilled note in Volume I of the *Arcana Coelestia* Index, he wrote: 'All knowledge is nuptial knowledge.'

For Swedenborg death takes nothing from man save his physical covering, and sex functions in the world of after-death as it does during this life. Thus, in heaven, each sex retains its identity; and there are marriages in heaven. The difference between these heavenly marriages and those on earth is that in heaven none but 'true' marriages are retained, for on earth there are both 'true' marriages in which there is a spiritual harmony between the partners, and 'false' marriages in which there is only physical attraction. In heaven, according to Swedenborg,

> 'If they can live together, they remain married partners; but if they cannot, they separate, sometimes the husband from the wife, and sometimes both from each other.'[1]

His treatment of union after death is especially interesting, for this was a matter which greatly exercised Patmore's mind. While the philospher stimulated his thinking here, he could not follow him in his conclusions, but came to hold fast to Catholic teaching. Swedenborg believed that if the earthly marriage had been a 'true' one, the surviving partner had no inclination to marry again. The conflict in Patmore's mind over his desire to marry again and yet to remain faithful to the memory of his first wife is seen in the ode 'Tired Memory', where it is treated not in Swedenborgian terms, but in those of loyalty, love and 'treason'. But his concern with the idea of the perpetuity of love after death, and the complicating factors of remarriage is reflected in the words already quoted from the postscript to *The Victories of Love*. 'The Plan of the Poem . . . involved . . . a final section on the subject of the hope which remains for individual love in death.' Both Swedenborg and Patmore strive for a way around Christ's words to the Sadducees:

> 'The sons of this age marry and are given in marriage; but those who shall be held worthy to attain to another age and the resurrection from the dead, shall neither marry nor be given in marriage, for they can die no more' (Luke XX, 27–28).

Swedenborg argues that Christ was not referring to human marriage at all, but to 'spiritual nuptials':

> 'By spiritual nuptials conjunction with the Lord is meant, and this is effected on earth; and when it has been effected on earth, it is also

---

[1] *Conjugial Love*, No. 49.

effected in the heavens; wherefore they are not married again, nor again given in marriage in the heavens . . . "to marry" denotes being conjoined with the Lord, and . . . to enter into nuptials denotes being received into heaven by the Lord.'[1]

This reasoning permits him to retain his conception of actual marriage between man and woman in heaven.

Emily's illness at the time of Patmore's writing of *The Victories of Love* made him think much of the possibility of reunion after death. The words he gives to Jane in Section VII of this poem show how carefully he had pondered over Swedenborg's argument:

> Poor image of the spousal bond
> Of Christ and Church, if loosed beyond
> This life!—'Gainst which, and much more yet
> There's not a single word to set.
> The speech to the scoffing Sadducee
> Is not in point to you and me;
> For how could Christ have taught such clods
> That Caesar's things are also God's?
> The sort of Wife the Law might make
> Might well be 'hated' for Love's sake,
> And left, like money, land, or house;
> For out of Christ is no true spouse.

When he wrote the first version of *The Betrothal*, Patmore was sufficiently in harmony with Swedenborg to say on the matter of 'Love's Immortality':

> My faith is fast
> That all the loveliness I sing
> Is made to outsleep the mortal blast,
> And blossom in a better Spring.
> My creed declares the ceaseless pact
> Of body and spirit, soul and sense;
> Nor can my faith accept the fact,
> And fly the various consequence.

But later he altered these lines, so that the Swedenborgian quality is minimized; and what is expressed might be the lyrical yearning of any lover for eternity of union:

> My faith is fast
> That all the loveliness I sing
> Is made to bear the mortal blast,
> And blossom in a better Spring.

[1] *Ibid.*, No. 41.

> Doubts of eternity ne'er cross
> The Lover's mind, divinely clear:
> *For ever* is the gain or loss
> Which maddens him with hope or fear.
>
> (*A.H.*, I, vii)

However, other passages retained in *The Angel* show clear effects of Swedenborg's teachings, as in:

> And thus, oh, strange, sweet half of me,
> If I confess a loftier flame,
> If more I love high Heaven than thee,
> I more than love thee, thee I am;
> And if the world's not built of lies,
> Nor all a cheat the Gospel tells,
> If that which from the dead shall rise
> Be I indeed, not something else,
> There's no position more secure
> In reason or in faith than this,
> That those conditions must endure
> Which, wanting, I myself should miss.
>
> (*A.H.*, II, xi)

Swedenborg saw the essence of true marriage as the union of love and wisdom, the basic principle which sustains all the world. Love is predominant in the woman; and wisdom in the man; the union of the two is essential to the spiritual development of either.

> 'The difference consists essentially in this,' says Swedenborg, 'that the inmost in the male is love, and its covering is wisdom; or, what is the same thing, it is love covered or veiled by wisdom; and that the inmost in the female is that wisdom of the male, and its covering is love thence derived; but this love is feminine love, and it is given by the Lord to the wife through the wisdom of the husband; whereas the former love is masculine love, and is the love of growing wise, and it is given by the Lord to the husband according to the reception of wisdom. Hence it is that the male is the wisdom of love, and the female the love of that wisdom.'[1]

So Patmore writes:

> '[Woman] is the sensible glory or praise of his spiritual wisdom . . . she only loves and desires to become what he loves and desires her to be; and beauty, being visible or reflected goodness, can exist in woman only when and in proportion as the man is strong, good and wise.'[2]

[1] *Conjugial Love*, No. 32.
[2] 'The Weaker Vessel', *Religio Poetae*, pp. 154–155.

On the relationship between man and woman, Swedenborg said:

'The male is born intellectual and ... the female is born volitional; or, what is the same thing ... the male is born into the affection of knowledge, understanding, and growing wise, and ... the female is born into the love of conjoining herself with that affection in the male.'[1]

and much the same idea is found in an early Patmore essay:

'The *affections* of the woman are developed beyond those of the man, pretty nearly to the same extent that the understanding of the man is developed beyond that of the woman.'[2]

So it is not hard to detect the traces of Swedenborg in such passages of *The Angel* as:

> Were she but half of what she is,
>   He twice himself, mere love alone,
> Her special crown, as truth is his,
>   Gives title to the worthier throne;
> For love is substance, truth the form;
> Truth without love were less than nought.
>
> (*A.H.*, I, v)

Although 'form' and 'substance' are terms used by the Scholastic philosophers, they are used no less frequently by Swedenborg, who often asserts that truth is the form of love and more: 'Love and wisdom are the real and actual substance and form which make the subject itself.'[3]

There are innumerable other passages throughout *The Angel* and its sequel which present ideas from Swedenborg, often in the language of the philosopher himself. For instance, Patmore's:

> Can ought compared with wedlock be
> For use? But He who made the heart
> To use proportions joy. What He
> Has join'd let no man put apart.
>
> (*A.H.*, II, vii)

may be compared with Swedenborg's:

'Conjugial delight, which is a purer and more exquisite delight of touch, surpasses all the rest on account of its use, which is the procreation of the human race, and thence of the angels of heaven. These delights attend the sense by influx from heaven, whence every delight is from use and according to use.'[4]

1 *Conjugial Love*, No. 33.
2 'German Lady Novelists', *North British Review*, Vol. VII, No. XIV, Aug. 1847, p. 371.
3 *Divine Love and Wisdom*, No. 40.   4 *Heaven and Hell*, No. 402.

Not only is conjugial love for Swedenborg the most pure of loves and the basic love, but it has a high analogy:

> 'Conjugial love has a correspondence with the marriage of the Lord and the church; that is, as the Lord loves the church, and desires that the church should love Him, so husband and wife mutually love each other.'[1]

Patmore employed the analogy between the love of marriage and that of God for the church, and, by extension (from his reading of the mystics), for the soul, so extensively that it can be illustrated by scores of passages, by the 'Psyche' odes, 'The Precursor', and by a large part of *The Rod, the Root and the Flower*. Although the analogy comes to Patmore from innumerable sources, ranging from the Bible to St. John of the Cross, Swedenborg was clearly one of the most important of these.

It is inevitable, in view of the rest of Swedenborg's teaching concerning marriage, that he should regard Christian monogamy as the only true kind of love-union. Patmore, of course, accepted this belief from his Christian faith, and not from Swedenborg. However, although he does not attack celibacy as such in his verse or prose, he takes a somewhat disdainful and patronizing view of it. Possibly he gained something of this attitude from Swedenborg, who was directly opposed to the whole idea of celibacy:

> The state of marriage is to be preferred to the state of celibacy.... Marriage is the fulness of man; for by means of it the human being becomes a full human being. In celibacy, all these things are wanting.'[2]

Whatever part such views played in determining Patmore's earlier attitude towards celibacy, they certainly helped to confirm him in his conception of the bliss of marriage as being so holy and so full of symbol that celibacy must be inferior. However, apart from the doctrinal considerations and such other factors as the example of his daughter Emily Honoria's life, he must sooner or later have come to see a certain incongruity in the strong condemnation of celibacy by a philosopher who never married, and to understand that the Catholic Church, in imposing celibacy upon the clergy, does not in fact deprive them of the 'higher marriage'—spiritual communion with God.

The teaching of Swedenborg on the chastity of the married state also appears to have strongly impressed Patmore. Swedenborg, seeing the love of marriage as the purest and most perfect of loves, concluded that 'truly conjugial love is chastity itself.'[3] 'The Vestal

---

[1] *Conjugial Love*, No. 62.   [2] *Ibid.*, No. 156.   [3] *Ibid.*, No. 143.

Fire', the early prelude in which Patmore hymns the beauty of married chastity, has already been quoted.¹ In many other places he expresses his belief in the chastity of marriage as against the Jansenistic or Manichaean contempt for, and distrust of, the physical side of marriage which he encountered in some of his reading, which he came in contact with, too, in his own age—even in his friends. Aubrey de Vere counselled suppression of the 'Psyche' odes; and other friends had criticized those parts of *The Angel in the House* which, in their view, celebrated too enthusiastically the delights of marriage. In 'Deliciae Sapientiae de Amore' Patmore includes among the virgins

> Young Lover true, and love-foreboding maid,
> And wedded Spouse, if virginal of thought;

and in the same poem he says:

> Love makes the life to be
> A fount perpetual of virginity.

'Purity', he wrote in a late essay, 'ends by finding a goddess where impurity concludes by confessing carrion.'² The emphasis he places upon the chastity of marriage, rare in his age, even among Catholic writers, suggests that it was Swedenborg who helped him to see its importance.

There are significant differences between Patmore's application of his principles of sex and marriage and the teachings of the Swedish philosopher on these matters; and a good number of the poet's concepts, especially with regard to the nature of the love of God for man, owe more to St. Bernard, St. Thomas Aquinas and St. Augustine. At the same time, his frequent expression in prose and poetry of so many of Swedenborg's ideas, so often in the exact language of the philosopher himself, justifies Patmore's being regarded as, after Blake, the most completely Swedenborgian of English poets.

---

¹ See above, Chapter I. ² 'Imagination', *Religio Poetae*, p. 107.

Later Influences on Patmore's Thought

IN THE LIBRARY of the British Museum, Patmore had unusual opportunities for studying the theological and mystical writers to whom his inclinations and his earlier reading led him. Despite delicate health, he was a diligent servant of the Library, and the Trustees acknowledged this by giving him a generous period of leave when his doctor insisted he should go abroad in 1863–1864, and by granting him an annual pension of £126 13s. 4d. on his retirement in 1866, after nineteen years of service. However, Patmore himself felt that he wasted a certain amount of time in reading the theological works which passed through his hands. His gifts of Sheridan manuscripts and, in 1880, of a very valuable set of the works of St. Thomas Aquinas were intended by him as an acknowledgement of the generosity of the Museum authorities and as compensation for the time he had spent there in reading and 'napping'.

It was probably in the British Museum Library that the poet first came across the writings of the Catholic mystics. Certainly he began to read Thomas Aquinas during his period there. As the years went by, his knowledge of the 'Angelic Doctor's' work, and that of other Doctors of the Church came to be very much greater than that of the average educated Catholic of his day, and certainly than that of any other poet of his time, with the possible exception of Hopkins. What he had learnt from Coleridge, Wordsworth, Emerson and Swedenborg remained with him, but these ideas were now blended with, and given new meaning by, concepts drawn from

Catholic theology. The more deeply he read, the more he became convinced that he had himself had insights into truth which paralleled those of St. Bernard, St. Teresa and St. John of the Cross, and that in St. Thomas Aquinas and St. Augustine were complete rational justifications of such insights—in other words, that he had been a mystic and a Thomist all along without knowing it. In retrospect, as we have seen, he was inclined to overstress his pre-Catholic Catholicism; he was inclined, too, to accept as Catholic truth any intuitions he thought valuable, however far from Christianity they at first seemed. In this, Patmore was merely expressing a concept which has become more familiar in our day than in his: 'All truth is Catholic truth.' That he found his spiritual home in the Catholic Church, that the writings of her Doctors and Saints gave him enduring satisfaction, and that they predominantly shaped the mood of all his later work is patent to any reader of the prose and poems written after his conversion.

He had no love for devotional books of the pietistic kind; and he preferred French books of devotion to English ones. After writing an enthusiastic note on the works of Marie Lataste, he said: 'There are no such books in English, but many in French. From a Christian point of view, we English are a poor lot compared with the French.'[1] He also had some shrewd criticisms to make of Thomas à Kempis's *The Imitation of Christ*, which he considered unfit for people who live in the ordinary relations of life.[2] Yet he found intellectual and spiritual nourishment in the Missal, which helped to deepen his religious faith as well as to confirm his Swedenborgian idea of the 'arcane' significance of the language of religion. The way in which the Church uses the Psalms and other Biblical passages to illuminate the 'mystery' of the various feast-days, and in which she binds together prophecies to provide a mystical focus at each point of the different religious seasons, excited him, and made him feel that he was right in emphasizing the symbolical significance of religious rites and utterances. Thanking a friend for a gift of a Missal he said that he had been

> 'astonished at the light which is thrown upon the Bible by the way the Church applies it. The collocation of prophecies, etc., for today is especially wonderful. "The thought that makes the monk and nun" glows darkly through them, as the heat glows through the shut doors of a smelting furnace.'[3]

Patmore's reading of St. Thomas Aquinas convinced him of the reasonableness of Catholicism. It is strange that the elaborate

1 Champneys, *Memoirs*, Vol. II, p. 80.   2 *Ibid.*, Vol. II, p. 86.
3 *Ibid.*, Vol. II, p. 82.

philosophical system built up by the Angelic Doctor did not alter his deep-rooted conviction that the truths of religion were 'self-evident', and part of 'the light which lighteth every man that cometh into the world'. Patmore's way was the way of faith, rather than of reason; and, though he was not 'anti-intellectual', he looked upon the affections and the conscience as sources of knowledge and enlightenment at least equally as important as that of reason in St. Thomas's sense. Ideas from the Fathers became so blended with his own apprehensions that he believed that what he had learnt he had in many cases already and always known. To be fair to Patmore's intelligence, however, it must be stressed that there is no fundamental change in his basic ideas from his first writings to his last; there is development and shift of emphasis, and a more profound conception of love in his later poems; but essentially, there is no incompatibility between the philosophy he earlier held, if a little vaguely, and that into which he matured.

Of all the Catholic writers whom Patmore studied, St. Thomas Aquinas was the one to whom he always accorded the highest place. Just when he began to read Aquinas is not certain; but it must have been some time in his early or middle thirties, since in his 'autobiography', just before he writes: 'when I had reached the age of thirty-five', he states:

'The study of the "Summa" of St. Thomas Aquinas ... greatly increased my Catholic sympathies by shewing me, better than I knew before, that true poetry and true theological science have to do with one and the same ideal, and that, much as poetry and theology seem to differ, they differ only as the Peak of Teneriffe and the table-land of Central Asia do.'[1]

Whatever the time of his first acquaintance with Aquinas, Patmore certainly embraced him with enthusiasm:

'I have bought,' he wrote, 'a fine edition of St. Thomas's "Summa", which has been a favourite book of mine all my life. It contains the *orthodox* view of every possible subject—and as the orthodox view nearly always turns out to be the right one, however contrary to one's first impressions, the book is a very valuable one, indeed. . . . No one, however violently prejudiced against Catholicism could *read* the "Summa" and not feel that he was in the presence of one of the greatest philosophic minds that ever existed.'[2]

The edition to which he here refers is the one he presented to the British Museum Library. The work, seventeen volumes in twenty-one, was the Dedication Copy to Pope Pius V of the first printed

<hr />

[1] Champneys, *Memoirs*, Vol. II, p. 52.   [2] *Ibid*, Vol. II, p. 86.

edition of the *Summa Theologica*, which was later given by the Pope to Philip II of Spain.

Patmore's enthusiasm for Aquinas was known to all his friends. Arthur Symons, for instance, testified: 'I think I never heard him speak long without some reference to St. Thomas Aquinas, of whom he has written so often and with so great enthusiasm.'[1] The Angelic Doctor is quoted often in his prose, in most cases being used in his customary aphoristic way, as in the opening of the essay on 'Ideal and Material Greatness in Architecture': 'St. Thomas Aquinas writes: "Great riches are not required for the habit of magnificence; it is enough that a man should dispose of such as he possesses greatly, according to time and place." As in life, so in art, and especially in architecture.'[2] And in *The Rod, the Root and the Flower* he is cited over a dozen times.

In particular ways Patmore's thought shows the direct impact of the *Summa*. The question of order and law as a basic principle of being became a central part of his later outlook; and this emphasis can have been derived from no other source than Aquinas.

Patmore believed that the pleasures of love 'take their vigour from control'; and that law in marriage deepens joy. Just as the limits of the arts give undiminished beauty, so those imposed by marriage give it, not monotony, but variety. Much of Patmore's teaching on marriage, as we shall see, is conceived in the light of this sense of law. His insistence upon an underlying imperative which controls both the universe and natural desires, and upon the fulfilment of man's nature and the production of beauty only in and through restraint owes something to Aristotle and St. Bernard, but most of all to Aquinas. A large part of the *Summa Theologica* is devoted to expressing the foundations of natural and moral law. Aquinas's teaching on the place of law in the universe was that there is not a single creature, animate or inanimate, which does not act in conformity with certain rules and in view of certain ends. While, however, animals and things obey these rules and move towards these ends without being conscious of them, man is aware of them, and his moral justice consists in his voluntary acceptance of them. Thus all the laws of nature, of morality and of society are particular instances of the same divine law, which, since it depends on the will of the eternal God, is itself eternal and the source of all other laws.[3]

---

[1] 'Coventry Patmore', *Figures of Several Centuries*, by Arthur Symons (London: Constable & Co., 1917), pp. 360–361.

[2] *Principle in Art*, p. 210.

[3] See Etienne Gilson, *The Philosophy of St. Thomas Aquinas*, translated by Edward Bullough (Herder Book Co., St. Louis, Mo., 1939), p. 327.

So far as man's acceptance of law is concerned, Aquinas held that men are accustomed to love gradually the good which they first desire for the sake of something else, or what they think is something else, and to come to will it for its own sake, recognizing it as the universal good and order which assures the individual good.[1]

All that Patmore wrote on the subject of law and man's obedience to it, in particular the ode 'Legem Tuam Dilexi', is in harmony with Aquinas's teaching. And St. Thomas's idea of vocation, which arises from the notion of law, forms one of the themes of *The Victories of Love*, wherein Patmore sets out his conception of vocation in marriage. Frederick marries Jane 'on the rebound' as a substitute for Honoria, whom he has lost to the poet, Felix Vaughan. But, living together as good husband and wife within the bonds of marriage, and surrendering themselves to its law, Frederick and Jane, through their trials, come to have for each other a perfect married love, and to recognize in it a reflection of the goodness of God and the result of their obedience to the matrimonial 'order'.

In 'Legem Tuam Dilexi', Patmore writes:

> And the just Man does on himself affirm
> God's limits, and is conscious of delight,
> Freedom and right;
> And so His Semblance is, Who, every hour,
> By day and night,
> Buildeth new bulwarks 'gainst the Infinite.

And St. Thomas says:

> 'Now in spiritual things there is a twofold servitude and a twofold freedom; for there is the servitude of sin and the servitude of justice; and there is likewise a twofold freedom, from sin, and from justice, as appears from the words of the Apostle (Rom. vi, 20, 22). *When you were the servants of sin, you were free men to justice; ... but now being made free from sin*, you are ... *become servants to God.* ... Since man, by his natural reason, is inclined to justice, while sin is contrary to natural reason, it follows that freedom from sin is true freedom which is united to the servitude of justice, since they both incline man to that which is becoming to him.'[2]

Patmore's keen awareness of a moral structure underlying all the activities of the just man and of the delight that comes from the

---

[1] See Etienne Gilson, *The Philosophy of St. Thomas Aquinas*, p. 333.
[2] *The Summa Theologica of St. Thomas Aquinas*, translated by the Fathers of the English Dominican Province (Burns Oates & Washbourne, 1924), Vol. 14, II, Q. 183, Art. 4, p. 152.

fulfilment of law shows the degree to which he had absorbed a fundamental element in Aquinas's teaching.

With this concept of law is connected that which both held of the body. Patmore exalted man's body, declaring it to be indeed holy, and setting this conception against that which denies the body its place in God's good universe. '"The human form divine"', he wrote in *The Rod, the Root and the Flower*. 'It is *actually* divine; for the Body is the house of God, and an image of Him, though the Devil may be its present tenant.'[1] In Aquinas the body, far from being a hindrance to the development of the highest spiritual powers of man, as Patmore might have believed had he followed Plato, is shown as in fact an aid to man's attaining the fullness of his divinely-appointed end. For St. Thomas regarded the body not as the prison of the soul, but as a servant and an instrument placed at its disposal by God. The union of the soul and the body is not a punishment of the soul but it is a beneficent link by which it can reach perfection. Gilson sums up Aquinas's teaching thus: 'The soul, being an integral part of the human composition, is constituted in its full natural perfection only by its union with the body',[2] while Patmore speaks of 'the Soul's blissful and immortal companion, the Body'.[3]

Patmore regarded man as a unity of soul and body in Aquinas's sense, and saw the flesh as worthy of a dignity it derived both from its union with the soul and from its sanctification by the Incarnation of Christ. In his emphasis on the Incarnation and its effects in the natural world and on the place the doctrine must hold in any consideration of the dignity of the human personality, he anticipated such poets as Charles Williams and T. S. Eliot, in whose verse the Incarnation is likewise a central concept. The Incarnation, as Patmore saw it, was the act by which man's body was wrought into the body of Christ and became the focal point at which finite and infinite meet. 'In His union and conjunction with Body,' he wrote, 'God finds His final perfection and felicity.'[4] So, on this premise, he saw all particular knowledge as falling into one Word, the Word made flesh, 'the synthesis of all things, and the Sabbatical rest of One Spirit in one sense.'[5] And in creating woman, God has shown to man that circumscribed infinity which reflects His own nature, since He is, Patmore says, quoting Proclus, 'the synthesis of Infinite

[1] *Rod, Root and Flower*, 'Aurea Dicta', LXXXVI, p. 41.
[2] *Philosophy of St. Thomas Aquinas*, p. 216.
[3] *Rod, Root and Flower*, 'Homo', XXXIII, p. 139.
[4] *Ibid.*, 'Knowledge and Science', I, p. 61.
[5] *Ibid.*, 'Aurea Dicta', CXLI, p. 52.

and Boundary'.[1] Woman is a 'little' Incarnation; she shows 'Heaven's bound';

> So that in Her
> All that which it hath of sensitively good
> Is sought and understood
> After the narrow mode the mighty Heavens prefer?
>> (*U.E.*, 'Wind and Wave')

Although the doctrine of the Incarnation plays a large part in the works of the Doctors of the Church, none devotes so much attention to it as St. Thomas, nor derives from an examination of the Mystery so many concepts about the nature of God and Man. Patmore, as a poet, does not follow Aquinas in his reasoning in detail, but, in saying that God finds 'His final perfection and felicity' in the Incarnation, he is restating what Aquinas wrote in the treatise on the Incarnation which opens Part III of the *Summa Theologica*:

> 'To each thing, that is befitting which belongs to it by reason of its very nature; thus, to reason befits man, since this belongs to him because he is of a rational nature. But the very nature of God is goodness. . . . Hence, what belongs to the essence of goodness befits God. But it belongs to the essence of goodness to communicate itself to others. . . . Hence it belongs to the essence of the highest good to communicate itself in the highest manner to the creature, and this is brought about chiefly by *His so joining created nature to Himself that one Person is made up of these three—the Word, a soul and flesh*, as Augustine says. . . . Hence it is manifest that it was fitting that God should become incarnate.'[2]

The paradox which limits God to the Trinity, and expresses itself in the Incarnate Trinity which St. Thomas describes, is recognized by Patmore in 'Legem Tuam Dilexi':

> Therefore the soul select assumes the stress
> Of bonds unbid, which God's own style express
> Better than well,
> And aye hath, cloister'd, borne,
> To the Clown's scorn,
> The fetters of the threefold golden chain.

While Aquinas is concerned with working out the doctrinal consequences of God made Man, Patmore is concerned with the wonder of it, and its corollaries as they bear on the dignity of the flesh. But he again and again echoes St. Thomas's statement: 'It pertains to the greatest glory of God to have raised a weak and earthly body to such sublimity.'[3]

---

[1] *Rod, Root and Flower*, 'Aurea Dicta', III, p. 25.
[2] *Summa Theologica*, Vol. 15, Part III, Q. I, Art. I, p. 5.
[3] *Ibid.*, Vol. 15, Part III, Q. 5, Art. 2, p. 89.

On marriage, Patmore is everywhere closer to Aquinas than were those of his fellow-Catholics who had become tainted with Jansenism. His attitude towards the permanence, the unity and dignity of marriage, and its divine origin, is Catholic, but more specifically Thomist. A good number of Catholic writers, from medieval times down to the present day, have regarded the sexual act in marriage as a consequence of the Fall, carrying thereby a taint, and being, even in the sacrament, a concession to the weakness of the flesh. However, St. Thomas argues, as more recent Catholic writers have emphasized, that the marital act can be, and in the right circumstances normally is, an act of virtue.[1] So fully does this coincide with Patmore's expression of the holiness of the body and the purity of marriage that there can be little doubt that he found in St. Thomas sanction for his quite un-Puritanical hymning of the pleasures of married love.

One of the strangest of the odes in *The Unknown Eros* is 'The Contract', in which Patmore, pursuing his theme of the relationship between virginity and marriage, imagines Adam and Eve pledging a 'mutual free contract of virgin spousals'. This virgin marriage, treated with insight and delicacy, is depicted as

> blissful beyond flight
> Of modern thought,

but as later broken through lust, in the wrong use of the married relationship, so that Mankind was sick at heart and could find no succour

> Until a heaven-caress'd and happier Eve
> Be join'd with some glad Saint
> In like espousals, blessed upon Earth,
> And she her Fruit forth bring.

In the *Summa*, Aquinas rejects the teaching of some earlier doctors of the Church that generation by coition is a consequence of the Fall. This, he says, is natural to man by reason of his animal life; but that Adam and Eve did not come together in Paradise, either because they were ejected from Eden shortly after the creation of Eve; or because, having received the general Divine command relative to generation, they awaited the special command relative to the time.[2] He goes on to argue that, had Adam and Eve not fallen, their vision would in time have gained its completeness, and they would have come together without shame. But, having sinned, the sense of shame and the lack of full control over the passions affected

---

[1] *Ibid.*, Vol. 19, Part III (Supplement), Q. 49, Art. 4, p. 153.
[2] *Ibid.*, Vol. 4, Part I, Q. XCVIII, Art. 2, pp. 347–348.

the temper in which, ultimately, they had relations. They felt, in short, with Patmore's small daughter, in her phrase that he often quoted, that marriage is 'rather a wicked sacrament'.

Patmore chooses to show the sin of Adam and Eve as consisting in the loss of a right attitude towards their desires. He does not say that the virtue consists in the voluntary denial of those desires, but in the health of their acceptance of them, and, in that health, practising a voluntary denial. For St. Thomas, the sin of the Fall was pride; but Patmore saw in the Biblical account an opportunity to expound the nature of virginity in marriage as consisting in the proper disposition and the control of lust. For all his praise of the fullness of marriage, he is aware with Aquinas that the sacramental quality of marriage does not lie in intercourse. 'The Contract', then, though it proclaims Patmore's own awareness of the place of restraint in marriage, with a hint that the harnessing of sexual energy may in fact increase man's spiritual awareness, at the same time clearly proceeds from the poet's meditation over those many passages concerning marriage in the *Summa Theologica*.

In such ways the reading of Aquinas contributed to the development of Patmore's poetic vision. The *Summa* gave him the knowledge of Catholic theology which is plain in his later writings; it provided him with innumerable poetic hints and suggestions and it supplied an intellectual superstructure for his faith, however much he may have believed it to be 'self-evident'.

Second only to Aquinas as an influence on Patmore's later work is St. Bernard of Clairvaux, whose treatise *On the Love of God* (*De Diligendo Deo*) and the eighty-six sermons he preached on the Canticle of Canticles gave Patmore his chief justification for plotting an analogy between the love of man for woman and that of God for the soul. Marianne Caroline Patmore translated *De Diligendo Deo* and selected passages from the *Sermons on the Canticle*. After her death, Patmore completed the work with further renderings from the sermons[1]; and it was the publication of this book, at Gosse's persuasion, which set him writing prose again after some twenty years. The saint's eloquent exegesis of the Song of Songs

---

[1] The book was published as *St. Bernard on the Love of God*, translated by Marianne Caroline and Coventry Patmore (C. Kegan Paul & Co., 1881). Patmore's prefatory note reads: 'My wife was occupied on this translation at the time of her death. Pp. 1–98 include her work; the rest is mine.' His own contribution, which begins with a translation of a portion of Sermon 34, covers just over 54 pages, roughly one-third of the book; but there is a remarkable harmony in style between his section and that of his wife. Without Patmore's note, it would be impossible to tell where one translator leaves off, and the other begins.

excited Patmore's poetic impulses, and *The Unknown Eros* is stamped with its mark. Not only the general concept of God's burning love for the soul and the soul's for God, expressed in terms of physical imagery, but the intense spirituality of the whole, the absence of 'eroticism' and the assimilation of the language of physical love into an austerely religious interpretation—all of these things made St. Bernard an inevitable model for the poet.

One of Patmore's favourite Biblical quotations was: 'That was not first which is spiritual, but that which is natural; afterwards that which is spiritual' (1 Cor. xv, 46), which he used to illustrate his conviction that married love is a forerunner and image of Divine Love. St. Bernard uses the same quotation for the same purpose in Chapter XV of *On the Love of God*. The Psyche odes and such essays as 'The Precursor', 'Dieu et Ma Dame' and 'Love and Poetry' might have had as their text St. Bernard's words: 'The love of God and of the soul can be expressed in no way so perfectly as by the mutual love of Bride and Bridegroom, all being in common between them, and neither having any separate possessions.'[1] Whereas St. Thomas interprets the relationship expressed in the *Song of Songs* as that between Christ and the Church, St. Bernard extended it to the individual soul,[2] and in this Patmore followed him.

Patmore found justification, too, for the sacredness of the body in St. Bernard, who said:

'Till the restitution of our bodies, our souls can never be swallowed up in God, which is their absolute perfection. . . . The soul which loves God profits by its poor, weak body, whether living, dead or

---

[1] *St. Bernard on the Love of God*, p. 60.

[2] Dean Inge writes: 'Bernard's homilies on the Song of Solomon gave a great impetus to this mode of symbolism; but even he says that the Church, and not the individual, is the bride of Christ' (*Christian Mysticism*, Methuen & Co., 1899, p. 370). In fact, St. Bernard writes: 'It is clear that all the words and praises of the Spouse in the Song are true of the Church, but it is not so clear how far each soul in grace may apply such things to herself. . . . Give me a soul who loves nothing but God, or whatever she ought to love for His sake. . . . I will not deny that such a soul is worthy of such regards and attentions from her Master, and, if it pleases her to boast of them, I see no reason why she should not do so. . . . When I find my spirit is open to the intelligence of Holy Writ . . . I cannot doubt that the Husband of my soul is present' (pp. 136–138). Dean Inge is anxious to prove that the 'employment of erotic imagery to express the individual relation between Christ and the soul is always dangerous', and thus minimizes the strength of the tradition in the Christian Church, overlooking such passages and others in St. Bernard in which the analogy is applied personally, although with cautions and admonitions which Patmore, for instance, does not always observe.

risen—living, by bringing forth with her fruits of penance; dead, by resting from its labour; risen, the two together attain the consummation of all joy. It is clear then that without the body the soul is not perfected; as in every state it is essential to her good.'[1]

'To the Body' contains a passage embodying the identical conception. Talking of the body after death, Patmore says:

> Thou must needs, for a season, lie
> In the grave's arms, foul and unshriven,
> Albeit, in Heaven,
> Thy crimson-throbbing Glow
> Into its old abode aye pants to go,
> And does with envy see
> Enoch, Elijah, and the Lady, she
> Who left the lilies in her body's lieu.

Both writers deal with the consuming fire of God. St. Bernard's words:

'But, consuming fire as He is, He burns sweetly and destroys happily, and is at once blasting and unction. When this fire in you has consumed the filth of sin and the stains of your vices, and purified and calmed your conscience, you experience a sudden and extraordinary expansion of the heart and an infusion of light, and you are able to understand the Scriptures and penetrate the mysteries of faith. This is the effect of a look of the Bridegroom, who thus makes your righteousness to shine as the noonday. But, so long as the ruinous walls of the body are standing, the light is seen only through cracks and crevices'[2]

appear to have been reflected in Patmore's writings in two ways. First, in the ode 'Eros and Psyche' he makes Psyche say:

> But, Oh,
> Can I endure
> This flame, yet live for what thou lov'st me, pure?

to which Eros replies:

> Himself the God let blame
> If all about him, bursts to quenchless flame!
> My Darling, know
> Your spotless fairness is not match'd in snow,
> But in the integrity of fire.

Secondly, he several times uses the image of the light shining through cracks and crevices, in, for instance, the statement that:

'The letter of Scripture is like the walls of a furnace, unsightly, and made of clay, but, to those who attend, full of chinks and crevices

---

[1] *St. Bernard on the Love of God*, pp. 47–48.   [2] *Ibid.*, p. 128.

through which glows the white heat of a life whose mysteries of felicity it is 'unlawful to utter".'[1]

There are many other parallels between the writings of the two men, of which the following are characteristic. In the ode 'De Natura Deorum', the Pythoness says to Psyche:

> O'ermuch thou mind'st the throne he leaves above!
> Between unequals sweet is equal love.

and Psyche answers her:

> Nay, Mother, in his breast, when darkness blinds,
> I cannot for my life but talk and laugh
> With the large impudence of little minds!

The source of this passage is almost certainly St. Bernard's:

'The time of Thine absence is short, indeed, if we consider our deservings, but very long to our desires. But the soul that loves is carried away by the ardour of the latter; she forgets her little merits and the majesty of her Lord. She thinks of nothing but her delights in His health-giving grace, and behaves familiarly with Him, recalling Him without fear or shyness, and demanding with confidence the restoration of her former pleasures.'[2]

On several occasions, the saint refers to the penitent Magdalene, saying, most notably: 'The penitent woman had her place at the feet of our Lord; another, if it be another, at His head'[3]; and, in the ode, 'Deliciae Sapientiae de Amore', we find:

> There of pure Virgins none
> Is fairer seen
> Save One,
> Than Mary Magdalene.

In 'De Natura Deorum', Psyche tells the Pythoness:

> He loves me dearly, but he shakes a whip
> Of deathless scorpions at my slightest slip.
> Mother, last night he called me 'Gipsy', so
> Roughly it smote me like a blow!

and St. Bernard writes of the soul, in her relations with God:

'The Lord thunders against His Beloved, not as Spouse, but as Lord; not that He is in anger, but because He desires to purify her by fear, and to make her thus capable of the vision for which she sighs; this vision being the recompense of the pure in heart.'[4]

[1] 'Attention', *Religio Poetae*, pp. 33–34.
[2] *St. Bernard on the Love of God*, p. 141.
[3] *Ibid.*, p. 87.   [4] *Ibid.*, p. 105.

In the ode 'Psyche's Discontent', Patmore makes Psyche proclaim that she is so absorbed in the love of Eros that she has neither fear nor awe of him:

> Shall I, the gnat which dances in thy ray,
> Dare to be reverent? Therefore dare I say,
> I cannot guess the good that I desire;
> But this I know, I spurn the gifts which Hell
> Can mock till which is which 'tis hard to tell.
> I love thee, God; yea, and 'twas such assault
> As this which made thee mine; if that be fault.

St. Bernard, speaking of the 'true marriage-contract' between God and the soul, writes:

> 'Nor need it be apprehended that the inequality of persons can render this union defective. Love knows nothing about respectful fear. Love consists in loving, not honouring. Astonishment, fear, wonder, are good for those to whom they are seasonable. The lover knows nothing of them.'[1]

The reference to inequality recalls Patmore's line:

> Between unequals sweet is equal love

in 'De Natura Deorum', as does another phrase of St. Bernard's: 'Is it not wonderful, for it is love that speaks, and love knows no inequality.'[2]

There are many other parallels, but I have given sufficient to indicate that the whole mood of the Psyche odes is coloured with the exegetical writing of St. Bernard, in which Patmore found a confirmation of his intuitions concerning the love of God for the soul, a justification for his use of erotic language in dealing with it and a wealth of imagery which he turned to his own purposes in *The Unknown Eros*.

Several writers on Patmore have drawn attention to the similarity between some of the odes in *The Unknown Eros* and the writings of St. John of the Cross.[3] Gosse says that when, in 1881, he found Patmore reading St. John's works with ecstasy, he had the impression that the poet had just recently discovered the Spanish mystic.[4]

But Frederick Page quotes from Patmore's note-book a sentence referring to the plan of *The Unknown Eros*: 'This poem to consist of a series of Poems on texts from the Canticles, and to contain

---

[1] *St. Bernard on the Love of God*, p. 148.   [2] *Ibid.*, p. 131.
[3] See, for instance, 'Coventry Patmore', by Rev. Henry E. O'Keeffe, *The Catholic World*, Vol. LXIX, No. 413, Aug. 1899, p. 651.
[4] *Coventry Patmore*, p. 241.

all the essential matter of St. John of the Cross.'[1] Although *The Unknown Eros*, as we have it now, does not carry out such a plan, the note makes it plain that Patmore had absorbed a good deal of St. John's teaching before he began to write his Odes. There is so much common to St. John of the Cross, St. Teresa of Avila, St. Augustine and St. Bernard which has become part of the tradition of Catholic mysticism that it is difficult, if not impossible, to single out the separate contributions of each to Patmore's poetry. It is in the later prose, perhaps, rather than in the Odes that St. John's teaching is chiefly evident.

In 'The Spiritual Canticle', wherein St. John annotates his *Songs between the Soul and the Spouse*, he writes:

'God is pleased with naught save love. . . . All our works and all our labours, though they be as numerous as possible, are nothing in God's sight, for by them we can give Him nothing, neither can we fulfil His desire, which is solely to exalt the soul.'[2]

Patmore's 'Dieu et Ma Dame' echoes this and similar passages:

'Again, as with a mortal lover, God does not require any service of external "charity", etc., from His beloved. Indeed, He complains, as He did to Martha, of all attempts to please Him otherwise than by giving Him her society and her person in contemplation.'[3]

In *The Rod, the Root and the Flower*, Patmore describes the enduring effects of the Incarnation and the relationship between the natural and the supernatural by saying:

'"Under the Tree where thy mother was debauched, I have redeemed thee." "We are healed by the serpent by which we were slain." It is by the natural desires that we were slain, and it is by the natural desires, made truly natural by inoculation with the Body of Christ, that we are ultimately saved. Religion has no real power until it becomes *natural*.'[4]

One of the stanzas of St. John of the Cross's *Songs between the Soul and the Spouse*, reads:

> Beneath the apple-tree
> There wert thou betrothed to me;
> There did I give thee my hand
> And thou wert redeemed where thy mother had been
> corrupted.

[1] *Patmore, A Study in Poetry*, p. 125.
[2] *The Complete Works of Saint John of the Cross*, translated and edited by E. Allison Peers (London: Burns Oates, 1943), Vol. II, p. 341.
[3] 'Dieu et Ma Dame', *Religo Poetae*, p. 164.
[4] *Rod, Root and Flower*, 'Aurea Dicta', LXXXIX, p. 42.

And the saint comments on these lines:

> 'Meaning by the apple-tree the Tree of the Cross whereon the Son of God redeemed human nature, and in consequence was betrothed to it, and consequently was betrothed to every soul, giving it for this purpose grace and pledges through the merits of His Passion. . . . For thy mother, human nature, was corrupted in thy first parents, beneath the Tree, and there likewise wert thou redeemed—namely, beneath the Tree of the Cross.'[1]

Patmore remarks of the union of the glorified soul with God:

> 'This wonderful doctrine of such a reduplicated reciprocity as the natural mind, even when supernaturally enlightened, can with difficulty receive, is necessarily involved in the truth that Our Lord and the regenerated Soul are two in one Body. "Such knowledge", cries David, "is too excellent for me; I cannot attain unto it" '[2]

which seems to have been prompted by what St. John of the Cross says of the Spiritual Marriage:

> 'The Spiritual Marriage, between the soul and the Son of God, her Spouse . . . is a total transformation in the Beloved . . . wherein on either side there is surrender, by total possession, of the one to the other in consummate union of love. . . . For even as in the consummation of marriage according to the flesh the two become one flesh, as says the Divine Scripture, even so, when this Spiritual Marriage between God and the soul is consummated, there are two natures in one spirit and love of God.'[3]

Such examples, which could be multiplied, make their own point. It is also possible that St. John of the Cross's mystical exegeses of his own poems moved Patmore to write his *Sponsa Dei*, and the essays 'Dieu et Ma Dame', 'The Precursor' and 'The Bow Set in the Cloud' which are, in effect, glosses upon his Psyche odes.

St. Teresa of Avila, on the other hand, is seldom quoted directly by Patmore, although she is named in several places,[4] and appears to be remembered in the line:

> Sheathe in my heart sharp pain up to the hilt

from the ode 'Eros and Psyche'.

It seems unlikely that Patmore knew much about St. Teresa's

---

1 'Spiritual Canticle', *Complete Works of St. John of the Cross*, Vol. II, pp. 143–145.
2 *Rod, Root and Flower*, 'Homo', VII, p. 110.
3 *Complete Works of St. John of the Cross*, Vol. II, p. 140.
4 E.g. *Religio Poetae*, p. 43; *Rod, Root and Flower*, p. 139.

life and character, however, since he does not include her, as he certainly should have included her, among those women

> 'whose qualities of mind and heart seem to demand a revision of its (the world's) conception of womanhood and an enlargement of those limitations which it delights in regarding as essential to her very nature, and as necessary to her beauty and attractiveness as woman.'[1]

Neither does he mention her in the essay, 'A Spanish Novelette'[2] in which he talks of the 'burning psychological insight' of the Spanish mind, and strongly recommends the works of St. John of the Cross. It is possible that, in spite of his claims that the theologian is as much a poet as the poet is, he was attracted to St. John of the Cross above St. Teresa because St. John wrote great lyrical poetry in addition to mystical treatises. However, despite the individual nature of their spirituality, these two Spanish saints have so much in common that it would be rash to attribute the source of many of Patmore's later images and apprehensions to one rather than to the other, or, indeed, in some cases to either, seeing that both drew generously for illustration and inspiration upon the Bible, and those Fathers and Doctors whom Patmore also studied.

At the same time, a brief examination of one ode, 'Eros and Psyche', should serve to show the extent to which the concepts of the Spanish mystics coloured Patmore's vision. Psyche muses upon the occasions of earthly love which have brought her intimations

> Of sudden wings
> Through delicatest ether feathering soft
> Their solitary beat.

She says that she has long wished to capture the lover whose presence she has felt, but that all her attempts to lure him have failed, and she cries:

> At last, of endless failure much afraid,
> To-night I would do nothing but lie still,
> And promise, wert thou once within my window-sill,
> Thine unknown will.

This is the state of passivity and surrender to the will of God which, the mystics agree, precedes full union with Him. St. John of the Cross writes of it thus:

> 'At this season of communication with God, it is fitting that all the senses, whether interior or exterior, be empty or idle, for, at such a time, the more they set themselves to work, the more they disturb the

---

1 'Mrs. Meynell', *Principle in Art*, p. 146.
2 *Principle in Art*, pp. 192–198.

soul. . . . Thus that which the soul does at this time in the Beloved is to remain in the delectable exercise of that which has already been wrought in it—namely, loving in continuation of the union of love. Let none, then, appear upon the hill; let the will alone be present in the surrender of itself.'[1]

Eros speaks to Psyche and reveals that he, too, seeks her with ardour, with more, in fact, than she seeks for him:

> Ah, Psyche, guess'd you nought
> I craved but to be caught?
> Wanton, it was not you,
> But I that did so passionately sue.

St. John of the Cross says of God's ardent desire for the soul: 'It must be remembered above all that if a soul is seeking after God, the Beloved is seeking it much more.'[2]

Psyche, rapturously greeting the coming of Eros, surrenders herself to her Heavenly lover and begs Him:

> Kiss me again, and clasp me round the heart
> Till fill'd with thee am I
> As the cocoon is with the butterfly.

This image of Patmore's comes from St. Teresa's vivid similitude of the silk-worm in the *Interior Castle* by means of which she develops her description of the Prayer of Union.[3] The silkworm is compared to the loving soul which feeds upon the mulberry leaves in the garden of the Church, and which, once full grown, spins its cocoon, and emerges from it a butterfly.

'Oh, then, my daughters!' she says. 'Let us hasten to perform this task and spin this cocoon. . . . Let the silkworm die. . . . Then we shall see God and shall ourselves be as completely hidden in His greatness as is this little worm in its cocoon. . . . And now let us see what becomes of this silkworm. . . . When it is in this state of prayer, and quite dead to the world, it comes out a little white butterfly. Oh, greatness of God, that a soul should come out like this after being hidden in the greatness of God, and closely united to Him, for so short a time.'[4]

However, although rejoicing in the love of Eros, Psyche fears that

---

[1] *Complete Works of St. John of the Cross*, Vol. II, p. 133.
[2] 'The Living Flame of Love', *The Mystical Doctrine of St. John of the Cross*, an abridgement made by C. H. (London: Sheed and Ward, 1936), p. 151.
[3] 'Interior Castle', *The Complete Works of Saint Teresa of Jesus*, edited by E. Allison Peers (New York: Sheed and Ward, 1946), Bk. V. Chap. 11.
[4] *Ibid.*, pp. 254–255.

her love might still be tainted with earthly love and asks to know
how she can be sure it is pure:

> Yet how 'scape quite
> Nor pluck pure pleasure with profane delight?
> How know I that my love is what he seems?

To this, Eros replies:

> 'Tis this:
> I make the childless to keep joyful house.
> Below your bosom, mortal Mistress mine,
> Immortal by my kiss,
> Leaps what sweet pain?
> A fiend, my Psyche, comes with barren bliss,
> A God's embraces never are in vain.

On the question of the fruitfulness of God's love as a test of its
reality, Saint Teresa says:

> 'For if the soul is much with Him, as it is right it should be, it will
> very seldom think of itself; its whole thought will be concentrated
> upon finding ways to please and upon showing Him how it loves Him.
> This, my daughters, is the aim of prayer; this is the purpose of the
> Spiritual Marriage, of which are born good works and good works
> alone.'[1]

In the embrace of Eros, Psyche rises to a pitch of ecstasy almost
too great to be borne, and she cries out for suffering to temper the
joy she feels:

> Bitter be thy behests!
> Lie like a bunch of myrrh between my aching breasts.
> Some greatly pangful penance would I brave.

St. John of the Cross talks about the 'trials and tribulations, wherein
the soul also desires to enter' when he says:

> 'Let us enter farther into the thicket. That is to say, into trials and
> afflictions, insomuch as they are a means of entrance into the thicket
> of the delectable wisdom of God; for the purest suffering causes and
> entails the purest knowledge, and, in consequence, the purest and
> loftiest joy which comes from deepest penetration.'[2]

Eros tells Psyche that she must endure the contact of his beauty
since these embraces are only the espousals, and nuptials yet await
her such as now she dare not guess. Psyche answers him:

[1] *Ibid.*, p. 346.
[2] 'Spiritual Canticle', *Complete Works of St. John of the Cross*, Vol. II,
pp. 166–167.

> Thy love has conquer'd me; do with me as thou wilt
> And use me as a chattel that is thine! . . .
> Nay, let the Fiend drag me through dens of guilt;
> Let Earth, Heav'n, Hell
> 'Gainst my content combine;
> What could make nought the touch that made thee mine!

In the same strain, St. Teresa writes:

> 'Do you know when people really become spiritual? It is when they
> become the slaves of God and are branded with His sign, which is the
> sign of the Cross, in token that they have given Him their freedom.'[1]

At the coming of the day, Eros bids farewell to Psyche, and says
that with his departing comes the penance she sought. To this she
replies in words which echo the imagery used by St. John and St.
Teresa of the 'dark night' in which the soul feels itself temporarily
deprived of the presence of God:

> Curs'd when it comes, the bitter thing we crave!
> Thou leav'st me now, like to the moon at dawn,
> A little, vacuous world alone in air.
> I will not care!
> When dark comes back my dark shall be withdrawn.

In such ways, the Psyche odes reflect Patmore's reading of
Catholic mystics, and employ ideas which belong in the main
tradition of orthodox mystical writing. The weaving into these
poems of so much of the contemplative experience of the saints,
expressed with such passion indicates that he felt himself akin, at
least poetically, to the mystics who gave him the greater part of his
imagery and most of his mystical 'psychology'.

St. Augustine was another writer whom Patmore read assiduously
during his later years, and to whom there are innumerable references
in the later essays. Patmore's library contained two copies of the
Confessions, and copies of the *Homilies on the New Testament*, the
Homilies on St. John, the *Homilies on the Psalms*, and several short
treatises, two in particular, *De Continentia* and *De Bono Conjugali*,
being much pencil-marked, with 'Sp. D.' often indicated in the
margin.[2] Patmore himself gives the clue to the main use he made
of St. Augustine in saying: 'The Saints, above all St. Augustine,
abound in epigrams.'[3] St. Augustine is referred to in his prose far
more often than any other philosopher, and his name nearly always
appears in the list of those whom Patmore offers as great guides,

1 'Interior Castle', *Complete Works of St. Teresa*, VII, iv, p. 346.
2 *Catalogue of the Library of Coventry Patmore.*
3 *Rod, Root and Flower*, 'Aurea Dicta', CXXIX, p. 50.

seers and philosophers. However, he uses Augustine mainly as a source of illustrative quotations to support some argument drawn initially from Aquinas, or one of his own 'corollaries'.[1] In *The Rod, the Root and the Flower*, some of the most striking of Patmore's sayings have their starting point in such a phrase. He says, for instance:

> 'The Angels gain credibility and human sympathy from the doctrine of their defect of absolute purity; and nothing has made the idea of the Blessed Virgin so amiable in my sight as the saying of St. Augustine that the only sin she is chargeable with is a little vanity in the consciousness of being the Bride and Mother of God.'[2]

One saying of the saint's particularly caught Patmore's attention; he uses it no less than four times in *The Rod, the Root and the Flower*. This—'Jesus Christ is the Bride as well as the Bridegroom; for He is the Body'—is just what might have been expected to have particular significance for him. In one place he joins it with quotations from his other sources in a significant statement of his ideas on the Incarnation as an image of man's relationship with God in contemplation and of the love between the sexes,[3] and on the title-page of *The Victories of Love*, he placed a sentence from Augustine which sums up the message he intended the poem to convey: 'Da quod amo; amo enim, et hoc tu dedisti'.

The whole tenor of Augustine's teachings, especially his anti-Manichaean attitude to the body, reinforced Patmore's already firmly shaped convictions, for he recognized that the general views of his own age on sex, marriage and the body had much in common with those of the Manichaeans in Augustine's day. In the essay 'Ancient and Modern Ideas of Purity', after referring to the outspokenness of the early Christian Fathers, notably Augustine, and contrasting this with the contemporary 'niceness of nasty thinkers',[4] he then goes on to say:

> 'The whole sphere of the doctrines of the early Church, like that of the great mythologies, revolved about mysteries which the modern Churches, in practice, absolutely ignore, but which nature, however

---

[1] E.g., 'Dieu et Ma Dame', *Religio Poetae*, p. 163.

[2] *Rod, Root and Flower*, 'Homo', IV, p. 107. Hopkins questioned Patmore's depiction of Honoria as taking pleasure in her lover's delight in her beauty—a kind of vanity which Patmore had said was not in Honoria—and Patmore replied, 'I meant Honoria's pleasure . . . a sense in which some great Doctor, Saint—I think St. Augustine—says that there was a little vanity in the Blessed Virgin.' (*Further Letters of Gerard Manly Hopkins*, p. 163, letter of Sept. 27, 1883.)

[3] 'The Bow Set in the Cloud', *Religio Poetae*, pp. 55–56.

[4] 'Ancient and Modern Ideas of Purity', *Religio Poetae*, p. 69.

improved by grace, absolutely refuses to ignore. The result is a practical Manicheism, which is as serious in its effects upon morals as it is treasonous to the truth.'[1]

The entire essay, as well as much in *The Rod, the Root and the Flower*, is a direct attack on Victorian prudery, and proceeds by arguments much like those of Augustine in *De Continentia* and elsewhere.

In Chapter IX of *De Continentia*, St. Augustine speaks of the 'madness' by which the Manichaeans attribute the flesh to some fabulous race of darkness, and contrasts it with St. Paul's injunction that husbands should love their wives, as Christ loved the Church. He continues by describing three similar unions; Christ and the Church, husband and wife, spirit and flesh, in which the former cares for the latter and the latter waits upon the former. All are good relations when the former as superior and the latter as subject, preserve the beauty of order—as Christ to the Church, so husband to the wife.[2] This is close to everything that Patmore wrote, not only on the various analogies of love, but also on the relationship between wife and husband; there is no reason to suppose that the concepts came to him from Augustine, but such teachings would be sufficient to make him mark the treatise generously, to use it in writing the prose *Sponsa Dei*, and to call St. Augustine as witness to many of his statements.

It is possible, too, that the idea hinted at in 'The Contract'—that through true continence man may attain to a heightening of his spiritual powers and learn profitably to re-direct 'sexual energy'— may have owed something to Augustine's words in *De Continentia*:

> 'Conjugal continence, indeed, usually abates the concupiscence of the flesh . . . only to such an extent that in the marriage itself it is not poured out in unmoderated licence, but that measure is observed, either that owed to the weakness of the spouse to whom the Apostle does not charge it by commandment, but to whom he yields it by indulgence, or that suited to the procreation of children. . . . But when continence does this, that is, when it moderates and in a certain way, limits the concupiscence of the flesh in married people, and orders its restless and inordinate motion, in a manner, to certain ends, it uses in a good way the evil of man whom it makes and wants to make thoroughly good.'[3]

---

[1] 'Ancient and Modern Ideas of Purity', *Religeo Poetae*, p. 71.
[2] 'De Continentia', translated by Sister Mary Francis McDonald, O.P., *Treatises on Various Subjects by St. Augustine* (Fathers of the Church Series, New York, Fathers of the Church Inc., 1952), Vol. 16, pp. 215–217.
[3] *Ibid.*, p. 225.

And so, on the matter of the two sexes, Augustine and Patmore are in accord. The sexes and the flesh, says the saint, are not as the Manichees urge, from the Devil but from God. The flesh is good since souls themselves are advised to imitate the harmony of its members.[1] Patmore puts it thus: 'The Soul is the express image of God, and the Body of the Soul; thence, it, also, is an image of God and "the human form divine" is no figure of speech.'[2] The detailed debt of Patmore to the Bishop of Hippo appears to have been less than his debt to Aquinas and St. Bernard, but there can be no doubt that the reading of such works as *De Continentia* strengthened his belief in what were to him the central truths of existence.

One further influence on the later Patmore differs from the others in her obscurity. This is Marie Lataste, the French peasant girl, and mystical writer. The single reference to her in the extracts from Patmore's papers published by Champneys is unfortunately undated; it runs:

'I am just now reading the Life of a peasant girl, Marie Lataste, who died only a few years ago. Her life was all grace and miracle, and her writings full of a living sanctity and vigorous perception of things hidden to the wise.'[3]

However, Frederick Page points out that among Patmore's notes for the odes are some transcripts from her French, and he claims, without producing any evidence in support, that 'she was Psyche, and I think we may say that the Pythoness was her confessor.'[4]

In fact, the Psyche odes disclose very little which is peculiar to Marie Lataste's writings. Psyche in the odes is a compound of many influences—Patmore's own daughter, for one, the Bride in the Song of Songs, the Greek myth itself, and the soul as St. Bernard and St. Teresa depict it. There is no characterization in the dramatic sense to suggest an identification with any particular person, and while it may indeed be possible that the French girl was one of many elements which went to form Patmore's Psyche, there is so little in her writings which may not be found in St. Thomas Aquinas, St. Augustine and St. Bernard, that it is difficult to agree that she played quite so important a part in the writing of *The Unknown Eros*.

Marie Lataste, born at Mibaste in the Landes district in 1822, was a poorly educated peasant girl, noted as an adolescent for her exceptionally virtuous and pious living. In 1839, she believed that

---

[1] *Ibid.*, p. 219.   [2] *Rod, Root and Flower*, 'Homo', XXXV, p. 142.
[3] Champneys, *Memoirs*, Vol. II, p. 80.
[4] *Patmore, A Study in Poetry*, p. 125.

Christ Himself appeared to her, and began with her a long series of conversations in which He acted as her instructor in the truths of religion and on matters of morality. Her revelations came to the attention of the parish priest, M. Darbins, who consulted with the Abbé Dupérier, professor of theology at the seminary of Dax. They persuaded the girl to set down her visions in written form. When the manuscript was studied by Dupérier and other priests, appointed for this purpose by the Bishop of Aire, they pronounced the works to contain nothing contrary to faith and morals, and said that they were calculated to do good to souls. In 1844, Marie Lataste became a postulant of the Nuns of the Sacré Cœur in Paris, and died in 1847, not having taken her final vows. The first edition of her writings was published in 1862—*La Vie et les Œuvres de Marie Lataste, Religieuse Coadjutrice du Sacré Cœur*—and this was the work which Patmore read. The Abbé Pascal Darbins, who edited the first four editions of this book, was the nephew of Marie Lataste's spiritual director, the Abbé Pierre Darbins, who supervised its publication.

To judge from the testimony of her English biographer and of her fellow nuns, Marie Lataste was a sensible girl of devout nature, with some of the characteristics of the typical 'sensitive'. Unhappily, it is now impossible to tell exactly what was the nature of her revelations, since it has been established that her written account was edited, recast and amplified by the Darbins, and possibly others. The great Jesuit authority on mysticism, the Abbé A. Poulain, writes:

> 'When Marie Lataste's *Works* appeared, the theologians, who had admired certain passages, ended by proving that they had been translated word for word from St. Thomas' *Summa*. They counted thirty-two passages of this nature. The objection was conveyed to the person who was supposed to have collected the revelations. He did not deny the fact, but replied majestically that, as Our Lord had inspired St. Thomas to write these pages, he could repeat them to Marie Lataste! Circumstances pointed, however, to a simpler explanation, which subsequent events tended to confirm.'[1]

This being the case, it is no wonder that Patmore, the devoted reader of St. Thomas, should have been attracted to Marie Lataste. That he was not the only English Catholic who accepted her works as authentic vision is shown by the strong partisanship in favour of

[1] *The Graces of Interior Prayer*, by R. P. A. Poulain, S.J., translated by Leonora L. Yorke-Smith (London: Kegan Paul, Trench, Trubner & Co., 1912), p. 339, note.

the revelations exhibited by Edward Healy Thompson who wrote her life in English and who translated her works.[1]

According to Marie Lataste, her record contained only what she heard from the lips of Christ. Yet her visions are very different from those of Swedenborg, for example. There is a certain amount of glimpsing of an orthodox Heaven, and occasional passages of not very complex symbolism, but there are no wonderful revelations. The writings consist largely of an elaborate detailing of Christian doctrine, and of traditional Catholic teachings on the active and contemplative lives. This is not surprising if they were largely tidied up, and perhaps in part actually written, by her priest advisers, but even allowing for a large amount of elaboration, the original 'revelations' were clearly more pedagogical than 'illuminative', and contained little which would not be familiar to any seminary student.

Father Terence L. Connolly has drawn attention to passages in Patmore's poems in which ideas expressed are paralleled by sections of Marie Lataste's writings.[2] One or two of these show an impressive similarity. For instance in 'The Wedding Sermon', Patmore writes:

> But if the flying spirit falls flat,
> After the modest spell of prayer
> That saves the day from sin and care,
> And the upward eye a void descries,
> And praises are hypocrisies,
> And, in the soul, o'erstrained for grace,
> A godless anguish grows apace;
> Or, if impartial charity
> Seems, in the act, a sordid lie,
> Do not infer you cannot please
> God, or that He His promises
> Postpones, but be content to love
> No more than He accounts enough.

Similar in sentiment and phrasing to these lines are the words which Marie Lataste attributes to Christ:

'You are mistaken if you think you do not love Me because you are unable to pray with attention because your mind is distracted and in a state of dryness, because your heart does not feel any tenderness for Me. When you find yourself in this state, remember what I said when

[1] *The Life of Marie Lataste* (Burns & Oates, Ltd., London, n.d.); *Letters and Writings of Marie Lataste* (London: Burns & Oates, Ltd., 1893). E. H. Thompson was an uncle of the poet Francis Thompson.

[2] *Mystical Poems of Nuptial Love by Coventry Patmore*.

I was on earth: "He who loves Me keeps My commandments"; for love is shown more by acts than by feelings. Feelings do not always depend upon yourself; sometimes I am pleased to withdraw from a soul to try it; but I do not prevent it from fulfilling My law and being faithful to My commandments. If sometimes a soul cannot testify its affective love, it can always testify its effective love.'[1]

At the same time, this counselling against distraction in prayer, and the drawing of consolation from praying even when the heart does not appear to be in it, is by no means peculiar to Marie Lataste. A great deal of St. Teresa's advice follows similar lines, in particular, Chapters XXI to XXIV of *The Way of Perfection*; while St. John of the Cross speaks in much the same terms.

Similarly, Patmore writes in the ode 'Pain':

> Choice food of sanctity
> And medicine of sin,

with which Father Connolly compares the following passage from Marie Lataste:

> 'God lays His hand heavily on the just and on sinners; on the just in order to facilitate their acquisition of greater merits; on sinners, to chastise them in their bodies and thus to save their souls by a sincere repentance.'[2]

However, neither of these passages contains anything which cannot also be found in Patmore's other sources. It is interesting, too, that while Patmore often refers in his essays to all the other writers to whom he was indebted he never refers to Marie Lataste. Nevertheless, the transcripts he made from her writings indicate that he must have been attracted by her expression of familiar truths, and perhaps by the whole idea of a young and illiterate peasant enjoying the great condescension of Christ appearing to her as Master and Tutor. The pedagogical role played by the Pythoness in 'De Natura Deorum' may just possibly derive a hint from Christ's attitude to Marie, as set out in the writings, or, as Page suggests, from the letters of Marie to her confessor. But the association is very tenuous and the half-flippant tone of the Pythoness is quite out of harmony with anything in the French girl's 'communications'.

Yet, Marie Lataste's teaching on marriage, as put into the mouth of Christ in the second book of her writings, must have made an impression on the poet, if only because it was identical with his

---

[1] *Letters and Writings of Marie Lataste*, Vol. I, p. 266.

[2] *Mystical Poems by Coventry Patmore*, p. 282. The passage comes from *The Writings of Marie Lataste*, Vol. I, p. 56.

own view. She stresses the holiness of marriage, saying that neither chastity nor purity is lost therein, so long as there is love of God, and dwells on the vocation of marriage, the need for restraint and continence in married love, and the importance of proper disposi- tions governing the relations between husband and wife—all topics close to Patmore's heart. That Marie thought of herself as a 'bride' of Christ is clear not only from her dying words, 'I am the Spouse of the Crucified Christ', but also from Sections IX to XI of Book XI in Volume II of her writings, which are devoted to 'The Graces which Jesus bestows on souls who choose Him for their Spouse; of the soul espoused to Jesus, and of the love of that soul for Jesus her Spouse', and similar topics. Of particular interest is Book XIII of Volume II, in which, following the tradition of the Church, Marie Lataste discusses God's dealings with Israel as a figure of His dealings with the soul, interpreting such Old Testament personali- ties as Moses, Pharaoh, Gideon, the Israelites and Noah in terms of mystical significance. Patmore's fondness for the 'arcane' significances of Scripture must have made him note especially this aspect of Marie's work.

Such elements, then, in the writings of the peasant girl, whatever their real origin, are so typical of Patmore's own thinking that it seems likely that her 'communications' helped to reinforce his convictions concerning marriage, the nuptial analogy, the value of the contemplative life, the mystical significance of chastity, and much else. It is the lack of anything strikingly original in her work, however, which makes it impossible to plot with certainty relations between Patmore's work and her own. The most that can be said is that she went with other writers, to shape attitudes in Patmore which were in harmony with Catholic doctrine, and yet were in the final analysis Patmorean.

Among other mystical writers studied by Patmore were St. Catherine of Genoa, St. Ignatius Loyola, St. Francis de Sales and St. Catherine of Siena. None of these had so deep an influence on him as Aquinas or Augustine, yet they too served in various ways to colour his thinking and enrich his poetry. The works of the two St. Catherines were in his library, and in the works of St. Catherine of Siena, a few passages of intimate Eucharistic doctrine are marked.[1] St. Catherine of Genoa is very seldom referred to in his prose, and when her name occurs it is in the most general of contexts. How- ever, one of the most important features of her teaching deals with Purgatory, and Patmore's ode, 'Pain' with its mystical treatment of suffering in this life and in the next world appears to be more

1 *Catalogue of the Library of Coventry Patmore.*

heavily indebted to her doctrine than to that of better-known Doctors of the Church. Patmore writes:

> Thou searest my flesh, O Pain,
> But brand'st for arduous peace my languid brain,
> And bright'nest my dull view,
> Till I, for blessing, blessing give again,
> And my roused spirit is
> Another fire of bliss,
> Wherein I learn
> Feelingly how the pangful, purging fire
> Shall furiously burn
> With joy, not only of assured desire,
> But also present joy
> Of seeing the life's corruption, stain by stain,
> Vanish in the clear heat of Love irate,
> And, fume by fume, the sick alloy
> Of luxury, sloth and hate
> Evaporate;
> Leaving the man, so dark erewhile,
> The mirror merely of God's smile.

This passage of the ode strongly resembles parts of St. Catherine of Genoa's writings which tell of the nature of the Purgatorial fire. For instance:

> 'The soul which, when separated from the body, does not find itself in that cleanness in which it was created, seeing in itself the stain, and that this stain cannot be purged out except by means of Purgatory, swiftly and of its own accord, casts itself in; and if it did not find this ordination apt to purge that stain, in that very moment there would be spontaneously generated within itself a Hell worse than Purgatory.'[1]

Patmore's image of the purging away of 'the sick alloy' in the fire of pain recalls another passage of St. Catherine's writings wherein she writes:

> 'Gold, when once it has been (fully) purified, can be no further consumed by the action of fire, however great it be; since fire does not, strictly speaking, consume gold, but only the dross which the gold may chance to contain. So also with regard to the soul. God holds it so long in the furnace, until every imperfection is consumed away. And when it is (thus) purified, it becomes impassible; so that, if, thus purified, it were to be kept in the fire, it would feel no pain; rather would such a fire be to it a fire of Divine Love burning on without opposition, like the fire of life eternal.'[2]

[1] Quoted in *The Mystical Element of Religion as Studied in St. Catherine of Genoa and her Friends*, by Baron Friedrich von Hugel (London: J. M. Dent & Co.), 1909, Vol. I, p. 285.　　　[2] *Ibid.*, p. 292.

Such similarities between 'Pain' and these teachings of St. Catherine leave no doubt that the saint was the inspirer of that particular poem. And further evidence is supplied by a short memorandum which is reproduced by Champneys:

> '*Mem.* Some works (like St. Catherine's treatise on purgatory) though not by any ordained teacher, have been accepted by the Church as almost canonical. This should be a final answer to my doubts as to my mission. (S. Ignatius' "Exercises" also.)'[1]

St. Ignatius Loyola also is referred to occasionally in Patmore's prose. Connolly suggests that the title of Patmore's ode 'The Standards' might have been prompted by one of the meditations in St. Ignatius's *Spiritual Exercises*, entitled 'A Meditation on Two Standards: the One of Christ Our Supreme Captain and Lord; the Other of Lucifer, the Mortal Enemy of Our Human Nature'[2]; and also that the opening lines of 'The Child's Purchase' may be an adaptation of St. Ignatius's prayer, the *Suspice*. Apart from such possible traces, however, there is very little of the characteristic spirit of St. Ignatius in Patmore's work, and certainly little of the militant missionary spirit of the Jesuits in his personality.

In addition to these Doctors and Saints of the Church, two other Catholic writers, Dante and Newman, supplied Patmore with inspiration and material. He read Dante in his youth, and retained the greatest respect for the Italian poet to the end of his days. In only one place is there a suggestion that he did not accept Dante uncritically, a passage in his essay 'Pathos', which runs:

> ' . . . how many a good piece of pathos has been spoiled by the historian of Little Nell by an attempt to make too much of it! A drop of citric acid will give poignancy to a feast; but a draught of it——! Hence it is doubtful whether an English eye ever shed a tear over the *Vita Nuova*, whatever an Italian may have done.'[3]

However, it is likely that here Patmore, often mischievous in his criticism, was gently gibing at his former friends, the Rossettis, since elsewhere he writes: 'The longer I live the more I am convinced that no one—since the Hebrew Prophets—has ever written religious poetry, except Dante.'[4] And he repeats this judgment in the ode 'Prophets Who Cannot Sing':

> At least, from David unto Dante, none.
> And none since him.

[1] Champneys, *Memoirs*, Vol. II, p. 69.
[2] *Mystical Poems by Coventry Patmore*, p. 222.
[3] 'Pathos', *Principle in Art*, pp. 41–42.
[4] Champneys, *Memoirs*, Vol. II, pp. 98–99.

He certainly looked upon Dante as one of the great 'seers', classing him in this respect with Swedenborg.[1]

He had his own way of appreciating Dante and of using him to back up his own convictions. Passages such as the following, in which Patmore bares his teeth, are among the most delightful exhibitions of personality in his entire work:

> 'It is . . . a vulgar error to consider Dante a melancholy poet. In the whole range of art, joy is nowhere expressed so often and with such piercing sweetness as in the *Paradiso*; and it flashes occasionally through the dun atmosphere of the other parts of the poem. The *Inferno* is pervaded by the vigorous joy of the poet at beholding thoroughly bad people getting their deserts; and the penances of purgatory are contemplated with the grave pleasure which is so often felt by the saner sort of persons, even in this world, under the sufferings they acknowledge to be the appropriate punishment of and purification from the sins they have fallen into.'[2]

Since Patmore admired *The Divine Comedy* so much, it is somewhat surprising that more echoes of the Italian poet do not appear in his writing. There are only a few passages which may owe something to Dante. For instance, Patmore's description of the 'living order' to which each soul aspires in order to fulfil its own beauty and felicity:

> 'This is his "ruling love", his individuality, the centre towards which his thoughts and actions gravitate, and about which his whole being revolves; while this individual being again travels about that greater centre which gives a common unity and generosity to all individualities'[3]

is reminiscent of the magnificent vision at the end of the *Paradiso* in which Dante sees all things revolving around and having their peace in God. It is possible, too, that portions of 'The Child's Purchase', the lines beginning:

> Life's cradle and Death's tomb!

and

> Mother, who lead'st me still by unknown ways,
> Giving the gifts I know not how to ask . . .

may have been suggested to Patmore by St. Bernard's hymn to the Blessed Virgin which opens the XXXIIIrd and last Canto of

---

1 'Swedenborgiana', *The National Review*, Vol. III, No. V, Oct. 1856, pp. 336–337.

2 'Cheerfulness in Life and Art', *Principle in Art*, pp. 8–9.

3 'Peace in Life and Art', *Principle in Art*, p. 32.

the *Paradiso*.[1] Patmore must have delighted in the fierce individuality of Dante, and in the poet's habit of putting in Hell priests and prelates he disliked; and he must also have sympathized with Dante's political career. The reason why comparatively little influence of Dante can be found in his work may be that the Italian poet's idealization of woman did not suit the more pragmatic mind of Patmore, who was, after all, mainly concerned with marriage, and not with an idealized Beatrice unattainable in this life. He respected Dante's poetic stature, his theology and human insight, but he could not follow him in his particular expression of love.

In the case of Cardinal Newman, Patmore's debt is more obvious and restricted. He keenly admired Newman's character and intelligence; and in *The Rod, the Root and the Flower* he paid tribute to the Cardinal in these words:

> 'The steam-hammer of that Intellect which could be so delicately adjusted to its task as to be capable of either crushing a Hume or cracking a Kingsley is no longer at work, that tongue which had the weight of a hatchet, and the edge of a razor is silent; but its mighty task of so representing truth as to make it credible to the modern mind, when not interested in unbelief, has been done.'[2]

Patmore met Newman once only; but they corresponded at intervals and Champneys prints two letters from Newman to the poet, one thanking him for a copy of the St. Bernard translation, the other for a copy of *The Unknown Eros*. There is, however, no evidence of close connection or intimacy between the two men. Patmore appears to have combined a strong regard for Newman as a person with some reservations about his religious views, which, in common with other Catholics of the time, he suspected of bearing traces of his former 'Protestantism'. For instance, he wrote:

> 'He never seems to me to have quite worked off his Protestantism. St. Evremond, I think, says that the Protestant and Catholic Spirits are distinguished thus; the Protestant is always thinking of not displeasing God, the Catholic is always thinking of pleasing Him, fear being the ruling motive in one, love in the other. Keble's Parish Sermons seem to me to be much more Catholic than Newman's.'[3]

Patmore's attitude, thus expressed, could mean little more than that, being himself temperamentally 'daring' and explosive, certain of truth, and convinced that his view was *the* Catholic view, he

---

1 See *Mystical Poems of Nuptial Love by Coventry Patmore*, pp. 292–293, 298.
2 *Rod, Root and Flower*, Preface, pp. 19–20.
3 Champneys, *Memoirs*, Vol. II, pp. 79–80.

found Newman's subtle, sensitive and rather devious, if thoroughly honest, mind difficult to understand, and not dreaming that the difference was primarily one of different temperaments, suspected that the Cardinal's outlook was not quite 'Catholic'. Yet he was never in danger of underestimating Newman's great contribution to English Catholicism, and he admired him as much as he disliked Manning. He wrote: 'In religion, what Newman has done for the Church of Rome, that Coleridge has done for the Church of England,'[1] and that, considering Patmore's devotion to Coleridge, was praise indeed.

Patmore did not care for *The Dream of Gerontius* as poetry, although he thought it a striking piece of imaginative psychology; and he felt that Newman was not really a poet at all, because his verse lacked the perfection of language which his prose had. But he read with unreserved admiration the *Essay in Aid of a Grammar of Assent,* and he took over parts of Newman's argument, especially that dealing with the 'illative sense', or the spontaneous divination by the mind in concrete matters that a conclusion is inevitable if it is felt to be 'as good as proved', and which operates with probabilities, including the matter of religious faith, with as great a care as that of a scientist dealing with mathematical fact. Newman's idea that there is a logical cogency in religious belief which goes beyond the scientist's logic, and that a 'rhetoric' of belief could be stated, Patmore used to support his own long-held concept that intuition is a form of spiritual reasoning which can produce results as true as those adduced by scientific logic.

The phrase which occurs so often in *Religio Poetae*—'real apprehension'—is borrowed from Newman, and the essay 'Religio Poetae' opens with a paraphrase of a part of the argument in the *Grammar of Assent,* except that Patmore substitutes the expression 'experimental assent' for Newman's 'notional assent':

'No one, probably, has ever found his life permanently affected by any truth whereof he has been unable to obtain a *real apprehension,* which . . . is quite a different thing from real *comprehension.* Intellectual assent to truths of faith, founded on what the reason regards as sufficient authority for, at least, experimental assent, must, of course, precede real apprehension of them, as also must action in a sort experimental, on faith of truths so assented to, but such faith and action have little effective life, and are likely soon to cease, or to become mere formalities, unless they produce some degree of vital *knowledge* or *perception.*'[2]

1 'Coleridge', *St. James's Gazette,* March 16, 1887; *Courage in Politics,* p. 85.
2 'Religio Poetae', *Religio Poetae,* p. 1.

The similarity between the terminology of the two writers on this topic may be seen from this brief quotation from the *Grammar of Assent*:

'Let the proposition to which the assent is given be as absolutely true as the reflex act pronounces it to be, that is, objectively true as well as subjectively, then the assent may be called a *perception*, the conviction a *certitude*, the proposition or truth a *certainty*, or thing known, or a matter of *knowledge*, and to assent to it is to *know*.'[1]

Similarly, Patmore's essay 'Real Apprehension' is a Patmorean application of other ideas in the *Grammar of Assent*. It opens with a quotation from Newman, and goes on to develop the Cardinal's distinction between real and notional assent:

'"Man", says Dr. Newman, "is not a reasoning animal; he is a seeing, feeling, contemplating, acting animal." To see rightly is the first of human qualities; right feeling and right acting are usually its consequences. There are two ways of seeing: one is to comprehend, which is to see all round a thing or to embrace it; one is to apprehend, which is to see it in part, or to take hold of it. A thing may be really taken hold of which is much too big for embracing. Real apprehension implies reality in that which is apprehended. You cannot "take hold" of that which is nothing. The notional grasp which some people seem to have of clouds and mares' nests is a totally different thing from real apprehension.'[2]

How much Patmore was indebted to Newman in this matter becomes plain if we compare the above passage with two sentences in which Newman discusses 'real apprehension': 'Real Apprehension is . . . in the first instance an experience or information about the concrete.'[3] 'Real apprehension, then, may be pronounced stronger than notional, because things, which are its objects, are confessedly more impressive and effective than notions, which are the subject of notional.'[4]

Patmore's reading, then, in theology, philosophy and mysticism was most unusual among the literary men of his age. Coleridge read more widely and deeply in philosophy and metaphysics; Newman in theology, philosophy and history; Arnold in classical literature, history and theology. But there is no other Victorian writer who can match Patmore's intimate knowledge of mystical literature and of the Doctors of the Church. In his interest in such writers and

[1] *A Grammar of Assent*, edited by Charles Frederick Harrold (New York: Longmans, Green & Co., 1947), p. 148.
[2] 'Real Apprehension', *Religio Poetae*, p. 77.
[3] *A Grammar of Assent*, p. 19.   [4] *Ibid.*, p. 30.

the use he made of them, he stands alone in his age, even among specifically religious poets; and he anticipated by many years that interest in such writers as St. John of the Cross, St. Teresa of Avila and St. Bernard which was to be displayed by several modern English poets.

Yet Patmore was more than just a passive receiver and adapter of other men's apprehensions. His reading played a large part in determining the direction of his thought, in indicating the lines along which his poetic vision developed, and in providing material for his essays; but all that he absorbed he remade to the demands of his strikingly individual personality, and bent to serve his own primary intuitions. However apparently incongruous and diverse his sources, he turned them all to his own end, that of the pursuit of truth, as he conceived the poet's duty to be. The working out of his own relationship to Catholic orthodoxy was no easy matter, and yet, despite some strain, and at perhaps a certain cost in equanimity, he achieved it. The result was to give him a group of poetic and religious doctrines, rather than a 'system', which, while receiving, as he believed, abundant confirmation from a wide variety of authorities, was particularly his own, and reflected his own unusual temperament and intellect.

PART THREE

THE ESSENTIALS OF PATMORE'S PHILOSOPHY

I

Leading Ideas

E HAVE SEEN that Patmore was not a systematic thinker, that he had neither the equipment of a philosopher nor the inclination to be one, and that it is unwise to try to force a coherent pattern on his apprehensions. Nearly all his suggestions and intuitions are valuable, and, taken together, they reveal a most individual temperament and an alert and venturesome mind. Yet, having accepted Christian dogma, and later Catholic theology, as the clearest expression of 'self-evident' truths, he was content to leave a good deal of religious thought unexplored, and to concentrate only on such aspects of it as suited his poetic purpose and his own spiritual inclinations.

In the discussion of his sources, some of Patmore's main ideas were touched upon. However, to demonstrate the individual colouring he gave to what he had taken from Aquinas, Swedenborg, Coleridge and others, I intend in this chapter to outline, not a 'system', but his leading ideas, to suggest the relationship between these ideas, and thus to indicate how Patmore's eclecticism enabled him to translate old truths into terms of his own living experience.

Champneys says that Patmore was one of those 'who rise from the technical to the spiritual, and, without repudiating or disparaging dogma, use it merely as a guide and support to thought which transcends mere definition.'[1] He points out that whenever matters

---

[1] Champneys, *Memoirs*, Vol. II, p. 24.

in dispute between the various Christian churches were discussed in the poet's presence, it was impossible to bring his mind down to the technical point at issue.

> 'He was', says Champneys, 'so exclusively occupied with great and far-reaching principles as completely to rise above controversial detail . . . . He (would) habitually override all considerations of mere matter-of-fact reasoning by reference to some great spiritual truth.'[1]

Patmore's concern with the 'corollaries' of, and not the reasons for, dogmas he accepted as merely common-sense must have made him a frustrating companion for anyone inclined to debate matters of Church history, practice and doctrine. As Champneys says (not wholly accurately, for Patmore never really left the earth, but was a man of an intensely practical nature, who rooted all his spiritual perceptions in phenomena), 'Things of the spirit were obviously far more real to him than aught perceptible to the senses.'[2] Champneys based his estimate as much on Patmore's conversation as on his writings. The general impression his recorded utterances, his letters and his note-books give is that Patmore was a man of absolute religious faith, and yet at the same time one with not the slightest instinct for proselytism.

The standpoint of Patmore, that he *knew*, while others simply *opined*, covered not only the nature of genius and of poetry, the symbolism of the Bible, the love of man for woman and of God for the soul, but also the 'leprosy' of Gladstone, the 'betrayals' of Disraeli, and the defects of democracy. His temperament made it inevitable that he should place his political certainties on the same plane as his religious certainties, but this was in some ways unfortunate for his poetic reputation, in that the scorn of some critics for his 'reactionary Toryism' has extended to other concepts which had, at least, a traditional and psychological backing such as his political views did not. The coherence of his outlook was emotional, not rational. Like so many Victorians, he was unable rationally to justify the workings of his conscience. Yet his work does convey a sense of the importance and the urgency of certain spiritual concepts. This is not because he convinces by argument, but because his constancy, rooted in character, establishes a special point of view. From a study of his work, the reader, as Patmore hoped he would, may learn to cultivate a particular attitude to God and man, in which both are seen in a new perspective. It is a matter

---

[1] Champneys, *Memoirs*, Vol. II, pp. 24–25.   [2] *Ibid.*, Vol. II, p. 30.

of 'seeing', which is, in Patmore's case, a matter of 'feeling' rather than of being rationally persuaded.[1]

In sum, then, Patmore regarded himself as a poetic 'seer'. But the basic experiences he sets out, although distinctive to himself, he believes to be capable of attainment by all, given the right disposition. Although he is a humanist, there is no late Renaissance humanism in him; his humanism is that of the Middle Ages. He never sees man as potentially God nor does his imagination extend, as does Rimbaud's, or Poe's in *Eureka*, to thinking that the poet is in actual fact God, making and destroying universes. For him, man is 'Creation's and Creator's crowning good'. Because he sees in him a glory which has not passed away from the earth, but which is the reflection of the glory of God, he eschews both the Manichaean outlook of English Puritanism, and post-Renaissance secular humanism. Hence, in this, as in much else, he was divorced from the general tendencies of his age; and, partly as a result, looked forward to new discoveries both in psychology and in the things of the spirit which were to come as a consequence of a dissolution of Victorian complacency and spiritual pride.

That Patmore's habit of expressing his conception of 'right seeing' and 'real apprehension' in unphilosophical language and with the confident tone of one who knows beyond all shadow of doubt could be irritating to one with a trained philosophical mind is seen from Gerard Manley Hopkins's reaction to the essay 'Real Apprehension'. On the whole politely, but nevertheless with a touch of acerbity, Hopkins objected not only to the text from Newman: 'Man is not a reasoning animal; he is a seeing, feeling, contemplating, acting animal', which he felt Patmore had taken too much in earnest, but also to Patmore's apparent denigration of reason. To Hopkins's rather overwhelming analysis, Patmore had little answer, save:

'I agree with most, perhaps all of what you say. . . . Its drift, however, was not so much to expound Newman's "text", as to make an indirect attack upon the great popular fallacy that a thing must be "understood" in order to be a discernible reality.'

And he added, with a touch of that humility which shows itself many times in his correspondence with the Jesuit:

'I have little or no paternal affection for the disorderly children of my brain, and am, and always have been, even thankful to any one who has the goodness and courage to knock them on the head. I have a

---

[1] See John Freeman, 'Coventry Patmore', *The Quarterly Review*, Vol. 240, No. 476, July 1923, p. 134.

"real apprehension" that this is not quite as it should be, though I do not yet quite "understand" my defect.'[1]

In the light of this admission, even if we discount disinclination on Patmore's part to indulge in the close defence Hopkins's reasoning called for, Patmore's attempts to justify the essential 'rightness' of his apprehensions are seen to be based on feeling, rather than on reason. The circumstances of his upbringing and education, as well as the nature of his mind, had much to do with this tendency to rationalize; and it was an awareness of this in himself, as much as the natural caution of the Catholic layman, which made him disclaim, in the preface to *The Rod, the Root and the Flower*, either originality or system in the 'teachings' contained in the book. And he reveals the same sense that he is expressing his experiences and a vision of truth rather than a 'philosophy' when he writes of the soul genuinely in love with God:

> 'The utterances whereby she endeavours to draw others to her wisdom are interjections, doxologies, parables, and aphorisms, which have no connecting unity but that of a common heat and light.'[2]

Knowledge acquired by study can provide illustration of basic truths; but the truths themselves can be acquired only by the intuition of the uncontaminated soul. Once the mind has become aware of such truths, it will find in man and the universe a vast number of parallels and correspondences whose chief value is to confirm what the soul already knows.

Such a view is that of the poet rather than that of the philosopher, although for Patmore the philosopher and the poet acquire their insight into truth by essentially the same process. Both are men 'after God's own heart'. He is not thinking of the activity of thought when he speaks of 'intuition' or 'real apprehension', but of the surrender of the soul to love in its simplicity, for he believes that through the love of God and of woman, man comes to understand basic truths of being. Despite his endeavour to give a colouring of philosophical logic to his view of 'apprehension' in such essays as 'Attention' and 'Real Apprehension', he is, in fact, only describing, out of his own experience, the poet's 'wise passiveness' before natural phenomena. The poet in contemplation is submitting himself to the facts of human life and Nature, seeing them anew. In 'The Wedding Sermon' he writes:

[1] *Further Letters of Gerard Manley Hopkins*, pp. 239–242.
[2] 'A People of a Stammering Tongue', *Religio Poetae*, p. 49.

And fathom well the depths of life
In loves of Husband and of Wife,
Child, Mother, Father; simple keys
To what cold faith calls mysteries.

For him, such facts of human existence are 'simple keys', because, while faith may leave truths mysteries, love unlocks and reveals all. When Patmore spoke of seeing, he implied faith, and the confirmation of dogma through love and faith. 'For fidelity does not *discover* dogma,' he wrote, 'but only enables the faithful, in proportion to their faith, to confirm it with absolute personal assurance.'[1] He was fond of quoting in his essays the Authorized Version text of the Epistle to the Hebrews, xi, 1 : 'Now faith is the substance of things hoped for, the evidence of things unseen.' The word 'evidence' in this text clearly meant much to him.

When Patmore discussed the methods and philosophies of other writers, he often took the occasion to defend his own position by implication. Nowhere in his writings does he give a clearer picture of his own development and of his own attitude towards intuitions than in what he says about Maine de Biran, whom he describes as

'a man whose whole life was occupied in making and recording observations of his actual psychological experience, with a characteristic horror of any thing which was not either spiritual fact, or an immediate and obvious deduction from it; the consequence, of course, being that the more he observed and the more he aspired towards the higher life to which his observations led him, the farther did he become removed from that philosophical sphere which delights in logical schemes and "complete acts", and the more did he find himself involved in mental states and perceptions of truths which logicians will always be at a loss to make much of so long as we see "as in a glass darkly".'[2]

Not all men, however, are able personally to confirm dogmas. Real contemplatives and seers, be they poets or mystics, may thus apprehend them, but most men must hold them by faith.

'The mass of mankind must receive and hold these things as they daily receive and hold a thousand other things . . . by faith; their real apprehension in such matters extending for the most part only to the discernment of the reasonableness of so receiving and holding them.'[3]

In this way Patmore reconciled his strong belief in the value of individual insight with belief in the authority of a teaching Church.

[1] 'Christianity An Experimental Science', *Religio Poetae*, p. 42. See also, 'A People of a Stammering Tongue', *Religio Poetae*, p. 47.
[2] 'De Biran's Pensées', *The National Review*, Vol. XI, No. XXI, July 1860, pp. 146–147.
[3] 'Real Apprehension', *Religio Poetae*, p. 82.

He regarded it as natural that only very few should be able to receive self-evident truth. This fact does not invalidate individual apprehensions, but points to the need for some authority to transmit them to mankind at large.

However, even the sensitive soul and the unusually virtuous man cannot realize these 'self-evident' truths without contemplation. Lacking this, such men may remain as blind as the mass of their fellow-men. Before God can be apprehended in His creation, the senses must be disciplined, and the mind directed towards Him. In its highest form this contemplation is the experience of the great mystics; it is the 'simple and perceived contact of the substance of the Soul with that of the Divine',[1] and its effect is

> 'like the photographic plate which finds stars that no telescope can discover, by simply setting its passively expectant gaze in certain indicated directions so long and steadily that telescopically invisible bodies become apparent by accumulation of impression.'[2]

The faculty for seeing 'realities' is one which the child possesses by nature and instinct, and which, of men, the poet, the saint and the mystic alone frequently recapture. This service is more pleasing to God and more fruitful for the soul than active service.

Pure love, expressed in this undistracted surrender to God, not only yields insights more fundamental than those which can be obtained by scientific investigation or by being busy Martha-like, but is also, in the long run, more beneficial to humanity than arduous labour. In support of this, Patmore quotes St. John of the Cross: 'An instant of pure love is more precious to God and the soul, and more profitable to the Church, than all other good works together, though it may seem as if nothing were done.'[3] This is love on the highest plane, but even in its simpler forms, as with youthful first love, the spiritual sight is sharpened, and insights are given in the fullness of loving another which cannot be arrived at by other means. Love sees in the commonest things manifestations of wonder and delight which are in fact the basic truths of all being:

> Not in the crises of events,
>   Of compass'd hopes, or fears fulfill'd,
>   Or acts of gravest consequence,
>   Are life's delight and depth reveal'd.

---

[1] *Rod, Root and Flower*, 'Magna Moralia', XV, p. 160.
[2] 'Real Apprehension', *Religio Poetae*, p. 81.
[3] *Rod, Root and Flower*, 'Aurea Dicta', XXI, p. 31.

The day of days was not the day;
  That went before, or was postponed;
The night Death took our lamp away
  Was not the night on which we groan'd.
I drew my bride, beneath the moon,
  Across my threshold; happy hour!
But, ah, the walk that afternoon
  We saw the water-flags in flower!

(A.H., I, viii)

The man in love, the poet, the child, the saint—these are all 'seers'.

His sensitivity to childhood insights is expressed as early as 1844, in one of the sonnets in *Poems*, a sonnet which also indicates his faith in a contemplative's ability to arrive at truth beyond logic and argument; and begins:

> My childhood was a vision heavenly wrought.

In 1857, he wrote, in words which as in his Prelude, 'The Revelation', link childhood and first-love as sources of intimations of eternity:

> 'Heaven, or at least as much as our hearts can contain of it, is revealed to us in the visions of childhood and of early love. But the world assures us that our visions are naught, and accordingly we learn in time to desecrate and forget them; and many of us find in after years, with bitter remorse, that we have shut out heaven from our hearts by ways of life which are no more than practical assertions (in violation at first of the sweet instincts of youth) that these visions were indeed but shadows, or rather far less; for shadows are at least the figures of realities, and indications of their whereabouts. By accepting those young intuitions with grateful minds, as the first and best gifts of the Giver of all good things ... we might have prolonged the joy of childhood into man's estate ... and the light and immortality which have been externally revealed, would have found each of us happier than, in this life at least, they have much chance of making us. How much of the miserable addition which we all make to our original taint, might be prevented by a right reverence, taught by the Great Teacher of men Himself, for childhood, it is hard to conceive.'[1]

Likewise, in his otherwise pedestrian biography of 'Barry Cornwall', he takes the opportunity offered by Cornwall's description of a childhood infatuation and its effects in bringing him to maturity to emphasize the fundamental importance of such infantine passions in the history of poets. It may well be, he says, that the imaginative

[1] 'Emanuel Swedenborg', *Fraser's Magazine*, February 1857, p. 175.

glory with which poets celebrate the idea of love results from their having experienced the fullness of passion in the innocence of childhood and represents the retention in manhood of the happy memory of that experience.[1]

In all Patmore wrote about the intuitions of childhood over a period of more than half a century, he never deviated from his early conviction that they are among the most precious insights that human beings can attain. In *The Rod, the Root and the Flower*, he says again merely what he had said in his first volume of poems: 'None attains the promised land "except those little ones who ye said should be a prey", i.e. the perceptions attained in and preserved from childhood and youth, which the Tempter is always endeavouring to destroy.'[2] It is in keeping with such ideas that he should also have considered that genius possesses, in addition to the proper balance of masculine and feminine elements, essentially the same innocence as that of childhood. As the perceptions of children and of lovers are linked, so, too, are those of childhood and those of genius. Indeed, in his capacity for innocent acceptance and uncomplicated seeing, the child *is* a genius. The genius's power of seeing things in their living relationship he considers a virtue rather than a talent, whose condition is an interior simplicity and absolute faith which is the result of the survival of a childlike mental innocence. Unfortunately, after their infancy, men see little of the reality and beauty of things because they see only what they think they ought to see, whereas reality and beauty are always unforceable and largely unaccountable.[3]

Patmore, however, does not believe that men must *be* children, or that it is possible to retain in adulthood all the apprehensions of the child without a corresponding loss. His essay 'Simplicity' contrasts the three simplicities, that of the child, that of genius and that of wisdom, finding that while the paradisaical vision of the first is conditioned by the innocence of ignorance, genius consists in the possession of the faculty of unitive apprehension in maturer years, but now with consciousness or the power of reflection; and the simplicity of age has as its great condition innocence which has been retained through, or recovered during, the struggles of manhood.[4] Patmore's treatment of the vision of childhood is based upon a full appreciation of the gains of manhood, as well as of the inade-

---

[1] *Bryan Waller Procter (Barry Cornwall), An Autobiographical Fragment and Biographical Notes* (Boston: Roberts Brothers, 1877), pp. 36–37.

[2] *Rod, Root and Flower*, 'Aurea Dicta', XXXVI, p. 32.

[3] See 'Out-of-Doors Poetry', *St. James's Gazette*, July 9, 1887; *Courage in Politics*, pp. 35–36.   [4] 'Simplicity', *Religio Poetae*, pp. 64–67.

quacy of the apprehensions of a child when faced with the moral problems of life. Because, with poetic logic, he links childhood, knowledge, love, genius and God, with a man's awareness of the demands and problems of life, and because he draws upon a singularly rich childhood of his own, he is the only Victorian poet who treats children and their world without sentimentality.

Among the intuitions which he attributed initially to his childhood were the concepts of law, and of limitations. The literary sources of, and parallels to, these ideas have been discussed, and it remains to show how pervasive they were, and what characteristic forms they assumed in Patmore's mind. His conscious and deliberate assertion of the excellence of law and sanctions in life and in the universe is both more articulate and more moving than Tennyson's compulsive praise of law. Patmore passionately believed that authority and 'form' begin in law, and that the joy and beauty of art, as well as of love, proceed from underlying laws which govern the nature of both. The limitations in each case are the causes as well as the conditions of their particular excellences. Without law, love is dead, empty, carnal and frustrating. Restraint and balance are bulwarks against satiation and excess; love is controlled by a harmony which he describes on more than one occasion by the analogy of planetary motion.

Patmore's belief in law makes him the poet of domestic love, in contrast to the kind of Romantic love inherited from the Troubadours, and perhaps beyond them from the Catharists, that love which chafes against the restraints of marriage. Patmore saw monogamy, domesticity, husbandly and wifely affection not as accidents, but as the essence, of love; so he was able to praise the controls which deepen it. The bonds of love do not constitute a compromise imposed by the laws of society on man's passion, so that order might follow and disorder be prevented, but they are eternal and immutable laws of nature; even God Himself, in the Christian paradox, is limited in His infinity to the 'form' of the Trinity, and further limited, and at the same time fulfilled, in the humanity of Jesus Christ.

Thus Patmore saw in married love the fulfilment of passion, and not its negation. For him, passion differs from love in that it scorns bonds; it is a restless, boundless desire, which, disdaining law, is without limit or form, while love has a form, to which it owes its obedience and its distinction. He summed up his conception of law, both as it applies to marriage and to the universe, again using his favourite image of planetary order, in the Prelude 'Joy and Use':

> Can ought compared with wedlock be
>   For use? But He who made the heart
> To use proportions joy. What He
>   Has join'd let no man put apart.
> Sweet Order has its draught of bliss
>   Graced with the pearl of God's consent,
> Ten times delightful in that 'tis
>   Considerate and innocent.
> In vain Disorder grasps the cup;
>   The pleasure's not enjoy'd but spilt,
> And if he stoops to lick it up,
>   It only tastes of earth and guilt.
> His sorry raptures rest destroys;
>   To live, like comets, they must roam;
> On settled poles turn solid joys,
>   And sunlike pleasures shine at home.
>   (*A.H.*, II, vii)

The same idea is also found in a prose passage:

> 'In vulgar minds the idea of passion is inseparable from that of dis-
> order; . . . and the great decorum of a passion, which keeps, and is
> immensely increased in force by, the discipline of God's order, looks
> to them like weakness and coldness. Hence the passions which are the
> measure of man's capacity for virtues, are regarded by the pious vulgar
> as being of the nature of vice; and, indeed, in them they are so; for
> virtues are nothing but ordered passions, and vices nothing but
> passions in disorder.'[1]

Passion, therefore, is not a diabolical force; it is God's gift. But it
must be controlled by God's law, in which case it will return to God
as a virtue; if uncontrolled it shows before Him as a sin:

> In Godhead rise, thither flow back
> All loves, which, as they keep or lack,
> In their return, the course assign'd
> Are virtue or sin. . . .
>   (*V.L.*, 321)

The ode 'Legem Tuam Dilexi' is Patmore's most complete
poetic statement of his principle of law. Here he says that everywhere in nature there are compulsive forces, which are held in
check only by law. The fallen angels craved infinity, and so were
damned:

> Nor bides alone in hell
> The bond-disdaining spirit boiling to rebel.

[1] *Rod, Root and Flower*, 'Magna Moralia', II, p. 146.

> But for compulsion of strong grace,
> The pebble in the road
> Would straight explode,
> And fill the ghastly boundlessness of space.

Apart from the anticipation of the release of atomic power, with a suggestion of the theological implications of the use of such power, this passage has special interest in that Patmore gives the source of the image in his essay 'Imagination':

> 'Another child, a year or two older, lay stretched on a gravel path, staring intently on the pebbles. "They are alive," he cried, in the writer's hearing, "they are always wanting to burst, but something draws them in." '[1]

It is tempting to see that child as Patmore himself, as indeed it might well have been.

Since law and control are sources of order and of the greatest joy, man, says Patmore, seeks true freedom in self-imposed limits. Hence the justification of monastic orders, whose function he describes in the same ode, linking it with asceticism in general and with restraint in desires and passions. By one of those leaps of vision which distinguish him as a poet, he applies the same 'philosophy of limits' to pain. In 'Legem Tuam Dilexi', he suggests that the punishment by pain of the fallen angels is a limit which actually imposes relief against their desire for divinity and infinity:

> And God, for their confusion, laugh'd consent;
> Yet did so far relent,
> That they might seek relief, and not in vain,
> In dashing of themselves against the shores of pain.

The opening lines of the ode 'Victory in Defeat' are in the same vein. However, his attitude towards pain is very different indeed from the algolagnic reactions of Swinburne. He was enough of a psychologist to know the piquancy of pain in love, the edge that may be given to the purest love by the submission to physical and spiritual pain on behalf of the beloved; and this psychological reality is expressed by Psyche when she calls for some 'greatly pangful penance'. Yet there is no sado-masochism here, for Patmore sees pain not as an element adding extra keenness to unrestrained pleasure; it is a necessary restraint on delight; the real lover accepts it voluntarily both as an offering of love and as a mark of submission to the reality of limitation. Pain is a good, like love, because it is one of the limitations placed on man's being, a bulwark

[1] 'Imagination', *Religio Poetae*, p. 105.

against the horrors of infinity, and because, too, it is a law, which, in the mystery of man's relationship with God, blends into the ecstatic joy of his love.

So Patmore can defend asceticism on the grounds that the refusal of disordered liberty to the senses and feelings sharpens and elevates them. A man who accepts control in love may obtain from the slightest tokens of favour offered him by his beloved an intensity of happiness which the sensualist, who continually indulges himself, can never know, even in his most abandoned moments.[1] And he applies the same principle of law and control to literature, when he says:

> 'The laws of metre are like the laws of life in this, that the affections and passions evoke music by a tender strain upon them which never breaks them. The bad poet, like the bad man, trifles with such laws for the sake of mere excitement and escape from monotony, stretching these formal limits without the excuse of true emotion, and breaking them rather than suffer the *ennui* of his own dullness.'[2]

Much of his interest in metrics, which reached its fullest expression in his *Essay on English Metrical Law*, and part, at least, of his fondness for the restrictions of the iambic metre, can be traced to this devotion to the rule of law.

Like happiness, beauty also is life expressed in law. Thus in architecture, Patmore sees the perfection of architectural form in adherence to what he considered to be permanently true laws of construction and the use of materials, and hence he finds in Gothic the finest of architectural styles:

> 'As the inexhaustible torrent of upward life is checked peacefully, but with no denial of infinite *potential* aspiration, in the square-headed tower, so the same reconciliation of life with law without the least detriment to either—that reconciliation which is the consummation of Christianity—is expressed even more completely in the more essentially decorative details of pointed architecture.'[3]

Patmore's mind abominated vague concepts of infinity and the whole idea of boundlessness. Hence 'Legem Tuam Dilexi' opens with the words:

> The 'Infinite'. Word horrible! at feud
> With life, and the braced mood
> Of power and joy and love.

---

[1] 'Unnatural Literature', *St. James's Gazette*, Feb. 26, 1887; *Courage in Politics*, pp. 127–128.
[2] 'Goldsmith', *St. James's Gazette*, Jan. 16, 1888; *Courage in Politics*, p. 64.
[3] 'Architectural Styles', *Principle in Art*, p. 256.

And the splendid beginning of 'Wind and Wave' similarly speaks of the need of bounds to give direction to the Divine force, both in created things and in the love of woman:

> The wedded light and heat
> Winnowing the witless space,
> Without a let,
> What are they till they beat
> Against the sleepy sod, and there beget
> Perchance the violet!
> Is the One found,
> Amongst a wilderness of as happy grace,
> To make Heaven's bound;
> So that in Her
> All which it hath of sensitively good
> Is sought and understood
> After the narrow mode the mighty Heavens prefer?

One of his statements, that the poet knows 'as Plato knew, that God Himself is most falsely described as infinite', is at first sight more than a little disconcerting. Yet he goes on to say:

'God is the synthesis, as Proclus declares in his treatise on the Fables of Homer, of "Infinite" and "Boundary", and is excellently intelligible, though for ever unutterable, by those who love Him.'[1]

Clearly he wishes to suggest, not that God is limited to and by His creation, but that man's vision of the great Reality of God is limited by his own inability to grasp abstractions, and that God, by offering Himself to man in the Incarnation and in the other visible analogies of His creation, becomes 'credible' to mankind.[2]

This idea is closely related to the important place the body holds in his vision and, through the body, the Incarnation. In this way his mystical attitude contrasts most sharply with Donne's Platonic notion that love is of the soul, and independent of the body. Donne's experience of love in this sense is profound and inspiring, as such poems as 'The Undertaking' and 'The Ecstasy' show; but few love poems could be more different than these from Patmore's 'De Natura Deorum' and 'To the Body', in which the body is not only accepted, but joyed in. In the Incarnation Patmore found the answer to the problem which concerned him so deeply (and which he had observed Maine de Biran grappling with),[3] that of the relationship

---

[1] 'Religio Poetae', *Religio Poetae*, p. 5.
[2] See *Rod, Root and Flower*, 'Aurea Dicta', CXVI, p. 47.
[3] 'The extraordinary dependence of the moral nature of Maine de Biran upon corporeal conditions made the nature of the connection between soul and body an ever-present problem to him.' ('De Biran's Pensées', *The National Review*, July 1860, p. 149.)

between the soul and the body. The body protects man against the horrors of infinity and abstraction in which nothing is intelligible or graspable. Both soul and body together make up that 'unit' which he saw at the heart of being. The body itself contains, thought Patmore, a duality, which exemplifies this unity between soul and body:

> 'The body ... seems to be expressly formed for that cohabitation and communion of two Persons (whose union is a third) which Scripture and the Church declare that it is made for. . . . There are two brains, in which Science has traced the separate indwelling of the legislative and executive functions, two systems of nerves, active and sentient, two sides of the body, obscurely but decidedly distinguished in their activities, two souls with two consciences, the rational and emotional, a heart with a double and contrasted action, and endless other dualities and reciprocities ... and withal a unity arising from co-operation which makes the body itself as clear an echo of the Trinity as the soul is.'[1]

Thus the truth of life is to be found in the body—the 'form'—and he is never more in earnest than when he speaks of the body, not only as the temple of God, 'little sequester'd pleasure-house for God and for His Spouse', but as the place wherein man may and can seek God. Love leads us to explore the body in reverence and with restraint; and it is through such love developed in the body that each sex comes fully to discover its own being. The body is:

> Form'd for a dignity prophets but darkly name,
> Lest shameless men cry 'Shame!'

So, in the dogma of the resurrection of the body, that gloriously epitomized by the Assumption of her

> Who left the lilies in her body's lieu,

Patmore sees the final dignity of the flesh of mortal men.

Francis Thompson, in saying that it is a consequence of Patmore's principles 'that in the study of the analogies of the body, man has a key to the knowledge of God, so far as such knowledge applies to his own needs',[2] did not go as far as Patmore does. Patmore meant something more than that the analogies of the body would help man to understand God. By respecting the body, by loving it as the second element of man, a partner with the soul, by entering, in the light of such knowledge, into the fullness of human love, man comes to realize the possibility of contact between the finite and the Infinite. Patmore accepts the advice of St. Paul in its com-

[1] *Rod, Root and Flower*, 'Homo', II, p. 104.
[2] 'Patmore's Philosophy', *Literary Criticism by Francis Thompson*, ed. T. L. Connolly, p. 213.

pleteness: 'Glorify and bear God in your body' (I Cor. vi, 20).
Man's body derives its final sanction of holiness from the Incarnation, in which God Himself taking form in a human body, made
flesh sacred beyond man's powers of understanding. The spirit
craves for union with and eternal captivity to what is not spirit, and
the higher the spirit the greater the craving. The infinite condescension of God and His vast love for the soul is shown in His
desire for union with Body, where He finds 'His final perfection
and felicity'.[1]

This is dangerous ground on which to tread, unless armed with
the caution of a theologian; the fusion of the spiritual and the
erotic, though expressed only by closely-guarded analogies, is
almost certain to be misunderstood by some. Hopkins, de Vere,
Greenwood and others were disturbed by Patmore's teaching on
the body. Yet Patmore seems to have realized himself the immense
difficulty of imparting his intuitions about the 'corollaries' of the
Incarnation without seeming to be advocating a kind of religious
eroticism, or a species of spiritual materialism. The burning of
Sponsa Dei, his attempt to set out the main implications of the
nuptial analogy as he saw them, may well have been prompted by
his realization of the inadequacy of his metaphors to express the
spiritual truths. So he was content to leave the 'doctrine' in the
hints and illuminations of the essays, the odes, and the aphorisms,
some of which are startling indeed, if not interpreted in the light of
other sayings of the same kind. 'So give me to possess this mystery
that I shall not desire to understand it',[2] seems to have been one of
the most heart-felt, as well as one of the most significant, of his
later aspirations.

What he says about the Incarnation itself is clear. It is the act
whereby God 'has taken hold' of man:

'the Highest has found His ultimate and crowning felicity in a marriage
of the flesh as well as the Spirit; and in this infinite contrast and intimacy of height with depth and spirit with flesh He, who is very Love,
finds, just as ordinary human love does, its final rest and the full
fruition of its own life; and the joy of angels is in contemplating, and
sharing by perfect sympathy with humanity, the glory which humanity
alone actually possesses.'[3]

Because the Incarnation saves us from 'an abstract Christ', man
may now 'see the disc of Divinity quite clearly through the smoked

[1] *Rod, Root and Flower*, 'Knowledge and Science', I, p. 61.
[2] *Ibid.*, 'Aurea Dicta', XXVIII, p. 30.
[3] *Ibid.*, 'Knowledge and Science', VIII, p. 68.

glass of humanity, but not otherwise'.[1] From the dogma, Patmore drew several corollaries. One of these concerns sacrifice and suffering in relation to sanctification. In his later years, he formulated conceptions different from those implied by his statement that the 'human form divine' is no mere figure of speech. The Crucifixion is, says Patmore, 'the consummation of the descent of Divinity into the flesh and its identification therewith; and the sigh which all creation heaved in that moment has its echo in that of mortal love in the like descent.'[2] Thus, to share in the Resurrection and the Incarnation, man must also share in the Crucifixion. The body must surrender itself wholly to God before the Incarnation can be renewed in it. For the Incarnation is 'not . . . an historical event which occurred two thousand years ago, but . . . an event which is renewed in the body of every one who is in the way to the fulfilment of his original destiny.'[3]

Yet the benefits of this 'renewal' of the Incarnation cannot be obtained without the surrender to God of what man holds dear:

> In Will and Mind
> 'Tis the easy path so hard to find;
> In Heart, a pain not to be told,
> Were words mere honey, milk, and gold;
> I' the Body 'tis the bag of the bee;
> In all, the present, thousandfold amends
> Made to the sad, astonish'd life
> Of him that leaves house, child, and wife,
> And on God's 'hest, almost despairing, wends,
> As little guessing as the herd,
> What a strange Phoenix of a bird,
> Builds in this tree,
> But only intending all that He intends.
>
> ('The Open Secret')

The body must learn obedience before it can share in its high destiny and before the soul can discern good and evil. Once the body has been rejected as containing nothing good in itself, then the mind grasps good, which thenceforth takes the place of truth, for truth is, in effect, only a schoolmaster to lead men to the natural possession of God. From this point the body becomes the helpmate and glory of the spirit.[4] Hence the ecstasy of the mystic's awareness of the eternal working of the Incarnation is tempered by the know-

---

[1] *Rod, Root and Flower*, 'Aurea Dicta', CL, p. 54.
[2] *Ibid.*, 'Magna Moralia', XLVIII, p. 196.
[3] *Ibid.*, 'Homo', XIX, p. 124.
[4] Cf. *Rod, Root and Flower*, 'Homo', XVII, p. 122.

ledge that God's will must be submitted to in everything. Man does not have to deny his own nature to share in the joy of God's love, for 'Nature fulfilled by grace is not less natural, but is supernaturally natural'.[1] However, he must attain spiritual control and obedience, for the law of God is not an arbitrary law imposed by a tyrannical Jehovah from without, but a reflection in the soul of man of God's very nature. Man seeks bonds as God Himself did in becoming man, and in doing so fulfils himself as his Creator did. Any criticism which finds undisciplined eroticism in Patmore's work can do so only by completely ignoring the clearly set out concepts of asceticism, discipline and control, of which his poetry and prose are full.

Because Patmore saw the body sacramentally, he was able to see the rest of Nature in the same way. Nature is not truly natural without the supernatural; in external Nature, man can detect, if he has the pure and innocent eye, those likenesses by which spiritual realities may be rendered credible to people of inferior perception. Nature offers a series of symbols, parables, and rites; these are correspondence-identities which bear eternal witness to the central truths of Christian doctrine. In his own words:

> 'God clothes Himself actually and literally with His whole creation. Herbs take up and assimilate minerals, beasts assimilate herbs, and God, in the Incarnation and its proper Sacrament, assimilates us, who, as St. Augustine says, "are God's beasts".'[2]

The blind of spirit are those who refuse to acknowledge that 'Heaven Earth, Sea, and Hell witness with a thousand voices the secret which is the sole felicity of man; and almost all men refuse to hear.'[3] This 'Open Secret', the sacramental aspect of Nature, which gives the nuptial analogy, with other analogies, to the loving soul, was, he felt, the only knowledge worth having; and yet this knowledge was denied, deliberately overlooked, or simply not seen, by professional philosophers and scientists. Thus he came to deride the methods and many of the findings of Victorian science.

Traces of his youthful scientific interests remain in various analogies and images scattered throughout his poems. However, in three of the odes, 'The Two Deserts', 'Sing Us One of the Songs of Sion' and 'The Cry at Midnight', as well as in places in his prose, he is bitter about the blindness of scientists. 'Modern science', he writes, 'goes towards the truth, as, when we walk

---

[1] *Ibid.*, 'Aurea Dicta', XVII, p. 28.
[2] *Ibid.*, 'Knowledge and Science', II, p. 62.
[3] *Ibid.*, 'Aurea Dicta', VIII, p. 26.

towards the sinking sun, the world while we walk rolls the other way.'[1] He did not deny that scientific enquiry could and did produce useful information; it was the exploitation of that information to which he objected. So he mainly attacked spurious science, science which passed across its borders to explain away Christianity, and to undermine traditional ethics. Unlike other writers of his time, such as Tennyson and Arnold, who were perturbed by or infected by the materialism of Victorian science, Patmore maintained that genuine science is not incompatible with religion. One of the most balanced statements of the relationship between science and religion to be written by any Victorian is found in *The Rod, The Root and the Flower*. The unperturbed manner in which Patmore assimilates such things as Evolution and Biblical 'Higher Criticism' into the general Christian pattern, and in which he shows the dogmatism of Victorian science as more intransigent than religious dogmatism contrasts with the spiritual turmoil of other Christian writers confronted with the same scientific claims. He writes:

'The modern Catholic looks on, with serenity, at the advances of physical science, ready to admit and glad to make use of all its permanent discoveries, and to confess that they may greatly modify or possibly invalidate, not Revelation, but some practically unimportant points in the customary reading of the letter of Revelation. He is, however, naturally somewhat contemptuous of, and indignant at, the shameless effrontery of physicists in setting forth hypotheses as established truths, and the equally shameless abandonment of them, without apology, when they have fallen, as most of the most famous and, for the time, infallible theories have done, before a fuller knowledge. . . . Nor can it be said that the increase of knowledge of Nature has been so great as much to modify the externals of faith. The history of creation, regarded by some in very early ages as probably 'mythical', has, indeed, been proved to be certainly so, but the myth includes teaching of much more significance to us than the supposed history, and every one should be glad to discover that the aim of the writers of Scripture was not to satisfy an idle curiosity about facts which do not concern us. The doctrine of evolution promises to be of very easy assimilation by the Church; and recent considerations on the nature of "matter" and "substance" have made the doctrine of the "Real Presence" much more naturally credible than it could have seemed at the time of the Council of Trent.'[2]

At the same time, the contemporary passion for scientific truth appeared to him to be defective in that, while denying truth to

[1] Champneys, *Memoirs*, Vol. II, p. 66.
[2] *Rod, Root and Flower*, 'Knowledge and Science', XXX, pp. 91–92.

Revelation and to the intuitions of the mystics, it required itself something of the same initial intuition before any great discoveries could be made. Without God, he believed, the real direction of science and the import of its discoveries cannot be realized by men. He points out that while science is popularly believed to consist only of the observation of facts and the application of discursive reason to them, there has been, in great scientists like Kepler, Newton and Faraday, something more—vision and inspiration. In fact scarcely any scientist worthy of the name does not bring to his data an intuitive quality which transcends the strictly logical procedure.[1]

Science, therefore, must be judged on a spiritual plane. Its main use was not, as most of the Victorians thought, to explain or to 'explain away', but to provide man and especially the poet with analogies which would enable him better to comprehend *real* truths. Everything that is, natural phenomena, man and art, has value only in so far as it is close to God and to His purpose. Hence, Patmore can write:

> 'Parables and symbols are the only possible means of expressing realities which are clear to perception though dark to the understanding. . . . Natural sciences are definite, because they deal with laws which are not realities, but conditions of realities. The greatest and perhaps the only real use of natural science is to supply similes and parables for poets and theologians.'[2]

He does not mean merely that the greatest value of science lies in its confirmation of spiritual truths. The fundamental reality is the spiritual one. Since 'God clothes Himself actually and literally with His whole creation', science, which is the description of phenomena, describes, without realizing it, correspondences of God, and presents a type of incomplete knowledge which the spiritual sight must receive mainly, if not wholly, as parables. In a materialistic age which offered almost nothing to such a mind as Patmore's, he showed his independence of its science either by attacking its misuse or by treating it as if it were of small consequence by comparison with the knowledge acquired by spiritual insight. After the great fact of the Incarnation all other knowledge appeared to him to be of little importance save in so far as it confirmed that fact.

The most important of the spiritual analogies which he regarded as confirmed by science and the experience of the saints was that of sexual duality in the universe. Everywhere in nature this pattern is to be found.

[1] 'Seers, Thinkers and Talkers', *Religio Poetae*, p. 89.
[2] 'Love and Poetry', *Religio Poetae*, p. 141.

'And nature goes on,' he writes, 'giving echoes of the same living triplicity in animal, plant and mineral, every stone and material atom owing its being to the synthesis or "embrace" of the two opposed forces of expansion and contraction. Nothing whatever exists in a single entity but in virtue of its being thesis, antithesis, and synthesis, and in humanity and natural life this takes the form of sex, the masculine, the feminine, and the neuter, or third, forgotten sex spoken of by Plato, which is not the absence of the life of sex, but its fulfilment and power, as the electric fire is the fulfilment and power of positive and negative in their "embrace".'[1]

So human perfection cannot be discovered in its fullness in any one sex, but only in a union of both. The angels in heaven offered him a useful 'analogy' of sexual duality. Swedenborg writes: 'For in heaven two married partners are not called two, but one angel; this is meant by the Lord's words, "that they are no longer two, but one flesh".'[2] The title of *The Angel in the House*, incidentally, gains extra significance if read in the light of this statement of Swedenborg's which must certainly have been in Patmore's mind when he selected the title. He uses more than once the bisexuality of the angels, as depicted in traditional theology, to support his theory of man's relationship with God in terms of sex.[3]

This notion of fundamental duality tends to become 'the universal symbol' in his work, although it is not always expressed in sexual terms. For instance, he finds the same principle in magnetic attraction and repulsion:

'God is the great, *positive* Magnet of the Universe, and whatever, in the Universe, aspires to approach Him must assume the *negative*, the feminine, or passive and receptive aspect.'[4]

The same double aspect he traces in the twofold constitution of man, in whom he discovers two consciences—the rational or male conscience, that commands man to act according to laws he believes to be right, and the sensitive or female conscience that persuades man to good, whose existence appears to him to approach the reality of a double personality in one being.[5] Poetry, too, in the fullest sense, and in fact, all genius, is double-sexed in that in really great minds the two sexes are reconciled into something like the 'homo'. In man, who is the image of God, genius is the third creative sex which contains and is the two others.

1 'The Bow Set in the Clouds', *Religio Poetae*, p. 54.
2 *Conjugial Love*, No. 50.
3 E.g. 'Dieu et Ma Dame', *Religio Poetae*, p. 160.
4 *Rod, Root and Flower*, 'Homo', XV, p. 120.
5 'Conscience', *Religio Poetae*, pp. 73–74.

Frederick Page once claimed that this conception of Patmore's 'is not to be called sexual except by a metaphor; a metaphor derived from any other instance of the same principle would be as valid.'[1] But to deny that Patmore did actually think of the antithesis, thesis and synthesis in terms of sex is to go against the evidence of nine out of ten of the contexts in which he discusses the basic forces in life and nature. It is quite true that while believing that in sex was the most important manifestation of the duality, he also thought in terms of a wider principle, almost Hegelian in its implications. Yet the emphasis he placed on sexual duality is one of his most distinctive features as a writer, and if he indeed felt that this was but one manifestation of opposition and reconciliation, he often writes as if it were the only one.

In any case, Patmore suggests that man's rational and emotional nature reveal a duality which reflects the two sexual elements. In both man and woman 'homo' is potentially present, since each sex contains in itself the natures of both sexes. From the spiritual point of view, sex is only an expression of the relationship between these elements. The love of a man and a woman is the most striking, as well as the most common, instance of the manifestation of the opposition and of its reconciliation which the created world has to offer. Through love, the 'homo' is completed, and the original spiritual unity of the sexes found again in the being 'two in one flesh'.

This idea is summed up in a passage in *The Rod, the Root and the Flower*:

> '"Woman", says Aquinas, "was created apart, in order that the distinction of sexes" (in the *homo*) "might be the better marked, and in order that the man and the woman herself" (who is also a potential *homo*, or entire humanity) "might be induced to attend above all to that which is their worthiest contemplation", i.e. the reflection in themselves of the nature of God, whereby, as the Church says, "He has fruition in Himself". Hence, in heaven and sometimes even on earth, the separation ceases; man and woman having each become the fully conscious *homo*, or duality of sex in one being, and a real image of Him who said, "Let us make Man in *our* image." The external man and woman are each the projected *simulacrum* of the latent half of the other, and they do but love themselves in thus loving their opposed likenesses.'[2]

In the logic of Patmorean analogy this concept leads up to the nature

[1] 'Coventry Patmore—Points of View', *The Catholic World*, Vol. CXIII, No. 675, June 1921, p. 386.
[2] *Rod, Root and Flower*, 'Homo', I, p. 103.

of the Trinity Itself which he finds is most easily approached under the analogue of 'homo':

> 'The mystery of triple Personality in one Being, the acknowledgement of which is the prime condition of a real apprehension of God, may be best approached by the human mind under the analogue of difference of sex in one entity.... By the Church the Second Person is represented as the "glory" of the "Father" who is Christ's "Head" as Man is the glory of his Head, Christ, and Woman the glory of Man, who is her head. The individual Man, the *Homo*, is the image of God, in so far as he is a substantial reflection of the Love, the Truth, and the Life, which last is the "embrace" of Truth and Love, as the Holy Spirit is said by the Church to be the "embrace" of the First Person and the Second.'[1]

In heaven the marriage relationship cannot persist because here the soul is united to God, of whose love all earthly loves have been only the shadow. After death the soul is in the same relation to God as on earth woman is to man. Only if the love of God is seen as spousal love, in terms of the 'homo', can such sayings as 'The proper study of mankind is woman'[2] and 'If the Son is the Bride of the Father and the Husband of the Church, it follows that the male soul may be the Bride of Christ and the Husband of the female'[3] be seen as more than freakish paradoxes. To God, the great positive, masculine force, the soul is the receptive, feminine force. And the meeting of God and the loving soul in the spousal relationship is the 'mystic rapture' which Patmore hymns in his preludes to *The Angel in the House* and in *The Unknown Eros*.

Although the principle of 'homo' is not original with Patmore, his application of it certainly is, especially when he reverses the analogy and applies the traditional idea of the soul as 'the Bride of Christ', together with the implications of 'homo', to the ordinary relations of married people. It is in this 'converting of the proposition', and his expressing of it in poetry, as much as in his 'corollaries' that his claim to originality lies. But before this attitude towards marriage is analysed, some consideration must be given to the place he allotted to women in his scheme.

'As it is between Man and Woman, so it is between Christ and Man, who is *His* "Glory", and between God and Christ, who is God's "Glory".'[4] Woman is man's 'glory', as man is God's 'glory', and as Jesus Christ is the 'glory' of the Father. Woman, too, is the 'body', from the analogy which links man and woman as an entity with body and soul as an entity.

---

[1] 'The Bow Set in the Cloud', *Religio Poetae*, pp. 53–54.
[2] Champneys, *Memoirs*, Vol. II, p. 77.   [3] *Ibid.*, Vol. II, p. 76.
[4] *Rod, Root and Flower*, 'Homo', X, p. 113.

'According to Christian theology', says Patmore, 'it was the Second Person, the "glory" of God the Father, who took on actual womanhood, or "body" in the body of the Blessed Virgin, and who imparts the same to all who partake of the same body in the Holy Sacrament; and accordingly it is said by St. Augustine, that "Christ is the Bride as well as the Bridegroom, for He is the Body".'[1]

Patmore's idea that sex is the essential relation made him oppose any doctrine which seemed to disturb it. Since few aspects of his thought have aroused more protest than his seeming desire to 'keep woman in her place', as the phrase might have been understood by a Mr. Pontifex or a Mr. Moulton-Barrett, the matter is worth discussing in some detail.

Perhaps the most direct attack on Patmore's attitude towards women has come from Miss Virginia Crawford, who has much to say in praise of his genius and his poetry, but who also writes as follows:

'I would say that he never gave a thought to the feminine soul save in its relation to man. A wife was indeed to be the Angel in the House, but only on condition of remaining always within it, and of spending her life seated at the feet of her lord.'[2]

Others (for instance, Sir Arthur Quiller-Couch and Arthur Symons) have felt the same about Patmore's ideas on the status of women; while even in his own day, Patmore found reviewers taking him to task for them.

C. C. Abbott in his introduction to the Hopkins–Patmore correspondence pays tribute to Patmore's genius, but is unable to rank him as a great poet because of what he calls 'his Sultan-like conception of woman and her sphere'. Abbott's difficulties are bound up with Patmore's 'conception of love and the place of woman in that love, and so question the very fibre of his thought'.[3]

On the other hand, Patmore has not lacked his champions in this regard. A good deal of Osbert Burdett's *The Idea of Coventry Patmore* and of Frederick Page's *Patmore—A Study in Poetry*, is devoted to the defence of the reasonableness of Patmore's conception of woman and of her function. More recently, George N. Shuster has presented a view of Patmore's concept of the place of woman which might be taken as a reply to the criticisms of Miss Crawford and of Abbott. Although Patmore's verse often seems to imply a

[1] 'The Bow Set in the Cloud', *Religio Poetae*, pp. 55–56.
[2] 'Coventry Patmore', *The Fortnightly Review*, Vol. 75, No. CCCCX, Feb. 1, 1901, pp. 309–310.
[3] *Further Letters of Gerard Manley Hopkins*, Intro., pp. xxv-xxvii.

feudal relation between the sexes, he writes, subjection is, in fact, exacted only in love. Love is fundamentally an art, with its own inexorable rules, and Patmore's poems are treatises on this art. The woman is the material to which the plastic conception—man— comes seeking expression. 'Unless she remain even as clay, and he keep his winged status as idea, there shall be no saving the union from ultimate disfiguration.'[1]

For the most part Patmore's poems present a view of woman which is both kinder and more realistic than some of his prose remarks would suggest that he held. Honoria is admired, but unsentimentally admired. She is anything but an idealized conception, and when she is compared, as Patmore intended that she should be, with Jane, what is seen is a picture of womanhood which is indeed full of psychological realism. However, some of the essays, for instance 'The Weaker Vessel' and 'Margaret Fuller Ossoli', and such statements as 'If there's anything that God hates utterly, it is a clever woman',[2] imply a Pasha-like stand which makes it easy to understand Miss Crawford's feminine indignation.

Yet there is not the slightest evidence to suggest that Patmore treated any of his wives with the domineering tyranny of the legendary Turk. On the contrary, the domestic happiness he enjoyed with them and the tone of his letters to them and of theirs to him indicate that he was a wise and understanding husband with no undue sense of his 'rights' as a 'reflection of God'. The fact seems to be that Patmore never quite reconciled what his intellect told him was a reasonable deduction from his premises of 'homo' and of the nuptial analogy with what his experience told him about women and marriage; that his poems, reconciling emotion and intellect more successfully than his prose does, express a more judicious, and on the whole truer, view concerning women's place; that because of his endeavour in his prose to apply rigidly a theory of man and woman even when the facts were against him he tends to go to extremes in presenting a case against 'masculine women' and 'feminine men'. The magnificent presentation of feminine psychology in *The Angel in the House* both softens and to some extent justifies his attitude towards women; it is difficult to take seriously the ferocious polemics of his prose comments on 'feminism'. He is forced again and again to admit exceptions to his abstract conception of womanly talent and virtue, as in the cases of Madame de Hautefort and Alice Meynell, in both of whom he

---

[1] 'Patmore—A Revaluation', *Commonweal*, Vol. XXIV, No. 26, Oct. 23, 1936, p. 605.
[2] Champneys, *Memoirs*, Vol. II, p. 78.

finds the qualities which by strict theory should reside in manly men alone.

In the concept of 'homo' woman's part, since she is 'marr'd less than man by mortal fall'[1]; is, spiritually, more important than his. Woman is thus because she is, as 'the weaker vessel', an unreasonable being; man finds her attractive because she is unreasonable.

> 'It is "of faith" that the woman's claim to the honour of man', writes Patmore, 'lies in the fact of her being the "weaker vessel".... It is a great consolation to reflect that, among all the bewildering changes to which the world is subject, the character of woman cannot be altered; and that, so long as she abstains from absolute outrages against nature —such as divided skirts, free-thinking, tricycles and Radicalism— neither Greek nor conic sections, nor political economy, nor cigarettes, nor athletics can ever really do other than enhance the charm of that sweet unreasonableness which humbles the gods to the dust and compels them to adore the lace below the last hem of her brocade! It is owing to this ineradicable perfection that time cannot change nor custom stale her infinite variety.'[2]

Quite early, Patmore drew a distinction between men and women with regard to their affections. An essay written in 1847 contrasts the casual nature of a father's feeling for his children with a mother's particular tenderness. While the affection of one is probably as great as that of the other, in the first case it rises little above the character of an instinct, in the second it has come to be a conscious feeling. Thus he concludes that a woman's affections are developed beyond those of a man, as a man's understanding is developed beyond that of a woman.[3] Because of this richness of affection, and because of her greater sensitivity to the value of human feeling, woman is a constant reminder to man of those mysteries of love and being which lie beyond the scope of reason—Pascal's 'reasons of the heart'—which man is otherwise likely to ignore since they are not discoverable by the reason alone. She reveals to man new depths within himself, and enables him to complete himself as his understanding enables her to complete herself. As his spiritual witness and conscience, woman conveys to him an awareness of divinity which he realizes in this life in love, the love of marriage in particular. Thus Patmore is not using a conventional hyperbole,

---

[1] *Angel in the House*, Bk. 1, Co. IV, Prelude 1, p. 83.
[2] 'The Weaker Vessel', *Religio Poetae*, pp. 147–148.
[3] 'German Lady Novelists', *North British Review*, Vol. VII, No. XIV, Aug. 1847, pp. 370–371.

but simply stating his belief in the special mission of woman when he writes:

Her face
Is the summ'd sweetness of the earth,
Her soul the glass of heaven's grace,
To which she leads me by the hand;
Or, briefly all the truth to say
To you, who briefly understand,
She is both heaven and the way.

(*A.H.*, II, ix)

Much of what appears at first sight to be sentimentality, of language and emotion, in the earlier poems, is Patmore's recognition of the special spiritual function of womanhood. In the field of grace, and of the supernatural destiny of mankind, he gives woman the higher place, since she 'desires the infinite, man the finite. She is the continent of the infinite, making it conscious and powerful by limitation.'[1]

The relationship of man and woman, then, as Patmore sees it, is based upon a difference of functions, to which he gives the name of 'inequality'. But we must understand just what he implied by the term. God, the masculine force, desires the soul, the woman, and this is an act of condescension, a union of high with low, a conjunction of opposites. By the logic of his analogy, then, Patmore believed that all happiness in love is the result of the union of unequals. He writes:

'*Between unequals sweet is equal love*; and the fact is that there is no love, and therefore no sweetness, which is not thus conditioned; and the greater the inequality the greater the sweetness. Hence the doctrine that infinite felicity can arise only from the mutual love of beings infinitely unequal—that is, of the creator and the creature. Inequality, far from implying any dishonour on either side of the mutual compact of love, is the source of honour to both.'[2]

The health and the harmony which come from the balance of these inequalities in love can be found only if man and woman keep their respective natural places, and recognize the indispensable role that each sex plays in relation to the other. The man must be 'manly' and the woman 'womanly'. He dislikes 'emancipated women' whose leading feature, he claims, is their emancipation from the Christian faith.[3]

[1] *Rod, Root and Flower*, 'Aurea Dicta', CLIII, p. 55.
[2] 'Thoughts on Knowledge, Opinion and Inequality', *Religio Poetae*, pp. 133–134.
[3] 'The Social Position of Women', *North British Review*, Vol. XIV, No. XXVIII, Feb. 1851, p. 526.

Woman forfeits her prerogative when she abandons her gentleness. This is the theme of such Preludes as 'Honour and Desert':

> O Queen, awake to thy renown,
>   Require what 'tis our wealth to give,
> And comprehend and wear the crown
>   Of thy despised prerogative!
> I, who in manhood's name at length
>   With glad songs come to abdicate
> The gross regality of strength,
>   Must yet in this thy praise abate,
> That, through thine erring humbleness
>   And disregard of thy degree,
> Mainly, has man been so much less
>   Than fits his fellowship with thee.
> High thoughts had shaped the foolish brow,
>   The coward had grasp'd the hero's sword,
> The vilest had been great, hadst thou,
>   Just to thyself, been worth's reward.
> But lofty honours undersold
>   Seller and buyer both disgrace;
> And favours that make folly bold
>   Banish the light from virtue's face.
>   (*A.H.*, II, iv)

At her best, faithful to her womanliness, woman is for man a mirror in whom he sees reflected the true 'glory' of his being which nothing else can so clearly show him. But when she is untrue to her God-given nature, she can become a snare and a trap.

In all such utterances is implied that view of love as the *ars amandi* to which George N. Shuster points. The idea of love as an art practised by husband and wife, not according to the notions of Victorian sentimentality, nor to the codes of modern 'marriage manuals', but through respect and understanding by each partner of the other's spiritual and emotional resources, is prominent in Patmore's outlook, and it was on this 'art' that he relied to maintain the health and harmony of marriage. Because he thought that husband and wife should not take each other for granted, he admired, to the horror of his friends, the novels of Crébillon *fils* and other French 'boudoir' novelists, seeing in them at least glimmers of the idea that love must be cultivated with tenderness, delicacy and understanding of the psychology of the spouse.

Despite the emphasis in Patmore's verse on the dignity of woman, the exaggerations, paradoxes, and occasional testiness of his prose writings on women and their 'rights' tend to create an impression that he feels a genial contempt and respectful pity for womankind.

Yet there is, in what he says of the social rights of women, a good deal more realism and durable good sense than was usual in his day. He believed firmly in a natural difference of function and capacity between the sexes, and it is not untrue to his major thesis to suggest that often when he used 'inequality' he meant rather 'difference'. In his stress on this difference, he believed that he was elevating, not degrading womanhood, as he thought feminist ideals were doing. By being fully 'womanly', woman fulfilled her destiny as the indispensable complement of man, and as a constant witness to the mysteries of life and the realities of Heaven.

This position of woman as the final and visible reflection of the beauty of God is another thing entirely, in Patmore's mind, from her social status. The idea of social independence for woman he declared to be completely opposed to nature and reason. He deplored the influence its advocates were gaining, for such people were, in his eyes, the real obstacles to improvement in woman's social condition. The 'emancipated woman . . . would prove to men that she is as good as a man, by shewing them that she is as bad.'[1] Not that woman is to be regarded as a useless doll, a Nora in her prison-house. In the essay in which this sentence appears, Patmore reveals himself as a serious critic of Victorian methods of feminine education. He stigmatizes as the basic reasons for feminine discontent '*a defective education* and afterwards *an inactive existence*'.[2] The type of education given to women in his day, he says, is based on a narrow view of life itself, making worldly advancement the chief aim. Since marriage is the only way most women can gain such advancement, showy accomplishments are emphasized and more solid learning is acquired only with a view to its market-value. Men are dazzled by such accomplishments, and thus, in their way, prevent women from aiming at higher attainments. He doubts whether the French 'mariages de convenance' are not superior to English marriages entered into by a woman called upon to feign false feelings she does not possess, or to excite those to which she cannot respond. Those who regard Patmore's ideal of womanhood as a soft, complacent, mindless creature would find it hard to reconcile such a view with his own words which follow:

'A great mistake has been made by many writers of both sexes, who confound *weakness* with tenderness, and *want of character* with gentleness. It is common to compare a woman to a clinging plant, who can live only with the support of a noble tree; but such should not be the relationship of the sexes. Weakness can never be beautiful, either

1 'The Social Position of Women', *North British Review*, Feb. 1851, pp. 527–528. 2 *Ibid.*, p. 532.

morally or physically; and though the feminine type may possess greater softness and more feeling, it must be active, firm and healthy, or it cannot be beautiful.'[1]

The betterment of women's education, that is, giving her a fair share of intellectual training, as opposed to the cultivation of drawing-room accomplishments, will, he says, not only make for greater social usefulness for unmarried women, but will assist in married happiness. A thoroughly uncultivated woman may be a pleasant toy, or a good domestic drudge; but she will never be her husband's most valued companion, nor his most loved friend.

This striking plea for better education for women does not mean that Patmore favours the breaking-down of traditional domesticity. On the other hand it shows that in his emphasis elsewhere on the 'inequality' of women, he is concerned with a spiritual principle and with the relationship of the sexes in love. Far from being 'harem-minded' in his attitude to women, he asserts the special gifts and the spiritual resources of womankind, and actually propounds a scheme for her educational and intellectual betterment far in advance of the ideas of many of his contemporaries. The most charming and most gracious of Patmore's essays on woman is the piece on Madame de Hautefort. Any misunderstandings which his more polemical essays may create as to his real attitude towards the opposite sex must be modified or removed by the conclusion of this piece, which may fairly be taken as summing up all his ideas on this matter, and which ends:

'The happiness and dignity of man and woman require, not a confusion, but a complete distinction, of their relations; and the title of the "weaker vessel", being, on the best authority, the woman's peculiar title to honour, is not to be forgotten and ignored, but to be contemplated and loved.'[2]

Later in his life, Patmore, as already indicated, came to consider the place of the Blessed Virgin Mary in the Christian scheme more closely than he had done before; and to recognize in her the fulfilment of all his ideas concerning the body, the Incarnation and the nature of woman. 'The Blessed Virgin, "the holiest and humblest of creatures",' he said, 'crowned with the glory and honour of bearing God in her womb, is the one woman in whom the whole

---

[1] *Ibid.*, p. 535.
[2] 'Madame de Hautefort', *Principle in Art*, pp. 189–190. This essay appeared originally under the title of 'Madame de Hautefort and her Contemporaries' in *The National Review* for October 1856.

of womanhood has been more or less reconstituted and perfected.'[1] At the beginning of 'The Child's Purchase' he celebrates his finding in her the reconciliation of virginity, the love of God, married love, motherhood, and the perfection of the nature of woman.

By bearing the Son of God, the Blessed Virgin became the very highest example of the contact between the divine and the human. She gave bound, shape, 'credibility' to an infinite God; through her God becomes intelligible, and he who honours her honours all women as well as her Son. She is the prototype of all good, pure, natural women. Her humble reception of the message of the angel showed the way to all men and women who acknowledge with faith and humility the fact of God's marriage with the flesh and his coming to the individual soul.

> 'Those who fear to call Mary the "Mother of God",' he asserts, 'simply do not believe in the Incarnation at all; but we must go further, and believe His word when He rebuked the people for regarding her as exclusively His Mother, declaring that every soul who received Him with faith and love, was also, in unison with Her, His Mother, the Bride of the Holy Spirit.'[2]

Since in the Blessed Virgin, womanhood is perfected, and the marriage of God and man is consummated, she is in truth the 'second Eve'. Even more, 'The B.V. is co-redemptrix with Christ. His visit converts the soul to acknowledge the truth and to obey it in intention, destroying the old Adam. Her visit converts the body, giving gentle disposition and affection, destroying the old Eve.'[3] Again, she is the mirror of virginity, and the perfect example of chastity in marriage, as well as a model for the celibate; as Patmore writes in 'Deliciae Sapientiae de Amore':

> 'Hail Virgin in Virginity a Spouse'!
> Heard first below
> Within the little house
> At Nazareth;
> Heard yet in many a cell where brides of Christ
> Lie hid, emparadised.

His concept that 'Lover and Mistress become sensibly one flesh in the instant that they confess to one another a full and mutual complacency of intellect, will, affection, and sense, with the promise of inviolable faith',[4] and that all that follows after is, in the words of

---

[1] 'Dieu et Ma Dame', *Religio Poetae*, p. 159.
[2] *Rod, Root and Flower*, 'Knowledge and Science', VIII, p. 68.
[3] Champneys, *Memoirs*, Vol. II, p. 66.
[4] *Rod, Root and Flower*, 'Magna Moralia', V, p. 149.

Aquinas, 'an accidental perfection of marriage', he finds completely fulfilled in the Virgin marriage and the Virgin birth.

The notes for 'The Marriage of the Blessed Virgin' which Frederick Page has transcribed leave no doubt as to the importance Patmore attached to Catholic teaching concerning the Blessed Virgin. The work was to be the crown and the summing-up of his former writing. It is an indication of his nature as a poet that the proposed poem was not to enter the 'breathless ether of divinity' either, but was to be treated in terms of a Patmorean realism, the same realism which saves *The Angel in the House* from sentimentality. Page says: 'Patmore's subject was to have been the literal marriage of the Jewish sixteen-year-old girl to a Jewish carpenter of forty-five.'[1] Even in this poem, however, the focus of attention was to be on the Incarnation and its significance. One of his notes reads:

> *This marriage as the perfection of human marriage and as affecting all humanity by being so is the subject of the Poem.*[2]

And when Patmore abandoned his project, at least one of the reasons behind his breaking off was a realization that it was a subject containing so many implications that he could not encompass it and do it justice. But although he did not complete more than the prologue to what he felt was to be his greatest work, he expressed in this section his recognition that the 'Lady Elect' was the crown of womanhood, and the one creature who gave all his life's work purpose and meaning:

> Mother, who lead'st me still by unknown ways,
> Giving the gifts I know not how to ask,
> Bless thou the work
> Which, done, redeems my many wasted days,
> Makes white the murk,
> And crowns the few which thou wilt not dispraise,
> When clear my Songs of Lady's graces rang,
> And little guess'd I 'twas of thee I sang!

[1] *Patmore, A Study in Poetry*, p. 129.   [2] *Ibid.*, p. 134.

II

The Doctrine of Love

FEW OTHER ENGLISH POETS have written so much of love as
Patmore did, and certainly none has found so much lyrical inspiration in marriage. He alone was inspired to take the common round
of Victorian domesticity, and to pierce through the externals to the
heart of nuptial love with an understanding which spiritualized the
accidents in the course of celebrating the holiness of the substance.
Since he was dissatisfied with the kinds of love set forth by Dante
and Plato, and since he hated abstractions, it was inevitable that he
should have found married love to be the only kind which completes
the identity of the 'homo', that satisfaction of personality which each
sex seeks in the other. He believed, with 'real apprehension', that
marriage is indeed 'a great sacrament', and hence that the 'outward
sign of inward grace' is to be sought, not in any idealized Romantic
love, nor in the socially-conditioned ideals of Victorian domesticity,
but in the realities of family life, common to every age, and including the commonplaces of his own as typical of the facts of
marriage in any age. It did not matter to Patmore that earlier poets
had passed over married love as unsuitable for poetry because of its
ordinariness. On the contrary, one of the most original features
of his own view of love lies in his turning the commonplaces of
marriage to advantage in his lyrical expression.

He was, in everything, a realist. Vague ideas of love had no more
attraction for him than vague ideas of God. To have meaning, as
well as mystery, love must proceed from the actuality of human
experience. 'Love is rooted deeper in the earth than any other

passion,' he writes; 'and for that cause its head, like that of the Tree Igdrasil, soars higher into heaven.'[1] In fact, for Patmore, the closer love came to true humanity and to the essential nature of created beings, the more esoteric its implications. His description of the nature of poetry in an essay written in 1856 may be read as a justification of the kind of subject-matter he used in *The Angel in the House* and its sequel.

'Poetry,' he says, 'so far as it relates to moral and intellectual truth, has the somewhat paradoxical recommendation of having to do mainly with truisms. . . . All the greatest poets seem to have been equally partial to commonplace themes, as well in incident as in moral; for these reasons, among others, that moral truth is usually important in proportion to its triteness; that the poet is doing his noblest work in resuscitating moral truths from the inert condition of truisms and conferring upon them a perennial bloom and power. . . . The poet more than justifies his adoption of truisms and stale legends by his mode of dealing with them; he shows that, in such things, acknowledged and spoken of by all men, there are more and deeper meanings than may be fully expressed or comprehended by any man.'[2]

Before, then, we can assess the success or failure of Patmore's poems of wedded love, we must know exactly what his aim was. Most of those who welcomed *The Angel in the House* accepted the poem for what, on the surface, it was—a pleasant novelette in verse in which a conventional love-story ran a conventional course, interrupted, a trifle annoyingly, perhaps, by somewhat baffling 'accompaniments' (later 'preludes') dealing with various aspects of love and marriage; this despite the fact that in the Prologue to the first edition (1856) of *The Betrothal*, Patmore had written, in lines later cancelled:

> The Song should have no incidents,
> They are so dull, and pall, twice read:
> Its scope should be the heart's events;

Swinburne parodied its commonplaces in 'The Person of the House'; while Edmund Gosse described the domestic poems as written by 'this laureate of the tea-table, with his humdrum stories of girls that smell of bread and butter', who was, he added, 'in his inmost heart the most arrogant and visionary of mystics'.[3] Yet Patmore

---

[1] 'Love and Poetry', *Religio Poetae*, p. 142.
[2] 'New Poets', *Edinburgh Review*, Vol. CIV, No. 212, Oct. 1856, p. 339.
[3] 'Poems by Coventry Patmore', *The Athenaeum*, No. 3059, June 12, 1886, p. 771. A letter from Patmore to Gosse concerning this review is especially interesting in view of the fact that the poet is often represented as keenly sensitive to criticism: 'We were greatly pleased with the praise, and no less

knew just what he was about; that his philosophy led him apparently to confirm the normal Victorian view of marriage conceals the fact that he arrived at his conclusions from premises vastly different from those of most of his contemporaries, and also that the implications of his idea of nuptial love, missed completely by those who read *The Angel in the House* for its 'story', its contemporary 'props', or its sentiments, actually extended into a transcendental realm undreamt of by the writers of sentimental novelettes.

Patmore's doctrine is esoteric, not only in *The Unknown Eros*, where the removal of the period details shows the philosophy naked, and where the shift of emphasis has markedly changed, but in all his major poems from *Tamerton Church-Tower* onwards. Whereas many earlier poets had tried to express the inwardness of love, its fervour and passion, by removing it from earth, or from the restraints of law, Patmore set out to show that, within the limitations of Christian Marriage was to be found the most rapturous joy and the fulfilment of all human passion; and that in an exploration of the facts of marriage there lay as much material for poetry and as much chance for psychological subtlety as in the description of defeat, disillusionment and extra-marital adventure. He aimed to show that the constant purity of marriage enshrines a miraculous variety; and that, far from dying, love in marriage can, and should, flower and expand with the years. Hence, by placing the familiar in an unfamiliar light, by exploring the moods, the paradoxes and the realities of pre-marital and marital love, with insight, tenderness and candour, he defends Christian marriage with an unmatched originality.

Patmore did not accept the sacramental nature of marriage because it was a Christian dogma. On the contrary, by intuition and then by his experience of an ideally happy marriage he arrived independently at the sacramental view, and accepted Catholic teaching on marriage because his experience had convinced him of its truth. Gosse insists, and rightly, that 'his transcendental adoration of wedded love was originally neither a rule of theology nor an argument of morals, but was a symptom of purely individual lyricism.'[1] He did not acquiesce in the conventional middle-class attitude of his time towards marriage, which, he saw clearly, substituted sentimental compensations and conventional emotional

amused by the blame. You should have heard the inextinguishable laughter with which your description of "Honoria" and "Amelia" as "girls smelling of bread and butter" was received. My wife suggests that, in the next edition, the name of "Honoria" should be changed to "Butterina".' (Champneys, *Memoirs*, Vol. II, p. 257.)

[1] *Coventry Patmore*, p. 39.

reactions for the ecstatic acceptance of an indissoluble union of mind, heart and body which alone, in his view, meant a true marriage.

He knew, too, that in English verse, the particular character of married love had hardly ever been expressed. Even Robert Browning, who might have seemed the Victorian poet best qualified to write lyric poetry on the theme of wedded love, barely glances at it in one or two brief pieces, while his great poem, *The Ring and The Book*, although it is dedicated to, and intended to enshrine, the memory of his dead wife, his 'lyric love', presents a spiritualized and 'abstract' love which has more in common with that of Dante than with that of Patmore. Yet Patmore, it has been suggested, was in love with the idea of marriage rather than with any of his wives. One critic, for instance, has written, 'He loved Woman, rather than women.'[1] This is a half-truth. It was because Patmore loved a woman that he was able to love Woman; it was because he loved a spouse that he was able to love espousals. It is the firm, clear, accurate depiction of the actualities of the lover's, the husband's, the beloved's, and the wife's emotions in *a* marriage that lends conviction to his ideas on marriage. In the course of this delineation, Patmore specifically recognizes the mood of being 'in love with love', and isolates it as an early stage in Vaughan's love:

> Whene'er I come where ladies are,
>   How sad soever I was before,
> Though like a ship frost-bound and far
>   Withheld in ice from the ocean's roar. . . .
>
> Then is my sadness banish'd far,
>   And I am like that ship no more.
>   (*A.H.*, I, ii)

However, this mood is part of Vaughan's outlook before he selects Honoria and sees her as *the* woman, after which all his love and thought are concentrated on her. There is, in short, not the slightest vagueness about Patmore's portrayal of married love, however subtle and complex the moods he reveals in the 'Preludes'; its nuances, its joys, its sacrifices, its compensations, its trappings, are faithfully rendered.

It is customary to regard those poems in *The Unknown Eros* which deal with Divine Love as his finest and most individual achievement. Splendid though they are and fully his own, these share with other poems, by Crashaw and St. John of the Cross, for

---

[1] 'Coventry Patmore', by W. K. Fleming, *Life and Letters*, Vol. IV, No. 1, January 1930, p. 36.

instance, a common subject. It has been traditional in Catholic theology to depict the love of the soul for God and of God for the soul in terms of the language of human love. However, Christian writers have been less ready to regard marriage as in itself holy. To be sure, Augustine, Aquinas, and other Doctors of the Church stressed the sacramental character of matrimony, and its importance as a means of sanctification. But, despite this, the other words of St. Paul that 'it is better to marry than to burn' and the writings of such misogynistic Fathers as St. Jerome have created an opposing tradition, largely the product of a celibate consciousness, which regards marriage as a kind of sop to man's concupiscence, tolerable only because it perpetuates the race. Thus the tendency has been to use the vocabulary of human love to describe the relationship of God to the soul, but not to reverse the process and treat of human love as an analogue of Divine love, nor to suggest that, if there is in fact any basis for the Divine analogy, then human love must be in its way holy. It is Patmore's distinction that he made the process a two-way one, and restored the dignity of wedded love as both symbol and prophecy of the love between Christ and the soul.

He saw married love, too, as a fundamental, indeed, an indispensable, element in civilization. No abstract concept could, he believed, work the results in refining manners, in establishing courtesy of behaviour, comeliness of demeanour and civility, which are among the marks of man's superiority to the beasts. Love is for him 'the nursling of civility', whose civilizing power he describes in the Prelude of that name. Married love, then, provides both the sanction and the source of man's social life. In the family, love welds together the sexes and parents and children in a harmony which offers a pattern for society as a whole. If the true husband and the true wife come to realize the fullness of love in each other, this supplies them with a revelation which can extend the Kingdom of God on earth.

In view of his desire to recharge the whole idea of marriage, it is ironical that Patmore should have been regarded so widely as the 'typically Victorian' singer of Marriage. Throughout the domestic poems is a consistent, underlying emphasis on the sacredness of the body, the purity of sexual love in marriage and the natural joys of the flesh which shocked readers when it was presented plainly in *The Unknown Eros*. It is to Tennyson, with his evasions and his compromises on sex that we must turn to find that view of domesticity which most closely agreed with the outlook of a middle-class public, not to a poet nourished on Swedenborg, St. Augustine, St. Bernard of Clairvaux, Aquinas and St. John of the Cross.

Patmore himself had not the slightest doubt that he had stumbled upon a hitherto unexplored subject; his enthusiasm for the theme of *The Angel in the House* is sufficient to show that he was not merely concerned with writing inoffensive *vers de société*. His early poems contain in embryo the ideas which were to mature in *The Angel*; *Tamerton Church-Tower*, in particular, reaches out towards the longer poem, and is a necessary step on the way towards it, as *The Victories of Love* is towards *The Unknown Eros*. But it was not until 1854 that he really realized just what he wanted to do in poetry. Aubrey de Vere has left a vivid account of Patmore's joy at his discovery. Calling on de Vere one day in a state of unusual excitement, Patmore announced that he had found the one particular theme for poetry—not Love as a caprice of fancy or an imaginative passion, but 'that Love in which . . . all the Loves centre, and that Woman who is the rightful sustainer of them all', who had seldom been sung sincerely and effectually. And he had found not only the theme, but, he asserted, the perfect form for it.[1] And that Patmore was convinced that this poem would be of singular importance when the proposed six parts were completed is seen from the words of Alfred Fryer in a letter to H. S. Sutton: 'He thinks of writing a poem to be *the* poem of the age, but half doubts his own powers. I tell him that *the* poem of the age *we* expect from his pen and that, it seems to me, he has quite genius enough to write it.'[2]

The Prologue to *The Angel in the House* proclaims his conviction that in selecting married love as his subject he was taking the most meaningful topic about which a poet could write:

> Learn that to me, though born so late,
>   There does, beyond desert, befall
> (May my great fortune make me great!)
>   The first of themes, sung last of all.
> In green and undiscover'd ground
>   Yet near where many others sing,
> I have the very well-head found
>   Whence gushes the Pierian spring.

For this poet, the kind of love delineated in the domestic poems is valuable not only in itself, but also because it reveals to man a principle which can be found in all human experience. The honest lover is awakened to the beauty and mystery of the universe. Patmore does not try to explain the mystery, but tries to show how it can be apprehended as a reality in the bonds which bind human beings together. He writes:

[1] Champneys, *Memoirs*, Vol. I, pp. 159–160.   [2] *Ibid.*, Vol. I, p. 95.

'The relation of man and woman, besides being the first and strongest of human ties, is the source from which they all spring; and a miscomprehension of the nature of the primary relation necessarily involves error in the understanding of those which are derivative.'[1]

His emphasis on marriage as the fruition of love came simply from his conviction that only in this union of soul and body is the sacramental nature of love fulfilled. This kind of love requires an external sanction so that man will be assured of its reality. The blessing of the Church, Patmore realized, was its sanction of a generally recognized human relationship, for he knew and made much of the fact that it is the partners, not the priest, who administer the sacrament of Matrimony. However, as a natural corollary of his view of law, marriage could have no real validity unless it was conceived of as a permanent union, for in the permanence of love lies the secret of its delight, as well as the condition of its freedom.

Married love, for him, was *creative love*, as all the sacraments are creative, if man co-operates with the grace offered him in them. And like all other sacraments, too, marriage has its ritual and its liturgy. 'Love supersedes all the sacraments', one of Patmore's favourite quotations from Augustine, expresses what he felt about the priority of love, but it also implies that in love, as a supreme sacrament, there is a ritual which is an integral part of all sacraments. His keen sense of the ceremony of marriage made his poetic analysis of courtship and married life, in Gosse's words, 'a breviary for lovers'.[2] Patmore's account of the ceremonies of married love has been painstakingly analysed by Osbert Burdett, who has gone through his early poems section by section, pointing to the psychological subtlety and the depth of understanding they reveal.[3] We need select only the main aspects of Patmore's treatment to show how he regarded the relationship of husband and wife, and the duties and responsibilities of each sex.

To begin with, for marriage to keep its mystery and beauty, it must, he believed, be based not only upon mutual sacrifice, but also upon the 'great and gracious ways' of which he speaks in the ode Departure. There must be reverence and awe in marriage, not the near-contempt of an easy familiarity, for

> intimacy in love is nought
> Without pure reverence
>
> (*V.L.*, II, xii)

[1] 'Madame de Hautefort', *Principle in Art*, p. 191.
[2] *Coventry Patmore*, p. 82.
[3] *The Idea of Coventry Patmore* (Oxford University Press, 1921).

When, in the happy early days of the betrothal, Felix and Honoria take one of their first outings together, Felix notes that as the intimacy grows, so, too, does the courtesy:

> And in the eternal light I saw
>   That she was mine; though yet my heart
> Could not conceive, nor would confess
>   Such contentation; and there grew
> More form and more fair stateliness
>   Than heretofore between us two.
>
> (*A.H.*, I, viii)

At the same time, a balance must be struck between excessive awe and excessive familiarity. As over-familiarity ignores the mystery of love; so, too, over-much idealization can smother its ardour. The husband must regard his love as an art to be cultivated, a ritual to be observed with tact and prudence. For, Patmore points out with his customary shrewdness, a woman can give only half her love to a man who is totally absorbed in her to the exclusion of other interests:

> Such honour, with a conduct wise
> In common things, as, not to steep
> The lofty mind of love in sleep
> Of over much familiarness;
> Not to degrade its kind caress,
> As those do that can feel no more,
> So give themselves to pleasures o'er;
> Not to let morning-sloth destroy
> The evening flower, domestic joy;
> Not by uxoriousness to chill
> The warm devotion of her will
> Who can but half her love confer
> On him that cares for nought but her;
>
> (*V.L.*, 'Wedding Sermon')

The ceremonies of love, then, the pattern of gracious acknowledgement of the demands of the other's personality, mutual respect manifesting itself in courtesy on both sides, these make up an essential theme of the poems of domestic love. This might appear simply to reflect the ceremonial of a middle-class Victorian household. But Patmore is expressing in terms of his own time and place an aspect of love which has been recognized by all poets—its ritual. And since woman is the 'glory' of man, a constant reminder of the divine to him, the honour given instinctively to her by civilized men Patmore explains as an unconscious recognition of her place in the divine plan. In addition, of course, the ceremonies of marriage are another form of constraint by which man preserves the force of

his love and prevents it from running out into the marshes of lust
or indifference.

So, in one of his 'Preludes', he sets out with grace and delicacy
the counsel of 'Love Ceremonious':

> Keep your undrest, familiar style
>   For strangers, but respect your friend,
> Her most, whose matrimonial smile
>   Is and asks honour without end.
> 'Tis found, and needs it must be so,
>   That life from love's allegiance flags
> When love forgets his majesty
>   In sloth's unceremonious rags.
> Let love make home a gracious court;
>   There let the world's rude, hasty ways
> Be fashion'd to a loftier port,
>   And learn to bow and stand at gaze;
> And let the sweet respective sphere
>   Of personal worship there obtain
> Circumference for moving clear,
>   None treading on another's train.
> This makes that pleasures do not cloy,
>   And dignifies our mortal strife
> With calmness and considerate joy,
>   Befitting our immortal life.
>
> (*A.H.*, II, iii)

Marriage, then, is not 'a man's affair' only. Vaughan, as the married
lover, tells himself

> Her manners, when they call me lord,
> Remind me 'tis by courtesy.
>
> (*A.H.*, II, xii)

Marriage entails sacrifice on the husband's part as it does on the
wife's. The man may seem, too, to be the pursuer, and the active
partner, but in reality the woman, both before and after the
wedding, is at least equally the pursuer, bent, in her more indirect
way, on fulfilling her destiny as a spiritual and as a biological being.
The prelude 'The Chace' skilfully shows how the woman, wearied
'with an ill unknown', sighing for love, yet half-afraid, is bewildered, repelled and gradually won by the man; and then herself
advances, and employs her more delicate arts. The more she
retreats and flies, the more, in fact, she advances, so that

> Should she be won,
> It must not be believed or thought
> She yields.

Elsewhere, Patmore details the woman's method of pursuit in terms which seem to anticipate Shaw's *Man and Superman*:

> Without his knowledge he was won;
>   Against his nature kept devout;
> She'll never tell him how 'twas done,
>   And he will never find it out.
> If, sudden, he suspects her wiles,
>   And hears her forging chain and trap,
> And looks, she sits in simple smiles,
>   Her two hands lying in her lap.
>
> (A.H., II, viii)

Light though the touch be here, and in other preludes in which the deeper implications of the sex relationship are touched upon, he is making the serious point that, although the male, with his more obvious aggressiveness appears to be the active creative force in wooing and in loving, woman, too, although more subtly, is also creative and in her way assertive. He would be in complete agreement with those contemporary psychologists who attribute some of the failures in marriage to frigidity on the part of the woman, and who believe that the idea that the woman should be a completely passive creature, emotionally and physically, is false to the demands of her true nature. In Patmore's view it is the function of the male to draw out the womanhood in his mate, so that she responds with her own creative femininity.

The perpetuation of this relationship throughout married life is not only the product of an art, but also the fruit of a vocation diligently persisted in. There is something elusive in marriage; it is a paradox of love that it is always to be fulfilled, yet never is; and the lover is driven ever to pursue in the hope of coming closer to the heart of the mystery. Patmore noted of Sir Kenelm Digby, in his marriage with Venetia Stanley: 'His ardour . . . appears to have been increased, rather than diminished, by possession'[1]; and it was this mystery of never quite satisfied pursuit, yet constant increase, of love, that made him consider that every winning in marriage must be preceded by a wooing (another point in which he is in accord with contemporary writers on the 'techniques' of marriage). Only if this part of the 'ritual' is observed will the continuance of love and its increase be assured. His married lover asks:

Why, having won her, do I woo?

---

[1] 'Sir Kenelme Digby—His Character and Writings', *The Gentleman's Magazine*, May 1848, p. 483.

and answers himself:

> Because her spirit's vestal grace
> Provokes me always to pursue,
> But, spirit-like, eludes embrace. . . .

> Because, though free of the outer court
> I am, this Temple keeps its shrine
> Sacred to Heaven; because, in short
> She's not and never can be mine.
>
> *(A.H.*, II, xii)

So Felix Vaughan, after ten years of marriage, can find himself only at the threshold of delight.

The pattern of wooing and wedding given in *The Angel in the House* is incomplete; only when it is joined with that shown in *The Victories of Love* can Patmore's rounded philosophy of love be seen. Together, both poems offer a view of conjugal relations quite opposed to Romantic conceptions of 'soul-mates' and 'elective affinities'. Although *The Angel* outlines the blissful prelude to a blissful marriage of the kind the poet had himself enjoyed, he knew thoroughly well that a marriage of mutual ecstatic love, persisting with undisturbed increase, was the exception, not the rule; and that it is in the development of love through sacrifice, adjustment, and the alternating assertion and surrender of the male and the female egos, that the fulfilment of the nature of the average marriage is found. Even in *The Angel*, which ostensibly offers no serious impediment to the happiness of the lovers, there are many intimations that the success of marriage does not depend upon a sense of affinity, nor on comfortable material circumstances, nor even on a harmony of tastes, education and outlook, but upon the unshakeable fidelity of husband and wife to their vows, even though it would appear, in the frequent disillusionment of marriage, that an irreparable mistake had been made:

> You loved her, and would lie all night
> Thinking how beautiful she was,
> And what to do for her delight.
> Now both are bound by alien laws!
> Be patient; put your heart to school;
> Weep if you will, but not despair;
> The trust that nought goes wrong by rule
> Should ease this load the many bear.
> Love, if there's heav'n, shall meet his dues,
> Though here unmatched, or match'd amiss;
> Meanwhile, the gentle cannot choose
> But learn to love the lips they kiss;

> Ne'er hurt the homely sister's ears
> With Rachel's beauties; secret be
> The lofty mind whose lonely tears
> Protest against mortality.
>
> (*A.H.*, II, v)

Patmore was keenly aware of the disillusionment that often succeeds the complacency of ante-nuptial love, and knew that the love which preens itself 'like the Pharisee' often sustains a rude shock in the actualities of married intimacy. Thus there is a law of vocation in the married relationship as there is in the religious life. A man and a woman who marry not for 'love', but for a secondary, not necessarily unworthy, reason, may, if they are faithful to their vows, receive the grace of true conjugal love.

The two kinds of lover are clearly described in the domestic poems. The prelude 'The Lover' tells of the man who

> meets, by heavenly chance express,
> The destined maid; some hidden hand
> Unveils to him that loveliness
> Which others cannot understand.
>
> (*A.H.*, I, iii)

And in 'The Wedding Sermon' is found he who marries without experience and without the compulsion of an overpowering love:

> A youth pursues
> A maid whom chance, not he, did choose,
> Till to his strange arms hurries she
> In a despair of modesty.
> Then simply and without pretence
> Of insight or experience
> They plight their vows. The parents say:
> 'We cannot speak them yea or nay;
> The thing proceedeth from the Lord!'
> And wisdom still approves their word;
> For God created so these two
> They match as well as others do
> That take more pains, and trust Him less
> Who never fails, if ask'd, to bless
> His children's helpless ignorance
> And blind election of life's chance.
> Verily, choice not matters much,
> If but the woman's truly such,
> And the young man has led the life
> Without which how shall e'er the wife
> Be the one woman in the world?
> Love's sensitive tendrils sicken, curl'd

Round folly's former stay; for 'tis
The doom of all unsanction'd bliss
To mock some good that, gain'd, keeps still
The taint of the rejected ill.

'Love is a recent discovery,' writes Patmore, 'and requires a new law. Easy divorce is the vulgar solution. The true solution is some undiscovered security for true marriage.'[1] The passage quoted above, from 'The Wedding Sermon', reveals where that security lies—in a realization of the permanent nature of the union, the freedom which bonds give and the sacramental graces of a vocation persisted in.

The Victories of Love sets out the development of love in a marriage by no means as fortunate as that of the Vaughans. Frederick's marriage to the humble Jane is complicated, not only by her lack of refinement, but also by Frederick's continued love for Honoria and his jealousy, even after marriage, of the successful Felix. As, in the unity of married life, and through the loss of two of their children, affection steadily grows, they attain a completeness of identification neither would earlier have thought possible.

So far as children are concerned, Patmore's conviction was: 'The best use of the supremely useful intercourse of man and woman is not the begetting of children, but the increase of contrasted personal consciousness.'[2] Children are the stay and the means of the consolidation of marriage, as well as its first purpose. They are, nevertheless, as much for love as for their own sakes:

> babes, chief fount
> Of union, and for which babes are
> No less than this for them, nay far
> More, for the very bond of man and wife
> To the very verge of future life
> Strengthens, and yearns for brighter day,
> While others, with their use, decay;
> And, though true marriage purpose keeps
> Of offspring, as the centre sleeps
> Within the wheel, transmitting thence
> Fury to the circumference,
> Love's self the noblest offspring is,
> And sanction of the nuptial bliss.
>
> (*V.L.*, 'Wedding Sermon')

Like the sleeping centre of the wheel, the procreation of children gives 'fury' or impetus to family life, yet, both in and through the

---

[1] *Rod, Root and Flower*, 'Aurea Dicta', CXXXV, p. 51.
[2] 'Distinction', *Principle in Art*, p. 63.

children, between husband and wife, as between parent and children, and between the children themselves:

Love's self the noblest offspring is.

Patmore's view of purity and virginity was intimately related to his idea of marriage. Having no love for that negative 'purity' which is the product of fear, and not of love, he did, however, have great regard for that pure virginity which represents conscious surrender of the good of married love so as to pursue the contemplative way of the 'divine nuptials'. But, in contrast to involuntary purity, purity in its strict sense is to be sought, he believed, in love sanctified by the sacrament of matrimony. The state of wedded lovers in a pure marriage is the highest point of the state of virginity. Control of passion and subordination of the will reveal depths of purity in married love, for marriage is a battle-ground, menaced all the time by custom and use, by opportunities for excess, by an intimacy easily abused. It calls, in the normal round, for an almost heroic strength. 'If you wish to be commonly good, the easiest, indeed the only way, is to be heroically so,'[1] Patmore writes. But the exercise of purity in marriage leads up to a peace and joy which comprise the greatest felicity mortal man can attain.

'Deliciae Sapientiae de Amore' proclaims the virginity which is a part of all pure love, whether directed towards a wife or a husband, or towards God. And here none is fairer than Mary Magdalene. For Patmore considered that virginity could be regained by penitence and turning to God in love, since the only sin which can not be forgiven is persistent and unrepentant unfaithfulness. As the shepherd gives special attention to the lost sheep, God loves with a special love the soul that repents and renews its purity; so, too, in the right disposition, human love may be increased by a total repudiation of past faults:

Love makes the life to be
A fount perpetual of virginity.

Thus he finds a place in his philosophy for the 'fallen woman' sentimentalized by Victorian writers. He saw beyond the conventional attitude towards the girl 'betrayed' and realized that it was, like the attitude towards the death of small children, a kind of compensatory gesture, a conscience-salving for the abuses of Victorian society. To some extent the much-prized 'purity' of Victorian womanhood was dependent, in social terms, upon the

[1] Champneys, *Memoirs*, Vol. II, p. 76.

amount of contempt levelled at her 'fallen' cousin and at the prostitutes. In the only passage in his printed works in which he discusses the matter, Patmore offers comfort to the 'woman betrayed' by suggesting in a paradox which, while it does not justify the sin, almost says *O Felix culpa!*, that such a lapse as hers may be the occasion of grace and love unknown by those who with hypocritical smugness abhor her state:

> Behold the worst! Light from above
>   On the blank ruin writes 'Forbear!
> 'Her first crime was unguarded love,
>   'And all the rest, perhaps, despair.'
> Discrown'd, dejected, but not lost,
>   O, sad one, with no more a name
> Or place in all the honour'd host
>   Of maiden and of matron fame,
> Grieve on; but, if thou grievest right,
>   'Tis not that these abhor thy state,
> Nor would'st thou lower the least the height
>   Which makes thy casting down so great.
> Good is thy lot in its degree;
>   For hearts that verily repent
> Are burdened with impunity
>   And comforted by chastisement.
> Sweet patience sanctify thy woes!
>   And doubt not but our God is just,
> Albeit unscathed thy traitor goes,
>   And thou art stricken to the dust.
> That penalty's the best to bear
>   Which follows soonest on the sin;
> And guilt's a game where losers fare
>   Better than those who seem to win.
>   (*A.H.*, I, xi)

There is a rather curious unpublished note among the Patmore papers in the Princeton Library which indicates that he did not always find it easy, in the ordinary business of living, to maintain his high ideal of womanhood. The crotchety side of his temperament, which usually spares man's 'glory', provoked perhaps by some domestic disagreement or a realization of inner tension, here extends itself in a caustic comment on the nature of woman. Since the poet never committed it to print, it is unfair to take it as revealing a considered point of view on women in general; yet it is of some importance in expressing his conviction that marriage must be based upon 'mutual integrity' of love, in placing the chief blame for woman's downfall on the wrong attitude of man, and in giving another statement of his views on the 'woman betrayed'. The note reads:

'The worst men respect woman more than the best women respect themselves. A man, however degraded he may be, has a secret horror of an innocent young woman allowing the last intimacies to a man whom she does not passionately love; but the innocent young woman, with full knowledge, usually yields, without remorse, the sanctities of her person to any man, whose companionship is not actually repulsive, in order to "improve her station" and to get a house and babies of her own. The man she regards as an *accident*. This proves that she has really no consciousness of personal sanctity, which is indeed so horribly outraged, if only she could see it, by bodily conjunction without mutually passionate love, that—though it would not do to preach the doctrine—it is absolutely true that adultery, with such love, is far less essentially immoral than the most exemplary marriage without it. The only consolation for this state of things is in the recollection that sanctities which are wholly undiscerned are not interiorly profaned by external outrage, and that these poor young women are to be pitied, rather than condemned. I am told that a favourite exhibition in the lower theatres of Paris is that of a female infant who, hoisted on the shoulders of a man, sings obscene songs. But so shameless, so pitiable and often so blameless is the position of most good married women in Europe. America alone yearns for better things, though she seeks, in facility of divorce, what can only be legitimately and effectually cured by the formation of a popular conscience that marriage is more shameful and irreparable than any other form of sin unless it has been at least initiated in mutual integrity of love. The blame is chiefly man's, for woman learns herself from him, and she will only begin to respect herself when she is made to feel that all available men reverence her person as something inviolable and divine, and require that she should in like manner reverence herself.

"Ah, wasteful woman, etc."'

This view of loveless marriage is much more extreme than anything in his published writings; it is unlikely that Patmore would have been prepared seriously to defend (even apart from whether or not it would do 'to preach the doctrine') his statement that 'adultery, with such love, is far less essentially immoral than the most exemplary marriage without it.' At the same time, the note helps to establish that his view of married love was different, in basic respects, from the conventional view of his age.

The key to Patmore's distinctive idea of love and to an understanding of the difference in emphasis between his earlier and his later poems may be found in these few lines from 'The Wedding Sermon':

For all delights of earthly love
Are shadows of the heavens, and move
As other shadows do; they flee
From him that follows them; and he
Who flies, for ever finds his feet
Embraced by their pursuings sweet.

The basic justification for fidelity in marriage, the key to the mystery of nuptial union and the explanation for the fact that even in the most happy of marriages, man's questing spirit of love is never completely fulfilled, lies in the doctrine that 'Nuptial love bears the clearest marks of being nothing other than the rehearsal of a communion of a higher nature.'[1] Marriage is the precursor to a higher mystery, the union of the soul with God, of which love it is a parable. This is the supernatural hypothesis on which his glorification of married love firmly rests.

As has been shown, it is, in Patmore's view, one of the conditions of love's development that it should have to conquer desire, frigidity, custom, convention and all other kinds of difficulties. But a more basic reason for the frustrations of even the happiest love is that it is only the foreshadowing of a greater love never to be satisfied on this earth. The soul

> sick longing breeds
> For marriage which exceeds
> The inventive guess of Love to satisfy
> With hope of utter binding and of loosing
> endless dear despair.
>
> (*U.E.*, 'Sponsa Dei')

As he puts it in 'The Precursor':

'Every one who has loved and reflected on love for an instant, knows very well that what is vulgarly regarded as the end of that passion is, as the Church steadfastly maintains, no more than its accident. The flower is not for the seed, but the seed for the flower. And yet what is that flower, if it be not the rising bud of another flower, flashed for a moment before our eyes, and at once withdrawn, lest we should misunderstand the prophecy, and take it for our final good?'[2]

The pattern of wooing and winning, losing, wooing and winning again, only to lose again, the pursuit of her who 'spirit-like, eludes embrace' has its psychological reference, of course, and springs from Patmore's own experience and close observation of the 'ritual' of marriage, but, like almost everything else in *The Angel*, it has its supernatural reference as well. On that level, the elusive-

---

[1] 'Love and Poetry', *Religio Poetae*, p. 144.
[2] 'The Precursor', *Religio Poetae*, pp. 15–16.

ness of the spouse, the fact that man can never *quite* know and possess his wife, that, however intimate the communion, the lovers never wholly merge, that love ever promises more than it performs, are, for Patmore, empirical proofs that wedded love is but the preliminary to the nuptials of the soul with the Creator.

He brings every aspect of married life into harmony with this idea. The disappointment in marriage of the ecstatic expectation of courtship may be the greater as the love is greater:

> The more, indeed, is love, the more
> Peril to love is now in store.
>
> (*V.L.*, 'Wedding Sermon')

But if the maximum happiness is to come out of such a realization, both lovers must accept the fact that in each other is not the ultimate reality of love, but only a semblance and an anticipation:

> So, loyally o'erlooking all
> In which love's promise short may fall
> Of full performance, honour that
> As won, which aye love worketh at!
> It is but as the pedigree
> Of perfectness which is to be
> That our best good can honour claim.
>
> (*V.L.*, 'Wedding Sermon')

Therefore, that the 'course of true love never did run smooth' was not for Patmore an indication of love's imperfection so much as a living proof that nuptial love is the base of the ladder which leads up to the eternal nuptials. If there are problems and mysteries in such an analogy, why should there not be?

> The truths of Love are like the sea
> For clearness and for mystery

begins 'The Wedding Sermon'. Thus the constant refrain of his entire treatment of love is:

> Though love is all of earth that's dear,
> Its home, my children, is not here:
> The pathos of eternity
> Does in its fullest pleasure sigh
>
> (*V.L.*, 'Wedding Sermon')

And he saw so clearly the direction in which his poetic impulse was leading him that he could write, early in *The Angel in the House*:

> This little germ of nuptial love,
> Which springs so simply from the sod,
> The root is, as my song shall prove
> Of all our love to man and God.
>
> (*A.H.*, I, vi)

By relating married love thus closely to Divine love he redeemed love from the spiritual and physical adultery which some poets had offered as its fulfilment; and he was able at the same time to face the physical facts of marriage with a frankness and tact not easy to match in his time. The sexual intimacies of marriage were not, in his eyes, ludicrous, or the mere source of animal gratification but actually godlike, for they were, in semblance, the way of God Himself with the human soul and with His universe. This way was wonderful to him, not because it is divorced from human experience, but, on the contrary, because it is so deeply rooted in it:

> How long shall men deny the flower
> Because its roots are in the earth,
> And crave with tears from God the dower
> They have, and have despised as dearth. . . .
> (*A.H.*, I, vii)

Only when man accepts the Reality of God's love as mirrored in, and as proceeding from, the 'reality' of every day will he refrain from thinking and speaking of love in terms of a debilitating abstraction. The Church itself has not been without fault in this, in his view, for it has been infected with the puritanism of the Reformation, and has thus under-stressed or thrust aside implications which the poet regarded as self-evident:

> 'That human love which is the precursor and explanation of and initiation into the divine', he writes, ' . . . has been so deeply branded with the charge of impurity which its celestial candour rebukes in its mortal subjects that modern preachers and pietists have studiously ignored or positively condemned as carnal and damnable the greatest of all graces and means of grace.'[1]

If, then, the theme of the revelatory and anticipatory character of earthly love is an essential element in *The Angel* and *The Victories*, what is the difference between his treatment of love in these earlier poems and in *The Unknown Eros*?

Some critics take it for granted that the earlier poems deal with human love, and the later ones with Divine love. The strongest opponent of this 'easy antithesis' is Frederick Page, who devotes a great part of his *Patmore—A Study in Poetry* to the establishment of an essential continuity in Patmore's thought and work. He writes:

> 'The poem with the theological title is supposed to deal with married love as purely physical, domestic and social as it can be among pro-

---

[1] *Rod, Root and Flower*, 'Magna Moralia', p. 197.

fessing Christians; and in the poem with the mythological title Eros and Psyche are God and the Soul. Thus the summarist deftly reverses the telescope in which Patmore shows us God as Eros.'[1]

He points out that in a note-book of 1861, Patmore wrote: 'It must be impressively shown that Felix and Honoria also look to Heaven for the fruition of their love',[2] and that he made notes for a poem to be called 'The Wife in Heaven'. The coherence of Patmore's work, Page finds in 'Dieu et ma Dame', adding that the writers of handbooks have reversed the order, and think they have indicated the time sequence of his thought, whereas, in fact, God, Nature, Woman, Man are all actual and intervolved.[3]

Page's point is surely sound; as the quotations from *The Angel* and *The Victories*, which have been given above, should be sufficient to show, in writing his poems of domestic love, Patmore had always in mind the supernatural experience which runs through and beyond marriage. Yet, in destroying the illusion of a dichotomy between *The Angel* and its sequel on the one hand, and *The Unknown Eros* on the other, Frederick Page tends to blur the fact that between the two groups of poems there is, if not a change in philosophy, certainly a marked change in tone and emphasis. Unquestionably Patmore believed much the same when he wrote the later poems as he did when he wrote the earlier ones, yet, after his conversion, his reading of Catholic theology and mysticism so enriched his knowledge and his imagination that the final truths rather than the immediate ones excited him more, and those ideas of the nuptial analogy, presented epigrammatically or in almost gnomic phrases in *The Angel* became in *The Unknown Eros* vibrant, intense, uttered with lyrical intoxication. It might be said that, while in the early poems the human aspect of his philosophy is chiefly stressed, in the later poems the divine aspect is stressed. As Osbert Burdett has it: 'The Odes, therefore, provide the transcendental philosophy, which is built upon the data of experience, and these data it is the delight of The *Angel* to provide.'[4]

He elevated and spiritualized human love in *The Angel in the House*, and humanized Divine Love in *The Unknown Eros*. In the later work is no celebration of an abstract desire, but a revelation of a personal intimacy, the secret experience of one who was himself passing upwards from the joys of married love to another, higher love. This, for Patmore, is the goal of life and the heart of its mystery, the burning heart of the Universe. And only those who

---

[1] *Patmore, A Study in Poetry*, p. 12. [2] *Ibid.*, p. 104. [3] *Ibid.*, p. 127
[4] 'Coventry Patmore', *Dublin Review*, Oct.–Nov. 1919, p. 255.

have on earth understood and experienced love can have any conception of, or are in a fit condition to obtain, the love of God. For, as he writes: 'Divine love and sweetness cannot exist where there has been no knowledge of natural love and sweetness.'[1]

The intimacies of the lovers in *The Angel* and its sequel are paralleled in the Psyche odes by the intimacies of God with the soul. Patmore saw nothing incongruous in this analogy; on the contrary, the intimacies of bodily love have, in his view, validity and sanction only as they have their transcendental parallel. The essay 'Dieu et ma Dame' traces some of the main analogies, 'say rather identities', between Divine and human love. As Swedenborg found in Biblical passages endless correspondences, level upon level of significance, so Patmore believed that such analogies could be prolonged almost indefinitely. There is essentially no difference in mode, although a difference in height and reference, between the love of man for woman and that of God for the soul. And, to attain the latter, the former love must be not rejected, but accepted and treasured as the precious initiation into the destined end of man. The heroine of the domestic poems is not, then, Honoria or Jane; it is the bisexual 'Angel' of Love; it is 'homo', as it is manifested in the union of bodies and minds which marriage alone makes possible. So, the heroine of the Odes is Psyche, the soul, the bride of God, also 'homo'. And the heroine of all the poems is seen at length to be the Blessed Virgin Mary, who attains the fullness of human love in her virgin marriage with Joseph, the perfection of motherhood in the home at Nazareth, and the fullness of Divine Love in bearing the Divine Child of her Child, God Himself.

Patmore characteristically reinforces the nuptial analogy by symbolical significances drawn not only from the mystics, but also from the Bible, the Liturgy and Catholic dogma. In *Religio Poetae* he refers to the Miracle at Cana, as an analogy of the Incarnation and of the Eucharist.[2] And, in affirming the reality of God's intimacy with the soul, he again used the analogy of the Eucharist:

> 'Should any believing reader object that such thoughts as I have suggested to him imply an irreverent idea of the intimacies of God with His elect, I beg him to remember that in receiving the Blessed Sacrament with the faith which the Church demands, he affirms and *acts* a familiarity which is greater than any other that can be conceived.'[3]

The essential orthodoxy of Patmore's thought, even in such an apparently daring analogy, is pointed by some remarks of Paul

---

[1] 'A Safe Charity', *St. James's Gazette*, Aug. 27, 1887; *Courage in Politics*, p. 50. [2] 'Religio Poetae', *Religio Poetae*, p. 9.
[3] 'Dieu et Ma Dame', *Religio Poetae*, p. 174.

Claudel, who, without reference to those passages of Patmore in which marriage is related to the Eucharist, makes the comparison on his own account, and calls in Bellarmine as witness.[1]

In one of his last poems, written in 1882, he summed up his entire conception of married love, of the 'homo', of the love of God for the soul, and of the relation of the sexes to each other and to God, by means of the image of the triune Angel. This poem was originally entitled 'Scire Teipsum', but renamed 'The Three Witnesses'. Of it Patmore wrote to Gosse: 'They (the verses) may be taken . . . as expressing the rewards of virginity—attainable even in this life—in the supernatural order.'[2] But it is more than that, a vision of the blessed in communion with God, and a symbolical presentation of human love, in a remarkable synthesis of his leading ideas:

> Musing I met, in no strange land,
> What meet thou must to understand;
> An Angel. There was none but he,
> Yet 'twas a glorious company.
> God, Youth and Goddess, one, twain, trine,
> In altering wedlock flamed benign.
> The Youth i' the midst did shadowy seem,
> Till merged in either blest extreme,
> But could, by choosing, each way turn,
> And, with God, for the Goddess burn,
> Or vanish in the Goddess quite,
> To be, with her, the God's delight;
> And, whether he chose Hers or His,
> He glow'd at once with either's bliss.
> The head was Godhead without guile,
> A solar force, an infant's smile;
> Breasted the Wonder was and loin'd
> With Man and Woman's beauties join'd;
> And thence, O, moonlike and most sweet,
> The Goddess brighten'd to the feet,
> Which, when they felt the one the other
> Felt each like Cupid and his Mother.
> Unwearying, since I caught that sight,
> Him have I praised by whose word's might
> The Heavens and the Earth did breathe
> And the gay Waters underneath.

The Angel in the poem is, of course, Love—single, but containing God, Man and Woman. The 'altering wedlock' in which the Youth-Man could merge in 'either blest extreme' refers to the earthly

---

[1] 'Lettre sur Coventry Patmore', *Positions et Propositions*, Vol. II, p. 31.
[2] *Coventry Patmore*, pp. 161–162.

nuptials into which man enters as husband and the heavenly nuptials in which man's soul enters as bride. So, too, the Goddess—Woman —is bride to the husband, and, as a soul, bride to God. Man can look either way, to God or to the woman, with a love of the same nature, and since both male and female souls are female to God, who is the masculine force, so the Goddess, woman, is, like the man, the 'glory' and the delight of the Creator's love. In 'homo' each partakes of the other's nature. When man loves God, the glory of God is reflected in him; when he loves woman, his glory is reflected in her. God, too, as the poem indicates, is revealed in the sun, or nature, and in the innocence and the acceptances of childhood. The androgynous nature of the Angel is a mark of the nature of 'homo'; but it is also a sign of God Himself, who, as Patmore says, contains in Himself 'the Divine Manhood and the Divine Womanhood'.[1]

[1] *Rod, Root and Flower*, 'Homo', XI, p. 115.

PART FOUR

ASPECTS OF PATMORE'S PROSE

I

The Writer of Prose

WHEN P. G. PATMORE FLED TO FRANCE to escape his creditors, Coventry, unfitted for any other kind of work, turned to writing periodical articles for a living, beginning with contributions to *Douglas Jerrold's Shilling Magazine*. Later, when he was installed in the British Museum Library, the smallness of his income, the demands of a growing family and his wife's long illness forced him to continue such work. Determined to be a poet, he dreaded at first that, being without a profession, he might be 'compelled, *faute de mieux*, to take to that of a literary hack and magazine writer'.[1] His prose reviews and articles were, for him, impediments to the cultivation of poetry, and, as he came to deprecate his first volume of poems, so, too, he was accustomed to look down on his early prose.

When his second marriage in 1864 brought him financial security, he was vastly relieved to be able to give up prose entirely, save for the perfunctory life of 'Barry Cornwall' written in 1877 out of a sense of obligation to Mrs. Procter. However, after the publication, in 1884, at Gosse's instigation, of Marianne and Coventry's translation of St. Bernard, Patmore was persuaded to embark upon a long series of articles, for various papers, chiefly the *St. James's Gazette*. Between March 1885 and August 1888 he contributed over one hundred articles to the latter journal. Thus, apart from the

1 Champneys, *Memoirs*, Vol. I, p. 64.

'Cornwall' biography and the St. Bernard translation, neither characteristic, Patmore's prose falls into two distinct periods, separated by about twenty years. Almost all the pieces collected in his various volumes were written after 1885: *How I Managed and Improved My Estate* (1886), an account of his work on his Sussex property, Heron's Ghyll; *Hastings, Lewes, Rye and the Sussex Marshes* (1887), a largely descriptive work; *Principle in Art* (1889) and *Religio Poetae* (1893), consisting very largely of articles which originally appeared in the *St. James's Gazette*. *The Rod, The Root and the Flower*, a gathering of new material, aphorisms and very brief essays, appeared a year before his death.

Altogether about two hundred periodical articles can be identified as either positively or almost certainly Patmore's,[1] essays ranging from the forty-page pieces he wrote for the *Edinburgh Review* to three-page articles for the *St. James's Gazette*. Of these, almost all written after 1885 have been reprinted; but of those produced between 1845 and 1866 only two appear in later collections— 'Madame de Hautefort', and 'English Metrical Critics', which, as 'Essay on English Metrical Law', formed an appendix to the *Collected Poems* of 1886. The remainder, almost half of Patmore's total output, remain uncollected from the various journals in which they originally appeared. Patmore himself told Buxton Forman that he wished his name to be connected with only five of these early pieces, including the 'Essay on English Metrical Law' and 'The Sources of Expression in Architecture'.[2] However, Frederick Page has noted that on the manuscripts of several other articles Patmore has written 'Reprint entire' or 'Reprint in part', including his interesting essay on Tennyson's *Maud* and *In Memoriam*, a criticism of the 'Spasmodics' and a piece on de Biran's *Pensées*.[3]

Despite Patmore's own concentration on his later prose, the early pieces are important as revealing the birth and development of his main ideas. These essays are often, in the manner of the day, inordinately lengthy; he was accustomed to use the books he was given to review as the occasion for a substantial discussion of some aesthetic principle, sometimes only vaguely related to the books themselves. The style, too, is by no means as disciplined as that of the later essays; it is often wordy where the latter are concise, and repetitive where they are direct. At the same time, these articles have been unfairly neglected. Apart from their often great intrinsic

---

[1] See Bibliography, in which a complete list of Patmore's essays is given, together with the evidence for ascription.

[2] Champneys, *Memoirs*, Vol. I, p. 109.

[3] See Appendix, *Courage in Politics*.

interest, with their shrewd literary criticism and their enunciation
of critical principles, they are also valuable as showing the consistency of Patmore's thought on questions of art, literature and
religion, and as disclosing his especial interest in metrical theory and
his working out of the concepts of subject-matter and technique he
was to employ in his major poems.

In the prose of the second period there is little change in fundamental outlook, but a natural marked increase in religious and
mystical discourse. The chief difference is a stylistic one, and lies
in the greatly increased tautness of expression. However, while few
of the early essays deal directly with politics, several of those written
after 1885 reflect the Toryism Patmore developed in his days of
financial security, and were produced with the encouragement of
Frederick Greenwood, the editor of the *St. James's Gazette*, and a
friend of Patmore's, many of whose opinions he shared. The
literary articles, which still predominate, show less concern with
technical problems and more with the values of poetry. After
Greenwood resigned from the *St. James's Gazette*, Patmore wrote
only a few articles, mainly for the Meynells' *Merry England*, and the
Anti-Jacobin; but concentrated his attention on the editing of the
collections and on the production of new material to round them
out.

Patmore's prose is always readable, energetic and free from affec-
tation. His early style is somewhat in the tradition of 'journal
rhetoric', with frequent long periods, a touch (but no more) of the
pontifical, and with a certain tendency to hammer home a point by
repetition. Yet it is never artificial, self-consciously rhythmical nor
loaded with poetic figures. He was always concerned with what he
was saying, and with saying it as lucidly as possible. He is brimming
over with ideas, especially on art and poetry, which often so excite
him that he will seize the least excuse to discuss them. His prose
always suggests 'masculine force' (to use one of his favourite
critical labels) and vigour. For instance, in an essay on Tennyson's
The Princess, he writes:

> 'Art, then, properly so called, and as it differs from mere imitation, is
> always, in a certain degree, metaphorical and enigmatical; consequent-
> ly, when the meaning of a work of art is just, the work may be said,
> not so much to inculcate, as to be, the truth; and where it is appreci-
> ated, it acts, not by giving "information" in the modern sense of the
> word, but by informing, in the sense in which the word was used by
> the accurate and thoughtful writers of the sixteenth and seventeenth
> centuries; that is to say, by inducing the mind actively to take upon
> itself for the time at least, a new and excellent shape, namely, that of

the artist's work, as the only clue to the comprehension of it. The open recommendations to holiness of any other preceptor than art, are likely to be heard and understood without being adopted, the mind is able to perceive their beauty and can derive a lazy satisfaction from its contemplation, without at all becoming the thing contemplated; but art is like religion in the treatment of her votaries. She helps those who strive to help themselves.'[1]

There is nothing impersonal about this style. Patmore's personality comes out in his certainties, his high moral code, his ideals of good literature, his stress on principles, but also in his irony and humour, sometimes gentle, more often sardonic, and in his gift for paradox and epigram.

His humour and his sharp-edged wit enable him to make many telling critical points, as in his delightfully ironical description of 'Spasmodic' poetry,[2] his analysis of Longfellow's *Psalm of Life* ('It is flattering to find that one's most commonplace opinions are thought worthy of being expressed with such emphasis')[3] and in many of his architectural pieces. His illustrative imagery, used with sparing skill, catches the attention of the reader and helps to 'fix' the argument. Elizabeth Barrett Browning's imagination is 'not sufficiently weighted with rule', he writes, so that it 'pitches, like a kite without a tail'[4]; Longfellow has 'no sufficient feeling of the fact that a poem is like the mirror of a telescope in this—that it is *the last rub which polishes it* and makes it capable of reflecting the heavens.'[5] So, too, his keen wit enables him to strike out many sentences which have the weight and feel of a good epigram: 'Simplicity is not the absence of intricacy, but its solution'[6]; 'Beauty is sustained by truth, as the poppy by the corn'[7]; 'Mr. Bailey flogs the vices and follies of the age with a rod of rushes pickled in milk-and-water.'[8]

There are touches of impatience and testiness in these early essays; and now and then marked prejudices intrude. Yet, these qualities rarely irritate; they merely offer evidence of a mind that

[1] 'Tennyson's *Poems—The Princess*', *North British Review*, May 1848, p. 50.

[2] 'New Poets', *Edinburgh Review*, Vol. CIV, No. 212, Oct. 1856, p. 344.

[3] 'American Poetry', *North British Review*, August 1852, pp. 404–405.

[4] 'Mrs. Browning's Poems', *North British Review*, Vol. XXVI, No. LII, Feb. 1857, p. 448.

[5] 'American Poetry', *North British Review*, August 1852, p. 402.

[6] 'Tennyson's *Poems—The Princess*', *North British Review*, May 1848, p. 51.

[7] 'Ruskin's *Stones of Venice*', *British Quarterly Review*, Vol. XIII, No. XXVI, p. 489.

[8] 'The Decay of Modern Satire', *North British Review*, Vol. XXIX, No. LVIII, Nov. 1858, p. 517.

knows itself and of rugged common-sense. The faults are an excessive wordiness—Patmore would certainly have extensively revised them had he republished any—a tendency, inevitable in hasty periodical articles, to repeat the same ideas in different essays, and, now and then, a perfunctoriness about the critical judgments. At the same time, there can be no doubt that the man who wrote them also wrote *Religio Poetae, Principle in Art* and *The Rod, the Root and the Flower.*

Of the essays in these later volumes, Arthur Symons wrote: 'Only in the finest of his poems has he surpassed these pages of chill and ecstatic prose.'[1] Yet Hopkins was much less enthusiastic. Patmore, like Newman, he said, did not so much write prose as think aloud with pen to paper. This process, he avowed, excluded the belonging technique, the belonging rhetoric, the own proper eloquence of written prose:

> 'Each thought is told off singly and there follows a pause and this breaks the continuity of the *contentio*, the strain of address, which writing should usually have. . . . You too seem to me to be saying to yourself, "I am writing prose, not poetry; it is bad taste and a confusion of kinds to employ the style of poetry in prose: the style of prose is to shun the style of poetry and to express one's thoughts with point." But the style of prose is a positive thing and not the absence of verse-forms and pointedly expressed thoughts are single hits and give no continuity of style.'[2]

In making this criticism, Hopkins is assuming that all prose should conform to the older type of 'persuasive' prose, and that the ideal style is that which combines sublimity of thought with certain rhetorical and rhythmical effects—a kind of prose which Patmore had no intention of producing, and which, had he been capable of it, would, in any case, have been inappropriate to his purposes. In an essay on Sir Thomas Browne, he shows that he is well aware of the difference between the kind of writing Hopkins was disappointed not to find in his work, and that which he actually produced. Modern prose he traces to the pamphleteering of the seventeenth century. Pre-revolutionary prose, he says, employed a varying flow of music, which aimed at convincing the feelings, as the words themselves the understanding. 'The best post-revolutionary prose appeals to the understanding alone, and is, as a rule, and in proportion to its perfection, an exquisite craft, but no fine art.'[3]

[1] *Figures of Several Centuries*, p. 362.
[2] *Further Letters of Gerard Manley Hopkins*, pp. 231–232.
[3] 'Sir Thomas Browne', *St. James's Gazette*, April 1, 1886; *Courage in Politics*, p. 55.

Style was for Patmore what Newman, in fact, called it, 'a thinking out into words'. He is concerned primarily with clarity of expression, rather than with graces; yet the flexibility of his style, within its self-imposed limits, is illustrated by the essential difference in tone between 'Religio Poetae', where the seriousness of his theme urges Patmore to a pitch of intense and forceful expression, and the collected group named 'Architectural Styles', in which a cogent argument is developed out of a great number of technical details handled with easy skill. Hopkins does, however, put his finger on a weakness in Patmore's prose. Some of the later essays, such as 'Dieu et ma Dame' and 'Seers, Thinkers and Talkers', have the air of slackly organized strings of aphorisms, and appear to be almost an intermediary form between the firmly constricted critical essays and the dicta in *The Rod, the Root and the Flower*. There is, however, even in such essays, a progressive movement of thought; and they do have a clear, if rather loose, structure. Because Patmore believed that mystical apprehensions must be to a large degree expressed aphoristically, he found it less easy to write structurally taut essays on such topics than on literary and political ones. But, even if the difference were greater than it is between the styles in the two kinds of essay, Hopkins was hardly justified in generalizing on the basis of the two or three essays Patmore sent him. Patmore wrote in a style which was not the norm in his age, at least for professional literary men. Newman is almost the only other considerable contemporary prose-writer who was using a development of the older 'plain style' tradition, in which plain statement, logical sequence and a shunning of extraneous ornament are some of the chief results aimed at. Patmore's work had no affinity with the 'poetic prose' of his admired Jeremy Taylor, and of such of his friends as Ruskin. His purpose is to set out, as clearly as the nature of the subject will allow, personal judgments, and provocative insights woven into the form of expositions, and to jolt his readers into a re-examination of familiar responses and phenomena by a skilful use of paradox.

The Jesuit's more scholastically trained mind would have liked more formal presentation of ideas as well as more 'belonging rhetoric'; he is impatient with Patmore's leaps of thought, with his taking something for granted because he has already written about it, not once, but a dozen times before. Moving as he does from his base of 'self-evident' truths and riding his hobby-horses a little hard, Patmore at times certainly gives the impression of authoritarianism. Where Newman patiently reasons out his premises and proceeds from there, Patmore often assumes his premises and plunges straight into one of his 'corollaries'. He is thus, on occasion, wayward and fallacious; yet these very things, combined with his use of the plainest language, give his prose a piquancy and a vitality such as, to a modern reader, much of the self-conscious prose of, say, Pater does not now possess. The 'graces' which Hopkins apparently missed in the older poet's prose are the very things which render much Victorian writing virtually unreadable today. In sum, then, Patmore aimed at the beauty of precision and not at the beauty of elaborate arrangement and rhythmical effects. It is significant that he had the greatest respect for the bare style of Aquinas:

> 'Aquinas is to Dante as the Tableland of Thibet is to the Peak of Teneriffe; and the first is not less essentially a poet, in the sense of a Seer, because his language is even more austere, and without ornament than that of the latter.[1]

The later essays, then, written in a vigorous, provocative style, rich in the concentrated experience of a life-time of reading and meditation, covering a wide range of subjects, from political theory, critical analysis and descriptions of Nature to metaphysical discussion; they mingle outrageous paradox and piercing insight, lofty impersonality and marked individuality, severe common-sense and ineradicable prejudice, startling leaps of mystical speculation and the plainest of moral teaching. Their confident tone sometimes stimulated immediate reactions, especially on political matters. 'Thoughts on Knowledge, &c' provoked vigorous dissent from both the *Spectator* and the *Guardian*. To the charges that he confused the 'elect' with the 'select', he replied in the essay 'Distinction', wherein with irony and sarcasm he defends his position and sets out his conception of individuality. This is a revealing personal statement, in which it is impossible not to recognize that Patmore is enjoying himself hugely, and secretly relishing that picture of himself drawn by his critics as an aristocratic scorner of the mob. Yet, in it, he also shows a spirit of half-joking raillery, of 'chaff', as he called it. The same kind of half-humorous defence of his intuitions, both Champneys and Gosse record, characterized much of his conversation. Such a mood must be kept in mind lest the reader of 'Distinction' take wholly seriously his castigation of democratic ideas and his disdain of the mob.

Not all his friends, Alice Meynell and Frederick Greenwood among them, understood this impish quality in Patmore, and it must be admitted that sometimes his irony was apt to become a

---

[1] 'Religio Poetae', *Religio Poetae*, p. 7.

little heavy-handed. In most of his articles, of course, he was not 'chaffing', but engaged in a serious presentation of his ideas. Aubrey de Vere used a revealing phrase when he described *Principle in Art* as using the '*Affirmative* as distinguished from *Demonstrative* method'.[1] 'Affirmative' is a good name for the later prose, in which Patmore writes as 'prophet', 'seer' and 'poet'. The smooth combination of long and short sentences shows his firm control of his material, and reinforces the impression of the language itself that here is someone with something positive and important to say. Like the earlier ones, these essays are enlivened by a judicious but most felicitous use of imagery, much of which springs from close observation of Nature. Emerson, for instance, could not see 'that a religion of which there is nothing left but an "over-soul" is much the same as a man of whom there is nothing left but his hat',[2] while women unclothed of the sentiment of surrounding manhood 'are as unsightly a spectacle' as the animal called a hermit-crab, 'when, by some chance, it is ejected, bare, comfortless, and unprotected, from the shell of its adoption.'[3]

The Rod, the Root and the Flower is largely transcendental epigram and paradox, but irony and scorn tinge the other late prose, as, for instance:

> 'It cannot but soften the most religious tradesman's heart to find that his brother-tradesman, who holds the Catholic faith, will, as a rule, cheat as readily as he will himself; and such differences of opinion as the holding by one party that lying is a venial sin and detracting a mortal one, and, by the other, that the guilt of these actions is exactly the reverse, cease to be injurious to amicable relations when it is observed that Catholics and Protestants as a rule are equally given to lying and detracting.'[4]

Patmore's prose, then, has genuine distinction and more virtues than the usual concentration on four or five essays from *Religio Poetae* reveals. In the preface to *The Rod, the Root and the Flower* he says of his own writing that it has been found by some 'as Fuseli said of Blake, "D——d good to steal from"', and indeed some of his ideas have unobtrusively found their way into later works through the writings of such of his friends as Francis Thompson, Alice Meynell, Aubrey de Vere and even Ruskin. It is almost certainly the matter—the esoteric ideas, the metaphysics—of some

1 Champneys, *Memoirs*, Vol. II, p. 339.
2 'Emerson', *Principle in Art*, p. 118.
3 'The Weaker Vessel', *Religio Poetae*, pp. 157–158.
4 'How is it to End?', *St. James's Gazette*, March 23, 1887; *Courage in Politics*, p. 26.

of the later essays that causes his prose to be little read today, save for the highly charged *Rod, Root and Flower*. There is, however, a possibility of the revival of his best prose, which will stand beside some of the finest written in his own time, and above a good deal of the most highly praised written since. His violence, his exaggerations and his more extreme paradoxes have been somewhat softened by time, but his prose still conveys the impression of a forceful and original personality and a very keen, if somewhat eccentric, mind; while essay after essay gives off a real heat.

His writing shows a particularly subtle use of simple words, and has a clear air of authority. Though he has a tendency to confuse invention with apprehension, and some of his expositions contain disconcerting leaps, he is never dull; the interplay of wit and insight is remarkable. In the best of Patmore's later essays there is that felicity of style and distinction of thought which is usually associated with the word 'classic'.

II

The Literary Critic

<hr>

'MR. PATMORE DOES NOT AIM AT "APPRECIATION"', but at the elucidation of principles', wrote Francis Thompson in a review of Patmore's *Religio Poetae*,[1] thus succinctly stating the main difference between his own criticism and that of the older poet. Whereas Thompson is a fairly typical nineteenth-century 'appreciator', whose weakness as a critic lies in his lack of a body of principles and a consistent critical standpoint, Patmore is always concerned with the search for generally valid critical criteria, and with the relationship between form and content. He is 'Classical' in his criticism, as Thompson is 'Romantic'.

As his interest in mysticism developed, Patmore became more inclined to seek symbolical meanings in literature, and to proclaim the seerdom of the poet. These ideas were not incompatible with his early beliefs about the moral function of literature; but are a logical development from them. As in his poetry, there is a consistency of outlook in Patmore's critical writing which allows it to be treated as a unit. On the other hand, he made no attempt to bring his critical principles together into a coherent body of doctrine. He wrote in one of his later essays:

> 'There already exists, in the writings and sayings of Aristotle, Hegel, Lessing, Goethe, and others, the greater part of the materials necessary for the formation of a body of Institutes of Art which would supersede and extinguish nearly all the desultory chatter which now passes for

[1] 'A Poet's Religion', *Merry England*, Sept. 1893. Reprinted in *Literary Criticism by Francis Thompson*, p. 211.

criticism, and which would go far to form a true and abiding popular taste. . . . The man, however, who could put such materials together, and add such as are wanting, does not live; or, at any rate, he is not known.[1]

Patmore certainly did not believe that he was that man. Many of his important critical comments were made in the course of book-reviewing; much that might have rounded out his ideas he left unwritten, and a good deal of his earlier criticism is tentative rather than final, showing him working out his own attitude towards poetry. The conclusions to which he came, especially in the articles written in the 'forties, were derived from both his poetic practice and his study of literature. Then, too, in his later years mystical inclinations and a critical intellectualism were in somewhat unequal balance in his mind, leading at times to paradox and contradiction. Hence it is unfair to the poet to attempt to make a water-tight formal system out of his critical suggestions. Nevertheless he was in the main consistent, even if incomplete; he was clear-headed; and his critical writings together approach as closely to a statement of critical aims and criteria as do those of any other writer of his age who was not primarily a critic. Patmore had much to say which was of the greatest value to criticism, some of it of enduring significance.

He had little use for what is sometimes called 'impressionistic criticism', 'emotional criticism', as he named it. 'True criticism', he wrote, 'appeals to the intellect, and rebukes the reader as often as it does the artist for his ignorance and his mistakes.'[2] From the beginning he emphasized the basic importance of the clear enunciation by the critic of rational grounds for his judgments. In what is almost certainly his first printed article, he says:

'To promulgate sound principles of criticism is one of the most serviceable offices that can be performed to literature. There is in everything a positive as well as a relative excellence. To judge of positive excellence requires a knowledge of the principles and elements of the thing criticized, whilst to judge comparatively is a mere empirical test applied according to the experience and capacity of the individual.'[3]

In contemporary periodical criticism, he felt there was excessive subjectivity and a lack of attention to formal and technical matters. Criticism such as that of Swinburne in Britain and of Victor Hugo in France represented the kind of 'creative' criticism against which

---

[1] 'Principle in Art', *Principle in Art*, p. 5.   [2] *Ibid.*, p. 2.
[3] 'Leigh Hunt's "Imagination and Fancy"', *Douglas Jerrold's Shilling Magazine*, Vol. I, Jan. 1845, p. 90.

all his instincts rebelled. He was similarly distrustful of that criticism which uses literary works as an occasion for cloudy philosophical speculation, as well as that which is too much concerned with biographical detail and literary gossip, 'the "chatter about Shelley" sort of thing', as he calls it.[1]

Against, then, what he considered to be the emotionalism, the bias, the insipidity and the 'puffing' of contemporary criticism, Patmore set himself to enunciate the principles on which sound critical analysis of literature, art and architecture should be based. One of these concerns the moral function of literature and its affirmative quality. He asserts that 'art must have for one of its conditions, a *tendency* to elevate'[2]; and that 'the poet, in order to secure a high and permanent standing, must be in the habit of wielding his instrument to some noble end'.[3] The poet and the novelist have, therefore, not only an obligation to embody in their work their intuitions of the good and the beautiful, but they must also be able to move others to wish to make contact with such values. The common object of both religion and art should be the stimulating of men to the pursuit of the ideal life. Consequently, he believes that the responsibility of the writer for the health of his teaching is hardly inferior to that of the preacher.[4]

This emphasis on the moral function of art belongs largely to Patmore's early criticism. While he did not abandon his idea that art has a moral dimension, his later essays make it plain that he is not pleading for an overtly didactic literature. He writes, for instance:

> 'The old commonplace that "Art is essentially religious" is so far true as that the true order of human life is the command, and in part the revelation, of God; but all direct allusion to Him may be as completely omitted as it is from the teaching of the Board School, and yet the art may remain "essentially religious".'[5]

The implication is that the essential content of great art is moral or religious in that, without directly teaching or preaching, without even fully comprehending the moral values implicit in their work, the great writers, the 'seers', by their understanding of human beings, and by their intuitive insight into the 'extra dimension' of existence, offer empirical proof of the reality of the truths expressed

[1] 'Coleridge', *St. James's Gazette*, June 13, 1887; *Courage in Politics*, p. 89.
[2] 'The Ethics of Art', *British Quarterly Review*, Nov. 1849, p. 442.
[3] 'Tennyson's *Poems—The Princess*', *North British Review*, p. 58.
[4] 'American Novels', *North British Review*, Vol. XX, No. XXXIX, Nov. 1853, p. 81.
[5] 'Bad Morality is Bad Art', *Principle in Art*, p. 22.

in religion. For, as Patmore has it, 'Bad morality is not a necessary condition of good art; on the contrary, bad morality is necessarily bad art, for art is human, but immorality is inhuman.'[1] There is an echo of Aquinas here, as there is also in his often-expressed view that 'order' and 'health' in literature, which proceed from an intuition of the laws of justice and truth and goodness, are the sources from which beauty springs. He writes in an essay on Goldsmith:

> 'There is no true poem or novel without "a moral": least of all such as, being all beauty (that is to say, all order), are all moral. . . . A "moral" is only inartistic when the artist has not sufficient strength of character and language to make it a real force, either as the kernel of disaster or felicity.'[2]

That is, although a literary work should be, in Patmore's sense, 'moral', it should not be 'moralizing'.

The greatest perversion of his function of which a poet can be guilty is to falsify the intuitions of youth, and to make light of the sacramental character of its love. Poets are the prophets of love, and are all the more powerful because, like the prophets of old, they are independent of the priests. The poet has no call to be a didactic counsellor or a social reformer. Indeed, the writer who turns aside from his task of embodying universal truth to immerse himself in strictly contemporary affairs must fail as a poet. It is not the poet's business to be a denouncer and reformer of abuses. He is the greatest of reformers, not because he expounds a programme, but because he embodies truth, justice, goodness in the form of beauty, and by doing so makes men love them.

> 'If he represents folly, vice, or any kind of uncomeliness, it is not in order to contemplate such evils in themselves, but in order to supply foils which shall set forth more strongly the irrefragable splendour of truth embodied in sensible loveliness.'[3]

In writing these words, Patmore apparently forgot his own political odes, with their topical references, their fierce Toryism and their burning invective, although he would probably have argued that the 'leprosy' of Gladstone was part of his own intuition into truth.

To be a true poet and faithful to his gift of seerdom, a man must co-operate with the grace of poetry. Patmore had a very clear conception of such a grace, considering poetic inspiration as parallel to

---

[1] *Ibid.*, p. 18.
[2] 'Goldsmith', *St. James's Gazette*, Jan. 16, 1888; *Courage in Politics*, p. 61.
[3] 'The Morality of "Epipsychidion"', *St. James's Gazette*, Nov. 13, 1886; *Courage in Politics*, p. 114.

the ecstasy of the saint, a point of view much like that expounded in more recent times by the Abbé Bremond in his *Prayer and Poetry*. The poet's intellect, thought Patmore, 'seems capable of a sort of independent sanctification'.[1] And of essentially religious art, he says:

> 'But the mere *intention* of the artist is not enough to make it so. When Homer and Milton invoked the Muse they meant a reality. They asked for supernatural *'grace'* whereby they might interpret life and nature.
>
> "By grace divine, not otherwise, O Nature, are we thine"
>
> says Wordsworth. This gift without which none can be a poet is essentially the same thing as that which makes the Saint.'[2]

This does not mean, of course, that the poet must in fact be a saint, or that the 'grace' of poetry has the same effect on the spiritual life of the poet as has supernatural grace. The degree of grace which suffices to make art good and beautiful may leave the poet himself unaffected. But even in the works of poets who have a false conception of the purpose of art, or who are themselves very little like saints, one may find passages which show that, in writing them, the poets were in fact under the influence of divine grace, and which alone, in Patmore's view, establish their real claim to be called poets. In sum, 'The Poet is, *par excellence*, the *perceiver*. . . . He occupies a quite peculiar position—somewhere between that of a Saint and that of Balaam's Ass.'[3]

This view of the nature of the poet derives, at least in part, from the theories of the earlier Romantics, but it is opposed to that of such later Romantics as Shelley in its refusal to allot to poetry the functions of religion and law-making, or to the poet the role of the priest. Although Patmore often appears to claim for the poet's insights the same kind of infallibility as he acknowledged in the dogma of the Catholic Church, he is always concerned to distinguish between the prophetic and the priestly functions. For instance, writing of Aubrey de Vere's poetry, he says:

> 'The poet is a prophet, not a priest, and the two offices have, from the earliest times, been wholly independent, even when they have not been antagonistic. The prophet has ever been to the truly universal Church, which includes all such as love the living truth with an ardour which "supersedes all the sacraments", what the priest has been to the "visible" body.'[4]

1 'Religio Poetae', *Religio Poetae*, p. 3.
2 'Bad Morality is Bad Art', *Principle in Art*, p. 22.
3 'Religio Poetae', *Religio Poetae*, pp. 2–3.
4 'Aubrey de Vere's Poems', *St. James's Gazette*, July 16, 1887; *Courage in Politics*, p. 155.

The language in which Patmore expresses these convictions reveals the effect of his later reading. Yet, save that he has adopted a more theological terminology, there is little in his later views on the nature of poetry which differs from the ideas contained in the essay, The Ethics of Art, written in 1849.

Few poets have held a more exalted view of their art than did Patmore. 'Poetical integrity', as he called it, was genuinely precious to him. On one occasion he wrote:

> 'I am the only poet of this generation, except Barnes, who has steadily maintained a literary conscience. . . . Though, of course, I may not be a competent judge of how good my best is, I am sure that I have given the world nothing but my best.'[1]

While the preface to the 1886 Collected Edition of his poems reads:

> 'With this reprint I believe that I am closing my task as a poet, having traversed the ground, and reached the end which, in my youth, I saw before me. I have written little, but it is all my best; I have never spoken when I had nothing to say, nor spared time or labour to make my words true. I have respected posterity; and should there be a posterity which cares for letters, I dare to hope that it will respect me.'

From such utterances, and similar ones scattered through Patmore's prose, it is easy to understand why what impressed Arthur Symons most when Patmore talked to him of his poetry was not what the poet said of technique, but 'the profound religious gravity with which he treated the art of poetry, the sense he conveyed to one of his own reasoned conception of its immense importance, its divinity.'[2]

Patmore saw that the integrity of a poet does not reside in his active life, which is judged socially, but is to be inferred from what he writes, for, while his actions may belie him, his words do not. A poet may fail to bring his external life into harmony with his interior desire, but his poems will reveal what he inwardly is, for in poets the power of language is so developed as to expose the very soul with a faithfulness of which the writer is often only partially conscious. Hence a writer cannot force the note and remain true to his vision. If he tries consciously to say 'fine things', instead of 'rendering his whole utterance a single true thing', or if he polishes over-much instead of relying on 'inward labour and true finish of passion', he violates integrity.

Real poetry, then, for Patmore, cannot be produced by men who

---

[1] Champneys, *Memoirs*, Vol. I, p. 261.
[2] 'Coventry Patmore', *Figures of Several Centuries*, p. 365.

are gifted only with clear observation and technical expertness. He believed that predominance of form over energy, and concern with language and imagery before human significance are sure signs of shallowness and interior corruption.[1] Fundamentally, poetry must be based on the feelings:

> 'Be the theme of the poet magnificent or humble, be it his purpose to justify the ways of God to man, or to publish the praise of the "small celandine", it is certain that, in order to sing, he must first feel. Poetry is truth or fact of properly human import and general intelligibility verbally expressed so as to affect the feelings.'[2]

However, at the same time, people can usually feel in art only in so far as simple perception exceeds the conscious understanding in any particular direction. Those used only to the analytical approach may not feel beauty which is appreciated by uneducated people. Yet, in a mature culture, this faculty may be suspended at will, and the educated man thus be able to respond to the beauty felt by children and ingenuous adults.

In effect, literature is controlled not by technique or fanaticism, but by inspiration; and, underneath every work of art there are laws which determine matter and form, which, in fact, condition the expression of particular feelings in different forms but of which the artist is by no means necessarily conscious. In all his criticism, Patmore is reaching out towards an *organic* conception of poetry, in which form and content are integrally related, and in which the completed work has a unity which is also its individuality. Everything he wrote about 'style' indicates that the organic concept constituted his ideal of poetry. His criticism of such writers as Rossetti and the later Tennyson shows that his dissatisfaction with them arose from his sense of a great disproportion between their technical skill and what they had to express. His own Odes represent, indeed, one of the most successful attempts in his age at an organic form of poetry.

That 'inward labour and true finish of passion' he admired were the products of that self-discipline which he saw as a part of the poet's creative personality.

His constant emphasis is on interior finish, a care with the execution so complete that in the poetic process all traces of workmanship are removed, and idea and expression become one; the ideal being, as one of his stray phrases has it, 'the song that *is* the

1 'Poetical Integrity', *Principle in Art*, pp. 45–46.
2 'New Poets', *Edinburgh Review*, Vol. CIV, No. 212, Oct. 1856, pp. 339–340.

thing it says'.[1] Poetry meant to be valued for its ingenuity or its purely verbal beauty was repugnant to him. Perhaps part of his difficulty in appreciating Hopkins's poetry was his feeling that the Jesuit's manner drew attention to itself rather too aggressively. For Patmore, the personality revealed in the highest kind of poetry is something other than a manner; it is a reflection of the poet's real self, which can be expressed only when freakishness and coarseness have been removed. His consistently high praise of William Barnes's poetry undoubtedly arose from a conviction that in Barnes's work the delicate and intangible traits which express personality are invariably revealed.

Temperamentally opposed to the freakishness of Bailey and the 'Spasmodic' school, to the intricately empty music of Swinburne, to the garrulousness of William Morris and to the overpolished verses of Rossetti, he always preferred the comparatively modest, small but perfect piece to the long and uneven work. Reviewing one of Robert Bridges's earlier works, he made a valuable distinction between the 'tense' and the 'intense' in literature, which reveals his distaste for Romantic frenzies and artificial poetic hysteria. The 'tense' he calls 'the vulgar counterfeit' of the real thing, 'an extravagant and unreal mockery of the intense, as hysterics are of true passion'. And he continues: 'In everything infinite, even in infinite sorrow, there is peace; and the true master of the intense in art is never so much disturbed by his subject as not to be able to express it with sincerity and grace, and to "temper extremities with extreme sweet"'.[2]

One of Patmore's criticisms of Keats is that he was defective in the assimilation of the sensual as opposed to the sensuous. He tests Keats and other poets by Milton's definition of poetry as 'simple, sensuous and passionate'; and keeps before him a critical ideal based upon harmony between the 'objective' and the 'subjective' elements in poetry. He believes that Blake, Keats and Rossetti, in different ways, destroy such an equilibrium. Yet in his view such a balance by no means excludes the personal element. On the contrary, it alone enables a poet to express his individuality without becoming incoherent or using chaotic forms:

'Whenever the poet enables us to see common and otherwise "commonplace" objects and events with a sense of uncommon reality and life, then we may be sure that this divine light is present . . . if we carefully analyse any very successful lyric or idyll which at first strikes

[1] *Rod, Root and Flower*, 'Aphorisms', p. 217.
[2] 'Eros and Psyche', *St. James's Gazette*, Dec. 31, 1885; *Courage in Politics*, pp. 149–150.

us as being simply a glorification of the "commonplace", we shall most often discover that it has some "motif" . . . which has this double quality of novelty and slightness, although the events and ideas which are set in play by that "motif" are of the most simple and ordinary kind.'[1]

Such passages as this reveal the intimate connection between Patmore's critical theories and judgments and his own poetic practice. The lines just quoted are, in their way, a justification of both the theme and the technique of *The Angel in the House* and *The Victories of Love*, as well as a recognition of the defects and limitations of that kind of 'popular' poetry to which *The Angel* and its sequels were believed by most of their readers to belong.

Despite some minor inconsistencies which are perhaps inevitable in one who did so much periodical reviewing, the general tendency of Patmore's criticism is against the current of popular middle-class reading, against the 'aesthetic' type of poetry, against excessive emotionalism, and towards moderation, control and unobtrusive finish.

His mature ideas on what constitutes the highest kind of literature appear in particular in two later essays Emotional Art and Peace in Life and Art. The first points out that, in the highest art, the emotions are assimilated into a vision which transcends them and which approximates to a sublime good sense. But Patmore is careful to indicate that he is not speaking of didactic art, for 'the ideals of the greatest artists are the morality of a sphere too pure and high for "didactic" teaching'.[2] The distinctive quality of great art, he asserts, is 'peace'—a quality higher than the ordinary emotions which are called for, or which a reader feels called upon to exhibit, before most literary works.

'Joy, and pathos of its privation, are the "pain" and "pleasure" of art, poetic "melancholy" and "indignation" being the sigh of joy indefinitely delayed and wroth at the obstruction of its good by evil. These form the main region of the lyric poet. But as joy and pathos are higher than pleasure and pain, being concerned with the possession or privation of a real good, so in *peace*—which is as much above joy as joy is above pleasure, and which can scarcely be called emotion, since it rests, as it were, in final good, the *primum mobile*, which is without motion—we find ourselves in the region of "great" art.'[3]

And this 'peace' is the most precious gift the arts can give to man. It is no negative, passive thing. It is the 'living order' which all

[1] 'William Barnes, the Dorsetshire Poet', *Macmillan's Magazine*, June 1862, p. 156.

[2] 'Emotional Art', *Principle in Art*, p. 27.   [3] *Ibid.*, pp. 28–29.

great art aspires to express, and it involves 'in its fullest perfection, at once the complete subdual and the glorification of the senses, and the "ordering of all things strongly and sweetly from end to end"'.[1] As in life, so in art. The words of Aquinas, 'perfect joy and peace are identical', lie at the heart of Patmore's concept of literature and of conduct. Even in his metrical theory the basis is one of rest and resolution, not one of conflict and tension, as it is in that of Hopkins. In literature of the highest kind, he believed, the expression of pain and pleasure can never be an end in itself, but is always a means to the attainment, or the glorifying, of peace.

There is little that is original in Patmore's critical theory; Aristotle, Hegel, Ulrici and others are the obvious sources of most of his important ideas. Yet what he drew from such authors he tested by his own instinct and fused with his knowledge of theology and mystical literature, so that there is a distinctly individual turn to his enunciation of principles. He is completely free from modishness, and, if his praise of a writer happens to coincide with the general verdict, one can be certain that Patmore has reached his conclusion independently. So discriminating is his taste that it is a matter for regret that he did not ever write a complete book of literary criticism, for such a work may well have had the distinction of his 'Essay on English Metrical Law'. The collected essays suffer from an appearance of scrappiness and the lack of following-through of ideas. However, Patmore is a critic who cannot be neglected. His constant emphasis on the need for principles in literature, and his shrewd assessment of the basic weaknesses in later Romantic writing make him one of the few critics of his time who anticipated modern critical trends. In his conception of great literature as achieving a degree of impersonality beyond the ordinary emotional responses, in his stress on the classical 'point of rest', in his recognition of order and control in successful but apparently lawless verse, he looks forward to the writings of such critics as Eliot and Leavis. Despite changes in taste, and shifts in values, which outmode some of his premises, a large part of his general critical statement still stands.

There was, however, at least one distinctive and original contribution made by Patmore to literary criticism, and this was the application of the principle of sexual duality to literature. Only Osbert Burdett, in *The Idea of Coventry Patmore*, and Paull F. Baum[2] have realized what an important part Patmore's sexual theories

---

[1] 'Peace in Life and Art', *Principle in Art*, p. 33.
[2] 'Coventry Patmore's Literary Criticism', *University of California Chronicle*, Vol. XXV, 1923, pp. 244–260.

played in his criticism. Baum draws attention in this regard to a passage from Patmore's essay on Keats, in which he divides poets into two classes; one, that in which intellect prevails, governing passion and evolving beauty and sweetness as accidents, and which he names 'masculine'. The other class, in which he places Keats, is 'feminine', in which beauty and sweetness are essential, and the truth and power of intellect and passion the accidents. In all the great poets, he says, there is a feminine element. However, the difference lies in which element has the mastery:

> 'In Keats the man had not the mastery. For him a thing of beauty was not only a joy for ever, but was the supreme and only good he knew or cared to know; and the consequence is that his best poems are things of exquisite and most sensitively felt beauty and nothing else. But it is a fact of primary significance, both in morals and in art . . . that the highest beauty and joy are not attainable when they occupy the first place as motives, but only when they are more or less the accidents of the exercise of the manly virtue of the vision of truth. There are at fitting seasons a serene splendour and a sunny sweetness about that which is truly masculine, whether in character or in art, which women and womanly artists never attain—an inner radiance of original loveliness and joy which comes, and can only come, of the purity of motive which regards external beauty and delight as accidental.'[1]

Mr. Baum comments on this passage: 'This not only points clearly to the great weakness of Keats's immaturity, but it illustrates its own point. For it is a masculine idea, expressed with a vigour which has also the accident of beauty.'[2]

Patmore's use of the sexual principle as a means of literary discrimination is based upon his idea that genius possesses a double-sexed insight. Even in his earliest essays, he treated of literary work as exhibiting to a greater or lesser degree masculine or the feminine characteristics. In his analysis of *The Princess*, published in 1848, he sees Ida as 'representative of the passive or feminine principle of the intellect, in a condition of total independence of, and opposition to, powers of higher activity and authority'.[3] Since genius is double-sexed, the great artist is he in whose personality both elements are in a state of equilibrium, the grace of the feminine being tempered with the intellectual strength of the masculine. Masculine law is the theme of all true poets; feeling is

---

[1] 'Keats', *Principle in Art*, pp. 77–78.
[2] 'Coventry Patmore's Literary Criticism', p. 249.
[3] 'Tennyson's *Poems—The Princess*', *North British Review*, May 1848, p. 69.

the 'feminine inflection' of this law, without which it has no poetic life. Patmore recognizes that all genius is essentially energy or vigour, which proceeds mainly from the masculine side, and gives sublimity and scope, while the feminine gives grace, purity of feeling, meticulousness. One is large, encompassing, imperfect; the other, small, exact, nearer perfection. So he finds in Mrs. Meynell's essays, 'the hall-mark of genius, namely, the marriage of masculine force of insight with feminine grace and tact of expression'[1]; and he writes of poetry in general: 'Poetry, in common with, but above all the arts, is the mind of *man*, the rational soul, using the feminine or sensitive soul, as its accidental or complementary means of expression.'[2] Hence, despite the charges he levels against Keats and Shelley of excessive 'femininity' and defective 'masculinity', he finds their quality as poets in the fact that the feminine aspect of a great poet is something other than woman—it is goddess. 'Keats and Shelley, in their best works, are wholly feminine; they were merely exponents of sensitive beauty; but into this they had such an insight, and with it such a power of self-identification, as no woman has ever approached.'[3]

The critical value of this sexual principle is seen in its application to individual authors. For instance, Patmore's assessment of Clough is more perceptive than that of most of his contemporaries. He sees the self-doubtings, the intellectual vagaries of Clough as little better than commonplaces, and detects in him an absence of intellectual toughness, which vitiates most of his work. He writes:

'The impressionable and feminine element, which is manifest in all genius, but which in truly effective genius is always subordinate to power of intellect, had in Clough's mind the preponderance. The masculine power of intellect consists scarcely so much in the ability to see truth, as in the tenacity of spirit which cleaves to and assimilates the truth when it is found, and which steadfastly refuses to be blown about by every wind of doctrine and feeling.'[4]

More revealing is his assessment of Tennyson. He wrote five lengthy articles on Tennyson's poetry, in which even though, when the essays were penned, Patmore was one of Tennyson's closest friends, looking up to him with an almost dog-like devotion, he put his finger on the aspects of Tennyson's poetry which prevent his best work from being quite of the highest order. In the 1848 essay on *The Princess*, Patmore makes the mistake of seeking more in the

[1] 'Mrs. Meynell', *Principle in Art*, p. 151.
[2] 'Emotional Art', *Principle in Art*, p. 24.
[3] 'Mrs. Meynell', *Principle in Art*, p. 149.
[4] 'Arthur Hugh Clough', *Principle in Art*, pp. 108–109.

poem than Tennyson intended to give, and of trying to fit the plan to a fancied allegory. He praises Tennyson's art and points to the many beauties incidental to the work; yet, at the same time, he sees in it a defect of spontaneity, a too-obtrusive 'over-polish', a want of unity and poetic purpose. What, in short, even at this early stage, he misses is that masculine power which gives both breadth and unity to poetry. The older poet's genius is, he thinks, essentially of the feminine order in that it is excessively artistic, but lacks intellectual strength. 'The gravest fault,' he finds, 'and one which seriously affects the value of the work, is the fact that it is *constructed upon*, rather than *inspired by*, the central idea.'[1] On the other hand, when, in 1850, Patmore writes of *In Memoriam* he devotes the bulk of the essay to a discussion of general principles of poetic technique. He finds the poem's chief merit in Tennyson's 'complete conquest and subdual of metre and language, to the service of thought and feeling'. In short, all the praise is for 'the admirable harmony and various poetic excellence' of *In Memoriam* and scarcely anything is said of the theme and content of the work save that it is characterized by 'thorough subjectivity'.[2]

There are gaucheries and misjudgments in Patmore's estimates of individual works by Tennyson, but in the main his final judgment is that of twentieth-century critics. Tennyson is *the* Victorian poet, and Patmore delicately recognizes this in writing of Tennyson's treatment of the medieval Arthurian tales in *Idylls of the King*:

> 'Mr. Tennyson does not always accept the situation with sufficient boldness, but sometimes palliates, with modern reasons, certain points in a course of conduct which, in its whole character, belongs to and is only made tolerable by a mythical antiquity, and which is not repulsive to our feelings only because it is inexplicable or incredible to them.'[3]

While everywhere acknowledging Tennyson's superb technical skill, Patmore finds him deficient in creative energy, in expression of the deeper passions, in intellectual content, and in power of integration. Carefully though he qualifies it, his categorizing of Tennyson's work as 'feminine' must be taken in the light of the sharper definition he was to give to this term in a literary context as denoting an important lack in the poetry of his friend.

The same criterion is applied to, among others, Shelley and Rossetti. His chief complaint against the latter is the 'constant

---

1 'Tennyson's *Poems—The Princess*', *North British Review*, May 1848, p. 72.

2 'In Memoriam', *North British Review*, August 1850, pp. 549–551.

3 'Tennyson's *Idylls of the King*', *Edinburgh Review*, Vol. CX, No. 223, July 1859, p. 248.

high-pressure' he finds in Rossetti's work, a stress which gives 'an impression of cold instead of warmth, as if the fire had a salamander instead of a heart at its centre'.[1] This suppression of emotion and calculation of effect suggest to Patmore elaborate artificiality in poeticizing, where real feeling is carefully concealed, rather than expressed. He finds confirmation of this view in the mannerisms, so frequent in Rossetti's verse, of which he says:

> 'Style, which is the true expression of the poet's individuality . . . is almost suffocated in Rossetti's most characteristic work, by voluntary oddities of manner and by a manifest difficulty in so moving in the bonds of verse as to convert them into graces.'[2]

In sum, Rossetti's work, to him, is 'tense without being intense'— it has a preponderance of the feminine quality and a deficiency in the masculine quality.

Perhaps the most rewarding application of the sexual principle is found in Patmore's essay on Francis Thompson. Although Patmore respected the work of a poet who was to become, to some degree, his disciple, his judgment on Thompson's work is balanced and judicious, and forms an interesting contrast to claims made subsequently for Francis Thompson's poetry by some of his co-religionists. He points unerringly to Thompson's weaknesses— his lack of taste and control, his over-lush language, his detachment from reality. He praises highly the metrical qualities of Thompson's poetry, his wide vocabulary and his music, but adds:

> 'The masculine intellect . . . is as conspicuous and, alas, as predominant in Mr. Thompson's poetry as it is in that of Crashaw and Cowley. The feminine element, which is as essential to perfect poetry as a crust is to a pie, is in insufficient presence. Profound thought, and far-fetched splendour of imagery and nimble-witted discernment of those analogies which are the "roots" of the poet's language, abound; but in the feminine faculties of "taste", of emotion that must have music for its rendering, of shy moderation which never says quite so much as it means, of quickness to "scent the ridiculous from afar", of the dainty conscience which sets "decorum" far above all other duties and knows that in poetry the manner is much more important than the matter, since manner is beautiful in itself, whereas, without it, it is no matter where the matter may be since it fails to express itself with feminine *feeling* and perception; in these qualities Mr. Thompson's poetry is as often deficient as is that of his two eminent predecessors. Even the barest sublimity cannot be adequately rendered in poetry without some measure of the chaste and timid reticence of womanhood. Mr. Thompson throws about him "handfuls of stars" and swings the earth

---

[1] 'Rossetti as a Poet', *Principle in Art*, p. 103.   [2] *Ibid.*, p. 99.

as "a trinket from his wrist"; but these are very cheap sublimities compared with Aeschylus's

"Slow is the wrath of gods, but, in the end, *not weak*."[1]

'Cheap sublimities' is a shrewd phrase, for the general effect of Thompson's poetry is, in fact, to reduce the cosmic and the sublime to the status of playthings, and his verse, as Patmore was quick to see, has in it much of the lack of definition and vague feeling from which the 'Spasmodics' suffered.

In other essays, even when Patmore's language does not reflect a direct application of the principle of sexual duality, it is clear that he is assessing the value of literary works by the kind of sensibility displayed in them. He made no attempt to apply the masculine–feminine analogy rigidly; yet at the same time it offers a useful critical tool with which to define the character of the work of particular authors. It is one indication of his critical astuteness that, in more recent times, some critics have again begun to examine poetry and fiction in the light of the masculine and feminine duality of genius. We do not have to accept Patmore's general theory of sex to recognize the value of this analogy in isolating strengths and weaknesses in literature.

On his general critical achievement, however, there is considerable agreement among even the most friendly of his critics that, stimulating as he is in his exposition of principles, his weakness lies in his application of those principles. Frederick Page, for instance, writes: 'The morality of *Tamerton Church-Tower* is as sound as Patmore's principles in art, and like them, only wrong in its application.'[2] Percy Lubbock speaks of the 'exaggeration' which 'ran riot in his literary and artistic criticisms'[3]; while the usually wholly partisan Osbert Burdett warns intending readers not to approach the essays by way of those on individual writers.[4]

The most completely destructive discussion of Patmore's critical work, however, comes from Dr. Richard Garnett. Garnett was responsible for the statement: 'He had no perception of the sublime in other men's writing, or of the ridiculous in his own'[5]; which, because of its epigrammatic character, has been quoted so often as to become almost the standard verdict. Epigrams rarely give the

---

[1] 'Francis Thompson, a new Poet', *Fortnightly Review*, January 1894; *Courage in Politics*, pp. 159–160.

[2] *Patmore*, A Study in Poetry, p. 56.

[3] 'Coventry Patmore', *The Quarterly Review*, April 1908, p. 368.

[4] 'Coventry Patmore (1823–1896)', *The London Mercury*, Vol. VIII, No. 45, July 1923, pp. 290–291.

[5] *Dictionary of National Biography*, Vol. XXII, p. 1122.

whole truth; most, however, have enough truth in them to make the statement at least ponderable; this phrase of Garnett's is almost completely false. Although he had almost as many prejudices as Dr. Johnson, Patmore was often both shrewd and just in assessing his subjects, and his admiration for the great writers of Europe was forcefully expressed on many occasions. His essays on Shakespeare, his many tributes to Milton, Wordsworth and Coleridge, his praise of Matthew Arnold and of Robert Bridges, his vigorous defence of Thackeray's realism, his regard for Burns and Barnes, his admiration for Dryden and Dante—these surely more than balance his underestimating of Blake and Keats and his blindness to the virtues of Browning. As for the suggestion that Patmore was unaware of the 'ridiculous' elements in his own work, such a judgment not only overlooks Patmore's keen, if sardonic, sense of humour, but it exaggerates the number of 'banalities' in his poems and completely mistakes the nature and purpose of the 'furniture' in them.

However, the comment in question represents only a briefer restatement of a point of view advanced by Garnett in an earlier essay, written in 1896. Here he begins by postulating a dichotomy between the earlier poems and *The Unknown Eros*, going on to say:

> 'In the critical department of Mr. Patmore's work a corresponding duality exists, perhaps best defined by the remark that he belongs to the exceedingly small class of men who have a stronger hold upon and a more lively apprehension of principles existing in the abstract than of principles embodied in individuals.'[1]

He praises Patmore for his 'constant and quiet enunciation of subtle truths', but deplores his 'imperfect grasp of, or frigid indifference to, the actual works which he professes to be criticising.'[2] This point he illustrates by selecting first of all the essay on William Barnes which is reprinted in *Principle in Art*, and which he criticizes as being all *ipse dixit*, with not a single line of Barnes quoted in confirmation or illustration: 'The essay, therefore, is wholly ineffective as concerns its professed purpose, and we can attribute the failure to nothing but Mr. Patmore's indifference to persons in comparison with principles. His admiration for Barnes is sincere, but tepid; the man is nothing to him in comparison with the views which he can be made to suggest.'[3]

There are several facts which nullify Garnett's charges. The first is that this essay on Barnes is only one of five pieces which Patmore

---

[1] 'Living Critics. V. Mr. Coventry Patmore', *The Bookman*, Vol. IX, No. 54, March 1896, p. 180.
[2] *Ibid*.   [3] *Ibid*., p. 181.

wrote on the poet and which, taken together, constitute a thorough appreciation of his poetry; one of them, in fact, written for the *North British Review* in November 1859, is almost overloaded with quotations, in addition to which it discusses Barnes's use of dialect, and its importance in the general poetic effect, his similarity to, and difference from, Wordsworth and Burns, his use of simple subjects, his descriptive power and the delicacy of his love-poetry. Another essay, in *Macmillan's Magazine* for June 1862, covers much the same ground, and quotes generously from Barnes's poems and prose. In sum, these articles make up the most substantial and detailed appraisal of William Barnes and his poetry produced by any critic in the nineteenth century. The extent to which Patmore, contrary to Garnett's assertion, considered the man and the text as well as the principles may be gathered from such a typical comment as this:

> 'Seldom before has the precept "look in thy heart and write" been followed with such integrity and simplicity; and seldom before have rural nature and humanity in its simpler aspects been expressed in verse with fidelity so charming. We breathe the morning air while we are reading . . . a commonplace in the verses of Mr. Barnes is respected, because we are sure that it was penned by him with no commonplace feeling.'[1]

Whatever else such judgments may be, they are certainly not 'tepid'.

Although Patmore doubtless over-estimated Barnes's poetry, he was ahead of his time in appreciating the beauty of Barnes's simplicity, the warmth of his sentiment, and the metrical skill underlying apparently elementary forms. After one reads Patmore's careful analysis of the distinguishing characteristics of Barnes's verse and his glowing tribute to him, Garnett's assertion that 'the man is nothing to him in comparison with the views which he can be made to suggest' becomes ludicrous. It may be suggested that Patmore is to blame for selecting the most general of his essays on Barnes for inclusion in *Principle in Art*, and that, on the evidence offered there, Garnett was justified in complaining of the absence of quotation and of detailed critical treatment. Yet the title of the book is, after all, *Principle in Art*; the essays in it were brought together simply because they *do* emphasize general literary principles.

Garnett's chief complaint, however, is that Patmore has too much of a 'reserved attitude' towards great writers. This again is not

---

[1] 'William Barnes, the Dorsetshire Poet', *Macmillan's Magazine*, June 1862, p. 160.

borne out by the facts. Patmore, in fact, errs at times, as in the case of Mrs. Meynell, by too great an enthusiasm for his subject. Nor did writers have to be well known to be admired by him. He found much to praise, for instance, in the early poems of Robert Bridges. While few of his contemporaries were seemingly aware of the existence of the Provençal poets, Patmore wrote a discriminating and appreciative essay on the Troubadours, especially Cadanet, whom he calls 'one of the world's truest poets'. He lauded the virtues of the *Anti-Jacobin*, which, he said, contained the 'latest specimens of satire which is likely to stand the test of time'.[1] He wrote in almost ecstatic terms of Goldsmith's *The Vicar of Wakefield*.[2] Although he was repelled by the novel of Thomas Hardy which he called 'Jude the Obscene', he was devoted to his other novels, and accurately gauged Hardy's potentialities as a poet when he wrote, long before Hardy turned to verse:

'His love of nature is so passionate and observant, that it is impossible to read him without a sense that he is in some degree wasting his powers and experience by expending them upon prose. No poet has ever discovered more acutely or expressed more forcibly, tenderly, and daintily the inexhaustible beauties of wood, heath, field and lane.'[3]

The greatest critical blunders Patmore made were his assessments of Blake and Keats—blunders for which, it is clear, no commentator is prepared to forgive him. He found some passages in Blake full of great beauty and simplicity; but also said that his poetry 'with the exception of four or five lovely lyrics, and, here and there in other pieces, a startling gleam of unquestionable genius, is mere drivel',[4] and he suggests that Blake is much more important as an artist than as a poet. It is strange that Patmore does not appear to have recognized the Swedenborgian elements in Blake. Yet, even if he had, it is unlikely that he would have approved of Blake's assimilation, and adaptation, of the visionary aspects of Swedenborg. He was also a militant opponent of 'obscurity' in poetry, and it is possible that an attempt to grapple with Blake's *Prophetic Books* proved so frustrating that his exasperation extended to the rest of the mystic's work. In any case, the symbolism of Blake is admittedly difficult, even in the lesser poems, unless one

[1] 'The Decay of Modern Satire', *North British Review*, Vol. XXIX, No. LVIII, November 1858, p. 506.
[2] 'Goldsmith', *St. James's Gazette*, January 16, 1888; *Courage in Politics*, p. 61.
[3] 'Hardy's Novels', *St. James's Gazette*, April 2, 1887; *Courage in Politics*, p. 135.
[4] 'Blake', *Principle in Art*, p. 92.

has the key, and Patmore can hardly be blamed over-much for a lack of that appreciation which more recent knowledge of Blake's sources and symbols has helped to sharpen.

With reference to Keats, it is easy to see, from what has been said above of Patmore's attitude towards Keat's 'feminine' quality, that he would be deficient in sympathy for his poetry. He wrote: 'Let Keats try to assume the man . . . and all his life and power seem to shrivel and die, like the beauty of Lamia in the presence of Apollonius.'[1] There may be a grain of truth in this statement, but it hardly explains the baffling judgment, from one who prided himself on his knowledge of Shakespeare, that 'among real poets, Keats was the most un-Shakespearian poet that ever lived'.[2]

However, what he wrote about Shakespeare himself is extremely stimulating. A book on Shakespeare which Patmore planned as a young man was abandoned on reading Ulrici's *Shakespeare's Dramatic Art*, since there he found, he claims, that Ulrici had anticipated his main line of argument. He was rather prone to make such statements, and it is difficult not to suspect that there was at times a considerable amount of wishful thinking in them. However, in this instance, there is some evidence that he had developed original ideas about Shakespeare before reading Ulrici, since his essay on *Macbeth*, printed in *The Germ* in 1850, but which Patmore claimed to have written at the age of seventeen, is a most sensitive appreciation of the play.[3] It is also one of the first, if not the very first, essay to develop a hint from Coleridge that a plan to obtain the crown of Scotland by illegitimate means had been discussed by Macbeth with his wife before his first meeting with the witches. By a close analysis of the text, and a careful examination of the character of Macbeth, Patmore goes some way towards proving his point. However, as with a good deal of Shakespearian criticism, his thesis calls for a logical consistency and a watertight relationship between every detail of the dramatic structure in the play which it is most unlikely Shakespeare aimed at.

The main idea which Patmore and Ulrici share is that Shakespeare was not the objective playwright he had been generally taken to be, but that he was a great moral teacher, each of whose plays has as its basis some moral idea which is reflected over and over again in the plot, the characters and the language. According to Patmore, the plays of Shakespeare take place in a fairly rigid moral universe, and the characters' destinies are worked out according to their

---

[1] 'Keats', *Principle in Art*, pp. 79–80.   [2] *Ibid.*, p. 76.
[3] 'Macbeth', *The Germ*, Nos. 1–4. Reprinted by Thomas B. Mosher, 1898. Issue 3, March 1850, No. 11, p. 112.

acceptance or rejection of the underlying laws which condition this universe. By way of illustration, Patmore sets out the theme of *The Merchant of Venice* as 'the relation of the *letter* to the *spirit* of the law, and the various liabilities of man to dwell on the first and to neglect the last'.[1] The argument on this premise is close and ingenious, being worked out through the details of the play, and even finding symbolical confirmation in the disguises used. His main conclusion is:

> 'There are no heroes or heroines in Shakespeare's plays, that is to say, no one person constitutes the central interest. The chief interest is, or ought to be, found in the single but many-sided moral truths which they all pretty equally illustrate, and from their various relations to which they derive their proper significance. Viewed thus, the wonderful harmony of Shakespeare's plays ceases to be a mystery.'[2]

Such a view clearly owes something to Coleridge, but it is far from being merely Coleridgean. It has a distinctly modern ring, suggesting the recent assessments of Shakespeare's plays by E. M. W. Tillyard, Wilson Knight and Roy Walker. On the evidence offered by these two essays on Shakespeare, and the hints elsewhere in Patmore's prose, it seems likely that had the book on Tragedy ever seen the light, it may well have been a significant one.

One aspect of Patmore's approach to Shakespeare suggests the central weakness in his own criticism, that which prevents his critical writings, despite their often brilliant assessments and their striking obiter dicta, from being really influential. It is going too far to say, as Garnett does, that Patmore is incapable of enthusiasm for the works of other writers. At the same time, it is hard not to feel, again and again in his criticism, a deficiency in sympathy, not so much with the creative work of any one man, as with the vagaries of the creative spirit itself. Patmore's 'classical' inclinations, his instinct for 'normality' and his strong streak of practicality made him rather too severe on works which did not obey his hypothetical laws of aesthetics and caused him instinctively to distrust any strikingly individual form of expression. Arthur Symons puts it well when he writes: 'He hated the Protestantism of modern art, its revolt against the tradition of the "true Church", the many heresies of its many wanderings after a strange, perhaps forbidden beauty.'[3]

Associated with this is his tendency to try to draw too rigid

---

[1] 'Shakespeare', *North British Review*, Vol. XII, No. XXIII, Nov. 1849, p. 116.

[2] *Ibid.*, pp. 130–131.

[3] 'Coventry Patmore', *The North American Review*, February 1920, p. 272.

conclusions from aesthetic premises; to try to fit the work judged to his scale rather than to define its specific individuality. He recognized, indeed, that the great writer creates anew, but often what his instinct told him about the merit of a work conflicted with what he believed *should be* the end and aim of literature. In dealing with *The Merchant of Venice*, he tries rather to fit the play to a pre-conceived thesis than to accept and evaluate it as a whole. Patmore was not the first, nor will he be the last, to do this; but it is a weakness in several of his essays that he blames writers for not doing what he feels they should be doing, rather than assessing what in fact they have done. If a work was 'untidy', he held it deficient. The 'harmony' and 'interior polish' he sought were certainly lacking in most of his contemporaries; but in some—Browning, for one—there are a force, a power and an insight to which he was blind.

Patmore cannot be classed with the great English critics. Among his fellow-Victorians, Arnold, for example, surpasses him in insight, in comprehensiveness, in power, in taste and in fairness. The fragmentary nature of his work, a trace of perfunctoriness, his habit of identifying his personal likes and dislikes with literary axioms, the fact that there were several areas of literature of which he knew, or at least wrote, nothing, the absence of a consistent and well-rounded aesthetic—these are among his limitations. At the same time, he reaps the rewards of a confident, dogmatic critic, in that he is never evasive or obscure, nor seduced by novelty and sensationalism, and even his most questionable judgments contain important insights. He is capable, on page after page, of subtleties of judgment which far outweigh the inadequacies of some of his individual appraisals. For a man so full of bias in other directions, he is capable of the most generous and unexpectedly detached judgments. Above all, perhaps, he wrote always in a direct, sinewy prose which makes even the most outmoded of his appraisals still admirable reading. He did not aim at producing a well-rounded critical system, but at pithily, suggestively and forcefully restating basic truths about literature and about the relationship between art, life and religion, and this he did admirably. For this, as well as for his skilful application of the principle of sexual duality, for his illuminating phrases, and for his glancing insights, he deserves to rank high in the second level of English literary critics.

III

Architecture

PATMORE WROTE SOME TWENTY-THREE ARTICLES on various aspects of architecture, but his life-long concern with the subject was not merely theoretical, but practical as well. He extensively remodelled his Sussex home, Heron's Ghyll; and he built the Church of St. Mary, Star of the Sea, at Hastings. As he had had no formal architectural training, his interest was strictly that of an amateur; yet Basil Champneys, himself a professional architect, wrote, concerning Patmore's co-operation on the church at Hastings which Champneys designed: 'His knowledge of architecture was thorough, and, so far as I was concerned, displayed itself in the most satisfactory manner, in encouragement and appreciation, without interference.'[1] Tennyson, who had some knowledge of architecture himself, was impressed by Patmore's early essays on the subject; and Carlyle also admired them. Patmore wrote several articles on Ruskin's *Seven Lamps of Architecture* and *The Stones of Venice*. One of the latter delighted Ruskin, who wrote letters of thanks to Patmore in which he lauds his architectural knowledge.[2] And, in the same article, Patmore refers with pride to the fact that in the first volume of *The Stones of Venice* Ruskin quotes three times from an earlier piece of his[3] and accepts some of his views concerning Gothic decoration.

At one time, indeed, the poet contemplated writing a book on

[1] *Memoirs*, Vol. I, p. 337.   [2] *Ibid.*, Vol. II, pp. 286–287.
[3] 'The Aesthetics of Gothic Architecture', *British Quarterly Review*, Vol. X, No. XIX, August 1849, pp. 46–75.

architecture,[1] but this remained unrealized, like the proposed works on Swedenborg and on Shakespeare. His deep interest in the subject is shown, however, not only in his published articles but also in the letters he wrote to his friend Mrs. Jackson when in 1864, after the death of Emily, he travelled on the Continent. He spent a good deal of his time seeking out architectural specimens, on which he comments in a lively and even excited way.[2]

Patmore's architectural essays are anything but the enthusiastic yet superficial observations of a dilettante; they reveal a wealth of technical knowledge, with a thorough understanding of the use of materials known in his day, of structural methods and of both functional and aesthetic principles. The essay 'Sources of Expression in Architecture'[3] and the five essays grouped together as 'Architectural Styles' in *Principle in Art* represent his gift for exposition at its best; intricate technical detail is handled with ease and skill in illuminating discussions of the most fundamental aspects of architectural expression. His intimate interest in technique, both in poetry and in architecture, reveals the practical basis of his thinking; he is a craftsman, genuinely interested in mechanical detail, somebody quite different from the vague generalizer. His architectural sense shows in the structure of his odes, which are 'built up' and have the kind of pattern usually referred to as 'architectonic'. In one of his literary essays, indeed, he explicitly applies the principles of architecture to poetry when he counsels writers to 'follow, in poetry, the artistic law of architecture, which adopts, perfects and displays with the utmost degree of ostentation the essential, but nothing else.'[4]

Many aspects of his architectural thought are in advance of his age; for instance, his deploring the meaningless 'artistic' embellishment of public buildings, and his praise of the functional beauty of machines. 'Leave "style" to take care of itself,' he wrote (in words which anticipate Eric Gill's 'Beauty looks after itself'), 'as it always will, if you trust it. . . . What "fine art" that we could have time to understand on a railway journey could equal the beauty of the throbbing engines, or the admirably calculated reticulation and

---

[1] In a letter to E. Moxon, publisher of his first volume of poems, dated from the British Museum, December 3, 1852, Patmore writes: 'I am also about to publish a small volume on architecture, developing the views expressed by me in an article which appeared in *The Edinburgh Review* last year upon Ruskin. I should be glad to know if you would like to undertake its publication.' (Princeton University Library.)

[2] Champneys, *Memoirs*, Vol. II, p. 191.

[3] *Edinburgh Review*, Vol. XCIV, No. CXCII, October 1851, pp. 365–403.

[4] 'American Poetry', *North British Review*, August 1852, p. 418.

intersection of the iron lines at some great junction?'[1] He was vehemently opposed to jerry-building, to haphazard clusters of dwellings, and to the agglomerations of residences which constituted the rapidly growing metropolitan suburbs. London he called 'a vast open-air museum of models of the architecture of all times and countries'[2]; and he asked, 'Is it in ignorance and insensibility that our upper classes go on building in a style which expresses nothing but vulgar insolence, luxury and exclusiveness?'[3] Houses, in his view, should be built to last, not for a few years, nor for a life-time, but for centuries. Only thus, he believed, could nobility, dignity and grace be expressed in contemporary buildings, such things being excluded by the jerry-built dwellings most commonly erected at the time.

Discussing the 'ninety-nine year house' which he sees as the norm of contemporary London building, he expresses himself forcefully on the matter of architectural honesty in terms which have quite a twentieth-century flavour:

'This style is perfectly honest, and, as far as it goes, artistical. It is a true symbolical representation of the central idea. Just as "for ever" seems written on the face of every building of antiquity, so upon the faces of the 500 miles of flat, undecorated, baked-mud streets of London is written "for ninety-nine years". It was a bad thing when London streets first took to lying, and the thin walls of bilious-looking bricks hid themselves in plaster coverings of Greek and Palladian pretensions. But this falseness is quite shallow and excusable, when compared with that in which real materials assume forms whereof the main significance is an idea of duration totally at variance with the actual fact.'[4]

In a surprising number of ways, indeed, Patmore's views on architecture seem to be in harmony with aspects of the theories of such modern architects as Frank Lloyd Wright and Le Corbusier. For example, he welcomes the development of the apartment house, and sees in it one of the best solutions to the problem of metropolitan living: he recommends a greatly extended use of iron and glass for building, and praises the Crystal Palace on this score and on that of economy: he urges the use of plate-glass instead of the fashionable 'diamonds' or small-pattern glazing[5]: he anticipates the Eiffel Tower by pointing out the possibilities of using iron in a

[1] 'Ruskin and Architecture', *North British Review*, Vol. XXI, No. XLI, February 1854, p. 173.
[2] 'London Street Architecture', *The National Review*, Vol. V, No. IX, July 1857, p. 49.   [3] *Ibid.*, p. 68.
[4] 'Gothic Architecture—Present and Future', *North British Review*, Vol. XXVIII, No. LVI, May 1858, p. 354.   [5] *Ibid.*, pp. 357–358.

spire: 'A Gothic spire, which has never risen above 500 feet in stone, might easily attain a thousand in iron',[1] and he foresees a complete revolution in architecture from the extended use of the same material.[2] Honesty in the use of materials and the natural beauty that arises from the straightforward employment of them are for Patmore axioms of good architecture. Simplicity, above all else, should be the primary feature of good domestic architecture; he roundly condemns what he calls the 'cottage of gentility', the mock-Tudor type of structure. Ornamentation, he believed, should arise inevitably out of the building itself, and not be, as was common in his time, merely 'tacked on'. 'Strawberry Hill Gothic vanished like a nightmare', he writes, 'when Pugin for the first time authoritatively asserted and proved that architectural decoration could never properly be an addition to constructive features, but only a fashioning of them.'[3]

Patmore took architecture almost as seriously as he took poetry. For him, it was not merely a profession; it was one of the highest of the arts. At the centre of his admiration for Ruskin's writings on architecture was his recognition of the vast amount Ruskin had done to elevate the common notion of the art of building. One of the chief causes of the mediocrity of mid-nineteenth-century architecture, in his view, was the habit of regarding architects merely as professional men. He pleads forcibly for the acceptance of architecture as an art as well as a profession. Architecture, like all other fine arts, requires a special faculty; and technical knowledge, in Patmore's opinion, is by no means the main requisite for success in it.[4]

On the other hand, the detaching of such views from their context may give the impression that Patmore's writings on architecture have a more 'modern' flavour than in fact they possess. Like Ruskin, and even more like Pugin, Patmore is wedded to the Gothic style, which he sees not only as having an incomparable spiritual quality, but also as representing the culminating achievement of man's constructional genius. His conception of the ideal style for the Houses of Parliament, for permanent residences, and also for shops is the 'pointed' style—in fact, he believes that 'a combination of the Venetian and the Tudor-Gothic would produce a style of

[1] 'Gothic Architecture—Present and Future', *North British Review*, Vol. XXVIII, No. LVI, May 1858, p. 368.

[2] 'Character in Architecture', *North British Review*, Vol. XV, No. XXX, Aug. 1851, p. 495.

[3] 'Principle in Art', *Principle in Art*, p. 2.

[4] 'Sources of Expression in Architecture', *Edinburgh Review*, Vol. XCIV, No. CXCII, Oct. 1851, pp. 365–366.

house-building so exactly suited for London shops, that its adoption could not but immediately follow any alteration in the present system of land-leases which should render permanent building feasible.'[1] Gothic, in short, is as good for secular purposes as for religious ones and hence, logically, 'there is one class of building to which Gothic architecture might be applied . . . we mean farm-houses and farm-buildings.'[2]

For churches, Gothic is, of course, the only style worthy of serious consideration. In an article on the proposed Liverpool Cathedral he supports the plan for a Gothic building. 'What is the "significance" of Northern Gothic?' he asks, and replies, 'Its significance is Christianity, and only when Christianity is extinct will Gothic architecture become so.'[3] He is by no means blind to the particular excellences of other forms. For instance, writing of Japanese houses, he points out that the furniture and interior wall-decoration abound in beauties as peculiar as they are artistic.[4] Yet, so far as contemporary needs are concerned, he is the complete partisan of Gothic. To a great extent, his enthusiasm for the form springs from the same organic conception which lies behind his odes; Gothic, he feels, is the only architectural form in which all aspects—the structure, the use of materials and the decoration—unite in an organic whole singly expressing aspiration. Patmore's notion of 'organic architecture' looks forward, despite its different emphasis and its limitations, to what Frank Lloyd Wright achieves and calls by that name. Whereas Wright seeks to make each building 'grow' out of its surroundings as an aesthetic as well as a practical unit related both to environment and to the needs and character of its inhabitants, Patmore conceived of the ideal structure as an integrated Gothic entity, practical, economical and permanent, with beauty arising out of utility and out of the symbolic expression of the uplifting of men's hearts to God. The liberation from the 'box-style', however, which was proceeding in later Victorian architecture through the opening-up of corners and the development of variety in spatial relations, was appreciated by him. He roundly condemns the 'mud-hut style' of house-building—four brick walls with holes—and the 'slop-shop style' of jerry-built boxes,[5] and he

---

[1] 'London Street Architecture', p. 71.
[2] 'Gothic Architecture—Present and Future', p. 370.
[3] 'Churches and Preaching Halls', *St. James's Gazette*, March 10, 1887; *Courage in Politics*, p. 190.
[4] 'Japanese Houses', *St. James's Gazette*, April 13, 1888; *Courage in Politics*, p. 194.
[5] 'Ruskin and Architecture', pp. 174–176.

refers scornfully to the Londoner's 'preference of a foetid pig-sty of his own to a share of a palace which is also shared by others.'[1]

Although Patmore defends Gothic with technical arguments, fundamentally his preference is based upon his conviction that the form represents the most perfect use of spiritual symbolization that man has achieved in architecture. From his first essay to his last, he stresses the symbolic qualities of the major architectural modes. Not that he believed that the intention of the original builders of Gothic churches was explicitly symbolic or that the style was evolved as the expression of an abstract idea. Defending the symbolism of the Gothic church against Ruskin's criticism of the notion, he makes his position plain:

> 'The direct symbolization of sentiment is . . . among the most powerful and universal of human instincts. . . . But, granting as we do, that the symbolization of religious activity, by aspiring forms, may possibly not have been intended, or even perceived by the Gothic architects, in the works which they designed, we have shown that a consistent and co-operating series of those forms might, and probably did, arise from the natural desire to intensify an expression which was, in the first instance, the simple result of a peculiar constructive system. . . . While . . . we would discard from modern use the whole medieval system of *arbitrary* symbolization, we believe that we should be doing an injustice to Gothic architecture were we to refuse, with Mr. Ruskin, to perceive in its ancient examples an *artistic and essential* symbolism, which must retain its efficiency as long as the human mind retains its present constitution.'[2]

Patmore regards the three great styles—the Egyptian, the Greek and the Gothic—as 'the only three architectures of artistical integrity which the world has seen', using various relations of matter 'as the fittest symbols for the sensual, the intellectual and the spiritual mind'.[3] He considers it unlikely that any other mode would ever again rival them in symbolic character, for that character depended upon a constant reference to the great elementary fact of constructive weight of material. He can hardly be criticized for not foreseeing the development of the cantilever principle, and the weight-defying use of such materials as steel, glass and aluminium. As Patmore saw it, the lines and masses of the Egyptian style expressed simple weight and symbolized material power; the Greek temple expressed the resistance of gravity and hence symbolized

---

[1] 'Gothic Architecture—Present and Future', p. 374.

[2] 'Sources of Expression in Architecture', pp. 396–397.

[3] 'Ruskin's *Seven Lamps of Architecture*', *North British Review*, Vol. XII, No. XXIV, Feb. 1850, p. 326.

the balance of the material and the spiritual; while Gothic represented the spiritual completely, with its 'entire reversal of the primary characteristic of matter' and its shaft which 'flies up like a sheaf of arrows, without any reference to weight either suffered from or competently opposed, and loses itself in the lines of a roof which itself seems to soar.'[1]

The vivifying principle of Gothic is 'the graceful union of a spontaneous energy and a restraining law'.[2] As being the language of ideas, the elements of the 'pointed' style are beautiful in any position; but 'by their position in Christian buildings, their universal significance suffers, as it were, an apotheosis, and *they become appropriate and symbolical*.'[3] Hence, in Gothic architecture, Patmore saw exemplified the underlying law in all things, which does not hamper or destroy, but which gives unity, direction and meaning to art, to poetry, to life itself. The very same principles which he found at work in the married state and in the manifestations of poetic genius are superbly incarnated in Gothic, and in Gothic alone. This style renders all others obsolete, because it has emerged from the fullest development of Christianity, and expresses in stone that reconciliation of law and individual creativeness, of restraint and energy, of the material and the spiritual which the Christian religion teaches. He explicitly relates the 'pointed' style to his concept of the body, and shows how closely in his mind his architectural theory was connected with his pursuit of the sexual analogy, by writing:

'It may or may not be humiliating to admit that "the body has much to do with religion", that the sight of torrents of lines soaring from floor to roof-ridge helps the soul to soar in prayer, or that the surroundings of traceries and foliage expressly designed to symbolise life as moving freely in the strictest bonds of law conveys the peace of submission into the heart. It is a simple fact that it is so; and while it remains so, Gothic Architecture will continue to be the architecture of Christianity—a "phase" of mind which will in all probability be alive and active when our "modernism" has become a very ancient and forgotten thing indeed.'[4]

Like Pugin, Patmore was completely one-sided in his architectural medievalism, ignoring the Byzantine style, for instance, completely. Yet he was never irrational in his advocacy of Gothic, nor did he ignore architectural facts in his pursuit of symbolic

---

[1] 'Architecture and Architectural Criticism', *St. James's Gazette*, April 30, 1886; *Courage in Politics*, p. 180.
[2] 'The Aesthetics of Gothic Architecture', *British Quarterly Review*, Vol. X, No. XIX, August 1849, p. 66.
[3] *Ibid.*   [4] 'Churches and Preaching-Halls', p. 193.

significances, as may be seen from his discussion of the great architectural forms of the past in the essays grouped together as 'Architectural Styles' in *Principle in Art*. However, the Gothic church captivated him, because he saw it as a mighty triumph over the problem of mass and weight, expressing in stone the recognition of, but also the triumph over, the material by the spiritual. He calls it 'a great geyser of ascending life', and, in an inspired description says that Gothic

> 'is conscious of no task at all; but flies, without the least diminution of its substance, and without swelling under sufferance or gathering of strength by entasis at any particular point, to the commencement of the arch; where it divides itself, sending up the streams of its clustered shafts, some into the lines of the arch and others to the top of the clerestory wall; while others again follow the lines of the vaulting, there to meet like fingers joined in prayer, but still having no thought of the weight of the roof they really help to carry.'[1]

Patmore is indebted for the germs of his architectural theories to various writers: to Lord Lindsay; to Kugler's *Handbuch der Kunstgeschichte*; to Ruskin; to Pugin, whose name he always mentions with respect; and to George Gilbert Scott. However, his development of these ideas is decidedly original, and proceeds not merely from a close study of architectural theory, but from extensive observation and a reasonable amount of practical experience. His architectural writing, eloquent, enthusiastic yet reasoned, and full of well-ordered knowledge, is part and parcel of his general capacity for seeing the spiritual through material expression, and for finding symbolic analogies; yet it is tempered by his unfailing common sense. At times, in discussing the details of Gothic, he may appear to be hunting quincunxes, but his zeal never leads him into the kind of extravagance into which many of the neo-Gothic enthusiasts fell, for, as he once wrote: 'Mr. Ruskin has probably been sickened, as we have been, by the sentimental ravings on the subject of Gothic symbols.'[2]

The main weakness in Patmore's approach to architecture is his attempt rigidly to apply to all kinds of buildings the architectural 'laws' which he believed he had discovered and which he identifies in their fullness with one particular form. He makes no allowance whatever for differing tastes, nor does it appear to have occurred to him that an architectural style which may have been eminently suitable for ecclesiastical purposes is not necessarily either convenient or appropriate for a wide variety of secular and domestic

1 'Architectural Styles', *Principle in Art*, p. 253.
2 'Sources of Expression in Architecture', p. 396.

uses. He tends, in this instance, characteristically, to rationalize his own taste as a universal principle, and to find defective all architectural modes which do not conform to it. He does not appear to have envisaged the possibility that spiritual expression in church architecture would be possible in a form other than Gothic, but related to the culture of a different age and using new materials and new constructional means as Gothic was related to the culture of the Middle Ages and used the means and materials of that time. Yet, underneath all he writes of the spiritual appropriateness of the pointed style, there is more than a hint of that type of awareness which in the middle of the twentieth century has developed into the Catholic liturgical revival affecting church architecture and furnishings in a way by no means contrary to Patmore's general concept of ecclesiastical construction, if at odds with his particular application of it. And in his good taste, his militant opposition to ugly uniformity, to Victorian drabness and jerry-building, to ostentation, vulgar and meaningless ornament and cheerless makeshifts, his discernment and his sensitivity must be applauded.

IV

Politics

PATMORE WROTE ONLY ABOUT A DOZEN ARTICLES dealing directly with politics, which constitute one of the smallest groups on any one topic among his essays, but, taken together with the political odes in *The Unknown Eros*, they give a clear idea of his political outlook and of the issues on which he was at odds with the dominant social philosophy of the age. There is very little about politics in his early essays, and what there is, is fairly typical of 'liberal' sentiment in the 'forties. It is ironical to find the writer who became so politically pessimistic in later life writing in his twenties under the pseudonym of 'An Optimist' such Macaulayish sentiments as these:

> 'Oh, my friends, believe in progress—believe that mankind advances from bad to good—believe that evil is a night-phantom that will vanish before the light of a better day.... The faith in progress cannot be wrong; if we believe in it really, truly, heartily—we effect it.'[1]

As Patmore grew older, however, and especially after he became a Sussex property-owner, his politics hardened into an intransigent Toryism. His naturally authoritarian temperament found its inevitable political haven in a squirearchical system. He was intensely patriotic, believing that only a powerful and dominant England could preserve the peace of Europe. Despite his adolescent years in France and his visits to Italy, he appears to have known little about

---

[1] 'The Misanthrope', *Douglas Jerrold's Shilling Magazine*, Vol. II, No. VII, July 1845, p. 29.

the real state of affairs in European countries, and to have viewed all foreign governments with the suspicion of the typical squire of his day. In a time of national crisis, in 1852, he wrote to *The Times*, urging the formation of a Volunteer Rifle Corps, a suggestion which was later to bear practical fruit. Patmore used to say in later life that he was prouder of his part in the formation of the Volunteer Corps than of anything else he had done, save writing 'Amelia'. His interest in politics became keener with advancing years and as the policies of Gladstone, whom he hated, convinced him that England was being led down the steep slope of destruction. When he began to write for Greenwood in the *St. James's Gazette* he was overjoyed at the opportunity of being able to express his political opinions freely and trenchantly. When Greenwood retired from the editorship of the *Gazette*, Patmore toyed with the idea of founding a political paper of his own, to be called, possibly, *Tom o' Bedlam*,[1] but, because of his failing health and loss of energy, the project was not realized.

Few things Patmore wrote called forth more scorn from his contemporaries than his political essays and odes, which latter the *Athenaeum* damned as containing 'too much the scolding rhetoric of the platform, the mad gallop to nowhere of political or polemical passion.'[2] Even writers who have admired him in other respects find his political utterances distasteful. Hopkins, for instance, objected strongly to Patmore's reference to Disraeli in the ode '1867':

> In the year of the great crime,
> When the false English Nobles and their Jew,
> By God demented, slew
> The Trust they stood twice pledged to keep from wrong

which violent words refer, as Patmore's note to the poem shows, to his view that in 1867 'the middle and upper classes were disfranchised by Mr. Disraeli's Government, and the final destruction of the liberties of England by the Act of 1884 rendered inevitable'!

Patmore's Toryism cannot be attributed simply to his change of financial status and his 'vested interest' as a landed proprietor after his second marriage. Almost from the time of his marriage to Emily Andrews he showed unmistakable signs of an aristocratic temper, and of an intense dislike for the kind of parliamentary democracy which developed after 1850. To judge from the tone of his earlier writing, it seems that he had no quarrel with the condition of things

---

[1] Champneys, *Memoirs*, Vol. I, p. 387.
[2] 'The Unknown Eros', *Athenaeum*, No. 3291, Nov. 22, 1890, p. 694.

as they were in mid-century. But with the passing of the two later Reform Bills, he felt that England was doomed, because of the blow struck at the privileges and ruling power of the upper middle classes. His conception of society was essentially feudal. When he spoke of an 'aristocracy', however, he meant a squirearchy, in which traditions of education and breeding, together with the talent, rather than noble birth, gave the right to rule. Health in society, he believed, depended upon the recognition of differences between men and classes:

> 'All men', he wrote, 'are born believers in aristocracy. Who is there —out of the House of Commons—who does not hold the fundamental dogma of politics, that the best should govern? Modern democracy means nothing but the possession of the elective power by ignorant aristocrats: by those who desire that the best should govern, but who have no sufficient means of discovering the best.'[1]

Such views were the natural consequence of his intense individualism—his belief that, in words which he quoted from Maine de Biran: 'To be let alone in the grand need of society'[2] and his fear that the extension of state control and bureaucratic interference into the private lives of ordinary citizens would be a menace greater than more obvious social evils such as slums and exploitation of the labourer. Although, given his premises, his picture of encroaching bureaucracy may appear exaggerated, there is a startlingly accurate forecast in one of his essays of the Welfare State, of governmental 'snooping' and of the Puritanism of totalitarian governments. He fears, he writes, not the despotism of a single irresponsible tyrant, but

> 'the paltry and prying despotism of the vestry—the more "virtuous" the more paltry and prying—persecuting each individual by the intrusion of its myriad-handed, shifting, ignorant and irresistible tyranny into the regulation of our labour, our household and our very victuals, and, however "pure" in its abstract intention, necessarily corrupt in its application by its agents, since men, as a rule, are corrupt. . . . It will be a despotism which will have to be mitigated by continual "tips", as the other kind has had to be by occasional assassination. Neither the voter nor the inspector yet know their power and opportunities; but they soon will. We shall have to "square" the district surveyor once or twice a year, lest imaginary drains become a greater terror than real typhoid; we shall have to smoke our pipes secretly and with a sense of sin, lest the moral supervisor of the parish should

---

[1] 'Courage in Politics', *St. James's Gazette*, Mar. 19, 1888; *Courage in Politics*, p. 11.

[2] 'De Biran's Pensées', *National Review*, July 1860, p. 155.

decline our offer of half-a-crown for holding his nose during his weekly examination of our bedrooms and closets; the good Churchman will have to receive Communion under the "species" of ginger-ale—as some advanced congregations have already proposed—unless the parson can elude the church-warden with white port, or otherwise persuade him; and, every now and then, all this will be changed, and we shall have to tip our policemen and inspectors for looking over our infractions of popular moralities of a newer pattern. Our condition will very much resemble Swedenborg's hell, in which everybody is incessantly engaged in the endeavour to make everybody else virtuous.'[1]

There is much else in the essays in the same strain, making Patmore one of the minority in his generally complacent age who distrusted the kind of 'progress' offered by politicians and publicists. He felt that the rejoicings of Lord Macaulay and his like over the recent advances of mankind were exactly the same as those of a prosperous shopkeeper over the increase of his business,[2] and he refused to believe that material advancement not united to, or controlled by, an awareness of the need for ethical development could bring any real happiness to mankind.

His whole attitude towards the democracy he saw developing in England is summed up forcefully, if rather unpleasantly, in a memorable image:

'The other day, walking in a country lane, I saw what appeared at a little distance to be a dying animal. On a closer view it proved to be the carcase of a sheep which had in great measure been actually transformed into a mass of the soft, white, malodorous grubs known to anglers by the name of gentles. The struggles of these creatures to get at the food which they concealed produced a strong and regular pulsation throughout the whole mass, and gave it a ghastly semblance of breathing. The ordered state of England, according to its ideal, which for many generations has been more or less realised, compared with the sort of democracy to which we are fast drifting and have well-nigh attained, is much like the animal in which myriads of individual organs, nerves, veins, tissues and cells formed subordinated parts of one living thing, compared with this pulsating mass of grubs, each one of which had no thought but of its just share of carrion.'[3]

Here also his anti-mob sentiments are plain. He was sceptical of the supposed benefits of the education of the mass. An unorganized and enslaved multitude which must be, he felt, in the main self-seeking and unjust would only derive from education subtler means for

[1] 'A "Pessimist" Outlook', *Religio Poetae*, pp. 118–119.
[2] 'Possibilities and Performances', *Religio Poetae*, pp. 100–101.
[3] 'Thoughts on Knowledge, Opinion and Inequality', *Religio Poetae*, pp. 135–136.

developing covetousness and indulging vice. He had no faith whatever in the possibility of any improvement of the 'mass' as such,
but only in the improvement of individuals. He quite seriously held
that the people, far from desiring a spurious egalitarianism, actually
wished for, as much as needed, strong leadership and clearly-marked
social divisions.

> 'Not a ploughboy or a milkmaid', he wrote, 'but would feel without in
> the least knowing why, that a light had passed from their lives with
> the disappearance of social inequalities, and the consequent loss of
> their dignity as integral parts of a somewhat that was greater than
> themselves.'[1]

And at the conclusion of the same essay he makes the shrewd observation, especially pertinent to our own time:

> ' When conquest or revolution establishes the ever-inevitable political
> and social inequalities in new forms, it takes many generations of misery
> and turmoil to introduce into them the moral equality which renders
> them not only tolerable, but the source of true freedom and happiness.'[2]

While such thinking may appear to be the most extreme reaction-
ism, the violence of Patmore's language sometimes prevents the
reader from realizing that, under all his Coriolanus-like contempt
for the 'masses', there lies a firmly held concept of an organic
society, in which moral equality is the result of the recognition of
inequality of function and ability, and in which the rights of every
individual, of whatever station, are accorded the fullest respect. He
was convinced that Victorian ideas of progress and regimentation,
reducing men to a purely theoretical equality, were contradicting
the simple facts of nature, and, more, that by transforming human
beings into numbers or units they were robbing them of their
status as persons. In the 'mass', people *are* units; and to treat the
individual thus was to him the most monstrous of social heresies.
He saw the past as a kind of Golden Age, based possibly upon his
recollection of the placid times of his youth and upon memories of
eighteenth-century social theories, an age of an ordered society, at
peace, full of dignity and mutual respect and led by wise and just
men. This (if it ever existed) had passed, and England was falling
into a decadence for which the people were as much to blame as
their leaders.

On these and other matters Patmore knew that he ran counter to
the spirit of his times. Yet this, far from disturbing him, gave him,
as the ironical essay 'Distinction' shows, a kind of curious pride,

---

[1] 'Thoughts on Knowledge, etc.', *Religio Poetae*, p. 135. [2] *Ibid.*, p. 138.

the pride of a prophet who is confident that he is right because he is in a minority of one. He wrote once:

> 'The slavery of the man who spends his life in making perfectly round holes in needles, perfect points to pins, or perfectly smooth stones, is more real than that of the negro who submits to the lash. It is the slavery of the mind, from which it is the boast of the other that he is exempt.'[1]

The slavery of the mind which comes from dull uniformity was the ultimate horror which he saw emerging from current social and political disintegration; he believed that only the assertion of the will of idiosyncratic personalities would provide oases of freedom in a servile society. It is curious how strikingly, as Champneys has pointed out,[2] Patmore's political pessimism contrasts with his optimism in spiritual matters, and in matters of everyday life, especially as little of it can legitimately be attributed to the 'contempt of the world' which was sometimes found in medieval mystics. Towards the end of his life, even the recollection of a hypothetical 'Golden Age' seems to have faded, and he could say: 'We often mistake our own sweet childhood for the old time; which, had we lived in it, we should have found almost as intolerable as our own.[3] He was then content to be, in the words of one of his fragments,

> Exempt
> In the safe shadow of the world's contempt.

One of his practical proposals is of more than passing interest. In 1887, he wrote a letter to the *St. James's Gazette*, suggesting a European congress for the maintenance of peace, to be presided over by the Pope, whose loss of temporal power and whose consequent neutrality, no less than his spiritual prestige, appeared to Patmore to make him the only person likely to act as an impartial arbiter. In addition, pointing out that the sanctions of such a body must still be based upon force, he proposes an armaments pool and an international force under the control of the Congress to take punitive measures against transgressors.[4] Here, in germ, is the concept of the United Nations, and of such bodies as the North Atlantic Treaty Organization, suggesting that Patmore's attitude on such matters was by no means as impractical as some critics have believed. In fact, what seemed to many of his contemporaries to be

---

1 'Ruskin and Architecture', *North British Review*, Feb. 1854, p. 191.
2 *Memoirs*, Vol. I, p. 360.
3 *Rod, Root and Flower*, 'Aurea Dicta', XXVI, p. 30.
4 'How Is It to End?', *St. James's Gazette*, March 23, 1877; *Courage in Politics*, pp. 24–28.

most reactionary and unrealistic prophecies and proposals sound rather less absurd now in a world closer to Patmore's vision of the future than to Macaulay's.

His chief blindnesses in social matters were a certain lack of compassion, and a disbelief in the value of active works of benevolence, although, as his friends and family unite in asserting, he was personally the most charitable of men. But in an age of great humanitarian reforms, instigated by the zeal and idealism of selfless men, Patmore stood aloof, and could see only the shattering of a traditional social order. Perhaps his increasing interest in mysticism led him to regard the alleviation of social ills as irrelevant to true interior peace—as indeed a comfortably situated man could afford to believe. For him, the individual should, and could, work out his own destiny and achieve his own happiness in a hierarchical order in which each man knew his function and his place, in which wisdom and charity ruled, and in which nobility was pursued as a conscious end. But such an hypothesis ignored almost all the social changes which history was forcing upon Victorian society. The most perhaps one can say is that Patmore should not be too much blamed for setting his Golden Age in the past since nearly all his opponents always set it a little in the future.

At the basis of his political thinking was, inevitably, the sexual analogy. One of his letters to the *St. James's Gazette* is entitled 'How to Govern Ladylike Races'[1]; in the structure of society and in the relationship between nations he found the same masculine and feminine principles which, in his view, operated in life, art and literature. The proper organization of society he saw as analogous to that of a good marriage: 'When a whole nation comes to be mainly guided by the female or sensitive conscience, so far as it has any conscience at all, then great disaster is not far off.'[2] At the end of his essay on Madame de Hautefort he more specifically applies the sexual analogy to society in general, when, after discussing the complementary function of the sexes, he remarks how hopeful that reform would be that should begin where life begins, in the relation of the sexes, a misinterpretation of which for him implies an obscuration of all other relations, including the social ones.[3]

Just as in marriage, man supplies reason, intellectual strength and controlling power, while woman supplies sensitivity, moral force and emotional richness, so in society the feminine element is the masses, governed mainly by emotions, for, as Patmore quotes from de Biran, 'The sovereignty of the people corresponds, in

[1] *St. James's Gazette*, Dec. 29, 1885. [2] 'Conscience', *Religio Poetae*, p. 76.
[3] 'Madame de Hautefort', *Principle in Art*, pp. 190–191.

politics, to the supremacy of the sensations and passions in philosophy and morality.'[1] The masculine element, on the other hand,
is supplied by those who, by education, tradition and breeding,
have developed the right reason necessary for government. The
inequality between the sexes which is the source of delight in
marriage is similarly the spring of peace and order in society, for
'the immense and unalterable inequalities in the knowing faculties
of man are the source and in part the justification of that social
inequality which roughly and very partially reflects them.'[2] As man
is the 'head' of the wife, so the right reason of the governing class
is the 'head' of the state, and as the perfection of marriage results
from a recognition by each partner of the complementary function
of the other, so the perfection of the social order rests upon a
recognition by rulers and ruled of their different status, rights and
obligations.

Fundamentally, Patmore's view of social inequality is a moral
one. He foresees and fears the destruction of the ordered life of
England not only by mechanized civilization, but by the growing
'effeminacy' of democratic government. He based his opposition
to the agitation for equal social rights for women largely upon the
supposition that this would upset the balance of society, making
men more womanly and women more manly, and thus subject the
control of the nation's affairs more to emotion and passion than to
reason. As the political odes show, he blamed the older aristocracy
for surrendering their 'rights', just as he blamed men for the dissatisfaction of women. There were times, too, in which he felt that
the reason for the 'emasculate condition of the national mind' was
'our long continued and unparalleled national prosperity'. This
condition, he said,

'would disappear at once at the tonic touch of a great misfortune.
There are not a few, and those not the least wise and patriotic among
us, who begin to look forward to some such misfortune with hope, and
in whose eyes few calamities can be more terrible than the panic
apathy under which a great part of their fellow-countrymen are content
to be led by ambitious knaves and giddy fools towards a clearly
discerned destruction.'[3]

Political misanthropy could hardly go further than this.

Patmore's diagnosis of the state of England reveals the limitations
of his conception of social responsibility and of his knowledge of

[1] 'De Biran's Pensées', *National Review*, July 1860, p. 155.
[2] 'Thoughts on Knowledge, etc.', *Religio Poetae*, p. 132.
[3] 'Manifest Destiny', *St. James's Gazette*, Dec. 26, 1885; *Courage in Politics*,
pp. 10–11.

history. His political prose and poetry suggest crotchetiness, isolation and impotence. At the same time, his political views were based upon something deeper than an intense dislike of Gladstone and a desire to maintain property and privilege. However perverse and narrow some of them may appear to later eyes, they were at least founded upon a clear idea of the nature and function of the state, of the duties of rulers and ruled, and of the ultimate destiny of man, not upon expediency, or jingoism, or on the shopkeeper's vision of expanding profits. His prognosis may have been too pessimistic, and made too few allowances for inevitable change in the social structure, but it was by no means as far from the truth as his biographers, Champneys and Gosse, writing in the cosy, unsuspecting Edwardian era, imagined it to be.

V

Patmore's Theory of Prosody

ALMOST FROM THE TIME when his first book of poems was published Patmore showed a close interest in metrics and in the minutiae of poetic technique. Many of the reviews he wrote in the 'forties and 'fifties reveal him in effect working out the theories of English verse structure which he finally formulated in his 'Prefatory Study on English Metrical Law'. Probably it was Coleridge who originally inspired such investigations, for the first clear evidence of Patmore's special interest in prosody is a comment in an essay of 1848, quoting a manuscript note of Coleridge concerning the metrical function of accent, and an analysis in the same essay of a couplet from *Christabel*. But it is significant that the three essays in which Patmore gives most attention to his own concepts of metre are reviews of Tennyson's poems. The 1850 review of *In Memoriam*, in particular, contains the most complete exposition of his theories before the essay on 'English Metrical Critics'. On the many occasions on which the two poets walked and talked together in the days of their intimacy, questions of poetic technique must have had a large place in their discussions. Tennyson's knowledge of classical metres, his venturesomeness in the use of stanza forms, and his attention to the musical effects of language helped to encourage Patmore to develop his own metrical interests.

However, he was not content only to analyse his own technique, and that of his contemporaries, nor to follow Tennyson's example and precepts. He read very widely in technical works on English prosody, both standard authorities, and obscure writers to whose books his British Museum position gave him ready access. T. S. Omond, himself one of the most erudite of English metrists, called him 'a learned critic' of prosody,[1] and C. C. Abbott speaks of him as 'both curious and learned in prosody'.[2] In his 'Prefatory Study' Patmore refers not only to such works as Guest's *History of English Rhythm* (1838) and Mitford's *Essay on the Harmony of Language* (1774), but also to Dr. Burney's *History of Music*, O'Brien's *Ancient Rhythmical Art Restored*, Puttenham's *Arte of English Poesie*, Daniel's *Defence of Ryme*, and, most importantly, Joshua Steele's *An Essay towards Establishing the Melody and Measure of Speech* (1775), a virtually forgotten work which he may be said to have disinterred.

The most interesting of his earlier prosodical considerations deal with the relationship between prose and verse; with the nature of metre and rhythm, and the part played by the pause; and with the functional value of alliteration and rhyme. In all that he writes he is reaching out towards a conception of poetry as measured by temporal units instead of syllables, and towards the principle of 'isochronous intervals' he was to advance in the 'Prefatory Study'. In the 1848 essay on Tennyson, his chief technical points concern the power of rhythmical analogies and the choice of sounds in creating suggestion by indirect similitude. Dealing with the last of these, he shows his sensitivity to poetic effects when he analyses two lines from Coleridge's *Christabel* in terms which seem to anticipate Edith Sitwell's discussions of Pope's poetic texture:

> 'The brands were flat, the brands were dying,
> Amid their own white ashes lying.'

Here the cold vowels *a*, *i*, *o* are the only ones which are openly sounded, and of these *a* is repeated five times, and *i* three times; the *e* in the short *the*, preceding, as it does, the long syllable *brand*, is scarcely heard; the ear is wholly occupied with the eight cold vowels which occur in the long syllables of the eight feet that constitute these lines. The only effect of warmth is a very slight one, produced by the rapid succession of the consonants *b*, *r*, and *n*, *d*, in the word *brand*. Again, there is an effect of weight conveyed by the word *brand*, and to this effect we are invited to attend, by the repetition of it, and by the first juxtaposition and contrast of this word with other words, conveying the notion of softness and lightness; finally, the two ideas of lightness and weight are united, and the effect completed by the word *amid*, in which the sound passing through the soft *m* and its indistinct vowels,

---

[1] *English Metrists in the Eighteenth and Nineteenth Centuries* (O.U.P., 1907), p. 150.

[2] *Further Letters of Gerard Manley Hopkins*, p. xxix.

concludes in a heavy *d*; and completes, to a delicate ear, and a pre-pared mind, the entire picture of the weighty and smouldering brands, sunken through the light mass of ashes which remains after their un-disturbed combustion.'[1]

Fanciful though such an analysis may be, it does at least show a general awareness of phonetic effect and of the 'art which conceals art'.

In his appreciation of *In Memoriam* Patmore indicates, in speaking of the 'irregular ode', that he has already worked out the main outlines of his theory of isochronous intervals:

'Our impression of it is, that each line, however many syllables it may contain, ought to occupy the same time in reading, according to the analogy of bars in music. This view is supported by the best parts of the odes of Wordsworth and Milton, which may and ought to be read, each line into the same time; and also, by the necessity which has invariably been felt, for printing the lines in such a manner, that the reader shall know, beforehand, the requisite period to be occupied in the delivery of the line, and in the pauses by which it is to be preceded and concluded.'[2]

In support of this view he cites the irregular introductions to *L'Allegro* and *Il Penseroso*, stating that the lines of these introduc-tions ought not only to be read as regular bars themselves, but ought also to give the time to the whole of the lines which follow them.[3]

Rhyme and alliteration he regards as elements of genuine metre, the former being able to produce, he says, at certain fixed places 'an emphasis of sound which demands a corresponding weight of meaning'.[4] And, dealing with the pause, so essential to his own prosodic theories, he writes: 'Modern poets . . . require to be re-minded that a strong caesura ought always to occur at the conclusion of every verse of eight or more syllables.'[5] All of this clearly shows the trend of Patmore's thinking on metre. He is already a 'timer', and not a syllable-counter; and he sees rhythm and metre as explicable ultimately only in musical terms. Some time between 1850 and 1855 he seems to have discovered Joshua Steele's work, which asserts that verse is essentially a matter of musical rhythm, and applies musical methods to metrical notation, for, the next time he discusses metre, in the 1855 review of Tennyson's *Maud*, he makes very generous use of musical analogies. Passages in the poem, he says, might almost be called 'music without notes'; and the metrical foundation of the work as a whole he finds to be not syllables but

[1] 'Tennyson's *Poems—The Princess*', *North British Review*, May 1848, p. 56.
[2] 'In Memoriam', *North British Review*, Aug. 1850, p. 542.
[3] *Ibid.*, p. 543.   [4] *Ibid.*, p. 545.   [5] *Ibid.*

the number of accents in each verse. This he sees as 'a complete return to the Anglo-Saxon principle of isochronous bars, of which the filling up is left to the will of the poet.'[1]

In August 1857, the *North British Review* published a very long article by Patmore entitled 'English Metrical Critics'. With alterations, it was reprinted as 'Prefatory Study on English Metrical Law' as a preface to *Amelia* (1878) and later, under the title of 'Essay on English Metrical Law', as an appendix to the second volume of the 1886 collected edition of his poems. Students of prosody and practising poets have paid tribute to this essay. Omond, for instance, ranks it 'among the few papers of abiding value which the subject has elicited'.[2] A. E. Housman, writing of the 'latent base, comprising natural laws by which all versification is conditioned, and the secret springs of the pleasure which good versification can give', declares that 'a few pages of Coventry Patmore and a few of Frederic Myers contain all, so far as I know, or all of value, which has been written on such matters.'[3] And both Bridges and Hopkins, despite reservations about Patmore's theories, treated them with a respect which shows how deeply his 'Essay' impressed them.[4] Bridges tried to persuade Patmore to act as the mouthpiece for them all, and write a treatise embodying the principles of the 'new prosody'. In September 1883, he wrote to the older poet:

> 'The interest which you take in the grammar of English verse has led me to hope that you would not be disinclined to give an account in print of what Hopkins and I call the new prosody. . . . I think that—supposing the "new prosody" to be worth your attention—that the completeness of what you have hitherto written rather demands that you should treat this theory.'[5]

The project came to nothing, but the fact that the two younger poets should have seen in Patmore the writer most likely to be in sympathy with their prosodical ideas, and have visualized him as their collaborator in presenting them to the world, shows that they recognized the independence and originality of his theories.

Significantly, those poets and metrists who praise Patmore's 'Essay' are ones who think of metre in terms of time and not in terms of the emphatic stress of certain syllables, or of the number of syllables. When Omond writes that he regards it as inaugurating

1 'Tennyson's *Maud*', *Edinburgh Review*, October 1855, p. 515.
2 Omond, p. 156.
3 *The Name and Nature of Poetry* (Oxford University Press, 1933), p. 4.
4 See also Sydney Colvin in a letter to Patmore: 'the most luminous thing that has been written on that puzzling subject' (Champneys, Vol. II, p. 386).
5 Derek Patmore, *Life and Times*, pp. 191–192.

'the new prosody' he is referring to the kind of prosody of which he was one of the most able defenders, that which maintains that 'Verse depends first and always on time-rhythm; it "contrives its pattern of sounds in time".'[1] The 'Essay' is certainly one of the most important enunciations of the concept of the rhythm of a verse-line as arising from a grouping into units of sounds and silences, which produces the impression of temporal proportion. According to this concept, all feet are of equal duration, although the proportion between the *thesis*, the heavy or strong part, and the *arsis*, the light or slack part, may vary. For such theorists as Patmore, the number of syllables and pauses making up a foot can vary considerably so long as each foot takes the same time to pronounce.

Patmore begins his 'Essay' with a brief review of some of the earlier studies of metrics, pointing out what he considers to be their defects, but singling out for special mention Mitford, Guest and Steele. When he passes on to consider the essential nature of metre, his familiar concept of law emerges again in his description of versification as offering a necessary counterpoise to the 'great spiritualization' of language in poetry. 'The more vigorous and various the life,' he writes, 'the more astringent and elaborate must be the law by obedience to which life expresses itself'(221).[2] Language in good poetry should always seem to feel, but not to suffer from, the bonds of verse. Even prose and ordinary speaking, he points out, involve a good number of musical and metrical elements, which assume importance in proportion to the amount of emotion expressed. 'Metre', he concludes, 'in the primary degree of a simple series of isochronous intervals, marked by accents, is as natural to spoken language as an even pace is natural to walking' (224). He makes it clear, however, that he is referring to the 'common and intelligible delivery of prose', and asserts that 'verse itself is only verse on the condition of right reading'. The correct reading of both verse and prose, in his sense, is the recognition of the degree of measure whereby the passage is divisible into a certain number of bars, which, he claims, is natural and not artificial. In such a division accent is divided from accent by equal measures of time.

Unfortunately Patmore does not make clear just what he understands by accent. He writes:

'the only tenable view of that accent upon which it is allowed, with more or less distinctness, by all, that English metre depends, in

---

1 Omond, p. 240.

2 This reference and subsequent similar ones in this chapter indicate the page-numbers of the 'Essay' as printed in the 1886 collected edition of the poems.

contra-distinction to the syllabic metre of the ancients, is the view which attributes to it the function of marking, *by whatever means*, certain isochronous intervals' (230).

and a little later :

'There are two indispensable conditions of metre—first, that the sequence of vocal utterance, represented by written verse, shall be divided into equal or proportionate spaces; secondly, *that the fact of that division shall be made manifest* by an "ictus", or "beat", actual or mental, which, like the post in a chain railing, shall mark the end of one space, and the commencement of another' (230).

Thus, basing his idea of metre upon spoken delivery of verse lines, and, doubtless, upon contemporary methods of 'elocution', he identifies accent with ictus, and with musical accent. Accent answers, he says, to 'the character and conditions of accent in vocal and instrumental music' (231). For it is his conviction that the relationship of music to language goes far beyond that of mere similarity. '*Perfect poetry and song are, in fact, nothing more than perfect speech upon high and moving subjects*' (233).

The real difference, he considers, between ancient and modern metre consists in the modern rendering of 'the "accentual" division of time the *sole*, instead of merely the *main*, source of metre' (235–6). But, realizing that different syllables take different amounts of time to pronounce, he recognizes that pauses must be considered in any metrical scheme, and that in determining the form of a verse the silences are as important as the sounds. He draws attention to two types of pause, the metrical and the grammatical. However, when he says that the metrical pauses are usually much longer than the longest pauses of punctuation, adding that they are also 'almost entirely independent of them' (240), it is clear that he is ignoring all pauses save the terminal ones and the caesura, and that he visualizes every line containing an uneven number of feet as followed by a very long pause.

So far Patmore has been expressing with new force and lucidity ideas which he has adapted from Steele, O'Brien and others. He is now ready to announce what he believes to be his own unique contribution to prosody, which he puts forward with a certain sententiousness :

'Nothing but the unaccountable disregard, by prosodians, of final pauses could have prevented the observation of the great general law, which I believe that I am now, for the first time, stating, that the *elementary measure, or integer, of English verse is double the measure of ordinary prose*—that is to say, it is the space which is bounded by *alternate* accents; *that every verse proper contains two, three, or four of these metres,* or, as with a little allowance they may be called, "dipodes"; *and that there is properly no such thing as hypercatalexis*' (242).

This means, as he goes on to explain, that all English lines in common cadence are therefore dimeters, trimeters or tetrameters, and consist, when they are full, of eight, twelve or sixteen syllables. The theory of 'dipodes' implies that lines are measured by groups having the time of four syllables; when a line contains six or ten syllables it must be filled up with a pause equal to two syllables. But he allows in the irregular ode an almost unlimited liberty of catalexis and says that here the calalectic pause may vary from the time of two to fourteen syllables, justifying such a pause on the analogy of the pauses, or stops, in music (244). He regards the blank verse line as a trimeter, that is, a line which requires a silent foot, or a pause equal to a foot, to complete it. It was such aspects of Patmore's theory which led Hopkins to comment to Bridges that he thought Patmore 'pushes the likeness of musical and metrical time too far'.[1] Patmore's instinct is all for regularity, and for an underlying principle of uniformity and law, so that lines must be filled out, measures must go in sets of twos, variations must be explained as not really variations, and the iambic ode, once submitted to the law of pauses, must be described as 'erroneously called "irregular"' (244).

The remainder of the 'Essay' is taken up with a discussion of alliteration and rhyme. Neither of these, in Patmore's view, can be regarded as a mere 'ornament' of versification. Alliteration is a 'real and powerful metrical adjunct' and 'a very effective mode of conferring emphasis on the accent, which is the primary foundation of metre' (247). Taking the side of Daniel against Campion, he defends the metrical function of rhyme, and shows that it is a means of extending the limits and multiplying the symmetry of measure. All staves in poetry are in fact created by rhyme. He quotes Guest to the effect that rhyme 'marks and defines the accent, and thereby strengthens and supports the rhythm'. Only the transcendent genius of Milton enabled him to establish one kind of rhymeless narrative, in the face of the obstacles which absence of rhyme places in the way of the poet.

The 'Essay on English Metrical Law', like the rest of Patmore's prose, is lucid and more than a thought dogmatic. It expounds the temporal theory more clearly than any of his predecessors had done;

---

[1] *Letters of Gerard Manley Hopkins to Robert Bridges*, edited by C. C. Abbott (London: Oxford University Press, 1935), p. 119.

it is not loaded with new technical terms; it illustrates each point with well-chosen examples (although it may be felt, once or twice, that the examples offered are the *only* ones, rather than character-istic ones); and it goes right to the heart of prosodic problems. At the same time, the 'Essay' contains more than one mis-statement, and several rash generalizations, which betray Patmore's anxiety to make all English poetry conform to his hypothetical norms just as he wanted all other things to be explicable in terms of sexual duality. One wonders whether, unconsciously, he felt his 'dipode' to be the *homo* of verse, with the major accent the masculine element, and the minor accent the feminine, each complementing the other in due subordination to produce the harmonious rhythmical unit.

To say that Patmore's theories are by no means as original as he imagines them to be, is not to imply that they are all merely borrowed. Despite his acknowledgement of the work of others, his conclusions are the product of his own observations, thought and practice. Nevertheless, the temporal theory was very much in the air when 'English Metrical Critics' was written. Such works as E. S. Dallas's *Poetics* (1852), William Gardiner's *The Music of Nature* (1832), as well as the studies by O'Brien and Guest, all point in the same direction as Patmore's essay. Still, he deserves credit for having recognized the importance of the temporal theory and carrying it several stages further. And that his suggestion that others had accepted his ideas without acknowledgement is not wholly wide of the mark is seen from J. J. Sylvester's *The Laws of Verse* (1870), in which the notions of time as the basis of measure, and of the rhythmical importance of the pause, are advanced as if they are new and original discoveries. Further, in 1880 the American poet Sidney Lanier, in *The Science of English Verse*, was to provide the most elaborate and indeed the 'classic' statement of the temporal theory.

However, Patmore is led astray in some of his conclusions by his confusing word-accent and 'ictus', or musical beat. He writes that the ictus, although in English 'the *only* source of metre', has '*no material and external existence at all*, but has its place in the mind, which craves measure in everything, and, wherever the idea of measure is uncontradicted, delights in marking it with an imaginary "beat"' (230–1). His confounding word-accent and ictus leads him, then, to say that 'the marking of the measure by the recurrent ictus may be occasionally remitted, the position of the ictus altered, or its place supplied by a pause, without the least offence to a culti-vated ear.' This may be true of some kinds of spoken utterance, but it can hardly be true of the mental beat which gives poetry its rhythm. Had Patmore thought of metre as composed of isochronous feet instead of isochronous *intervals*, and conceived of each foot as containing *thesis* and *arsis*, he might well have escaped Hopkins's criticism of his 'unsatisfactory' treatment of English spoken accent.[1]

Again, when distinguishing between grammatical pauses and metrical pauses, Patmore suggests that:

> 'In beating time to the voice of a good reader of verse, it will be found that the metrical pauses are usually much longer than the longest pauses of punctuation, and that they are almost entirely independent of them' (240).

That metrical pauses are sometimes longer than the longest pauses of punctuation may be true. But the reading of verse is not determined by an antecedently established rhythmical pattern. A proper reading *discovers* the pattern, and in such a reading grammar, sense-pause and sense-emphasis help to determine accent and rhythm. The metrical scheme, including the pauses, cannot be developed independently of the grammatical structure, as indeed Patmore's knowledge of Milton should have taught him.

Patmore's recognition of the differing time-values of various syllables leads him to the conclusion that the proportion of metrical intervals between accent and accent is only 'general and approximate'; a conclusion with which Hopkins agreed. But as a consequence, Patmore is inclined to disregard the importance of all pauses, save the caesura and the terminal pause. He tends to throw all the weight of pause towards the end of the line, and will allow a final pause equal to an entire foot between the nominative and the governed genitive. So, too, grammatical periods may occur in the middle of an accentual interval without lengthening its time. 'In fact,' he writes, 'the "stops" or conclusions of grammatical clauses are rather marked by *tone* than *time*' (240).

His theory of 'dipodes' is even more difficult to accept. That all poets have been unconsciously obeying a hitherto unapprehended law of 'symmetry and quadrature', to use Hopkins's phrase, and that every line containing less than exact multiples of four syllables is catalectic, requiring to be filled out with pauses, are far-fetched conceptions. The example Patmore gives, from one of his own poems, does, in fact, appear to confirm his dipodic theory:

> How strange it is to wake
>   And watch, while others sleep,
> Till sight and hearing ache
>   For objects that may keep

[1] *Further Letters*, p. 178.

The awful inner sense
Unroused, lest it should mark
The life that haunts the emptiness
And horror of the dark.

This he offers as an instance of the six-syllable 'iambic' which he calls 'the most solemn of all our English measures'. Hopkins, discussing this part of Patmore's 'Essay' with Bridges, wrote:

> 'The principle, whether necessary or not, which is at the bottom of both musical and metrical time is that everything shd. go by twos and, where you want to be strict and effective, even by fours. But whereas this is recognized and insisted on in modern music, it is neither in verse. It exists, though, and the instance Pat. gives is good and bears him out.'[1]

All, in fact, that Hopkins wrote on metre indicates that, while he recognized that 'dipodes' could exist in certain circumstances, he did not accept them as a universal principle. Any attempt, indeed, to read all verse with the pauses necessary to complete the 'dipodes' would result in a funereal pace; in dramatic verse, especially, the principle would produce completely artificial isolation of individual lines. Frederick Page makes a gallant attempt to scan a portion of one of Patmore's odes according to 'dipodes'; but he admits that his reading does not convince himself.[2] This is not surprising, since it results in such grotesqueries as this:

: | Fo :—|r : crown'd : with | ro :—ses | al :l | :
'Tis | there : O | Love : they | keep : thy | fes :ti- | val : | :

and

And | na :—|—:me | : | :

Patmore's treatment of stress and time has caused some critics to assert that his metrical theories are at bottom identical with those of Hopkins. It has even been suggested that Hopkins took over Patmore's views *in toto*. For instance, Harold Whitehall goes so far as to say: 'Hopkins's sprung rhythm, and for that matter most of his running rhythm, follows Patmore's theories almost to the letter. Yet Patmore and Hopkins never saw how they complemented each other,'[3] while D. S. MacColl deplores the 'theoretical mess' which Hopkins and Bridges made of the matter of prosody, and alleges that Hopkins became 'an adept of Patmore's doctrine, merely

---

[1] *Letters to Bridges,* p. 119.   [2] *Patmore, A Study in Poetry,* p. 170.
[3] 'Sprung Rhythm': *Gerard Manley Hopkins,* by the Kenyon Critics (London: Denis Dobson Ltd., 1949), p. 41.

refining upon it at certain points'.[1] If these views are correct, it makes Patmore's inability to appreciate Hopkins's poetry very mystifying indeed. Patmore did his utmost to enter into the spirit of his friend's work, but he had to confess its difficulties insuperable. Perhaps a closer examination of the relationship between Patmore's theories and those of Hopkins may go some distance towards explaining this.

The letters exchanged between them, Hopkins's letters to Bridges and his 'Author's Preface' to his poems make it clear that each had studied metre with a different emphasis, and that, although in some matters they were completely in accord, their separate conclusions are almost diametrically opposed. The degree to which they differ is partially concealed by the uniformly courteous tone of their correspondence. It is noteworthy, however, that, while Hopkins always defended Patmore vigorously in his letters to Bridges, he is himself more critical of the older poet's work in this correspondence than he is in that with Patmore himself.

Patmore, at least, realized that the trend of Hopkins's metrical speculations and experiments led in an opposite direction to his own. 'I am conscious', he writes, in reference to Hopkins's poems, 'of my extreme slowness in taking fully in what is new. I suppose it comes of my all along having followed a single line of my own.'[2] Hopkins, on his side, felt the same, for he commented to Bridges, who had sent Patmore a manuscript book of the Jesuit's poems:

> 'Coventry Patmore has kept your MS. book a long time, as though it were to give himself the opportunity of repentance for not admiring all the poems, and indeed appears to look on his condition as one of guilt and near to reprobation—which is very odd of him. And I believe it will be of no avail and that like Esau and Antiochus he will not get the grace and is in a fair way to die in his sins.'[3]

And, in another letter, discussing Patmore's 'Essay on Metrical Law', he said: 'There are some things in this essay I do not find myself in agreement with, but on these I do not touch,' which suggests considerable reservations, especially if it is realized that the criticisms he does in fact offer refer only to Patmore's own arguments.

Hopkins was concerned with quantity in his concept of verse-rhythm, but by quantity he meant more than time. Length is associated in his mind with strength; as he writes in his 'Preface': 'In Sprung Rhythm, as in logaoedic rhythm generally, the feet

[1] 'Patmore and Hopkins: Sense and Nonsense in English Prosody', *London Mercury*, July 1938, p. 223.
[2] *Further Letters*, p. 204.　　　　[3] *Letters to Bridges*, p. 194.

are assumed to be equally long or strong and their seeming inequality is made up by pause or stressing.'[1] So, when he is explaining to Patmore how he differentiates *ictus* from spoken accent, he writes:

' . . . as suppose a man said in prose "a penniless adventurer is always in extremities"—this can be seen to run into alternate strong and weak beats, say iambs and trochees, according to where you begin scanning; and perhaps people wd. not notice that every other strong beat, every fourth syllable, that is, is really scarcely marked at all, so inevitably does the mind supply it. This indeed falls into double-iambic or double-trochaic feet, or in music bars of four time, in which the first accent is stronger than the second, but from the same kind of sentences may also arise the *blank stresses*, as I am accustomed to call them, of the ten-syllable line and other lines; for in fact in Milton few lines have five real stresses, one or two being blank, though in idea there are always five.'[2]

This shows that, whereas for Patmore rhythm is primarily a matter of time, and accents serve the function of marking time, for Hopkins rhythm is a matter of both time and stress, with the effort of stress looming large. His description of Sprung Rhythm in the 'Author's Preface' is given in terms of syllables and stresses, not in terms of equal or approximately equal intervals of time. He certainly did not accept the dipodic theory.

The basic divergence between the approach of the two poets to metre, even when on the surface they agree, is revealed by Hopkins's comments on the Alexandrine. Patmore had stated that the true Alexandrine 'as it appears in the Polyolbion' is a tetrameter having a middle and a final pause each equal to a foot. He regarded the Alexandrine at the end of the Spenserian stanza as a '*different verse, though including the same number of syllables; it is the mere filling up of the trimeter*' (262), and Hopkins writes:

'My theory of it (Alexandrine) is yours, that ideally every line has 8 feet, 8 stresses, but not equal—4 dimeters or bars of 2 feet each. Then at the pause in the middle of the line and at the end one of these 8 feet may be and commonly is suppressed so that 6 are left. This gives boundless variety, all of which is needed however to control the deep natural monotony of the measure, with its middle pause and equal division.'[3]

But though Hopkins says that he accepts Patmore's theory, he treats the Alexandrine in terms of stresses, not of isochronous intervals or

1 *Poems of Gerard Manley Hopkins*, Third Edition (O.U.P., 1948), Author's Preface, p. 8.
2 *Further Letters*, p. 180.   3 *Ibid.*, p. 212.

of dipodes. He is more interested in the variety which can be obtained by the disposition of stresses than he is in 'filling up' the line to obtain uniformity. Again, in his 'Preface', Hopkins gives as one of the reasons why Sprung Rhythm is the most natural of things, that 'it is the rhythm of common speech and of written prose, when rhythm is perceived in them.' Yet Patmore, quoting a passage from St. Jude, declares that all the accented syllables, in a right reading, would be severed from each other by 'equal measures of time' (226–7). Patmore would impose his isochronous intervals upon prose, while Hopkins would import something of the freer accentuation of prose into poetry.

Always aware of the relationship between stress and slack and between the rhythmical units, Hopkins sought for ways of producing tension, emotional power and the exhibition of contrast in his verse, while still retaining a rhythmical pattern. Patmore, on the contrary, was trying to find a means of avoiding monotonous agreement between word-accent and verse-beat while adhering to a fairly stable metrical scheme. It is not surprising, then, that the application of theories which some critics claim to be fundamentally the same resulted in poems as different as 'De Natura Deorum' and 'The Wreck of the Deutschland'. Apart from the elisions, the unusual words and combinations, and the somewhat extravagant markings which Hopkins used, the violent juxtaposed stresses, the startling fusion of line to line and the strange rhymes must have perturbed Patmore, who had reiterated so often in his criticism that good poetry is that from which all eccentricity and strangeness had been purged, and which is the product of 'interior polish', the art that conceals art. After reading Hopkins's poems several times, he was forced to confess that to the difficulties of thought and feeling in the poems Hopkins had added the difficulty 'of following *several* entirely novel and simultaneous experiments in versification and construction.' 'System and learned theory,' he adds, 'are manifest in all these experiments; but they seem to me to be *too* manifest.'[1] In this latter comment he may not have been wholly wrong. Even the most devoted admirer of Hopkins must admit that at times his innovations *do* force themselves too sharply forwards, and that the poetry is sometimes buried under the novelties. In a letter to Bridges Patmore said of Hopkins: 'His genius is, however, unmistakable, and is lovely and unique whenever he approximates to the ordinary rules of composition.'[2] The 'ordinary rules of composition' are Patmore's main concern. His prosodical theories, however novel they may at first appear, are in effect attempts to justify experiments

[1] *Further Letters*, p. 205.   [2] Champneys, *Memoirs*, Vol. II, p. 247.

within those rules. At bottom, he is much more conservative than either Hopkins or Bridges.

Both poets agreed that all the means of marking the harmonic pattern—especially rhyme and alliteration—are not superficial, but integral parts of a poem. Both regarded poems as organic wholes, 'the song that *is* the thing it says', both recognized the importance of time-values, and both were alive to the subtleties even in ostensibly simple prosodic structure. But they approached poetry from different ends, as it were. Hopkins's theory includes Patmore's principal ideas and transcends them. He accepted time as an essential part of the poetic order; he was sensitive to the relationship between poetry and music. But he gave at least equal place to other elements. He wrote to Dixon explaining that the new rhythm which had been long haunting his ear consisted 'in scanning by accents or stresses alone, without any account of the number of syllables, so that a foot may be one strong syllable, or it may be many light and one strong.'[1] Later he told Dixon that his practice was founded upon 'an easily felt principle of *equal strengths*'.[2] These and fuller explanations show Hopkins as unmistakably a 'stresser', rather than a 'timer'. He nowhere indicates that he accepts Patmore's idea that there are temporal measures existing apart from the basic relations established in the rhythmical structure. His problem is that of combining groups of varying numbers of syllables so that rhythm is felt as equivalent masses balanced against each other.

Fundamentally the differences between the two poets, which their differing attitudes towards prosody illustrate, were psychological. Each respected the other's judgment, intelligence and personality, while having distinct reservations about his poetry. Hopkins's defence of Patmore to Bridges, the time and care he expended on the detailed criticism of the older poet's work, his gentle, deferential tone in the correspondence, are sufficient indications of his regard for Patmore's personality and achievement. Patmore, on his side, although proud of his indifference to criticism, accepted Hopkins's 'subtle fault-finding' humbly and gratefully, and, after his death, paid him the most generous of compliments:

'Gerard Hopkins was the only orthodox, and as far as I could see, saintly man in whom religion had absolutely no narrowing effect upon his general opinions and sympathies. A Catholic of the most scrupulous strictness, he could nevertheless see the Holy Spirit in all goodness, truth and beauty; and there was something in all his words and manners

[1] *The Correspondence of Gerard Manley Hopkins and Richard Watson Dixon*, edited by Claude Colleer Abbott (O.U.P., 1935), p. 14.
[2] *Ibid.*, p. 22.

which were at once a rebuke and an attraction to all who could only aspire to be like him.'[1]

But, when the two poets met first, Patmore was sixty years of age, with his poetic work accomplished, while Hopkins was thirty-nine, with his spirit full of excitement at the prospect of poetic exploration. Patmore's mind was fixed on mystical matters and politics. He had moved too far away from his first feeling to dare any corrections to his verse which would involve rewriting of his earlier work, he told Hopkins. His tastes in poetry had long before been definitely formed, and he found it impossible to enter with sympathy into such a strange poetic universe as Hopkins's verse presented to him. W. H. Gardner suggests that he 'had written so many thousands of smooth octosyllables that not even the sinewy fluctuant Odes could obliterate the groove and prevent the canalization of his later views and responses.'[2]

Thus Patmore's 'deafness' to Hopkins's poems is not surprising after all. His fundamental traditionalism cut him off from the appreciation of the Jesuit's work. He sought for the 'point of rest' in his metrical theory, as he did in other forms of art, for the peace, order, law and harmony which he believed lay at the heart of every human activity. Hopkins sought for tensions, for stresses, for individuality. One valued smoothness; the other sharp contrasts and dynamic force. At bottom, in his metrical theory, as in his poetry, Patmore's Thomism is at odds with Hopkins's Scotism, for it is universals the older poet is seeking, not inscapes.

[1] Champneys, *Memoirs*, Vol. II, p. 249.
[2] *Gerard Manley Hopkins* (Martin Secker & Warburg, 1944), p. 206.

PART FIVE

DEVELOPMENT AND
ACHIEVEMENT IN PATMORE'S
POETRY

I

The Early Poems : Poetic Background

ATMORE'S YOUTHFUL POETRY is strongly deriva-
tive; the chief poetic influences, those of the older
Romantics and Tennyson, are very much what one
would expect to find in the works of a young man
beginning to write in the 1840's. So clear are the
echoes that it is at first difficult to understand the
reception of the early poems in some quarters, at
least, as being full of a new promise, and why the Pre-Raphaelites
were so enamoured of them as to elect the author as 'their' poet.
Patmore was to shed most of these conventional debts as he pro-
gressed towards the individual expression of *The Unknown Eros.*
Yet both in the character of most of the borrowings themselves, as
well as in the more original portions of these early poems, the
distinctive quality of his sensibility is shadowed forth. The sense of
the power and presence of Nature, the combination of lyricism and
moralizing, the uncomplicated verse-forms and the psychological
interest in human emotions, the eye for detail—all of these, shown
with more or less distinctness in the 1844 volume, were to remain
as part of his poetic universe. But between 1844 and 1854, when the
first part of *The Angel* was published, he abandoned the Romantic
symbolism, the youthful melancholy, the occasional lushness of
language and the ballad-themes of these pieces, and developed his
own particular expression of joy in love and peace in belief.

239

His poetry became more original in its inspiration, smoother and more technically skilful. As subsequently reprinted, the poems which were first published in the 1844 volume differ greatly from the originals. The River, despite the 'Aet. 16' which appears in all later editions, is so altered from the first version as to be almost another poem; and this is true, to a lesser degree, of almost all the other 1844 pieces. So, too, with his occasional poems. One rather curious piece dealing with a public execution, and called 'A Murderer's Sacrament', first published in *Douglas Jerrold's Shilling Magazine* in August 1845, was finally reduced to less than a quarter of its original length, and otherwise reshaped, then included in his collected poems as 'A London Fête'. Although there are manifest signs of true poetic feeling and precocious maturity of vision in the 1844 pieces, they are often technically clumsy. Patmore's ear for a defective line or a strained rhyme was at that stage far from keen, and Gosse not unfairly says that to read some of the early lyrics 'is like riding down a frozen lane in a springless cart'.[1]

However, Patmore's early articles, as we have seen, show his intense interest in prosody; and the changes he made in *The Angel in the House* before the 1863 edition reflect this careful and systematic study. The contrast between the gaucheries of the 1844 pieces and the music of *The Unknown Eros* is therefore the result both of increase in technical skill through practice in verse-writing and of an unremitting application to the mechanics of poetry. Patmore became aware quite early that he had no talent for intricate metrical forms. He abandoned the sonnet after three youthful experiments. And he wrote his poetry almost wholly in iambic feet. He turned this limitation into a virtue by perfecting the simple form of his earlier verse. He did not make the mistake of striving after ingenious effects, as Rossetti did, for example, and Woolner, whose poem *My Beautiful Lady*, intended as a kind of parallel to *The Angel in the House*, contains a mixture of blank verse, couplets and varying stanza forms. Neither did he aim at the grandiose utterance of the 'Spasmodics'. The metre of his 'domestic epic', one of the utmost simplicity, was deliberately selected because he recognized that it was the kind of form he could best handle.

As with metre, so, too, with language. Occasionally, in the odes, Patmore uses an unusual word (*Trophonian, photosphere, dilaceration, ingratiant*), but for the most part, even in the most 'philosophical' of them, his vocabulary is Wordsworthian in its unadorned character. He did not care for poetry which dealt largely in the out-of-the-way word or strange phrase. As he indicates in a letter to

[1] 'The History of a Poem', *North American Review*, March 1897, p. 286.

Sutton in 1847, his endeavour was to reach beauty, truth and pathos by the right ordering of simple words:

> 'I fear you underrate the evil effects that must result from an eccentric phraseology. Uncommon things must be said in common words, if you would have them to be received in less than a century. Common things derive advantage and seeming novelty from strange expressions; but if you really have any great new truth or truths to publish, depend upon it that an unaccustomed phraseology will seriously diminish the effect which you desire to produce.'[1]

The least pretentious of poets, he did not strive after a complexity of treatment beyond his reach; his concern is with 'style' and 'matter' rather than with 'form' in the narrower sense.

The mark of Tennyson on the 1844 pieces suggests that it was the publication of Tennyson's collected poems in 1842 which inspired Patmore to resume the writing of poetry after his first adolescent attempts. The Woodman's Daughter, in both mood and style, recalls Tennyson's Dora and The Gardener's Daughter; while Lilian, in theme and form, strongly resembles Locksley Hall. In fact, a contemporary critic, the American Thomas Powell, described the latter poem as 'a female counterpart to Locksley Hall',[2] and *Blackwood's* blasted it as 'an echo, both in sentiment and in versification', of the same poem.[3] It is significant that, while the setting of the other poems in the 1844 volume is vaguely medieval, that of Lilian, like Tennyson's poem, is contemporary. But other influences were at work in these early pieces. Although The River is in places reminiscent of Tennyson's Sir Galahad, its stanza-form also recalls that of The Ancient Mariner:

> Along, along, swiftly and strong
> The river slippeth past;
> The current deep is still as sleep,
> And yet so very fast!
> There's something in its quietness
> That makes the soul aghast.

Christabel, too, adds its contribution, as in Patmore's lines:

> The weak stars swoon; the jagged moon
> Is lost in the cloudy air;
> No thought of light! save where the wave
> Sports with a fitful glare,

---

[1] *Memoirs*, Vol. II, pp. 149–150.
[2] *The Living Authors of England* (New York: Appleton & Co., 1849), p. 111.
[3] 'Poems by Coventry Patmore', *Blackwood's Edinburgh Magazine*, Sept. 1844, p. 335.

which appear to have been suggested by Coleridge's:

> Amid the jagged shadows
> Of mossy leafless boughs
> Kneeling in the moonlight
> To make her gentle vows.

Keats is here as well, for the description of the windows of the manor-hall

> bright with shapes
> Of king and saint devout

in which

> The faded saints stare through the gloom,
> Askant, and wan, and blear;
> And wither'd cheeks of watchful kings
> Start from their purple gear

is a more sombre version of Madeline's casement in The Eve of St. Agnes.

In revising The River, Patmore eliminated the unpoetic name of Witchaire, the silent lover who watches outside the manor during his beloved's wedding-feast, and drowns himself in the river, and most of the detail of his melancholy vigil. In its final shape, this poem has considerable merit. The skilful use of repetition, the felicity of the descriptive detail, and the tone of gentle sadness give it a place among the better Pre-Raphaelite lyrics. Yet there is little in The River save the final reference to the river flowing 'calm as household love' which was to remain characteristic of the poet. The fashionable melancholy, the somewhat adolescent frustration, the medieval setting all vanish from his later work.

The Woodman's Daughter owes something, not only to Tennyson's idylls, but also, as Frederick Page recognizes,[1] to Wordsworth's Ruth. Patmore's poem tells of a woodman's daughter who is seduced by a rich man's son, and who, when deserted, loses her mind and murders her child. It is essentially a ballad-theme, which the stanza-form, almost identical with that of The River, and similar to that of Ruth, suits very well. The diction, too, is Wordsworthian with perhaps a trace of Tennyson. Lilian, later rechristened The Yew-Berry, again resembles Locksley Hall in metre, and also, in its form and treatment of dialogue, such poems of Elizabeth Browning as Lady Geraldine's Courtship. This monologue, spoken out of melancholy by a young man who has found his beloved unfaithful with his friend, is the weakest poem in the collection. Patmore told Bulwer Lytton that it was completed in 'unwarrantable haste'[2] for

---

[1] *Patmore, A Study in Poetry*, p. 30.
[2] Derek Patmore, *Life and Times*, p. 50.

the printer, which may mean that he wrote for it a prologue and epilogue in which Percy, finding a friend reading a French novel, tells him how his Lilian was corrupted by such books lent her by the treacherous Winton. Prologue and epilogue disappeared in the revisions, which is not surprising in view of such lines as:

> O heaven, then can I no where
>   Plant my hope, but there advance
> These literary panders
>   Of that mighty brothel, France!

The themes of these three poems—love unrequited, love betrayed and abandoned, and love deceived—clearly reflect young Coventry's state of mind after the rejection of his love by Miss Gore. Only in this mood did he touch upon the ballad side of the Romantic movement, and borrow from Wordsworth, Coleridge and Tennyson some of their melancholy elements. Yet they are typical of Patmore in that their common subject is love. Sir Hubert (later renamed The Falcon) retells the story from the fifth day of *The Decameron* of the impoverished knight who sacrifices his prized falcon to make a meal for his beloved. And the only other poems of interest in the 1844 collection are the three sonnets, accomplished, if hardly inspired, which treat of love and of two of the other themes which were to dominate his later poetry—the revelation of truth and the contemplation of God.

Patmore's next poem of consequence was *Tamerton Church-Tower*, begun in 1848, completed in 1849, but not published until 1853, by which time he was well into the writing of *The Betrothal*. *Tamerton Church-Tower* is written in quatrains in which iambic tetrameters alternate with iambic trimeters; it is the stanza of The River and The Woodman's Daughter with the last two lines removed and with each alternate line rhymed. For the metre of *The Angel in the House*, both the preludes and the narrative portions, Patmore simply filled out the second and fourth lines of the quatrain to make a rhymed iambic tetrameter quatrain. For *The Victories of Love* he used the same measure, but rhymed in couplets.

The temper of *Tamerton Church-Tower* is mainly sedately Tennysonian; but the predominance of natural scenery and the way in which it is related to the emotions of the characters recall Wordsworth, and particular parts of the poem suggest a more direct debt:

> The children 'gan the sun to greet,
>   With song and senseless shout;
> The lambs to skip, their dams to bleat;
>   In Tavy leapt the trout;

> Across a fleeting eastern cloud
> The splendid rainbow sprang,
> And larks, invisible and loud,
> Within its zenith sang.

Again, the story is a contemporary one. The narrator tells of a ride he took with his friend Frank from Tamerton to Plymouth to meet Frank's fiancée, Bertha. Here the narrator meets, woos, and marries Blanche. While the two couples are rowing on the sea, a storm comes up and Blanche is drowned. When the poet rides home to Tamerton the reverse journey is seen in a different emotional light as well as under different weather conditions. The poem is more meteorological than any poem of Wordsworth, but we are reminded of Wordsworth again by the end with its philosophical acceptance of life, as the hero draws consolation from his sight of the Tamar and from the song of an 'alms-taught scholar trim'.

Now and again, the imagery recalls Tennyson; for instance, in such lines as:

> Ere summer's prime that year the wasp
> Lay gorged within the peach,

but, above all, the increased smoothness of the versification and the way in which the lines, though printed in irregular narrative sections, fall almost regularly into self-contained quatrains show how much Patmore had learned from his friend. The contemporary setting of the poem, its concern with passion, sensuality, innocence, love and marriage and its mood of philosophic enquiry indicate the direction in which Patmore was to move to become completely Patmorean. Even clearer indications were given by two short pieces in the *Tamerton Church-Tower* volume, 'Honoria: Ladies' Praise' and 'Felix: Love's Apology', which were in fact portions of the work in progress, soon to be published as *The Betrothal*, the first part of *The Angel in the House*.

When Patmore selected for his poem of domestic love a vehicle so apparently commonplace as the octosyllabic quatrain he knew what he was about. His earlier experiments had made him master of this measure; and he felt it to be especially well suited both to the telling of a quiet story and to the lyrical and meditative comments on it, as well as to the particular kind of epigrammatic expression which is already evident in his early poems in such lines as:

> And in the maiden path she trod
> Fair was the wife foreshown,
> A Mary in the house of God,
> A Martha in her own.

There was a particular aptness, he believed, in describing a happy marriage in such a metre. Gosse relates that when he asked Patmore why he had chosen it:

> 'He replied that he did so of set purpose, partly because at that particular time the poets were diverging into the most quaint and extravagant forms, and he wished to call the public back to simplicity; but partly because it was a swift and jocund measure, full of laughter and gaiety, suitable, not to pathetic themes, but to a song of chaste love and fortunate marriage.'[1]

Whether or not he was right in this is a matter for later discussion. But his instinct for 'law' determined the choice of a regular metre, demanding clear and economical expression. And the skill with which he adapted this traditional form to psychological analogies, to lyrical expression, to epigram, to description, narrative and the flow of conversation reveals genuine versatility as well as an awareness of the limitations both of his own talent and of the form he had selected.

He laboured to perfect the lines of *The Angel in the House* in pursuit of 'interior finish', and gave over his polishing only when he was no longer really interested in poetry. His success may be measured by the fact that when modern critics speak of *The Angel* they take its finish more or less for granted; Sir Herbert Read calls it 'wit-writing of an extremely competent and felicitous kind'.[2] This emphasis on 'interior finish' and its application in *The Angel* indicate Patmore's strength as a poet, as well as his weaknesses, especially by comparison with Hopkins. Poetry is for Patmore very largely *instyle*; for Hopkins it is *inscape*. Despite his disclaimers, finish seems at times to be more important to Patmore than intensity of experience or quality of response. It is quite true that he thought highly, equally true that he felt deeply, and that poetic expression was a matter of high seriousness for him. Yet in his domestic poems, in particular, and even here and there in *The Unknown Eros*, there is more than a trace of verbalism, of spinning the experience out in 'poetic' words. Patmore's sensitivity to language was limited by his sensibility. The level on which he challenged the spirit of his times in the poetic field was not quite so fundamental as to eliminate certain conventional qualities. So his idea of 'interior finish' which makes the wit-writing of *The Angel* a rare achievement in his age, and gives it its particular charm, keeps the poem within the order of good, rather than of great poetry. It is individual, and stamped

---

1 'The History of a Poem', p. 287.

2 'Coventry Patmore', *The Great Victorians—2*, edited by H. J. and Hugh Massingham (Pelican Books, 1932), p. 392.

with Patmore's interesting personality, but its limitations are the limitations of his sensitivity not only to language, but to the whole nature of poetry.

Because what Patmore was trying to achieve in *The Angel in the House* was different from anything attempted before in English verse, he had no models for it such as had guided his earlier pieces. Each of the two books of the poem contains twelve cantos, and is preceded by a prologue centering round the poet Felix Vaughan and his wife, Honoria, whose courtship and marriage the poem pretends to celebrate. The whole concludes with an epilogue. Each canto contains an 'idyll' carrying the narrative portion, and preceded by brief lyrical poems or 'preludes', from two to five in number, which draw out the philosophical or psychological implications of the idyll.

Frederick Page gives a valuable clue to a possible precedent for the form of *The Angel* when he writes: 'The alternation of preludes and idylls constitutes an art-form unique in English, although perhaps owing something to Wither's *Faire Virtue*.'[1] With his taste for out-of-the-way works, especially those dealing with love, there is every likelihood that Patmore had read Wither's poem. And there are sufficient resemblances in form, tone and theme between *Faire Virtue* and *The Angel in the House* to indicate that, if he did not take Wither's poem as a 'model', he received more than one hint from it. *Faire Virtue*, or *The Mistress of Philarete* (1622), is an allegory of virtue, but throughout Virtue is treated as a real woman; she is described, and the wooing and winning of her recorded, with realistic psychological detail, as well as with all the conceits and cataloguings of Elizabethan poetry. Patmore's 'Angel' is love, the Swedenborgian 'homo' of a happy marriage, but Honoria herself is a real woman, and her wooing and winning is described realistically, in the setting of a conventional Victorian love-story. However, it is only Wither's description of love, its caprices, its pangs, its dedication, which is real. The setting and the 'furniture' of the poem are those of the literary pastoral, and it is written in the tradition of Spenserian Platonism, which, as we have seen, Patmore rejected. On the other hand, Patmore was always prepared to learn from all writers, whatever their philosophy, who had shown insight into the realities of love and marriage, so he makes use of Waring and Wither as readily as he does of Michelet.

Wither's shepherd Philarete gives an elaborate description of the body and soul of his beloved to a group of young women. Throughout the poem, the beauty and the purity of the lady Virtue are

---

[1] *Patmore, A Study in Poetry*, p. 81.

stressed, as also are the chastity of Philarete and the purity of his love. In form there is more than a little resemblance to *The Angel in the House*. The main body of *Faire Virtue* consists of description, narration and philosophical comment in seven-syllabled couplets. Interspersed at irregular intervals are groups of songs in varying metres which fulfil something of the same function as do Patmore's preludes. But *The Angel* is a 'tidier' poem than *Faire Virtue*. The relationship between the preludes and the idylls is more systematic in the former poem, and the metre is the same for both. There is a story, slight though it be, in *The Angel*, as there is merely a 'situation' in *Faire Virtue*, and the realism of the contemporary detail in Patmore's poem has no parallel in Wither's work. The most that can be said is that Patmore conceivably took a hint from the double form of *Faire Virtue*, and proceeded to elaborate it in his own individual way. On the matters of the concept of love and its graces, and the temper of the lover, as expressed in both poems, however, there are some interesting resemblances in detail which further illustrate Patmore's capacity for absorbing material for his poetry from literary sources.

There is the same tone in Wither's:

> If you truly note her face
> You shall find it hath a grace
> Neither wanton, nor o'er-serious,
> Nor too yielding, nor imperious;
> But with such a feature blest,
> It is that which pleaseth best
> And delights each sev'ral eye,
> That affects with modesty.
> Lowliness hath in her look
> Equal place with greatness took.

as in Patmore's:

> Within her face
> Humility and dignity
> Were met in a most sweet embrace.
> (*A.H.*, I, i)

and:

> And, ah, the heaven of her face!
> How, when she laugh'd, I seem'd to see
> The gladness of the primal grace,
> And how, when grave, its dignity!
> (*A.H.*, I, viii)

247

Even in his description of the 'chase' of love, Patmore appears to have remembered *Faire Virtue*; for he has:

> By secret, sweet degrees, her heart,
>   Vanquish'd, takes warmth from his desire;
> She makes it more, with hidden art,
>   And fuels love's late dreaded fire.
> The generous credit he accords
>   To all the signs of good in her
> Redeems itself; his praiseful words
>   The virtues they impute confer.
>   (*A.H.*, I, xii)

where Wither writes:

> If the heat of youthful fires
> Warm her blood with those desires
> Which are by the course of nature
> Stirred in every perfect creature,
> As those passions kindle, so
> Doth Heaven's grace and reason grow
> Abler to suppress in her
> Those rebellions, and they stir
> Never more affection than
> One good thought allays again.

These and several similar parallels indicate that *Faire Virtue* was one of the works at the back of Patmore's mind when he wrote *The Angel in the House* and *The Victories of Love*. The epistolary form of the latter poem does not give as much opportunity for the philosophical consideration of love as does *The Angel*, but in 'The Wedding Sermon' with which it ends there are further traces of Wither, for instance, Patmore's:

> In Godhead rise, thither flow back
> All loves, which, as they keep or lack,
>   In their return, the course assign'd,
> Are virtue or sin.

which seems to be a logical development of Wither's words:

> Virtues that most wonder win,
> Would converted be to sin
> If their flourishings began
> From no better root than man.

The whole tone of *Faire Virtue*, with its joyous and tender approach to love, is certainly like that of *The Angel*. Yet, when all that can be said is said about the relationship between the two poems, they are essentially different poems, with a different emphasis and a different purpose, and whatever Patmore borrowed from Wither he assimilated completely. Wither is, however, by no means the only seventeenth-century poet whose presence can be felt in the domestic poems. Because the revolutionary erotic philosophy and the proclamation of the dignity of the flesh are veiled by the seemingly pedestrian octosyllabic metre, the provincial atmosphere, the smell of violets, primulas and geraniums, Patmore's relationship with the Metaphysicals is far from obvious. Yet it is natural that he should have been drawn to them. Their interest in religion and love, their surface paradoxes and their inner paradoxes of thought and feeling, their sacramental view of Nature, must all have appealed strongly to him.

In *Lowe's Edinburgh Magazine*, between February and April, 1846, he published essays on Donne, George Herbert and Herrick. The impact of Donne's poetry on him may be gauged from the many reminiscences of it in *The Angel in the House*. For instance, the phrase, 'stranger than strangers', quoted in the 1846 article from Donne's *Satires*, appears in section 5 of 'The Cathedral Close', while the lines from A Valediction: Forbidding Mourning:

> 'Twere profanation of our joys
> To tell the laity our love

are echoed in both:

> Love blabb'd of is a great decline,
> A careless word unsanctions sense.
> (*A.H.*, I, xi)

and:

> . . . I would not have my mystery,
> From her so delicately hid,
> The guess of gossips at their tea.
> (*A.H.*, I, v)

Mario Praz, examining the relationship between the work of the two poets, sees Patmore as a nineteenth-century representative of the Metaphysical tradition.[1] Some of the parallels he has discovered

---

[1] 'L'Epopea del Quotidiano—"L'Angelo Nella Casa" di Coventry Patmore', Appendix to *La Crisi Dell'Eroe Nel Romanzo Vittoriano*, pp. 387–422. Dr. Praz is the first to draw attention to these resemblances between Patmore's poetry and that of the Metaphysicals. In this appendix he gives a considerable number of parallels, some of which I have used in this chapter. He does, however, confine his discussion to Patmore's debt to these poets, overlooking the relationship between his work and that of the prose writers I have discussed earlier, and leaving the impression that the Metaphysicals were the chief determining

may indicate merely that both Donne and Patmore drew upon the same theological sources to express not dissimilar views on love; but others are close enough to establish that Donne's poetry did become part of the later poet's inspiration. For instance, 'The Koh-i-Noor', as Praz points out, contains a good deal in Donne's manner. The conceit in:

> You have my heart so sweetly seized,
>   And I confess, nay, 'tis my pride
> That I'm with you so solely pleased,
>   That if I'm pleased with aught beside,
> As music, or the month of June,
>   My friend's devotion, or his wit,
> A rose, a rainbow, or the moon,
>   It is that you illustrate it.
> All these are parts, you are the whole;
>   You fit the taste for Paradise,
> To which your charms draw up the soul
>   As turning spirals draw the eyes.
>   (*A.H.*, II, viii)

recalls Donne's lines in 'The Good Morrow':

> . . . but this, all pleasures fancies be.
> If ever any beauty I did see,
> Which I desired, and got, 'twas but a dream of thee;

while both the line 'All these are parts, you are the whole', which may be compared with:

> Yet 'tis a postulate in love
>   That part is greater than the whole,
>   (*A.H.*, II, vi)

and the unusual image on the turning spirals, are characteristic of Donne's manner. His imprint is plain, too, on passages like the following:

> No fault of Love's but nature's laws!
>   And Love, in idleness, lies quick;
> For as the worm whose powers make pause,
>   And swoon, through alteration sick,
> The soul, its wingless state dissolved,
>   Awaits its nuptial life complete.
>   (*A.H.*, II, iv)

influences on Patmore's work. He implies, also, that Patmore's theory of love owes a good deal more to Donne than in fact it does. (While the present work was in the press, a translation of Dr. Praz's book, by Angus Davidson, was published by the Oxford University Press under the title, *The Hero in Eclipse in Victorian Fiction*.)

and:

> Because her womanhood is such
> That, as on court-days subjects kiss
> The Queen's hand, yet so near a touch
> Affirms no mean familiarness.
>
> (*A.H.*, II, xii)

Identical turns of phrase can be found in both poets. Where Patmore writes:

> But, now and then, in cheek and eyes,
> I saw, or fancied such a glow
> As when, in summer-evening skies,
> Some say 'It lightens', some say, 'No'.
>
> (*A.H.*, I, vii)

Donne had said in 'A Valediction: Forbidding Mourning':

> As virtuous men pass mildly away,
> And whisper to their souls to go:
> Whilst some of their sad friends do say,
> The breath goes now—and some say, no.

If Patmore found in Donne a vision in many respects akin to his own, we should expect him to have been particularly interested in 'The Extasie', in which Donne celebrates the sensual aspect of love. And, in fact, leaving aside the interesting similarity between the metre of this poem and Patmore's customary one, these lines from *The Angel*:

> The foolish zeal of lip for lip,
> This fond, self-sanction'd, wilful zest,
> Is that elect relationship
> Which forms and sanctions all the rest.
>
> (*A.H.*, I, vi)

express the idea in the latter part of Donne's poem:

> So must pure lovers' souls descend
> To affections, and to faculties,
> Which sense may reach and apprehend,
> Else a great prince in prison lies.
> To our bodies turn we then, that so
> Weak men on love reveal'd may look;
> Love's mysteries in souls do grow,
> But yet the body is his book.

The prelude 'The Revelation', in Canto VIII of Book I of *The Angel* (which title, like so many of Patmore's, has the Metaphysical ring), may contain another reminiscence of these same lines, with its reference to 'the book' which love offers to men. In many places too, where there is no direct mark of Donne, Patmore's verbal quibbles, his fondness for astronomical, legal and geographical imagery, and his sometimes awkward syntax suggest, if faintly, the earlier poet.

In *The Unknown Eros* there is intellectual and emotional striving, as there is in Donne's poetry, but Patmore's struggles are of a different order and handled according to his own personality. The two poets can hardly be compared with respect to tension and profundity of effect. Whatever aspects of Donne's vision appealed to Patmore, his own poetic pattern was shaped in accordance with the demands of his individual temperament. But he was clearly in sympathy with Donne's revolt against the elegant tradition which excluded from poetry the objects and language of everyday life. What he had already learned from Wordsworth, the Metaphysicals confirmed.

Here and there, as Praz also points out, traces of Marvell's poems appear to sound in Patmore's lines. But the temper of Herrick seems to have been more influential on him than that of any other Metaphysical poet save Donne. Patmore's own copy of the *Hesperides* is well-marked; and something of the atmosphere of Herrick's poetry seems to have communicated itself to *The Angel*. Patmore had quoted directly from the older poet in the later cancelled portion of the poem 'The Vestal Fire' the last lines of 'To Anthea':

> Know, the vestall fier
> Is not by mariage quencht, but flames the higher.

The fanciful description of feminine dress in the prelude 'The Tribute' has much in common in spirit with Herrick's 'Delight in Disorder', and a direct reminiscence of the same poem is found in Lady Clitheroe's words:

> The indolent droop of a blue shawl,
> Or gray silk's fluctuating fall,
> Covers the multitude of sins
> In me.

> (*V.L.*, I, xiii)

More important than such verbal borrowings is the fact that Patmore's poetry shows a Herrick-like instinctive joy in Nature and sheer delight in the identification of aspects of the human, natural and divine worlds. Patmore could not help but recognize, as few of his contemporaries did, the sacramental view of Nature expressed in Herrick's lyrics, and the vast amount of learning distilled in them. Herrick and Patmore are almost alone in English poetry in having written little unpretentious, seemingly fragile poems, in which, however, the results of wide reading and hard thinking have been integrated. In *The Angel in the House*, the warm, benignity of Patmore's view of woman, the natural gaiety before Nature, and the radiant glow of contented joy all remind the reader of Herrick. He may not have been a major influence on Patmore's verse, but it is highly probable that something of his spirit spilled over into the domestic poems.

In fact, the whole poetic attitude expressed in *The Angel* and its sequel recalls that of the major Metaphysicals—the dual acceptance of mundane reality and of a transcendental philosophy of love and being, the attempt to reconcile intellect and feeling, and the sense of loving joy. Like them Patmore tried both to render poetically the business of daily living, and to make the world of abstract thought perceptible to the senses. If the ways in which he resembles them are not fundamental, and if his poetry is 'cosier' than theirs, this must be attributed to the limitations of his own age, as much as to the limitations of his own sensibility. We cannot press the resemblances between Patmore and the seventeenth-century poets too far. Although they clearly did strike responsive chords in him, his ideas had already been formed before he read them. His poetry gains some of its flavour from the unexpected touches of the Metaphysical manner; but his work is in no sense an imitation of that style, nor a conscious attempt to translate their vision into Victorian terms. Yet there is a certain piquancy in realizing that there is a kinship between this mid-Victorian 'laureate of the tea-table' and a poet as strenuous and unconventional as John Donne.

Many works may have suggested to Patmore the actual story of *The Angel* and its sequel. The plot is simplicity itself, and hardly requires Frederick Page's elaborate explanation that Patmore took the plot of a novel by the Countess Hahn-Hahn, discarded most of the details and incidents, and inverted a portion of it.[1] It is possible that one of his purposes in *The Angel* was to show how a typical plot of current feminine fiction could be used to exhibit the fundamental elements of domestic love, the very things the titled authoress in particular rejected. Yet the story is so slender, and so different in its total effect from any work of the Countess Hahn-Hahn and her like, that Patmore might surely be given the credit for inventing it.

Felix Vaughan, poet and gentleman, returns to Sarum after six years abroad. Revisiting the home of Dean Churchill, he finds the three Churchill girls grown to womanhood. He falls in love with the

[1] *Patmore, A Study in Poetry*, pp. 63–66.

eldest, Honoria, courts her, declares his love and marries her. The poem describes the incidents of the courtship, the dawning and growth of love in both Felix and Honoria, the ball they attend, the love-letters Felix writes, his rather perfunctory attempts to work, the wedding and the honeymoon. Frederick Graham, Honoria's cousin, who had been in love with her, marries the patient Jane on the rebound. Mary Churchill remains unmarried. The managing Lady Clitheroe and Mrs. Graham, Jane's mother-in-law, emerge from their letters in *The Victories of Love* as interesting characters of the Trollopian kind. Yet, though there is a Trollopian atmosphere about Patmore's plot and characters, *The Warden* was not published until 1855, so there can be no question of Patmore's Dean reflecting Mr. Harding, or of Sarum Close owing anything to Barchester.

There is some force, however, in Page's suggestion[1] that the relationship of Frederick and Honoria and the pattern of *The Victories* developed, to some extent, by contrast out of Dickens's *The Battle of Life*. The title of Patmore's poem indicates a relationship between the two works, which is strengthened by his words in 'Faint Yet Pursuing':

> And what we have to gain
> Is, not a battle, but a weary life's campaign.

He was repelled by the false optimism and the sentimental unreality of Dickens's Christmas Book, and, in the course of reviewing it, laments that a noble title, suggesting a struggle such as is fought unrecorded every day, between temptation and duty, between passion and principle, should be profaned by Dickens's trite, improbable and sentimental tale. If Dickens really meant to portray a type of high-toned self-devotion, Patmore declares, how woefully he has missed his mark.[2] That Frederick and Jane may indicate Patmore's attempt to portray the 'lofty nature sorely tried' and the 'type of high-toned self-devotion' he missed in Dickens's book is more than likely. In this case, Dickens adds his stimulus to the many others which operated on Patmore's poetry.

Finally, in determining the nature of his story and its treatment, Patmore had another, more illustrious work in mind, Goethe's *Herman and Dorothea*. In one of his reviews of Tennyson's poems, he praises this work in significant terms:

'Goethe's *Herman and Dorothea*, a true domestic epic, has about as much incident in it as each of Mr. Tennyson's lovely Idyls; but what

---

[1] *Patmore, A Study in Poetry*, p. 72.
[2] 'Popular Serial Literature', *North British Review*, Vol. VII, No. XIII, May 1847, pp. 114–115.

makes this poem one of the noblest inspirations of modern times is the fullness and verity of the psychological commentary by which its slight thread of incident is illustrated.'[1]

The last portion of this sentence is at once a description and a justification of *The Angel in the House*. In detail there is nothing in common between Goethe's poem and Patmore's, save that in both cases there is a simple, pure love-story in scenes of middle-class domesticity, and that the slight tale is used as the occasion for a celebration of the domestic virtues. However, the background of *The Angel in the House* is one of peace and stability, while in *Herman and Dorothea* Goethe makes a striking contrast between the continuance of the ordinary business of living and loving and the turmoil of the Napoleonic Wars. It may be that Patmore saluted this contrast in Goethe's poem in the prelude 'The Song of Songs' which opens Book II of *The Angel in the House*. This, the only place in which the thought of war intrudes into the poem, was written during the Crimean War, and the theme is introduced only to be rejected:

> But men expect the Tale of Love,
> And weary of the Tale of Hate;
> Lift me, O Muse, myself above,
> And let the world no longer wait.

In form and theme, then, Patmore's early poems show the influence of his unusually wide reading. In every case what he borrowed from other poets became part of the Patmorean vision and manner. Patmore is no less original in his borrowings than he is in his wholly original writing.

---

[1] 'Tennyson's *Maud*', *Edinburgh Review*, Oct. 1855, p. 514.

II

The Early Poems: Theory and Practice

IN DISCUSSING *The Angel in the House*, many critics separate the 'preludes' from the narrative portions. The latter, it is said, make up what Ruskin called 'a funny little story', slight in substance, overloaded with period detail, shot through with sentimentalities and flawed with banalities. So tied to the commonplaces of life in a rather dull era, in short, is the 'plot' of *The Angel* that the work cannot be seriously considered as poetry. By contrast the 'preludes' are regarded as a set of pleasant, perhaps even exciting, little lyrics, to be plucked out from the whole like currants from a pudding. These, it is suggested, contain all that is of real interest in the poem. This attitude towards *The Angel*, that it 'lives by its Preludes',[1] raises two points fundamental to the appreciation of Patmore's early poetry—the purpose of the form of the work, and the degree to which he fulfilled that purpose. How valid, in short, are the criticisms made of the alleged banalities; how true is it to say, with Theodore Maynard, that the poem 'passed out of fashion with the Mid-Victorian millinery it so brilliantly describes'?[2]

There can be no dispute that the form, the setting and the story of *The Angel in the House* were chosen with careful deliberation. It

---

[1] *A Critical History of English Poetry*, by Herbert J. C. Grierson and J. C. Smith (Chatto & Windus, 1944), p. 453.

[2] 'Coventry Patmore', *The Freeman*, Vol. VIII, No. 184, Sept. 19, 1923, p. 32.

followed logically from Patmore's sacramental view of love that married affection had to be shown in poetry in its outward signs. The acceptance of the homely detail of married life serves two main purposes, that of demonstrating the universal truth of love *here and now* as well as *for ever*, and that of revealing the mystery and the beauty at the heart of ordinary things. In essence, Patmore's realism is much the same kind of realism as is found in the plays of Ibsen and Strindberg, a realism that is also a symbolism. Poetry has traditionally been hostile to the dress and the trappings of particular periods, or, at any rate, to the conventions of a comfortable society and to the elements of the domestic round. This, Patmore believed, was a betrayal of the very nature of love. To treat of love apart from the conditions of its incarnation was to turn a living emotion into a bloodless philosophical concept.

The question arises, then, is not the story of *The Angel* and its sequel more proper to the novel than to poetry? The courtship and marriage of Felix and Honoria, and the crises in the married life of Frederick and Jane surely constitute the stuff of fiction rather than of verse? The story of Patmore's poem is so slight, and devoid of incident that it would make the most unsubstantial of romantic novels. The significance of each happening lies not in the incidents themselves, but in their poetic realization. The essence of both poems is not the story, nor is it even the much-praised psychological analysis of the moods in love, but the lyrical vision of love which irradiates the mundane incidents, the special tone which makes the commonplace both beautiful in itself and an earnest of unimagined joys. Hence the 'idylls' or narrative portions, and the preludes are equally essential to the major purpose of *The Angel*. Without the story, slender as it is, the preludes would form merely a set of generalized lyrics dealing with 'Love' and 'Marriage'. Without the preludes, the implications of the narrative might well be missed, and the deeper significance of this particular wooing be much more elusive. They spread, as it were, a nimbus round the narrative.

Although the distinction between the preludes and the idylls is not as clear-cut as is often assumed, on the whole, the former deal with the more philosophical aspects of love. From one point of view they may be regarded as the distillation of Vaughan's mature experience of marriage, while the idylls form the retrospective re-creation of his impulses and emotions during the period of courtship. That the preludes are related to the narrative not point by point, but in general terms, is sufficiently indicated by the manner in which Patmore altered the relationship of several preludes and idylls in successive editions, and by a letter to Allingham in which he said:

> 'Tennyson...objects to the "Epigrams"[1]—but not before I had begun to object to them myself. So I shall put them out: thereby greatly increasing the simplicity of the form. I put them in as breaks, to prevent the idea of continuity or close relation between *The Idylls* and "accompaniments", but, on seeing the Poem in print, they do not seem to be necessary for this purpose.'[2]

The narrative is set, then, in the framework of the preludes, in which the more ideal concepts are embodied, while it is itself kept to a kind of glowing simplicity.

In *The Victories of Love*, the device of telling the story in the form of letters from six people is not as successful as the form of *The Angel*. Patmore has some difficulty in persuading the reader to accept the philosophical self-analyses of Jane, which seem, in poetical epistles, less probable than Pamela's prose disquisitions. The device of allowing the poet Vaughan to explore his own mind and sensations in *The Angel in the House* permits Patmore to 'distance' his own experiences and to keep himself out of the picture. But in *The Victories of Love* there is at times a too obvious co-opera-tion of the poet with each of his characters.

The project including *The Angel* and its sequel, as Patmore was aware, involved enormous difficulties, the greatest of which was the conventional belief that bourgeois marriage was *ipso facto* unpoetic material. Yet he had faith in his idea that if Wordsworth could make poetry out of leech-gatherers, rustic children and poor farmers, the domestic life of a married couple *could* likewise be made poetic. To his mind, a picnic on Sarum Plain and a walk in the Deanery garden were as proper settings for the heights of married love as the banks of the Nile were for the romantic passion of Antony and Cleopatra. How far did he succeed in making this idea poetically convincing? Is the common misreading of the 'domestic' poems justified by his ineptitude? Is Swinburne's clever parody The Person of the House a fair comment on his achievement?

Patmore has had his defenders, of course, but even these feel constrained to apologize for occasional banalities. Yet, to a great extent, the success or failure of *The Angel* and *The Victories of Love* depends upon the degree to which Patmore avoided bathos. Although details of contemporary life were essential to his particularizing of

---

[1] The name Patmore gave to epigrammatic quatrains which formed part of the preludes in the original *Angel*.

[2] *Letters to William Allingham*, edited by H. Allingham and E. B. Williams (Longmans Green & Co., 1911), p. 216.

love, his realism had to be, in the nature of poetry, selective. It is putting the cart before the horse to write, as Gosse did:

> 'The first thing it was essential for Patmore to do was to replace an element of realistic entertainment in the supply of which he could not hope to compete with Miss Yonge and Anthony Trollope, by delicate ingenuities of art and by a strain of consistent philosophy.'[1]

—as if Patmore decided on his story first and then looked around for a philosophy to fit it! Patmore does not put everything in. The details are selected in relation to the heightened sensibility of the lover. It is, in fact, surprising how fully the poet suggests the mores of his time through so *little* detail. He does not catalogue dresses, furniture, buildings; it is rather the *occasions* he depicts—occasions which are important because they are crises in love's development —the 'morning call', the picnic on Sarum Plain, dinner at the Deanery, going to church. In each case the detail is chosen, not for its sociological or its 'documentary' value, but as it bears upon the mood of the lover and his sharpened awareness of the life he looks at through the eyes of love.

Felix calls on Honoria in the morning; they walk together on the lawn, and he rides home with

> A load of joy and tender care.

He is brought back to the prosaic business of living almost at once, for

> whip-in-hand
> And soil'd bank-notes all ready, stood
> The Farmer who farm'd all my land,
> Except the little Park and Wood.

But when the business transaction is completed, he casts himself down on his bed, and admits to the love he now realizes he has come to feel for Honoria:

> Rising, I breathed a brighter clime,
>   And found myself all self above,
> And, with a charity sublime,
>   Contemn'd not those who did not love;
> And I could not but feel that then
>   I shone with something of her grace
> And went forth to my fellow-men
>   My commendation in my face.
>
> (*A.H.*, I, iv)

Between the experience and its full emotional realization, the detail of the payment of the rent intervenes, for life and business must go

[1] *Coventry Patmore*, pp. 80–81.

on; but even these things gain new point in the setting of the lover's delirium.

So, throughout *The Angel* and *The Victories of Love*, life is shown as the sum of trifles, and love itself as a complex of little things, in themselves meaningless, perhaps even a little ridiculous, to those who do not love, yet on which the metaphysical sense works to harmonize them with the sublime emotion of the preludes. To the eyes of the lover, all things connected with the beloved are of profound significance. Her dress, for instance, prompts the rhapsody beginning:

> Boon Nature to the woman bows:
> She walks in earth's whole glory clad,
> And, chiefest far herself of shows,
> All others help her, and are glad:
>
> (*A.H.*, I, iv)

which, as Osbert Burdett comments,[1] skilfully avoids any mention of a particular fashion, in the course of suggesting the quintessence of 'dress'. So, too, the delicate perfume of violets, the sweet odour of love which fills the consciousness of the lover in 'The Violets', springs from the tremendous trifle of Honoria's invitation to dinner, with its Postscript:

> Her sisters and she
> Inclosed some violets, blue and white;
> She and her sisters found them where
> I wager'd once no violets grew;
> So they had won the gloves. And there
> The violets lay, two white, one blue.
>
> (*A.H.*, I, v)

In the intoxication of his emotion, the lover sees all things as reflecting himself; the universe is suffused with the spirit of love, and the very motions of the stars respond to his mood. When Honoria is absent from home, Felix wanders at evening past the deserted Deanery. He wonders

> would her bird be fed,
> Her rose-plots water'd, she not by.

and as he moves away

> eastward grew
> In heaven the symbol of my mood,
> Where one bright star engross'd the blue.
>
> (*A.H.*, I, ix)

[1] *The Idea of Coventry Patmore*, p. 24.

Yet these are not the aspects of the poem which have been called into question. Where the poem sinks, it is claimed, is in the intractability of some of the 'business':

> The Ladies rose. I held the door
>
> Passing, they left a gift of wine
>   At Widow Neale's.
>
> I, while the shop-girl fitted on
>   The sand-shoes, look'd where, down the bay,
> The sea glow'd with a shrouded sun.
>   'I'm ready, Felix; will you pay?'
>
>   I write to say
> Frederick has got, besides his pay,
> A good appointment in the Docks;
> Also to thank you for the frocks
> And shoes for Baby. I (D.V.)
> Shall soon be strong.

Such are the lines which are condemned and parodied. Can these be called 'poetry' in any sense of the word? Does not their presence show the weakness both of Patmore's scheme and of his execution of it?

It is worthy of note, in the first place, that the lines quoted above are almost the only ones cited by Patmore's critics in illustration of his lapses, and the recurrent emphasis placed on them might be taken as a measure of his success, at least in the rest of the poem. We can dismiss the idea that such 'banalities' are the result of a lack of sense of humour on Patmore's part. He referred with wry irony to one of them in his essay, 'Distinction':

> 'I do think that when the *Guardian* charges me with the sin of having said nothing in *The Angel in the House* about the "Poor" the writer should have remembered the one famous line I have ever succeeded in writing, namely, that in which Mrs. Vaughan is represented as conveying
>
> > "A gift of wine to Widow Neale."
>
> I put it in on purpose to show that my thoughts were *not* wholly occupied with cultivated people, though I knew quite well when I did so that it must evoke from the Olympians . . . thunders of inextinguishable laughter.'[1]

For Patmore to succeed in his aim of portraying the whole character of married life, he had to include even the fatuities, or at

---

[1] 'Distinction', *Principle in Art*, p. 70.

least those things which would be fatuous were they not part of the mood of love. The sand-shoes episode is a test-case. The lines occur at the beginning of the idyll in the final canto of Book II of *The Angel*, which describes Felix and Honoria, on their honeymoon, about to visit Frederick Graham on his ship. The opening prelude, 'The Married Lover', establishes the mood of the canto:

> Why, having won her, do I woo?
>   Because her spirit's vestal grace
> Provokes me always to pursue,
>   But, spirit-like, eludes embrace.

And, in its context, the sand-shoes episode reads:

> I, while the shop-girl fitted on
>   The sand-shoes, look'd where, down the bay,
> The sea glow'd with a shrouded sun.
>   'I'm ready, Felix; will you pay?'
> That was my first expense for this
>   Sweet Stranger, now my three days' wife.
> How light the touches are that kiss
>   The music from the chords of life!

On this passage, Frederick Page comments that the last two lines, being a philosophical reflection, must reflect something, and goes on:

> 'That the incident was historically true of Coventry and Emily Patmore, and was not invented for Felix and Honoria Churchill, is a proof of Patmore's philosophical reflectiveness. And for the rest, the reader . . . will feel that he is much more occupied, in obedience to one of his predilections, with the sea and the sun than with the shop-girl, and critic as well as reader will accept the poetry of
>
> > Sweet Stranger, now my three days' wife.'[1]

W. H. Gardner calls the same lines 'poetically simple and ontologically subtle', suggesting that the words:

> down the bay,
> The sea glow'd with a shrouded sun,

'indicate the lover's deeper consciousness, as we see by the symbolic "shrouded sun" and its counterpart, the "sweet stranger". Thus the mystic-realist has the best of both worlds at the same time.'[2] In addition, it is clear that in this passage, Patmore is giving

---

[1] *Patmore, A Study in Poetry*, p. 98.
[2] 'The Achievement of Coventry Patmore—1. The Early Poems', *The Month*, Feb. 1952, pp. 94–95.

an empirical justification of the principle he announces in the prelude, that the ecstasy of love survives after its intimacies are known, and that the joy of marriage can transform this mundane transaction, and give it the dignity of a landmark. The purchase of the sand-shoes is a reminder of the responsibilities the married lover has undertaken, and an earnest of the tenderness which makes its own epochs out of things trivial to others.

One of the basic differences between *The Angel* and the domestic novels of the day is that whereas the latter ended with marriage, Patmore's poem shows the extension of love into and beyond marriage. And the 'ceremonies' of love with which he was so concerned include and justify such lines as

> The Ladies rose. I held the door

which is followed by

> And sigh'd, as her departing grace
> Assured me that she always wore
> A heart as happy as her face.

Such trifles are integral parts of the ceremony of love, reflections of the courtesy which lies at its heart. Love's etiquette is fundamentally the same from age to age, whether one holds doors or not.

> And do not chafe at social rules,
> Leave that to charlatans and fools

writes Frederick.

The selectivity exercised in *The Angel* is sensitive and delicate. The criticized lines are part of the texture of the whole poem; and as an organic whole *The Angel* shows that Patmore combined a keen sense of appropriateness with a wise innocence of outlook. Having elected to show married love in middle-class surroundings as no less love than that at the Tennysonian Court of King Arthur, his treatment of manners is natural and unforced. He would not have succeeded in his attempt to select what is valuable in the mid-Victorian way of life had he been lacking in humanity and humour. It is true that there is no rollicking humour in *The Angel*; but there is no pompous solemnity either. The early poems have a special tone which preserves them equally from pomposity and vulgarity—a temper compounded of brightness and light,[1] a tone of tender gaiety. There are pangs and fears in *The Angel*, but they are swallowed up in the gentle glow of love's delight. Passion is there, vibrating the poem, but it is controlled; purity also, but without prudishness. The spirit of *The Angel* is a unique combination of seriousness,

---

[1] The words 'bright' and 'light' themselves occur frequently in the poem.

tenderness and joy; it is indeed 'peace elate'. Predominantly its mood is that of

> But there danced she, who from the leaven
> Of ill preserv'd my heart and wit
> All unawares, for she was heaven,
> Others at best but fit for it.
> One of those lovely things she was
> In whose least action there can be
> Nothing so transient but it has
> An air of immortality.

> *(A.H.*, II, iii)

In this prevailing tone lies the special enchantment of the poem. Its style is inseparable from its substance; the sacramental vision conditions both, shedding

> penitential grace
> On life's forgetful commonplace.

The Victories of Love presents other problems. Few readers have found it as attractive as *The Angel in the House*; yet *The Angel* itself is incomplete without its sequel, the third and fourth of the projected six parts which were to end with 'a final section on the subject of the hope which remains for individual love in death.'[1] Patmore intended in *The Victories* to intensify the realism of his picture of marriage by balancing the harmonious happiness of the earlier poem with a study of an apparently ill-matched pair finding happiness through adversity. But, throughout, the story is counter-pointed with that of the maturing married relationship of Felix and Honoria.

By abandoning the preludes, Patmore involved himself in certain difficulties. There is no substitute in *The Victories* for the lyrical quality of the preludes—perhaps he thought it inappropriate to the nature of the theme—and the 'philosophical' comment has to be made part of the general statement. Also the particular character of the married life of Jane and Frederick demands a fuller depiction of domestic detail than was necessary in the earlier poem. Just as Patmore tried to catch the ring of conversation in *The Angel*, so he endeavours to capture the tone of correspondence in the letters of which *The Victories* is composed.

> Dear Mother—such if you'll allow,
> In *love*, not *law*, I'll call you now—
> I hope you're well.

[1] Postscript to *The Victories of Love* in *The Angel in the House* (Macmillan, 1863).

Throughout the second poem runs the thread of the same kind of illuminative comment as in *The Angel*. The ceremonies of love, for instance, have their due place. Felix writes to Honoria

> That intimacy in love is naught
> Without pure reverence.

So, too, nature is transformed in the lover's eyes:

> The clouds, the intermediate blue,
> The air that rings with larks, the grave
> And distant rumour of the wave,
> The solitary sailing skiff,
> The gusty corn-field on the cliff,
> The corn-flower by the crumbling ledge,
> Or, far down at the shingle's edge,
> The sighing sea's recurrent crest,
> Breaking, resign'd to its unrest,
> All whisper, to my home-sick thought,
> Of charms in you till now uncaught.
> <div align="right">(<i>V.L.</i>, I, xvii)</div>

And the same relationship between man and woman is enunciated by Jane as it was before by Felix:

> Image and glory of the man,
> As he of God, is woman.

However, in many ways, *The Victories* is closer to the nature of a novel than is *The Angel*. There are more characters, Jane, Frederick, Mary Churchill, Mrs. Graham, Lady Clitheroe, the Dean, to the forefront, and they are drawn, or rather revealed, more fully as individuals than any characters in *The Angel* save Felix and Honoria. There is actually more of a 'plot' as well, and if some of the dramatic possibilities in such a figure as Mary Churchill are only suggested, clearly *The Victories* contains the embryo of a novel at least as substantial as any of Charlotte Yonge's. Dean Churchill is typical of those characters who first appear in *The Angel* and are rounded out in its sequel. Something of a lay-figure in the earlier poem, he is revealed as a very Patmore in Orders when he delivers the 'Wedding Sermon' with which *The Victories of Love* ends, and which, with its remarkable summary of Patmore's nuptial philosophy, links the earlier poems to *The Unknown Eros*.

In the later poem the easy octosyllabic couplet encourages a certain looseness in the expression, and now and again the rhymes seem to have carried Patmore further than the thought demanded.

The didactic purpose, too, seems to loom larger here, so that the whole poem appears to lead towards, as well as to culminate in, the wedding sermon. Yet there is much more pure poetry in *The Victories* than is commonly allowed—a host of subtle thoughts delicately expressed, such as:

> But sometimes (how shall I deny!)
> There falls, with her thus fondly by,
> Dejection, and a chilling shade.
> Remember'd pleasures, as they fade,
> Salute me, and colossal grow,
> Like footprints in the thawing snow.
>
> (*V.L.*, I, xii)

and

> For 'gainst God's will much may be done,
> But nought enjoy'd, and pleasures none
> Exist, but, like to springs of steel,
> Active no longer than they feel
> The checks that make them serve the soul.
>
> (W.S.)

However, the special quality of *The Victories of Love* does not lie in its psychological acuteness, its deception of manners, its enunciation of a nuptial philosophy or even in the sharp-eyed observations of nature. It is found in the leading motif, which is pathos. Alice Meynell showed a sure instinct when she called her collection of extracts from Patmore's work *Poetry of Pathos and Delight*. For, as Patmore is the poet of the delights of marriage, so, too, is he the poet of a particular kind of poignancy, difficult to parallel in English poetry. Pathos is one of the principal themes of the first part of *The Unknown Eros*, but it is first enunciated in *The Victories of Love*. Much of the poem directly reflects Patmore's grief and desolation of spirit during Emily's illness. But the whole work is marked with pathos and grave melancholy.

The note is first sounded in the mood of Frederick, the rejected suitor, whose sense of irreparable loss colours his entire outlook:

> I do my work: the void's there still
> Which carefullest duty cannot fill.
> What though the inaugural hour of night
> Comes ever with a keen delight?
> Little relieves the labour's heat;
> Disgust oft crowns it when complete;
> And life, in fact, is not less dull
> For being very dutiful.
>
> (*V.L.*, I, viii)

It is developed after his marriage to Jane, when he compares what is with what might have been:

> I love this woman, but I might
> Have loved some else with more delight;
> And strange it seems of God that He
> Should make a vain capacity.
>
> (*V.L.*, I, xii)

And it tinges Jane's realization of Frederick's attitude and her attempts to accept her situation and to make the best of her marriage:

> And in his strength have I such rest
> As when the baby on my breast
> Finds what it knows not how to seek
> And, very happy, very weak,
> Lies, only knowing all is well,
> Pillow'd on kindness palpable.
>
> (*V.L.*, II, i)

The pathos reaches its fullest expression in the letters written by Jane to Mrs. Graham during her illness and to be read by Frederick after her death, and in Frederick's words to Honoria after his wife's death. The matter here is certainly matter for sentimental exploitation, but, although here and there the pathos tends to become soft and pulpy, the wit and common-sense with which the theme is handled make the poem for the most part communicate, not sentimentality, but what Alice Meynell calls 'vital and mortal pathos'.[1] While *The Angel* expresses the joy of a young lover and husband, its sequel is redolent of mature experience. The paradoxes and epigrams, the psychological insights, the 'metaphysical' images, lend freshness and new dignity to Patmore's basic idea that enduring love is based upon sacrifice and humility.

Yet it must be admitted that there is less memorable poetry in *The Victories of Love* than in *The Angel*. Lapses of taste and passages of sentimental commonplace indicate a slackening of that poetic tact which preserves the earlier work from banality. Patmore was too directly involved in the strain of Emily's long illness and the sorrow of her death to be able to transform these experiences into poetry without some signs of a divided mind and of the effort of composition. Possibly, too, he felt that this crisis in his life required the nobler form of the odes rather than the epigrammatic couplets of *The Victories of Love*. 'The Wedding Sermon', which is one of his

---

[1] *The Poetry of Pathos and Delight*, passages from Patmore's works, selected by Alice Meynell (Heinemann, 1896), Introductory Note, p. x.

most striking achievements, stands apart from the personal story, and is unashamedly didactic. Yet the complex abstract doctrine of love and marriage is expressed with such force and such concrete realization that it merits a high place in the poetry of statement. Though *The Victories of Love* is an 'imperfect' poem, it is nevertheless a poem, and not a versified novelette. There are many passages of fine poetry, of metaphysical vision, and of sensitive response to Nature, and, at its best, the poem, glowing with lyrical wit, has a distinctively Patmorean tone.

Together the two poems assert that poetry is capable of more than it was made to do in the hands of Tennyson and Browning. Patmore is in conscious revolt against the tired romanticism of most of his contemporaries. Where they are conventional and sentimental he tempers his sentiment with an astringent wit, which is that of the Metaphysicals, ingenious, subtle, crisply phrased. His early poems are full of gnomic expressions, everywhere showing the controlling intelligence:

> The lack of lovely pride, in her
> > Who strives to pleasure, my pleasure numbs,
> And still the maid I most prefer
> > Whose care to please with pleasing comes.
> > > *(A.H.,* I, ii)

and

> These cannot see the robes of white
> > In which I sing of love. Alack,
> But darkness shows in heavenly light,
> > Though whiteness, in the dark, is black!
> > > *(A.H.,* I, iii)

and

> She approach'd, all mildness and young trust,
> > And ever her chaste and noble air
> Gave to love's feast its choicest gust,
> > A vague, faint augry of despair.
> > > *(A.H.,* I, vi)

and

> She loves with love that cannot tire;
> > And when, ah woe, she loves alone,
> Through passionate duty love springs higher,
> > As grass grows taller round a stone.
> > > *(A.H.,* I, ix)

There are weaknesses, to be sure, in the diction of *The Angel* and its sequel, for Patmore had not sufficiently purified his vocabulary of conventional epithets. His favourite adjective is 'sweet', and others he overworks are 'light', 'bright', 'happy', 'blissful', 'noble', 'lovely', 'pure', 'dignified' and 'gracious'; while among the most frequently found substantives are 'joy', 'grace', 'pride', 'folly', 'bliss', 'loveliness', 'sweetness'. It is unlikely that these were simply concessions to popular taste. What is more probable is that the sustaining of a particular outlook through very long poems which have a deliberately limited range made exceptional demands on the language. Patmore's diction in *The Angel* and its sequel, in fact, is highly individual. Only a mannered style such as he developed could have sustained the tone of the poems. The reader becomes at times a little too conscious of 'sweet' words and looks and tasks, but in its context this epithet and others like it are always appropriate to the lover's mood. Stronger objections might be raised against such words as 'divine', 'heavenly', 'Heaven', 'angelical', 'saintly', 'celestial'. Yet these objections must be directed against the conventionally sentimental use of them, and not against Patmore's, for he meant, in fact, exactly what he said by each of them. When he writes:

> Those lesser vaunts are dimm'd or lost
>   Which plume her name or paint her lip,
> Extinct in the deep-glowing boast
>   Of her angelic fellowship,
>
> <div align="right">(<i>A.H.</i>, II, iv)</div>

'angelic' here points to the concept implicit in the title *The Angel in the House*. The 'angel' is the bisexual angel of love, the 'homo', and this is the 'fellowship' Patmore celebrates, not the sentimental equation of 'woman' with 'ministering angel'. If earthly love is indeed a rehearsal for a higher Communion, 'angelic' is strictly appropriate.

For the rest, Patmore's diction in these early poems is rinsed clean. Simple words, exactly placed, are saved from prattle and naiveté by the economy of expression. Sometimes an unusual word enriches his poetic statement, as in the exceptionally alliterated:

> Nor credence to the world's cries give,
>   Which ever preach and still prevent
> Pure passion's high prerogative
>   To make, not follow, precedent.
>
> <div align="right">(<i>A.H.</i>, I, i)</div>

and in:

> He prays for some hard thing to do,
>   Some work of fame and labour immense,
> To stretch the languid bulk and thew
>   Of love's fresh-born magnipotence.
>
> <div align="right">(<i>A.H.</i>, I, iii)</div>

Such words, like the paradoxical turns of thought, are pointers to the fact that the world of Patmore's domestic poems is not the world of album-verses and tea-table gossip.

The selected details of contemporary life, the epigrammatic type of statement, the 'metaphysical' wit, the combination of seriousness and gaiety in the manner, the carefully controlled diction—all add up to a distinctive Patmorean style. The intellectual alertness, the agile play of a refined sense of paradox, perhaps above all its other elements mark the 'domestic epic' off as something unique in its age. Even if it be granted that, on occasions, the expression sinks below the dignity of poetry, such blemishes serve only to emphasize the skill with which in the main Patmore, in maintaining simplicity, avoids both facility and dullness. While Adelaide Procter's poems and those of Elizabeth Barrett Browning are snared in the accidents of the time, Patmore's earlier poetry remains fresh and new because it is concerned only incidentally with these. Its real subject is 'the heart's events'.

III

The Structure of the Odes

IT IS LIKELY THAT, when Patmore abandoned his project for a long domestic epic, he did so as much because the metre had become monotonous to his increasingly critical ear after writing the hundreds of couplets in *The Victories of Love* as because the original inspiration passed from him when Emily died. To regard the choice of a new metre as wholly determined by a new kind of inspiration is to ignore the facts. Frederick Page is of the opinion that several of the odes in Book I of *The Unknown Eros* represent portions of the projected later sequels of *The Angel in the House*.[1] Whether or not this is true—and parts of Mr. Page's argument are strained—it is certain that some of the odes—'The Azalea', 'Departure' and 'A Farewell', for instance—were the direct product of Emily's sickness and death, and thus were conceived and written independently of the immediate expression of Divine Love which is supposed by some to have largely determined Patmore's change of poetic form.

Patmore himself resented the praise of the odes at the expense of *The Angel in the House*, and attributed the preference simply to the fact that *The Unknown Eros* was written in a less familiar metre.[2] Yet, while the difference between the earlier and the later poems is one of degree rather than of kind, the style of both books of *The Unknown Eros* indicates that, having moved further into transcendental fields of experience, and having also in his first wife's death known the poignant fullness of grief, he felt instinctively that the

[1] *Patmore, A Study in Poetry*, Chapter VIII.
[2] See, for instance, Champneys, *Memoirs*, Vol. I, p. 161.

'gay and jocund' measure of *The Angel* would be unsuitable for his deeper ecstasy and his naked sorrow. And *Amelia* to some extent tells against Patmore's suggestion that the metres of both early and late verse 'travel the same ground and at the same level', for it is graver and more solemn than any 'idyll' in *The Angel*, and has a touch of sweet melancholy of a kind not attained there.

The form Patmore used for his odes consists of a single poetic unit, without stanzas and bearing some resemblance to traditional ode forms. The length of the line varies from two to sixteen syllables. For instance, the first lines of 'Winter' consist, in order, of six, ten, six, six and twelve syllables. In all the odes rhymes are disposed irregularly; sometimes a pair of lines is rhymed, sometimes four or six lines rhyme alternately, sometimes several lines separate the rhymes. Only very occasionally does Patmore use a line which is neither rhymed nor assonanted. Extraordinarily flexible, the form is not, however, as it has been called, a 'rhymed free-verse'.[1] Though it certainly permits great freedom, the retention of rhyme, the manipulation of assonance and echo, as well as the calculated use of pause, give it a real shape. It is the practical expression of Patmore's conviction that verse should feel, but not suffer from, the bonds of law. All the odes in *The Unknown Eros* were deliberately composed, and their complex rhythms, although resting on an iambic base, bear little relationship to those of the domestic poems. Their inner principle of harmony satisfies the ear, but demands in the writer an especially delicate sense of rhythm and a firm integrity in the handling of words.

Various models have been suggested for the form of these odes. Patmore undoubtedly had Wordsworth's 'Immortality Ode' and Milton's earlier poems in mind, for while discussing the irregular ode in the course of his 'In Memoriam' review, he refers to these poems as establishing the isochronous principle.[2] He also frequently expressed his admiration for Spenser's Prothalamium and Epithalamium: the latter, he declared, was 'the most pure and exalted love-poem ever written'.[3] *Amelia* might very well be called Patmore's 'Prothalamium', since it has something of Spenser's blend of dignity and joy in its treatment of a similar theme. Milton contributed to the metre of *The Unknown Eros*, mainly through Lycidas, the irregular choruses of *Samson Agonistes*, and also the introductions to L'Allegro and Il Penseroso, to which Patmore specifically refers in the 'In Memoriam' article.

1 John Heath-Stubbs, *The Darkling Plain*, p. 135.
2 'In Memoriam', *North British Review*, Aug. 1850, p. 542.
3 'Ancient and Modern Ideas of Purity', *Religio Poetae*, p. 71.

The Structure of the Odes

W. K. Fleming claims that Patmore's 'catalectic' measure 'owes more to Cowley than the former cared to confess', adding that 'Cowley at his best, and Patmore, when his genius halts a little, are not far apart.'[1] Yet there is an essential difference between Cowley's odes and Patmore's. In the latter's poems, thought and music are closely wedded, and the movement of the line responds to the rise and fall of the emotion; in Cowley the form is a clumsy thing, imposed on the thought, and neither subdued to the feeling nor fused with it. In any case, Patmore made his attitude to Cowley's verse clear on several occasions. 'The climax of metrical insanity', he wrote, 'was attained by Cowley.'[2]

Crashaw seems a more likely model, for the nearest parallel in English to the temper and language of *The Unknown Eros* is to be found in Crashaw's sacred poems. Yet Gosse asserted that in 1881, four years after the publication of *The Unknown Eros*, he found that Patmore was not acquainted with Crashaw's poems and sent him a copy. This is confirmed by Patmore's letter of acknowledgement to Gosse, indicating that the poems were new to him.[3] It may seem strange that Patmore, so knowledgeable in mystical literature and poetry, should not have been acquainted with the works of Crashaw. Yet the fact is that he does not refer to Crashaw at all in his essays, not even in contexts which such a reference would illuminate. The resemblances between the two poets, then, must be the result of common sources, and of a devotion to the same mystical works.

Both Gosse and Page suggest an even earlier ancestry for Patmore's odes, the Italian *canzone*. In so far as the *canzoni* are the source of the form of the odes of Milton and Spenser, this is likely enough. But while the harmony of long and short lines derived from the *canzone* is something which persists up to Patmore, there is a great difference between the Italian form and that of the *Unknown Eros* poems. As F. T. Prince points out, the tradition of solemn odes in English derives less from the strict *canzone* than from the 'liberated canzone' of Italian lyric verse in the latter half of the sixteenth century. A *canzone* consisted of 'a complex, fully rhymed stanza of some length, repeated several times and followed by a shorter concluding stanza.' But in Tasso's *Aminta* and Guarini's *Il Pastor Fido*, a type of irregular lyric, with a sustained improvised pattern of rhymes and partially rhymed semi-lyrical passages of dialogue, helped to liberate Italian verse from the strict stanzaic

[1] 'Coventry Patmore', by W. K. Fleming, *Life and Letters*, Jan. 1950, p. 36.
[2] 'In Memoriam', *North British Review*, Aug. 1850, p. 541.
[3] Champneys, *Memoirs*, Vol. II, p. 253.

18—C.P. 273

pattern. It is suggested by Prince that Milton was acquainted with this 'liberated canzone' style and that *Lycidas* in particular owes much to it.[1]

The poems of William Drummond of Hawthornden provide the most likely link between Patmore's *The Unknown Eros* and the works of the Italian poets. There is no evidence that Patmore knew the latter at first hand. But Drummond's combination of long and short lines, his use of rhymes, and his language in some of his songs and madrigals produce an effect at times very like the music of *The Unknown Eros*, despite the fact that Patmore's line is more varied, his use of pause more subtle and the relationship of his line to the syntax of his often lengthy sentences more accomplished than anything in Drummond. There is a closer resemblance, for instance, between the following passages than between any part of *Lycidas* and Patmore's odes. One of Drummond's 'Songs' begins:

> Phebus arise,
> And paint the sable skies
> With azure, white and Red:
> Rowse Memnons Mother from her *Tythons* Bed,
> That Shee thy Cariere may with Roses spred.
> The Nightingalles thy Comming where each sing
> Make an eternall Spring,
> Giue Life to this darke World which lieth dead.

and Patmore's 'To the Unknown Eros' opens with these lines:

> What rumour'd heavens are these
> Which not a poet sings,
> O, Unknown Eros? What this breeze
> Of sudden wings
> Speeding from far returns of time from interstellar space
> To fan my very face
> And gone as fleet,
> Through delicatest ether feathering soft their solitary beat,
> With ne'er a light plume dropp'd, nor any trace
> To speak of whence they came, or whither they depart?

Drummond's longest lines are iambic pentameters, and his first and second lines form a broken iambic pentameter. Out of the eight lines quoted only two are really irregular lines, the third and the seventh, and these are both iambic trimeters. The lines from Patmore, on the other hand, contain in order six, six, eight, four, fourteen, six, four, sixteen, ten and twelve syllables.

---

[1] F. T. Prince, *The Italian Element in Milton's Verse* (Oxford: at the Clarendon Press, 1954), Chap. 5, 'Lycidas'.

Though there is some resemblance, therefore, between the work of the two poets, Patmore's odes are much less rigidly formal than those of Drummond. Like Milton, Drummond owed very much to Italian models, Tasso, Guarini and Marino among them; so that it might be said that if Patmore's odes do look back to the Renaissance Italian lyric, they do so only indirectly through Milton, Drummond and Spenser. Seeking a form in which he could achieve fluency of expression and reflect the rise and fall of powerful emotion, yet at the same time observe the laws of harmony and of rhyme, Patmore rejected Cowley's 'Pindarique' lawlessness, and taking hints from the great practitioners of the irregular ode, itself a product of the study of Italian poetry, set himself to refine and develop the form, producing his own characteristic type, which combined regularity with great freedom of movement.

What principles, then, do underlie the structure of his odes? Frederick Page suggests that the answer is to be found in W. P. Ker's description of the Italian *canzone* as based upon the harmony of the longer and shorter lines, in English the ten-syllable and six-syllable lines, which in Italian is eleven and seven.[1] In the same way, Page argues, as the hendecasyllable keeps the pre-eminence over the verse of seven by imposing its own time on the shorter verse, so Patmore's ten-syllable line, which, on his dipodic theory, makes a trimeter when completed by a two-syllable pause, imposes its own time on the shorter lines, even if they contain only six syllables.

It is true that a certain proportion of the shorter lines in *The Unknown Eros* are lengthened in their context so as to approximate in time to those longer lines which precede them. Page is able to demonstrate without difficulty that, in the case of alternating eight-syllable and six-syllable lines, the longer line determines the time of the shorter. Similarly, he cites a four-syllable line out of context:

> For chains and thongs
> And what belongs . . .

and makes his point about lengthening good by comparing the rapidity of this with the length of the same line as Patmore gives it:

> Reveres with obscure rite and sacramental sign
> A bond I know not of nor dimly can divine;
> This subject loyalty which longs
> For chains and thongs
> Woven of gossamer and adamant.[2]

---

[1] *Patmore, A Study in Poetry*, Chap. X, 'The Metrist'.   [2] *Ibid.*, p. 162.

But the matter is more complicated when it becomes a question of reconciling a ten-syllable line with a following two-syllable line or when he tries to answer Alice Meynell's objection against two successive lines of four and six, as in A Farewell, which add up to a heroic line. The time of A Farewell, Page argues, has been set by the solemn opening:

> With all my will, but much against my heart

and as the poem represents present emotion, the point-by-point expression of 'a continuing and increasing separation' is legitimately indicated by the separation of parts of the pentameter.

This is reasonable enough, and fairly sets out Patmore's practice. However, Alice Meynell had a further objection to make. 'Some of the short lines', she writes, 'are too abruptly short; it is not agreeable to stop with an emphatic rhyme upon a line of two syllables.'[1] Page counters this by quoting some lines from 'Legem Tuam Dilexi' beginning:

> What is the chief news of the Night?
> Lo, iron and salt, heat, weight and light
> In every star that drifts on the great breeze!
> And these
> Mean Man,
> Darling of God, Whose thoughts but live and move
> Round him. . . .

on which he comments:

> 'The reader will probably agree that the first two lines are not the ordinary octosyllabic couplet without end-pauses; they are, at least by Patmore's hypothesis, "trimeters". There must be a pause after "breeze". But how long? And what time-value has "these"? And what is its succeeding pause?—for a succeeding pause there is, and by no means, in Alice Meynell's words, "a pause that were best avoided". I cannot say, but I trust Patmore to know.'

Such a statement seems like an abandonment of theory to poetic instinct; and this is what we are forced to in any consideration of Patmore's practice in *The Unknown Eros*. For, while it is true that there is a pause before 'Mean Man', it is impossible to imagine that in any normal and effective reading of the poem the short line

> And these

could be made equal in time to the strongly weighted and pause-heavy

> Lo, iron and salt, heat, weight and light

[1] *Ibid.*, p. 157 (quoted from an article in *Merry England*, Dec. 1885).

On Mr. Page's own showing, the opening line of this poem:

The 'Infinite', Word horrible! At feud

sets the time of the rest of the ode, so that the tenth line, which consists of the single word 'Infinity', should have a similar time-value. Yet no form of stressing or pausing that is not unnatural and forced can fit this word-line into Patmore's dipodic system. Even if it were possible to accept such lengthy pauses as Page proposes for the lines

And these
Mean Man

the same argument can hardly apply to such later lines in the poem as

For none knows rightly what 'tis to be free
But only he
Who, vow'd against all choice, and fill'd with awe
Of the ofttimes dumb or clouded Oracle . . .

The necessary stress on 'he' which prolongs the second line cannot prevent a fairly rapid transition to the 'Who' of the next line, thus keeping 'But only he' comparatively short by comparison with the preceding and following lines.

What the precise musical organization of Patmore's odes is, appears to elude analysis as effectively as the choruses of *Samson Agonistes* have so far done. It is, however, clear that the careful choice of words and the disposition of emphasis do impart a solemn, stately tone to the poems, while the skilful use of pause, if it does not establish a formal regularity, does help to establish some kind of pattern. Perhaps the most important feature of the structure of the odes, which previous writers have overlooked, is the part played in it by rhyme. The importance which Patmore attached to rhyme has already been mentioned. Discussing the irregular ode he wrote in 1850:

'It has been excellently said that rhyme owes much of its charm to the fact of its containing a continual appeal to memory and expectation; and upon this saying we should found the rule that rhymes which recur at irregular and unexpected intervals ought always to be increased in number, in order to make up for the effect of their irregularity in weakening the force of that appeal. . . . Alliteration bears a very strong analogy to irregularly recurring rhyme. . . . It requires, however, extreme delicacy in its use.[1]

Irregular though the rhymes are in *The Unknown Eros*, they are not arbitrary. In any ode, the number of lines which neither rhyme

[1] 'In Memoriam', *North British Review*, Aug. 1850, pp. 544–545.

nor assonant is very few, and in some of the poems the rhyming is very close indeed. However, a rhyme is quite often suspended for such a long interval that only a careful examination of the pattern will reveal the relationship between apparently unrhymed lines. For instance, in 'Winter', 'most' at the end of line 3 is rhymed, or rather echoed, in lines 19 and 20, by 'crost' and 'frost'; while 'hoar' in line 44 is rhymed with 'or' in line 55. The whole rhyme-scheme of 'Winter' is as follows:

a a b c c d e e f f g g h i h i j k b b k d j l m l m n g n n d d i o o m
m p q p q p r h h s s t t (u u) n n r v

The (u u) indicates a partial rhyme or echo, 'adversity' and 'sigh'. The 'unrhymed' final line (56) ends in 'tranquil' which echoes 'well' and 'ineffable' in lines 47 and 48. And in the same line there are, in fact, two rhymes, one linked to the final word in the preceding line, the other wholly internal:

> Of ether, moved by ether only, or
> By something still more tranquil.

Out of the 107 lines in 'Legem Tuam Dilexi' there are 36 groups of couplets and three triple rhymes, and few of the other rhymes are separated by more than two lines. There is no doubt that in the odes Patmore did, in fact, put into practice his rule that 'rhymes which recur at irregular and unexpected intervals ought always to be increased in number.' Some critics have suggested that rhyme is superfluous in *The Unknown Eros*.[1] Yet it surely is a quite indispensable part of the total effect of the poems. Apart from the structural value of rhyme's 'appeal to memory and expectation', the additional stress which it gives to the emphatic ending of lines serves to attenuate the pause, and to help create an illusion of regularity.

Rather than isochronous intervals or equal pauses, it is this sense of symmetry, conveyed by rhyme and emphasis, as well as the comparative uniformity of most of the lines in any ode, which provides the basis of the harmony of the poems. Just as rhyme helps to establish the form, so does alliteration, which Patmore uses with the 'extreme delicacy' he says it requires. Line is often bound to line by an intricate system of alliteration. The pattern of f's, w's, l's and s's in this passage from 'Legem Tuam Dilexi' is characteristic:

[1] For instance, M. F. Egan in 'The Ode Structure of Coventry Patmore', *Catholic University Bulletin*, Vol. V, No. 1, Jan. 1899, p. 9.

> Surrendering, abject, to his equal's rule,
> As though he were a fool,
> The free wings of the will;
> More vainly still;
> For none know rightly what 'tis to be free
> But only he
> Who, vow'd against all choice, and fill'd with awe
> Of the ofttimes dumb or clouded Oracle,
> Does wiser than to spell
> In his own suit, the least word of the Law!

The consonants 'f' and 'h' weave in and out of this particular ode, giving special effectiveness to such lines as

> Straight to His homestead in the human heart

and

> Of the full heart with floods of honied love.

What we have in the *Unknown Eros* odes, in short, is a unique blend of subtly varied pause and stress, producing an effect of proportion, but given unity and shape by the use of rhyme and alliteration. In its freedom, as well as in its carefully calculated music, *The Unknown Eros* looks forward to Hopkins rather than back to Drummond.

The charge against Patmore of 'defective rhyming' is an old one. In the opening lines of 'To the Body', for instance, 'good' is paired with 'infinitude', and 'sky' with 'eternity', conjunctions which are all the more striking because of the exactness of the rhymes in the rest of the poem. Echo and assonance, however, were less familiar in Patmore's day than in our own; and such 'rhymes' can now be recognized as a conscious part of his varied musical organization. It is an interesting fact that several odes contain such 'echoes' in their first and last lines only. For instance, 'Saint Valentine's Day' has 'February' and 'marry' at the beginning and 'ecstasy' and 'die' at the end; 'Winter' opens with 'moved' and 'beloved'; 'Tired Memory' with 'insensibility' and 'dry'; and 'Arbor Vitae' with the unusual group, 'festoon'd', 'bound' and 'unsound'.

The form of the poems in *The Unknown Eros* is an intensely personal one, owing something to the great writers of English irregular odes who preceded Patmore, but essentially his individual variant of the tradition in which they wrote. To sustain its music requires much sensitivity and technical skill, so that, save in the rarest cases, a line does not end or a rhyme fall in any but a sense-emphatic place. In the main, the measure is solemn, taking its character from the longer, weighted lines, but it is capable of a certain grave gaiety, as in 'Psyche's Discontent'. It can be forceful and oracular as in the political odes, passionate and ecstatic as in 'Eros and Psyche' and 'Deliciae Sapientiae de Amore', meditative as in 'Magna est Veritas', or weighted with a profound sorrow as in 'Departure'. And to this varied use of the ode form, Patmore brings a sureness in handling the rhetoric of sentence-structure, and so leading the sense of his periods through the emphases of the form as to bind the odes together into organic units. 'To the Body', for instance, consists of three sentences only, the first being 37 lines long. In this way he achieved an organic poetry in which the form fluctuates, ebbs and flows according to variations in the thought and feeling.

The Unknown Eros odes cannot be bound to any theory, not even Patmore's. Their form is certainly not external and mechanical. The poems breathe and move with a life of their own. They achieve, as do all living things, a unique compromise between freedom and law, and so exemplify in their shape that principle of life which Patmore celebrates in the poems themselves. Francis Thompson's description of their metre is particularly apt. It is, he wrote, 'majestic, flexible and beautiful in a high degree, answering the feeling like the pulses of the blood.'[1]

[1] Review of *Coventry Patmore* by Edmund Gosse, *Athenaeum*, No. 4040, April 1, 1905, p. 390.

IV

The Unknown Eros

IN APRIL 1868, Patmore printed for private circulation a small volume called, simply, *Odes*, containing nine untitled poems, and without the author's name.[1] The lack of encouraging response from those who saw the volume led to his burning the remaining copies in 1870, save for one or two which his daughter Emily managed to put aside. However, between 1875 and 1877, eight odes appeared in the *Pall Mall Gazette* over the initials of C.P. In 1877 *The Unknown Eros* was published, containing thirty-one poems. This was followed in 1878 by an enlarged edition now containing forty-six odes, as well as 'Amelia'. Three of the odes, 'Psyche' (later renamed 'Mignonne'), 'Semele' and 'Alexander and Lycon', were excluded from the final arrangement of *The Unknown Eros* sequence, but included among his other poems. '1877', a bitter political ode, was omitted altogether.

The Unknown Eros was regarded by most of those who read it on publication as a miscellany, with no unity of idea or conception.[2] This view was encouraged by Patmore's own words in the Preface to the privately circulated nine odes:

---

[1] These Odes were later titled: 1. Prophets Who Cannot Sing. 2. Felicia (renamed, after Hopkins questioned the aptness of the title, 'Beata'). 3. Tired Memory. 4. Faint yet Pursuing. 5. Pain. 6. The Two Deserts. 7. Deliciae Sapientiae de Amore. 8. Dead Language. 9. 1867.

[2] Gosse, for instance, said of the nine original odes that they had 'a certain unity of method but of unity of subject there is very little' (*Coventry Patmore*, p. 126).

'I meant to have extended and developed this series of Odes until they formed an integral work expressing an idea which I have long had at heart; but feelings which are partly conveyed by the concluding piece[1] have discouraged me from fulfilling my intention, and I now print these fragments of the proposed poem for private distribution among the few persons who are likely to care for them as they stand.'

Without doubt, the idea Patmore had long had at heart was the completion of *The Angel* sequence, and the nine odes represent parts of the projected sequel to *The Victories*, which was to carry the idea of love from its earthly embodiment to transcendental heights. So much is indicated in the postscript to the 1863 edition of *The Victories* where he tells how Emily's death removed the inspiration and encouragement he needed to complete his project.

Accepting the nine odes as parts of the abandoned poem, then, Frederick Page endeavours to allot not only these but several of the later odes to various characters who appear in *The Angel* and its sequel.[2] He acknowledges the personal impulse behind 'The Azalea', 'The Toys' and 'Departure', but suggests that Patmore may have intended to put them into the mouth of Frederick, that all the poems of a widower, in fact, may well be his; that the poems on poetry should be Felix's, including 'Legem Tuam Dilexi', and that the political odes are Felix's speeches in Parliament or on the hustings. Although much of Page's argument is plausible, other parts appear strained, such as the attributing of 'Let Be!' to Mary Churchill, and putting 'Deliciae Sapientiae de Amore' into the mouth of Dean Churchill as a wedding sermon at the marriage of Mary and the widowed Frederick Graham.

It is likely that the early odes, at least, were designed in relation to specific characters. Yet the group of widower's poems is so much more personal than anything in his previous work that Patmore must have felt that it would be a kind of desecration to allot to fictitious characters utterances so immediately struck from his own poignant experience, such as 'The Azalea', with its deeply moving last lines; as the poet awakes from a dream that his wife is dead:

It *was* the azalea's breath, and she *was* dead!

That this is the direct lyrical transcript of an actual experience is shown by the note found among his papers: 'Last night I dreamt that she was dying; awoke with unspeakable relief that it was a dream; but a moment after to remember that she was dead.'[3]

[1] '1867', which reflects his depression at the political and social state of England.

[2] 'Dramatis Personae', Chap. VII of *Patmore, A Study in Poetry*.

[3] Derek Patmore, *Life and Times*, p. 156.

Although Patmore may, then, at one time have intended these poems to be part of his domestic epic, on consideration he must have felt that their intimately personal nature accorded better with a direct poetic expression of his entire philosophy, which is, in effect, what *The Unknown Eros* is, in its final form. However, the fact that it is possible to consider some of the odes as Page does helps to establish that there is no real division between the domestic poems and *The Unknown Eros*. As Patmore wrote to Arthur Symons in 1893:

'The meats and wines of the two are, in very great part, almost identical in character; but, in one case, they are served on the deal table of the octosyllabic quatrain, and in the other, they are spread on the fine, irregular rock of the free tetrameter.'[1]

There is another important element in *The Unknown Eros*. As we have seen, Patmore had been meditating as the 'crown and summing-up' of his former work a long poem on the Blessed Virgin Mary to express the fullness of his thought on marriage and virginity. He visualized for it a form like that of *The Angel in the House*, a blend of narrative and choruses, or dramatic and lyric sections, but in the metre of the odes. He intended it to be the most carefully woven of all his poems and the fruit of his long apprenticeship in poetry. 'The metre of the "odes"', he wrote, 'must be developed by a more copious and scientific use of rhyme; and in additional odes the requisite experiments should be tried before commencing the Poem.'[2] The only poem in *The Unknown Eros* which is obviously a portion of the proposed work is 'The Child's Purchase', subtitled 'A Prologue'. It is also possible that 'Regina Coeli', not included in *The Unknown Eros*, is another fragment. But there is evidence that Patmore had written other poems as part of the 'work in progress'. 'Three or four more Odes like the "Contract" and "Deliciae Sapientiae" I think will include all that ought to be attempted: the Series to be concluded and crowned with a great ode "To the Only Woman"',[3] he wrote to a friend.

In the light of this, it is likely that most, if not all, of the 'theological' poems in *The Unknown Eros* and one or more of the Psyche odes were intended either as part of, or experiments for, 'The Marriage of the Blessed Virgin', which he finally abandoned as beyond his powers. It would have been quite in accordance with the general scheme of 'The Marriage of the Blessed Virgin' for Patmore to have found a place therein for odes written independently

[1] 'Coventry Patmore', *Figures of Several Centuries*, p. 364.
[2] *Patmore, A Study in Poetry*, p. 140.
[3] Champneys, *Memoirs*, Vol. I, p. 251.

of it. In any case, there are sufficient indications of other intentions in *The Unknown Eros* to lead Frederick Page to say: '*The Unknown Eros and other Odes* is, then, a miscellany, representing at least one, and I think two, abandoned projects: "The Marriage of the Blessed Virgin" certainly, and the completion of the *Angel in the House*, perhaps.'[1]

Is, however, the word 'miscellany' appropriate? Is *The Unknown Eros* a mere assembly of fragments from other works? Patmore made relatively few verbal changes in the odes in their successive reprintings, but the final sequence of the poems, as it appeared in the collected edition, is the result of a thorough rearrangement of the original order. In this reshuffling he was seeking to impart a significant progression to the poems, to turn them from a miscellany into a coherent organic whole with a gradually unfolding theme. The ultimate shape the work assumed reveals a definite development of thought and mood; it sums up all his hopes and ideals, it surveys the whole field of his philosophy, and leads upwards to 'The Child's Purchase' as climax. Far from being a collection or a miscellany, *The Unknown Eros* is a well-rounded, integrated work, in which the individual poems, each in itself complete, take their place in a wider and more meaningful scheme.[2]

The Unknown Eros consists of a Proem and two books, the first containing twenty-four odes, the second eighteen. St. Paul's words: 'That was not first which is spiritual, but that which is natural; afterwards that which is spiritual' may be taken as defining the division between the two books, for the first deals mainly with what is 'natural' in man—his sorrows, his trials, his communion with Nature, his response to human love, his aspirations; the second chiefly with the 'supernatural' in him—his awareness of the Divine chastisement, his apprehension of God's presence, his desire for a deeper understanding of God's love, and the mystical union. Throughout both books are disposed poems which link them together—poems of philosophical speculation, poems of ordinary religious experience and others dealing with the nature of poetic utterance. Five main themes are woven into the first book—nature as a symbol of love, and the part it plays in man's spiritual progress;

---

[1] *Patmore, A Study in Poetry*, p. 119. Although in this book Mr. Page stresses the 'miscellany' nature of *The Unknown Eros*, he had set out a case for the unity of, and plan in, this volume in two essays: 'Coventry Patmore's "Unknown Eros"', *Catholic World*, Sept. 1917; and 'The Centenary of Coventry Patmore', *Dublin Review*, July 1923.

[2] I am indebted for some of the ideas on the plan of *The Unknown Eros* in the pages that follow to two articles by Eleanor Downing on 'Patmore's Philosophy of Love' (*Thought*, March and June, 1934).

human love both in its concreteness and as a premonition of divine love; the life of man in society, and its effect on the maturing soul; the consideration of the nature of truth, order and law; and finally, the theme of penitence, and of the spiritual preparation of the soul to receive the influx of divinity. Throughout several of these odes also runs the theme of virginity which is again taken up in the second book. And both books are shot through with references to trial and struggle, to conflict, fall and renewed resolution, as if to show the poet's realization that there is no easy path to the Beatific Vision, that the life of the spirit is a life of tension and battle, of loss as well as gain, of the sense of absence as well as the sense of union.

The Proem enunciates or hints at all these themes, and puts the whole work in the setting of its times. It is, Patmore says, 'a season strange for song'. Aware of the impact of political changes on England, he gloomily prognosticates the future of a land sunk in its 'last lethargy'; but ends with the hope that his voice will be heard in some happier time and with an invocation to the Holy Ghost:

> And Thou, Inspirer, deign to brood
> O'er the delighted words, and call them Very Good.
> This grant, Clear Spirit; and grant that I remain
> Content to ask unlikely gifts in vain.

The first three odes are all Nature poems, concerned with the seasons, spring, summer and winter, in which a Wordsworthian vision of living things is fused with his own vision of love. In each poem the season symbolizes one aspect of the phases of love. 'St. Valentine's Day' sings of the 'quick praevernal Power' of spring,

> Fair as the rash oath of virginity
> Which is first-love's first cry.

The earth breaking out from its winter covering is seen as a parable of the transformation of the cold austerity of virginity into the warm, fruitful response of mature love:

> Forget thy foolish words,
> Go to her summons gay,
> Thy heart with dead, wing'd Innocencies fill'd
> Ev'n as a nest with birds
> After the old ones by the hawk are kill'd.

'Wind and Wave', which follows, is a poem of the summer sea, with the 'immeasurable smile' of sunlight breaking on the heaving waves. In the image of the ocean responding at first in gentle ripples to the little breeze, gaining force and momentum and finally crashing on the beach, Patmore depicts the fruition of love, its consummation in marriage, and its surging on to the 'void sky-line and an unguess'd weal'. The stirring, gathering, final crashing and gentle ebbing of the waves are mirrored in the subtly fluctuating movement of the lines:

> And so the whole
> Unfathomable and immense
> Triumphing tide comes at the last to reach
> And burst in wind-kiss'd splendours on the deaf'ning beach,
> Where forms of children in first innocence
> Laugh and fling pebbles on the rainbow'd crest
> Of its untired unrest.

On another level, this poem may be taken as symbolizing the surge, climax and repose of the sexual act itself, in which case the images of the beach and the children gain an additional significance. Whether or not such a meaning was conscious with Patmore it is difficult to say, although the nature of his mind, and the complexity of his poetic expression permit of such a possibility. Nor is this the only poem in *The Unknown Eros* in which direct sexual symbolism may be discovered.

'Winter' depicts the blanketed silence of the season as 'not death but plenitude of peace'. Here is the spirit of love released from bodily desire, wrapped in the profound calm of the contemplation of God, and content with the assurance of a new birth. The tone is one of profound stillness, of immensely quiet serenity, beneath which the heart still beats strongly. The subject is quite simply the transformation of human love into contemplation, the consummation of the virginity of the spirit. 'L'Allegro', which is not included in *The Unknown Eros*, completes the cycle of seasonal poems with its picture of the joys of autumn. Rejecting

> the roaring wheel
> Of God's remoter service, public zeal

the poet chooses the better way of Mary. In the 'dreaming field and bossy autumn wood' he sees an image of Certitude, for Autumn is 'the Spouse of Honour, fair Repose'. Love, all passion spent, moves in the certainty of final peace, through a world of idle vanities, false gods and perverted thinking; consciousness of divine love makes such things fit only for man's 'idlest hour'.

Having dealt with love through the images of Nature in the first three poems, the poet turns to consider human love directly, and ten odes which follow show its pathos, its joys, its revelations and its consolations. These are the poems which many readers have found to be his most moving and most human, for in them are an unsullied purity of tone and a depth of poignant emotion which put them among the most touching poems in the language. Yet they are more than poetic realizations of Patmore's own private sorrow at the loss of his wife. In the pattern of *The Unknown Eros* they present the crises of human love, and show the revelation of its inwardness under the impact of grief, as well as the purgative effect of pain on the soul. They represent the apotheosis of the philosophy of *The Angel in the House*; the transcendence of death by love, the relationship between 'Life, Death, Terror, Love', the divine nature of love revealed as plainly in its sorrows as in its joys.

'Beata', one of the original nine odes, gains special significance from its place in the sequence. The single sentence which constitutes the poem develops the image of white light broken up by a prism into its constituent colours. The rays of infinite Heaven striking upon woman

> Renounced their undistinguishable stress
> Of withering white,
> And did with gladdest hues my spirit caress,
> Nothing of Heaven in thee showing infinite,
> Save the delight.

Like the opening lines of 'Wind and Wave', 'Beata' states Patmore's conviction that the Incarnation was necessary to teach men the nature of God, that love, no abstract thing, expresses itself in the concrete, and that to be knowable, all infinite things must be bounded by the finite. The image of the poem anticipates what he says in 'Dieu et ma Dame':

'Woman, that opaque surface in which the rays of Deity end, and from which they are reflected in all the multiplied splendours which they have gathered by being transmitted through the prismatic and refractive spheres that intervene.'[1]

Nine odes which follow distil the sadness of lonely, remembering love after the death of the beloved. 'The Day After Tomorrow' is, as Alice Meynell called it, a 'magnificent ode of reunion'.[2] Separated from his wife by death, the poet remembers the past delights of love, and sees them as an earnest of reunion in eternity. And in lines which suggest the time between Christ's death and resurrection he says:

> One day's controlled hope, and then one more,
> And on the third our lives shall be fulfill'd!

[1] 'Dieu et Ma Dame', *Religio Poetae*, p. 160.
[2] 'Coventry Patmore', *The Second Person Singular*, p. 97.

Here the terror of death is dissolved in the joy of eternal life. At the very beginning of the poetic consideration of love, therefore, Patmore sees married love as finding its perfect consummation in the Beatific Vision. 'Tristitia', asking that, if the lover be damned and his beloved saved, she promise

> Never, by grief for what I bear or lack
> To mar thy joyance of heav'n's jubilee,

is another declaration that love continues after death, and that in the certainty of the happiness of the beloved, even the most bitter agony will be tempered. Never from his soul, he says, can

> Such pleasure die
> As the poor harlot's, in whose body stirs
> The innocent life that is and is not hers.

In logical sequence comes the beautiful ode 'The Azalea', in which the husband, dreaming that his wife is dead, wakes, in the happy realization that it was a dream, then to the blinding awareness that she *is* dead. This poem is filled with the pain of separation, and the poignant agony of recollected joy. But the perfume of the azalea which pervades it is yet another symbol of the continuity of love. 'Departure' recalls the actual death of Emily and expresses the bewildered amazement of her grief-stricken husband in the face of the indifference of death, as she passes 'with not one kiss, or a good-bye'. 'Eurydice', using the myth of Orpheus's quest, portrays the husband dreaming that he searches for his wife in the nightmare of her need and finds her dying neglected, faintly seen, as the dead are in dreams. The mood is one of regret for things undone, the theme of too late, now she is

> Beyond love's cure,
> By all the world's neglect, but chiefly mine.

And then, in the poignance of his double recollection, in dream and waking, he finds 'after exceeding ill, a little good'.

'The Toys', one of the most familiar of the odes and the one which perhaps comes closest to sentimentality, gives, on the human level, a concrete instance of the widower's apprehension of the sustaining power of woman's love in the difficulty he finds in understanding his motherless children. Regret for a harsh dismissal of his child takes him to the nursery, where, gazing upon the boy's pathetic collection of treasures, he thinks of the greater charity of God towards the greater childishness of man. In its context, this poem is less 'soft' than it might appear in isolation, for it carries a stage further the conviction of the sustaining grace of God, and the awareness that all human love is a shadow of Eternal Love. 'Tired Memory', another very human poem, is full of remorse at the fading of the sharpness of love's recollection. The onset of a new love provokes the idea of treason, and disloyalty to the memory of the first love, as, in honest self-examination, he realizes that

> The strong rock of death's insensibility
> Well'd yet awhile with honey of thy love
> And then was dry.

In the heart, 'dead of devotion and tired memory', a new movement of sensuous delight is felt which compels him to examine the old love and the new in relation to each other. Patmore's psychological subtlety is nowhere more evident than in this poem. With complete absence of equivocation, the poet scrutinizes his own motives, recognizing the human weaknesses which flaw human love, and the impossibility of man, in this middle state, retaining unchanged the pristine memory of even the most perfect human love.

Thus far, the book has revealed the soul of love in Nature, expressed the joy and sorrow of human love and hinted at its fate in death, and considered the transitoriness of purely human affection. Recollections of this earthly love are to come again later, in two odes, 'If I Were Dead' and 'A Farewell', as if sometimes, in man's concern with the external world and with mystical contemplation, memories of past love disturbingly intrude. The first of these sees death as irrevocable parting and the second accepts the widening of the gap between living and dead. Father Connolly considers that 'A Farewell' indicates Patmore's breaking of his last bond with Emily by changing his religion.[1] This may indeed be one element in the poem, but the main emphasis is on final understanding, on the certainty that both, 'making full circle' of their banishment, will be finally reunited

> With tears of recognition never dry.

These two poems are interspersed among four odes which deal with 'public weal', and in which Patmore considers man's life in the community and the operation of God's providence therein. 'Magna Est Veritas' rejects the 'world's cause'. Yet it is not a pessimistic poem, but an expression of trust in Providence, for

> The truth is great, and shall prevail,
> When none cares whether it prevail or not.

The following odes, overtly political ones, must be approached in the attitude of 'Magna Est Veritas'. '1867', 'Peace' and '1880–1885'

---

[1] *Mystical Poems . . . by Coventry Patmore*, p. 191.

are dominated, too, by Patmore's concept of national honour, one which we accept in Shakespeare, and in the mood of war-time, but which many readers have been unable to accept from Patmore, since it is mingled here with political pessimism and intransigent Toryism. The intemperate tone of these odes forms a striking contrast to the dignified poignance of the immediately preceding poems. Yet they have a legitimate place in the plan of *The Unknown Eros*. Since Patmore was always aware of the social implications of love and its fundamental importance in the State, he could not, in a work concerned with the whole range of love's meaning and effects, ignore the milieu in which love was lived. The difficulty is that the political odes strike a partisan, rather than a universal, note. Instead of showing how love operates in public life as it does in private life, he offers mostly bitter recriminations. The tone is wrong; and reveals a marked defect in his sensibility. Yet these odes are not wholly lost in the lava of Patmore's prejudices. Based upon a passionate dislike of tyranny and a sense of the importance of individual freedom, they are not black Jeremiads, for they assert the conviction of future restoration and the certainty that God's will operates in history. There is, in fact, more than a touch of the mood of Léon Bloy in their combination of apocalyptic vision and ill-temper, as well as in the fact that Patmore foresees emerging from the coming turmoil, 'the Time of Grace', and asks that

> Christ's own look through
> The darkness suddenly increased
> To the gray secret lingering in the East.

The poetic search for evidence of God's hand and plan is then pursued into the realms of philosophy, as in the next two odes Patmore examines alternatives to his own concept of man and his destiny. 'The Two Deserts' rejects the claims made for science as a substitute for the spiritual vision. Contrasting the two 'deserts blank of small and great', the world of the telescope and that of the microscope, he prefers the life revealed by the latter to the dead grandeur of the skies, but prefers to either the familiar 'royal-fair estate' where

> Wonder and beauty our own courtiers are,
> Pressing to catch our gaze,
> And out of obvious ways
> Ne'er wandering far.

In 'Crest and Gulf', where the mood is more bitter, he pours scorn on 'the bitter jest of mankind's progress'. Yet, even here, we find, instead of a mere sterile cynicism, a vivid contrast between the transitory nature of earthly aims and the permanent world of eternal values where final issues are decided. Behind all history and man's rationalization of it he hears

> The fly-wheel swift and still
> Of God's incessant will.

These poems restate some of Patmore's most cherished convictions —the futility of man's effort without God's help, the need for control, so that, in working out God's will, man will use the full dynamic of grace, the concept that all created things lead, by analogy, to the world of the spirit, and the belief that all human knowledge is valuable only in so far as it points men to God.

The final five odes of Book I have been called *psalmi penitentiales*.[1] A preparation for the revelation of Book II, and a bridge between the contemplation of Nature and human life and the contemplation of the Deity, they reveal the spiritual resources of the soul undergoing the purgation essential as a preliminary to union with the Divine. 'Let Be!', a meditation on the impossibility of judging others, serves to temper the apparent hauteur of the political odes by showing Patmore's more truly charitable side:

> But not all height is holiness,
> Nor every sweetness good;
> And grace will sometimes lurk where who could guess?
>
> . . . Why should I clear myself, why answer thou for me?

Indications, too, are here of Patmore's struggle with himself in subduing his passions to his religion, his attempt, in a sense, to sublimate his sensuality:

> And that which you and I
> Call his besetting sin
> Is but the fume of his peculiar fire
> Of inmost contrary desire.

The mystery of grace is the theme of 'Faint Yet Pursuing', an ode which movingly states the sense of imperfection which comes to the most earnest seeker, and is analogous to the spiritual dryness of which St. John of the Cross speaks. 'Victory in Defeat' develops the same theme further, recording the alternations of success and failure which mark the soul's progress towards asceticism, and recognizing, with psychological acuteness, the pain that comes after the first ecstasy of surrender:

[1] Frederick Page in 'The Centenary of Coventry Patmore', *Dublin Review*, July 1923, p. 33.

> Ah, God, alas,
> How soon it came to pass
> The sweetness melted from thy barbed hook
> Which I so simply took;
> And I lay bleeding on the bitter land.

'Victory in Defeat' has something of the temper of Herbert's 'The Collar'. Frankly acknowledging his weakness, the poet meditates on the forgiveness of God and the depths of His grace, lest in his continual lapses he should despair:

> O God, how long!
> Put forth indeed Thy powerful right hand,
> While time is yet,
> Or never shall I see the blissful land.

But the thought of God's perfection, His fatherly care and His 'peace beyond surmise' sustains him.

'Remembered Grace' reaffirms trust in God's mercy. Even in the depths of apparent deprivation the soul remembers past evidences of God's love and cannot but see the marks of His power and His providence in the sacramental signs of nature. So faith in adversity and unfaltering trust are necessary for the soul who would be admitted to the intimacies of divine love:

> And, under the ever-changing clouds of doubt,
> When others cry,
> 'The stars, if stars there were,
> Are quench'd and out!'
> To him, uplooking t'ward the hills for aid,
> Appear, at need display'd,
> Gaps in the low-hung gloom, and, bright in air,
> Orion or the Bear.

At the end of Book I 'Vesica Piscis' gives a glimpse of the rewards of the faithful soul, in the first intimations of the immediate presence of God. Purged by its suffering, faithful in its trials, the soul is ready to approach the Deity directly. Patmore's image for the struggles of the dedicated spirit is Peter's unsuccessful fishing before his casting of the net in obedience to Christ's command once more filled his boat with the 'quick, shining harvest of the Sea'; and the discovery of the coin in the fish is man's discovery of God living in his own flesh.

In Book I of *The Unknown Eros*, then, Patmore moves logically from love found in Nature to love found in the flesh, in its dual aspects of joy and pain, thence to the social and philosophical referents of such a view of love, finally to the pursuits of divine love, in terms of human failings and aspirations, up to the first faint stirrings of the divine spirit felt in the soul of man.

The way is now prepared for a poetic exploration of the mysteries of the love of God. 'To the Unknown Eros', which opens Book II, shows by its joy and tranquillity a deepening of the mood of the work and a serene sense of approaching fulfilment. With the words

> What this breeze
> Of sudden wings
> Speeding at far returns of time from interstellar space
> To fan my very face,
> And gone as fleet,
> Through delicatest ether feathering soft their solitary beat

the soul recognizes the presence of the messengers of God, and prepares to respond to the will of the divine lover. At first the messages are enigmatic and only hint at

> A bond I know not of nor dimly can divine

but she knows that the way to union must lie in a detachment from earthly love, in a sacrifice for a greater gain. All the longing which she thought once to satisfy in Nature and in earthly love she now realizes can be satisfied only in God. 'The Contract' develops the notion of the attainment of divine love by sacrifice of earthly love through the presentation of the 'virgin marriage' of Adam and Eve. The implications of this ode in relation to Patmore's concept of virginity have already been discussed. It remains to say here that as part of the general plan of *The Unknown Eros*, 'The Contract' refers to the spiritual strength that comes from a voluntary renunciation of sexual intercourse, and, on another level, to that virginity of mind essential in all love, whether physical or divine. Like most of the other odes, it has also an immediate psychological significance; at its centre lies the idea generally described today as 'sublimation'. It is not to be taken as a serious exegesis of the first chapters of Genesis, but as a parable, using the story of Adam and Eve to describe the difference between pure love and lust, and to point up the weakness of man's flesh inherited from the choice of Eve. The last lines look forward to the fulfilment of the original pledge of Adam and Eve when 'a heaven-caress'd and happier Eve' will bring forth

> No numb, chill-hearted, shaken-witted thing,
> 'Plaining his little span,
> But of proud virgin joy the appropriate birth,
> The Son of God and Man.

In 'Arbor Vitae' and 'The Standards' Patmore expressly draws attention to the fact that, for the Christian, there is a guide from whom he may learn the way of God and by whose instruction he can confirm the truth of his own intuitions. He symbolizes the Church both as the tree of life and as a victorious army. These two odes plainly show the realism of his approach to organized religion. The Church is no ideal, perfect institution. The tree of life is deformed with gnarls and bosses, wreathed around with pagan mistletoe, thick with 'nests of the hoarse bird'—that is, her devotions are often childish, her ceremonial contains relics of pagan practices, her clergy are often vain and stupid. But the heart is sound, the tree continually renews itself and beneath the rough rind of its fruit is found nutritious meat. 'The Standards', prompted by English reaction to the declaration of the doctrine of Papal Infallibility, is a call to all Christians to uphold the authority of truth, and to mark the signs of the Church which show her divine origin. It is also an expression of confidence that the reprobation of men indicates the truth of her doctrines:

> The sanction of the world's undying hate
> Means more than flaunted flags in windy air.

Full of Biblical references and prophetic rhetoric, the ode ends with a vision from the Apocalypse.

After this recognition of the corporative nature of the Church and the part it plays in directing the soul towards God—a recognition not merely conventional but personally realized—Patmore turns directly to the vision of the soul as spouse of Christ, and since man is a duality, to the role of the body in the apprehension of God.

> What is this Maiden fair
> The laughing of whose eye
> Is in man's heart renew'd virginity?

he asks in 'Sponsa Dei'; and replies:

> What if this Lady be thy Soul, and He
> Who claims to enjoy her sacred beauty be
> Not thou, but God.

With this ode, we enter the highest reaches of Patmore's poetry. The way of Nature symbolism is abandoned for the nuptial analogy, and the fulfilment of the promise made in the early part of *The Angel in the House*:

> This little germ of nuptial love
> Which springs so simply from the sod,
> The root is, as my song shall prove,
> Of all our love to man and God.

'Sponsa Dei' and six of the odes that follow, including the 'Psyche' poems, represent the most complete poetic expression of the 'burning heart' of his nuptial philosophy.

'Legem Tuam Dilexi' sings of the joy that succeeds man's acceptance of the bonds of law, and the repudiation of the word horrible—'infinite'. It is logical that 'To the Body' should follow, for the body, 'wall of infinitude', and 'foundation of the sky', is the glorious limit of man. In his most mystical poems Patmore is still the humanist, accepting the wonder of the body and singing the Incarnation; and in this splendid ode he obeys the counsel of St. Paul, 'Glorify and bear God in your body.' But he also hymns the resurrection of the body; for man is complete only when the soul is reunited to its 'old abode'; until then the soul

> does with envy see
> Enoch, Elijah, and the lady, she
> Who left the lilies in her body's lieu.

Patmore, at least, would have found no quarrel with the dogma proclaiming the Assumption of the Blessed Virgin. After thanking God for the pleasures he has known in the body, Patmore turns in 'Deliciae Sapientiae de Amore' to celebrate the glory of virginity, including, as we have seen, all who are virginal in mind, and all the blessed in Heaven, for

> Love makes the life to be
> A fount perpetual of virginity.

No other poem of Patmore's so movingly expresses his conviction of the purity of love in law, and of the mystical dignity of virginity. Yet he is humble before his great theme, and no trace of the arrogance of the political odes enters in to flaw this piece of sustained lyricism. But the poems immediately before and after 'Deliciae Sapientiae de Amore' show his continual awareness of his age and of his physical surroundings. The placing of these odes seems designed to indicate that there is no reason why the mystic should be divorced from actuality; and that Patmore is quite aware of the need for the speculative mystic to keep his feet on the ground lest he lose himself in misty subjectivism. Another effect of 'Sing Us One of the Songs of Sion' and 'The Cry at Midnight' is to remind us of the difficulty of imperfect man's focusing with unflickering attention upon a single point of mystical absorption. Both poems, which appear like interludes among the poems of divine love and praise, reflect much the same mood as 'Crest and Gulf' in Book I.

'Sing Us One of the Songs of Sion' recalls the plight of the

Israelites during the Babylonian captivity. Identifying himself with them, Patmore asks

> How sing the Lord's Song in so strange a land?

And the strange land is the land of those who reject the old traditions, and who scorn the Christian God, in favour of a conventional deism or a pseudo-scientific rationalism. Although 'The Cry at Midnight', which follows 'Deliciae Sapientiae de Amore', is satirical in tone, it has a direct relation to the mystical poems. It rebukes the deists and agnostics who cannot conceive that the Creator—if there be a Creator—could possibly be concerned with the love of man, and think it blasphemy that some should say 'Our Bridegroom's near!' What, Patmore asks, is their norm?

> The Midge's wing beats to and fro
> A thousand times ere one can utter 'O!'
> And Sirius' ball
> Does on his business run
> As many times immenser than the Sun.
> Why should things not be great as well as small,
> Or move like light as well as move at all?

God's ways are not man's. He, not man, is the measure of all things, and His love for His creature is a mystery which neither philosophy nor science can solve. 'Auras of Delight' presents a calculated contrast to positivist thinking, this time in terms of a personal conviction of grace, a recollection of the intimations of divinity which come to man, particularly in childhood. At times, especially during the crises of adult life, the vision seems to have vanished, but never do they altogether die,

> Those trackless glories glimps'd in upper sky,

so that the sense of the holiness of pure love always determines, for those who have experienced it, their revulsion from lust.

Thus prepared for, the Psyche odes now crown the spiritual pilgrimage recorded in the earlier pages. Purged by suffering, disciplined by obedience to God's law, aware of the immensity of God and of her own insignificance, yet possessed by love for Him and convinced of His reciprocal love, the soul reaches out to embrace her God, and finds peace and the fulfilment of her destiny in union with Him. This, Patmore's attempt to record the apotheosis of human love, is at the same time the reflection of an intense personal vision. Two of the group of odes, 'Eros and Psyche' and 'Psyche's Discontent', are dialogues between Eros and Psyche, and one, 'De Natura Deorum', a dialogue between Psyche and the Pythoness.

In 'Eros and Psyche', the soul, weary of her apparently fruitless summonses to the Divine Lover, reaches the stage of passive receptivity and 'lies still'. As soon as she abandons her search, Eros comes, and she surrenders to the power and passion of his love. In the full flood of mystical-erotic expression the odes explore the nature of God's love, the intimacy between Creator and created, the mystery of His infinite condescension and the resources of the soul, which contains

> Some power, by all but him unguess'd,
> Of growing king-like were she king-caress'd.

This love, no negative thing, is positive and fulfilling, to be matched not in snow, but in the 'integrity of fire'. As its radiance begins to permeate Psyche, she cries at first:

> O, too much joy; O, touch of airy fire;
> O, turmoil of content; O, unperturb'd desire,

but submits completely to the will of her Lover, so that when He leaves her she is content in a love which, however widely shared, remains for her unique. Eros departs with an admonition that she delicately observe the intimacy of their relationship, lest it be profaned by misunderstanding:

> Bitter, sweet, few and veil'd let be
> Your songs of me.
> Preserving bitter, very sweet,
> Few, that so all may be discreet,
> And veil'd, that, seeing, none may see.

Psyche tells the Pythoness, in 'De Natura Deorum', of the visit of Eros, and of her fear that, if he does not return, she may be unable to remain faithful to him, for she remembers her past failings.

> Sadness and change and pain
> Shall me for ever stain.

But as the Pythoness reminds her of her own littleness and her immeasurable inferiority to Eros, she realizes that the especial joy of their union comes from this disparity. Only deliberate rejection of His love will hinder God's coming. He will forgive all else. And Psyche now knows that the severity and apparent harshness of Eros are salutary for herself and for her love. This Eros is not

> Our People's pompous but good-natured Jove,

that is, he is not the God of Victorian convention, the benevolent schoolmaster of sentimental piety. Although reverence in man's relation with God is necessary, inability to realize His love may cause excessive reverence to turn into fear:

> Knowst thou not, Girl, thine Eros loves to laugh?

Throughout this particular ode, Patmore strives to achieve a tone appropriate to the reverent gaiety of Psyche. But he writes with a colloquial playfulness which often falls short of what he intends. Hopkins, in fact, specifically objected to 'a certain jesting humour' which did not seem to him 'quite to hit the mark in this profoundly delicate matter'.[1] Patmore's intention is clear enough. He wants to show that, in opposition to Calvinist ideas, delight and gaiety are not incompatible with deep love and reverence for God. However, in such lines as these:

> Respectful to the Gods and meek,
> According to one's lights, I grant
> 'Twere well to be;
> But, on my word,
> Child, any one to hear you speak
> Would take you for a Protestant.
> (Such fish I do foresee
> When the charm'd fume comes strong on me)

the lapse of taste impairs the whole mood. Perhaps this in part reflects the difficulty Patmore found in visualizing himself as the receptive rather than the dominant partner in a love-relationship.

The final Psyche ode, 'Psyche's Discontent', finds the soul seeking respite from the love which has almost engulfed her. She begs that she be allowed to prove her love by her diligence in bearing

> The fardel coarse of customary life's
> Exceeding injucundity.

But her God-Lover replies that what he seeks for in her is not service, but love:

> Yea, Palate fine,
> That claim'st for thy proud cup the pearl of price,
> And scorn'st the wine,
> Accept the sweet, and say 'tis sacrifice!

Sharply and clearly, with reverence and yet with total involvement, the odes convey the intimacy of divine love. Despite an occasional touch of false rhetoric and now and then an incongruity of tone such as was noted in 'De Natura Deorum', they show, in the main, a combination of delicacy of feeling and subtlety of intellect.

[1] *Further Letters of Hopkins*, p. 199.

It is a mark of Patmore's sense of proportion that he should follow the Psyche poems with the ode on 'Pain', which opposes the Christian concept of the cleansing power of pain to both the Hedonism of some nineteenth-century writers and the algolagnia of Swinburne. Patmore is never concerned only with the fruits of the spiritual life, but always remembers their roots in human effort and in daily living. In this poem, he brings us back from the heights of mystic contemplation to the realities of human life, and yet goes beyond the fact of pain to the mystery of its relationship to 'joy and heart's delight'. The poet prays for strength and prudence, for help to resist the temptation to turn from pain to its 'pale enemy', pleasure. Here again we see Patmore's psychological perception in his realization of the thin barriers which separate bliss and suffering.

'Prophets Who Cannot Sing', which introduces 'The Child's Purchase', speaks of the inadequacy of poetry to do justice to the hidden life of the spirit. He is approaching his great final subject with humility. Although the tone is characteristically Patmorean, the theme of this ode has a good deal in common with those passages in the *Four Quartets* in which Eliot considers the limitations of language in the rendering of religious experience. Patmore's 'prophets who cannot sing' are not those without a vision to record, but those with a vision of the 'unveil'd heavens' so intense that it is inexpressible. Poetry, though the most piercing of the arts, produces songs which, by comparison with the reality, are 'tunes that nails might draw from slates'.

With this warning in our ears, we come to 'The Child's Purchase', his final poetic word on love and virginity. In the Blessed Virgin Mary he sees the perfection of virginity, of married love and of the love of God, as well as the supreme expression of the meaning of the Incarnation. The title of the poem is explained in the opening lines :

> As a young Child, whose Mother, for a jest,
> To his own use a golden coin flings down,
> Devises blithe how he may spend it best,
> Or on a horse, a bride-cake, or a crown,
> Till, wearied with his quest,
> Not liking altogether that or this,
> He gives it back for nothing but a kiss,
> Endow'd so I
> With golden speech, my choice of toys to buy,
> And scanning power and pleasure and renown,
> Till each in turn, with looking at, looks vain,
> For her mouth's bliss,
> To her who gave it give I it again.

Since every ordinary marriage is the symbol of union with God, the Blessed Virgin, the Mother of God, is the perfect exemplification of Patmore's nuptial philosophy and of his concept of limits. In the magnificent litany which is the core of the poem, he calls her:

Our only saviour from an abstract Christ.

Echoes from Dante, St. Bernard and the Bible are mingled in this hymn of praise to the Blessed Virgin, not only as the Mother of Christ, but also as the Second Eve forecast in 'The Contract', she in whom all womankind is raised up and glorified. Patmore is now ready to surrender his work to the judgment of Heaven, recognizing that, behind all that he has written of love, stood the hitherto unapprehended figure of the Virgin.

When clear my Songs of Lady's graces rang,
And little guess'd I 'twas of thee I sang!

She is the final paradox of all paradoxes, the 'rainbow complex in bright distinction of all beams of sex'; to whom God is 'Husband, Father, Son and Brother'. The 'rinsed and wrung' language of this ode, its dignity and its fusion of intelligence and sensibility make it a great religious poem, sincere, humble, yet full of daring insights.

The whole work closes with the eighteen lines of 'Dead Language', one of the original nine odes. Reflecting the melancholy mood in which those odes were written, it would appear to come a little oddly at the end of a sequence of poems which has ventured so far so daringly. Yet the ironical point it makes is typical of Patmore's realism. Should not such thoughts as this book expresses be 'decently cloak'd in the Imperial Tongue'? he imagines his monitor asking, to which he replies, 'Alas, and is not mine a language dead?' While in this final poem Patmore acknowledges the rejection of his later poetic vision by his age, it also, in the plan of *The Unknown Eros*, indicates his coming abandonment of poetry and his dedicating himself to religious and mystical speculation. It is not a lament over a lack of understanding, but a renewed assertion that the real significance of the odes lies hidden beneath the symbols, as the mysteries of the liturgy are hidden in the Latin.

Far from being a mere miscellany, then, compounded out of fragments from two unfinished, ambitious works, *The Unknown Eros* is a unified work, based upon a plan to which each ode contributes and in the context of which they gain richer significance. Together the odes outline 'the whole pedigree of love'.[1] Love as symbolized in Nature, love in its human reality, love in terms of social action,

---

[1] Osbert Burdett, *The Idea of Coventry Patmore*, p. 205.

and philosophy, love as penitence, are the themes of the first book. The second expresses lyrically the ecstasies of union with God, from the first intimations of His presence through the consciousness of the need for guidance, for self-abnegation, and the acceptance of pain, to the fullness of union. Both books are interspersed with reflections on the fluctuations of the spiritual life and on the duality of man. Full of 'wit' and of curious paradoxical turns of thought, which do not eliminate pathos but reinforce it, *The Unknown Eros* is a poem unique in its age.

The language of the odes is even more markedly Patmorean than that of *The Angel*. There is still his individual blend of concrete and abstract words, but the blend is not uniform throughout the work. The 'pathetic' odes are for the most part bare of elaboration, and have something of the same luminous simplicity as his earlier poems. The political odes are much more rhetorical, with the language showing signs of inflation. The vocabulary of the Psyche odes, and of those dealing with philosophical and religious themes, is compounded of words rich in Biblical and mystical associations and words of the utmost simplicity. Here is a mixture of almost ingenuous directness and intellectual subtlety which makes Patmore a genuine 'metaphysical'.

> But, lo, while thus I store toil's slow increase,
> To be my dower, in patience and in peace,
> Thou com'st like bolt from blue, invisibly,
> With premonition none nor any sign,
> And, at a gasp, no choice nor fault of mine,
> Possess'd I am with thee
> Ev'n as a sponge is by a surge of the sea!

Hopkins, defending Patmore to Bridges, once wrote:

'The faults I see in him are bad rhymes; continued obscurity; and the most serious, a certain frigidity when, as often, the feeling does not flush and fuse the language. But for insight he beats all our living poets, his insight is really profound, and he has an exquisiteness, farfetchedness, of imagery worthy of the best things of the Caroline age.'[1]

Though Patmore's mannered diction is a very different instrument from the highly charged word-relationships of Hopkins, Hopkins recognized the 'mastery of phrase' in Patmore which produced the tone the older poet desired. But the matter of frigidity is important. Do the odes lack passion? Does feeling appear at times to lag behind intellectual ingenuity?

This certainly cannot be said of the 'widower's' poems in *The*

---

[1] *Letters to Robert Bridges*, p. 82.

Unknown Eros, where the reader has a sense of overhearing the poet, of observing unawares the nakedness of private grief. But in the Psyche odes, there does not appear to be the same depth of passionate feeling as we find in the religious poems of Donne and Crashaw. That there is a sincere attempt at total immersion in the theme can hardly be doubted, on the evidence of flashes of pure beauty and feeling, but the reader is often aware chiefly of the force of Patmore's intelligence and of the delicacy of his insight. He is even in his most exalted odes primarily an intellectual poet. In every ode of Book II of *The Unknown Eros* the guiding principle of mind shows itself; there is rarely a full surrender to the urgency of feeling, even when it is demanded by the theme. Patmore is fundamentally anti-Romantic.

It is this element of unassimilated intellectuality to which Hopkins referred when he told Patmore that he had less of the 'tyke' in him than any other man he knew.[1]

Patmore's attempts at playfulness, especially in 'De Natura Deorum', but also in 'Psyche's Discontent', have a certain clumsy quality, a lumbering inappositeness. May this not reflect the difficulty Patmore found in contemplating the thought of surrender of himself as woman to God as man, when his own attitude towards women implied a kind of inferiority in them? To some extent, Patmore, like Milton, tried to reason himself into salvation. On the evidence of *The Rod, the Root and the Flower* he passed beyond this attitude, to one of complete acceptance. But in the second part of *The Unknown Eros* there are signs of his struggle to adapt himself, to fuse his emotions with his religion—in the prettiness of some images, in the commonplaceness of others, in an extravagance of tone, in a touch of obscurity, in the occasional failure to assimilate the details of erotic love into the celebration of the mystical union.

In this work Patmore made a daring attempt to treat love as both divine and as rooted in human reality—to have, as it were, the best of both worlds, in the Christian sense. Refusing to regard religious feeling as wholly ethereal in origin, he strove to relate the highest reaches of love to the body of man. He never relinquished his pure ideal, but the odes show the exceptional difficulty of expressing this ideal in poetry. Hence there is a conflict in his personality which gives a special piquancy to the second book of *The Unknown Eros*. The conflict is between Patmore's strong individuality—his independence of mind, his aloofness of temperament, his sensuality—and his ideal of religious experience and the most worthy life. He struggles continually to reach higher and higher levels in his poetry.

---

[1] *Further Letters of Hopkins*, p. 242.

Though his imaginative vision is high and constant, it is all the time accompanied by a process of intellectualization, and the two do not always fuse. When they do, as in 'Legem Tuam Dilexi' and 'To the Body', for instance, there is a unique blend of powerful feeling, sensuous and sensual experience, intelligence and sensibility. Such odes attain what Sir Desmond MacCarthy called an 'incandescent austerity'.[1]

The highest points of *The Unknown Eros* make Patmore a poet of the order of Donne, Crashaw, Hopkins and Herbert. Yet the work contains that dross which is the evidence of the intensity of his personal struggle. Throughout he is disturbed by memories of his first wife, which his later married happiness could not wholly eradicate; he is conscious of the difficulty of transmuting the experience of earthly love into divine love; he suffers not a little from the responsibility of his expanding knowledge of human passion. So paradoxes, invective, sardonic jests, difficult sayings, and rhetorical exaggeration break into the poems. A closer look at a characteristic ode from *The Unknown Eros* may give us a clearer idea of important aspects of Patmore's poetic sensibility. Sponsa Dei is not one of his best odes; it does not reach the height of the 'widower's' odes, nor of the best Psyche poems, but neither does it sink as often as the political odes. Representative of his average level of achievement in this volume, it shows the faults as well as the virtues of his later poetic style.

> What is this Maiden fair,
> The laughing of whose eye
> Is in man's heart renew'd virginity;
> Who yet sick longing breeds
> For marriage which exceeds
> The inventive guess of Love to satisfy
> With hope of utter binding, and of loosing endless dear despair?
> What gleams about her shine,
> More transient than delight and more divine!
> If she does something but a little sweet,
> As gaze towards the glass to set her hair,
> See how his soul falls humbled at her feet!
> Her gentle step, to go or come,
> Gains her more merit than a martyrdom;
> And, if she dance, it doth such grace confer
> As opes the heaven of heavens to more than her,
> And makes a rival of her worshipper.
> To die unknown for her were little cost!

[1] 'Coventry Patmore', *Criticism*, by Desmond MacCarthy (Putnam, 1932), p. 78.

So is she without guile,
Her mere refused smile
Makes up the sum of that which may be lost!
Who is this Fair
Whom each hath seen,
The darkest once in this bewailed dell,
Be he not destin'd for the glooms of hell?
Whom each hath seen
And known, with sharp remorse and sweet, as Queen
And tear-glad Mistress of his hopes of bliss,
Too fair for man to kiss?
Who is this only happy She,
Whom, by a frantic flight of courtesy,
Born of despair
Of better lodging for his Spirit fair,
He adores as Margaret, Maude, or Cecily?
And what this sigh,
That each one heaves for Earth's last lowlihead
And the Heaven high
Ineffably lock'd in dateless bridal-bed?
Are all, then, mad, or is it prophecy?
'Sons now we are of God,' as we have heard,
'But what we shall be hath not yet appear'd.'
O, Heart, remember thee,
That Man is none,
Save One.
What if this Lady be thy Soul, and He
Who claims to enjoy her sacred beauty be,
Not thou, but God; and thy sick fire
A female vanity,
Such as a Bride, viewing her mirror'd charms,
Feels when she sighs, 'Ah, these are for his arms!'
A reflex heat
Flash'd on thy cheek from His immense desire,
Which waits to crown, beyond thy brain's conceit,
Thy nameless, secret, hopeless longing sweet,
Not by-and-by, but now,
Unless deny Him thou!

The themes of this ode, that human love is a shadow of divine love, that the never-to-be-satisfied element in love comes from an instinctive awareness of this, and that all souls are feminine to God, are among those which appear in not dissimilar form in *The Angel in the House*. And the same kind of paradox as is found in the earlier work is also here, the idea that beneath the mundane details of love and courtship is 'the burning heart of the universe'. Yet the tone is

more elevated, and its control calls for a different kind of tact than
that which governed the gentle playfulness of *The Angel*. The lines

> If she does something but a little sweet,
> As gaze towards the glass to set her hair,
> See how his soul falls humbled at her feet!

which might not have been out of place in the lover's ecstasy in *The
Angel*, lend a touch of the commonplace to the higher statement of
the ode. This is the sort of thing that Hopkins felt not quite 'to hit
the mark'.

Some of the epithets are from stock—'sweet', 'fair', 'gentle' and
'divine'; and, save perhaps in the lines

> A reflex heat
> Flash'd on thy cheek from His immense desire,

the imagery barely escapes triteness. Patmore's analogy for the
soul's delight in its own beauty when it is loved by God:

> Such as a Bride, viewing her mirror'd charms,
> Feels when she sighs, 'Ah, these are for his arms!'

hints at a streak of coarseness in his sensibility. Although, in the
odes, he had largely passed beyond the clichés of the popular
religious vocabulary, he was not able wholly to dissociate himself
from conventional epithets of other kinds, which lend a touch of
literary vulgarity to some of the odes. One is tempted to attribute
this element to the state of the poetic vocabulary in the mid-
Victorian times. Patmore was not the only one among writers of
power and outstanding ability to fall foul of the 'vocabulary of the
heart'. For the present, it is relevant to note in Sponsa Dei the
touches of rhetorical exaggeration:

> To die unknown for her were little cost,

for instance; and the lack of concrete poetic detail. Patmore's
tendency towards generalization, marked in this poem, is both a
strength and a weakness. In 'Legem Tuam Dilexi' and 'Deliciae
Sapientiae de Amore' and other odes, the poetico-philosophical
abstractions have a genuine impressiveness, because the philosophy
from which they proceed is felt as a passionate experience rendered
with fitting dignity and breadth. But elsewhere, as in Sponsa Dei,
there is something of the verbal gesture, of the easy-way-out in
language.

On the other hand, the virtues of his style are evident in this ode,
too. One of these is the clarity of the central concept, the stiffening
which his philosophy gives to the idea, the poetic logic with which

the relationship between man's love for his 'Margaret, Maude, or Cecily' and God's love for man is worked out and the smoothness with which the experiences are linked. In the early part of the ode, we have an imaginative description of the exaggerated mood of the worshipping lover, who, even in his elation, recognizes that his beloved cannot satisfy his desire. Then, with the lines

> And what this sigh
> That each one heaves for Earth's last lowlihead
> And the Heaven high
> Ineffably lock'd in dateless bridal-bed

the transition is made between earthly and divine love, with the Incarnation seen as the great proof of the relationship.

The language is seldom inflated, and some of the phrasing is poetically inventive—'a frantic flight of courtesy', 'thy sick fire', 'tear-glad Mistress', 'a reflex heat'. More than this, the rhetorical control rarely wavers throughout. The opening lines are particularly sure in their statement. Among them

> With hope of utter binding, and of loosing endless dear despair?

is especially interesting. It contains a slightly clumsy inversion, yet its compressed paradoxical statement of Patmore's basic idea of the joy of limits shows the strong intellectual control behind the ode.

As a whole, Sponsa Dei is greater than the sum of its parts, and the same is true of many of the other odes. The most memorable of them are usually the most concrete, the 'widower's' odes and the 'Psyche' group, which deal with a particular situation, rather than with an abstract idea. Elsewhere *The Unknown Eros* indicates the difficulty Patmore found in expressing an intellectual experience in emotive terms. If *The Unknown Eros* is compared with the poems of St. John of the Cross, we see the difference between the work of a speculative mystic and that of a true mystic who was also a great lyrical poet. But the problem of the abstract subject is not the whole answer. There is a flaw in Patmore's sensibility, not one gross enough to invalidate his poetry, but apparent enough to keep his work in the second rank. It is partly a matter of emotional temper, partly one of too great a selectivity of experience, of over-assurance that he knew precisely what a valuable experience was, a touch, if you will, of spiritual complacency.

Yet, overriding this, throughout *The Unknown Eros* is the sense of struggle, of the battle to achieve harmony of thought and feeling, harmony of flesh and spirit; and finally, a confidence, trust and knowledge that ultimate peace will succeed the 'weary life's campaign'. And such knowledge is humble, not arrogantly haughty; it is a measure of the success of Patmore's war against himself that he can say, with manifest sincerity:

> Mother, who lead'st me by unknown ways,
> Giving the gifts I know not how to ask,
> Bless thou the work
> Which, done, redeems my many wasted days,
> Makes white the murk,
> And crowns the few which thou wilt not dispraise.

The Unknown Eros, then, is as complex and as serious a work as was written in England in the nineteenth century. It speaks to the twentieth century with a clearer voice than it spoke to Patmore's own age. The marks of strain and tension in it, and the struggle towards personal integration, give it an immediacy which most contemporary readers fail to find in Browning or Tennyson. The discipline Patmore exercises over his poetic expression in the odes is indicated by the demands he makes on his readers. His long, carefully-wrought sentences require close attention. Their syntax is rarely involved, but the thought is tightly-knit, closely-woven rather than uttered in lyrical outbursts. From this discipline and the organization of the thought, as much as from subject-matter, form and language, comes the curiously individual ring of the odes, that quality which Percy Lubbock describes as a 'union of severity——a certain noble gauntness—with a sensuousness that lavishes itself in such lovely and minute detail.'[1]

The very seriousness of Patmore's spiritual quest accounts equally for the disturbed and disturbing qualities of the odes and for their tender dignity. The revelation in *The Unknown Eros* of a complex spirit, individual, self-reliant, proud and even crotchety, struggling to submit himself to God, makes the work one of the most moving of religio-poetic expressions. Because they are so daring in their aim, the odes are at times extravagant, at others teeter on the edge of the absurd; yet the purity of Patmore's intention preserves them from banality. At their best they are in truth 'wedded light and heat'. Sometimes there is a storm of feeling here rather than a flooding of the spirit; sometimes thought and emotion are not fused; but in the better odes, and they are many, the poet seems to be poised on the brink of eternal silence, to be about to attain that divine tranquillity whose pursuit is so movingly recorded in this extraordinary work.

[1] 'Coventry Patmore', *The Quarterly Review*, April 1908, p. 371.

V

The Man and the Poet

==

THOUGH AN APPRECIATION of Patmore's ideas is essential to a just appraisal of his achievement, it is as a poet that finally he must be judged, as he would have wished to be. In essence, it is true, he is the poet of a single theme—love; yet not many poets who have taken all Nature and mankind as their subjects have plumbed a greater variety of poetic experiences. The gnomic qualities in his poetry and some of its 'metaphysical' elements have already been discussed. But Patmore is also an outstanding Nature poet, endowed with a clear eye for the significant 'little things' in the visible universe. Trees, flowers, skies, clouds, waves, the ocean, the varying scents of the seasons, the sweep of landscapes, are all mirrored in his lines:

> Where sunshine seems asleep, though bright,
> And shadows yet are sharp with night,
> And further on, the wealthy wheat
> Bends in a golden drowse.

> In nook of pale or crevice of crude bark,
> Thou canst not miss,
> If close thou spy, to mark
> The ghostly chrysalis,
> That, if thou touch it, stirs in its dream dark.

> (Of a rain storm)
> Till, sudden as it came, 'twas past,
> Leaving a trouble in the copse
> Of brawling birds and tinkling drops.

> The cock scream'd, somewhere far away;
> In sleep the matrimonial dove
> Was crooning; no wind waked the wood,
> Nor moved the midnight river-damps,
> Nor thrill'd the poplar; quiet stood
> The chestnut with its thousand lamps;
> The moon shone yet, but weak and drear,
> And seemed to watch, with bated breath,
> The landscape, all made sharp and clear
> By stillness, as a face by death.

At times, the descriptions of Nature have, in their exact simplicity, and in their use of colour, something of the quality of Barnes's verse:

> The leaves, all stirring, mimick'd well
> A neighbouring rush of rivers cold,
> And, as the sun or shadow fell,
> So these were green and those were gold.

At others, only the sophistication of synaesthesia can satisfy him:

> Skies bluer than the cuckoo's egg,
> And clearer than the cuckoo's call.

Yet, although there are Nature-references in plenty in the poems, and many charming passages of pure description, it is as a source of analogies for the nuptial relationship or for the personality of the beloved that Nature chiefly serves him:

> Our confidences heavenwards grew,
> Like foxglove buds, in pairs disclosed.

> And faith that, straight t'wards heaven's far Spring,
> Sleeps, like a swallow, on the wing.

> And there Amelia stood, for fairness shewn
> Like a young apple-tree, in flush'd array
> Of white and ruddy flow'r, auroral, gay,
> With chilly blue the maiden branch between.

Patmore drew for his images not only on Nature, but, as the Metaphysical poets did, on both homely human experience and curious out-of-the-way learning. He could write, with his distinctive pathos:

> His fondness comes about his heart
> As milk comes, when the babe is dead

and

> But fondness for her underwent
> An unregarded increment
> Like that which lifts, through centuries
> The coral-reef within the seas.

In one poem he could say:

> She pass'd, and night was a surprise,
> As when the sun at Quito dips

and in another:

> But likeness and proportion both
> Now fail, as if a child in glee,
> Catching the flakes of the salt froth,
> Cried, 'Look, my mother, here's the sea!'

Some of his images strike home chiefly by virtue of their 'wit', in the seventeenth-century sense:

> Alone, alone with sky and sea,
> And her, the third simplicity.

> To which your charms draw up the soul
> As turning spirals draw the eyes.

> Now from the matrix, by God's grinding wrought,
> The brilliant shall be brought.

> You'll find your strong and tender loves
> Like holy rocks by Druids poised,
> The least force shakes, but none removes.

Astronomy provides him with one of his most pervasive types of metaphor. Patmore's eyes are fixed on the heavens, literally as well as metaphorically; and he turns astronomical lore to poetic advantage more often than almost any other poet of his age:

> What in its ruddy orbit lifts the blood,
> Like a perturbed moon of Uranus,
> Reaching to some great world in ungauged darkness hid.

> Making each phrase, for love and for delight,
> Twinkle like Sirius on a frosty night.

> To him, uplooking t'ward the hills for aid,
> Appear, at need display'd,
> Gaps in the low-hung gloom, and, bright in air,
> Orion or the Bear.

Patmore is a genuine lyric poet, combining delicacy of response with economy of expression; he also possesses a power of epigrammatic writing rare in his age. Often his poetry has a Miltonic largeness and dignity, yet at the same time he retains, whenever it is appropriate, the ability to render minute detail. This command over precise detail caused the Pre-Raphaelites to admire his first poems; but they were unable to follow him into the more spacious universe of *The Unknown Eros*. It is this sense of concreteness which allows him, when rendering a powerful emotion, to detail the contents of his son's pockets or to catch exactly the scent of the azalea; it is his imaginative power which leads him beyond the concrete. As a poet, then, he combines in his work two virtually contradictory elements. When they fuse, his poetry has its own distinctive power of suggesting the mystery at the heart of the commonest objects; when they do not, he approaches sentimentality, mere prettiness or strained rhetoric. Although the swiftness of Patmore's intellectual apprehensions and the strength of his passions are sometimes at war, he seldom leaves the impression that he is 'making poetic gestures'. When the path along which he would lead the reader seems too rugged and uninviting, this is the result of a conflict between his poetic vision and his personal philosophy, not of facility or superficiality.

He did not compromise with his conscience. His high conception of the function of the poet would not permit him to publish anything save what he deemed to be his best. This regard for the dignity of poetry made him eschew rhetoric in *The Angel*, and use his own kind of rhetoric in *The Unknown Eros*. Striving for appropriateness of expression and 'interior finish', he avoided saying fine things for their own sake and always tried to make his utterance a whole and single thing. Did any poet of his day take his craft more seriously? Sir Herbert Read declares that 'no poet had a clearer understanding of poetic integrity, and no poet of the nineteenth century, Hopkins apart, struggled so ardently to achieve it.'[1] Far from clogging his verse with arcane significances and obscurities, he discourses on the great truths of love and life and death often with so little emphasis that readers may be (and clearly some readers have been) unaware that he has moved from the regions of ordinary perception. In his own day, critics and friends were baffled by certain difficulties in the odes largely because Patmore drew upon traditional sources of symbol, which were almost completely forgotten or ignored in his century. Modern readers, accustomed to a more overtly cerebral poetry than was the rule in Patmore's time, that, for instance, of

[1] *The True Voice of Feeling* (Faber & Faber), 1953, p. 89.

Hopkins, Eliot, Robert Lowell and others who also use analogies from the mystics to embody a similar kind of insight, do not find *The Unknown Eros* obscure. It is not an easy work, any more than, for that matter, the earlier, ostensibly simpler, poems are easy; but, once the particular character of Patmore's vision is understood, detailed interpretation presents few difficulties.

At the same time, the total effect of his poetry is one of unevenness. It is doubtful whether the conflict he waged with himself was ever quite resolved in his verse. For there is sometimes a lack of tautness in the odes, a weakening of verbal discipline, a banality of image, and a too easy surrender to rhetorical abstractions. Yet, although these defects in his poetic genius prevent him from being classed with the greatest poets, they should not obscure his particular excellences, nor should they prevent recognition of the fact that Patmore understood, as few poets had understood since Coleridge and Keats, the need for an organic structure in poetry. Poetry was not a matter of mere artifice to him; it was a matter of finding the form which would most fittingly embody his vision, and of making each piece a rounded, self-subsistent whole. In his own way he was concerned, not with what Coleridge called 'Cold notions—lifeless technical rules', but with 'living and life-producing ideas, which shall contain their own evidence.'[1] In pursuit of the exact transmission of that which is within the thing, Patmore tirelessly corrected and recast his poetry. Yet on this point there is an apparent conflict of evidence. Gosse would have it that Patmore had no gift of imaginative storage, that he was essentially an improviser, that he 'could only write when the intolerable inspiration descended upon him.'[2] Champneys and Garnett also suggest that Patmore composed very quickly. Patmore's own words substantiate such statements. For instance, he once wrote to a friend: 'My best things were written most quickly. "Amelia" took four days; "Deliciae Sapientiae de Amore" two hours, several of the best odes even less. But I have often spent days and weeks in working up a short passage to the level of the best. The first Book of the "*Angel in the House*" took only six weeks in the writing, though I had thought of little else for several years before.'[3]

However, even on this evidence we cannot facilely deduce that Patmore was a hasty writer. He meditated long on his work, as he indicates, before setting pen to paper. Although the first book of

[1] 'On Poesy or Art', *Biographia Literaria with Aesthetical Essays*, ed. J. Shawcross (Oxford University Press), Vol. II, p. 258.

[2] *Coventry Patmore*, p. 214.

[3] Champneys, *Memoirs*, Vol. I, p. 261.

The Angel may have taken only six weeks to write in its original form, it was more than twice that number of years in the revision. Despite, too, Patmore's claims to have written the odes so quickly, the British Museum manuscript of *The Unknown Eros* shows that he systematically rewrote the poems, seeking the exact word and the precise cadence; that they did not come to him fully-grown out of the air. For instance, one of the early drafts of 'Wind and Wave'—which may not be the first—reads as follows:

>   shine
> The swift-winged ~~light~~ and heat,
> Darting through witless space
> Without a let,
> What are they till they beat
> Against the sleepy clod, and there beget
> Perchance the violet?
> ~~Mans~~ Love is nothing or base,
> Until the One be found.
> And wanton limit any joy and pride
>   desert   as happy
> Out of a wilderness of equal grace
> Decree Her for its bride
>   To be Lives
> ~~And be~~ its Bride and Bond
>   Henceforth to be in Her
> ~~From that time hence~~
> All which in heaven is sensitively good
> By him is understood
> ~~Only in her~~
> ~~(So subtle Heaven ordains~~
> ~~And this great worship gains~~
> ~~With small offence~~
>   After
> ~~And if~~ The narrow mode the mighty Heavens prefer)
>
> She, as a little breeze

The final form of these lines, after other drafts, is:

> The wedded light and heat
> Winnowing the witless space,
> Without a let,
> What are they till they beat
> Against the sleepy sod, and there beget
> Perchance the violet!

> Is the One found
> Amongst a wilderness of as happy grace,
> To make Heaven's bound;
> So that in Her
> All which it hath of sensitively good
> Is sought and understood
> After the narrow mode the mighty Heavens prefer?
> She, as a little breeze

The first five lines, doubtless formed in the poet's mind as the starting point of the poem, have undergone comparatively little change, and that in the direction of alliteration and more exact epithets; but the remaining fifteen lines in the first draft have been reduced to eight, and the thought much more tautly expressed.

Incomplete though the British Museum manuscript is, the erasures, substitutions, cancelled pages and abandoned sections show that Patmore worked over his odes with great care, and that he certainly had nothing in common with the popular conception of the poet as one who waits until the lightning strikes and then writes without further consideration. Neither did he write when he had nothing to say. His output is comparatively small beside the rows of fat volumes of his poetic contemporaries; and as a result rather less of his writing has to be discarded to reach the essential ore. When he felt he had said all that was in his heart, he gave up writing verse. He respected poetry too much to try to force the note. This poetic integrity acts as a kind of ground-base to his poetry, and, for the reader who comes to know and love his particular tone of voice, helps to win acceptance of his idiosyncrasies and even sympathy with his occasional flatness. Behind all he wrote is the sustaining force of a distinctive personality, an intriguing and highly individual spirit. There is an elusive 'I' in Patmore's work which fascinates, even when the reader finds himself repelled by certain angularities of thought and a lack of resilience.

The dignity and austerity of this personality at first sight appear to conflict with contemporary impressions of Patmore as a man. His many-sided character has been amply documented by Champneys, Gosse, Garnett and other friends and is generously revealed in his letters. In his exhaustive biography, Champneys gives more of the essential Patmore than does Gosse. The latter, knowing Patmore only in his later years, and always on the look-out for a 'character' to exploit, aims at a balanced estimate, but frequently misjudges Patmore (in the matter of alleged broken friendships, for instance) and over-emphasizes his idiosyncrasies and crotchetiness. Yet out of the biographical details there does emerge a picture of a man different from either the sentimental poetaster superficial readers imagined had penned *The Angel*, or the haughty aristocrat and arrogant mystic of certain critics. That he was a complex character no one has doubted. He was ascetic in his life, even when he enjoyed squirearchical prosperity, and fastidious in his dress and personal habits. As a father his will was law, but he was never excessively severe. His son by his third marriage called him 'a loving husband, a kind father and a good friend'.[1] He loved his children, although he did not always understand them, and became estranged from his eldest boy, Milnes. He was a warm and generous friend, maintaining close relations over many years with Carlyle, Ruskin, Woolner, Dykes Campbell, Greenwood and many others. It is true that he moved away from the Pre-Raphaelites, largely because their interests developed in a different direction, and that his friendship with Tennyson was broken off. But, in the latter case, it is clear that the break came through a misunderstanding in which neither was more to blame than the other. Perhaps the quality of Patmore's personality is best seen from the fact that he won the devoted attachment of men as different in character and outlook as Francis Thompson and the egregious Frank Harris.

He had a love of paradox and of baiting the more prudish of his friends. His most pointed shafts were aimed against sentimental humanitarians, teetotalers, people who gave to animals the affections they denied to men, and all who would try to regulate humanity into goodness. His waggish humour on the subject of cherished Victorian conventions, his trenchant conversation, his calculatedly provocative exaggerations, and his tendency to think in terms of hyperbole, no less than his leaving 'prudery to the Puritan half-believers',[2] disconcerted many of his acquaintances and still baffle those who think it impossible that a Victorian who was, moreover, the 'laureate of wedded love', could have had so puckish a sense of humour. Yet these external qualities, of which Gosse makes so much, did not obscure for his intimates the essential fineness of his spirit. They recognized that beneath the apparent disdain and intolerance in the disproportionate utterances was a nature tender, full of human sympathy, intellectually candid and sensitive. Gosse declared that he had 'rarely touched such pure intellectual enjoyment' as when in Patmore's company,[3] while de Vere was impressed

[1] 'Coventry Patmore: A Son's Recollections', by Francis J. Patmore, *The English Review*, Feb. 1932, p. 135.
[2] 'Coventry Patmore', *Contemporary Portraits (Third Series)*, by Frank Harris (New York, 1920), p. 204.
[3] *Coventry Patmore*, p. 158.

by 'the sensitive and impassioned character of his intellect'.[1] Champneys saw as his basic qualities 'the essential geniality of his nature . . . the depth of his affections, and . . . the loyalty of his friendship'.[2] Neither a bigot nor a prig, Patmore valued plain-speaking above platitudes, and sincerity above social conventions. He was confident in his faith and in his vision, and because he really did see life differently from other men, he gives an impression of intolerance on ideas, but never about the men who held them. He was a mixture of tenderness and vehement likes and dislikes, of clear spiritual vision and practical business wisdom, a man of conflicting humours, and, like his poetry, paradoxical.

All that he said and wrote, however, indicates that his allegiance to spiritual truth was consistent and high; that his will was dedicated to the pursuit of good. The seeming arrogance of some of his essays and utterances tends to conceal Patmore's essential humility. He was not lured by self-confidence to attempt work beyond his range, and if he felt satisfaction with his achievement, it was with a knowledge of his limitations. Never afraid of being in a minority of one, forthright in his assessment of his contemporaries, he nevertheless submitted with grateful acknowledgement to Hopkins's 'careful and subtle fault-finding'. Making no claims to originality as a thinker, he was always careful to acknowledge the sources on which he drew, and in the preface to *The Rod, the Root and the Flower* he wrote:

'I make no ridiculous pretence of invading the province of the theologian by defining or explaining dogma. This I am content with implicitly accepting, my work being mainly that of the Poet, bent only upon discovering and reporting how the "loving hint" of doctrine has "met the loving guess" of the souls of those who have so believed in the Unseen that it has become visible. . . . I should be horrified if a charge of "originality" were brought against me by any person qualified to judge whether any of the essential matter of this book were "original" or not. Mine is only a feeble endeavour to "dig again the wells which the Philistines have filled." '[3]

Despite the high value he placed upon the function of the poet-prophet whose intellect seemed to him capable of a kind of independent sanctification, he never confused the office of the poet with that of the priest, nor did he claim a special moral privilege for poets.

'That which is unique in the soul is its true self, which is only expressed in life and art when the false self has been surrendered wholly. In

---

[1] Champneys, *Memoirs*, Vol. I, p. 96.   [2] *Ibid.*, p. 396.
[3] *Rod, Root and Flower*, pp. 19–20.

saints, this surrender is continual; in poets, etc., it is only in inspired moments.'[1]

Such avowals, if put against all he wrote of the capacity of the poet for special insights into truth, temper his autocratic stand with a note of genuine humility. He knew well that it was possible to be a good poet and very little of a saint. His spiritual certainty came from his belief that 'There can be no absolute certitude about the impressions of the senses or the inferences drawn from them. There can be about moral and spiritual things.'[2] A conviction of inner truth, and not personal arrogance, led him to speak as a prophet. He believed, in short, that through his intuitions he had discovered truths which men had forgotten or were too blind to see, and which they would recognize only when they dared believe their own eyes. And with regard to truth, he followed the counsel of Augustine: 'What you do not understand, with submission wait for, and what you do understand, hold fast with charity.'[3]

His attitude towards his adopted religion is especially revealing. Some writers have seen him as a singularly independent Catholic. 'He always held very original views about religion',[4] writes Derek Patmore; and Frank Harris declared that he 'was always too insubordinate to be a representative Catholic'.[5] On the whole, Champneys, despite his admittedly imperfect knowledge of Catholicism, gives a fair assessment of Patmore's relationship to Catholic orthodoxy. At the same time, the two Catholics whose advice on matters of religion he acknowledges in his preface are Baron von Hügel and Rev. George Tyrrell, both Modernists, and both concerned with highly individual interpretations of doctrine for which Tyrrell was later excommunicated. At one stage, Champneys compares Patmore to Tyrrell 'for a spirituality which rises above the controversial sphere'.[6] The comparison is valid to the extent that both were deeply interested in the mystical significances of Christianity, but Patmore's sense of the concrete and the importance he attached to the doctrine of the Incarnation prevented him from falling, as Tyrrell did, into a wholly symbolizing religion which reduces Christianity to a process of myth. In all ways, Patmore is closer to the heart of orthodox Catholicism than Tyrrell.

After his conversion, he never deviated from his allegiance to the

---

[1] *Rod, Root and Flower*, p. 219.
[2] 'Thoughts on Knowledge, Opinion, etc.', *Religio Poetae*, p. 123.
[3] Quoted, *Rod, Root and Flower*, 'Aurea Dicta', XXXIII, p. 31.
[4] Preface to *Rod, Root and Flower*, p. 16.
[5] 'Coventry Patmore', *Contemporary Portraits (Third Series)*, p. 201.
[6] *Memoirs*, Vol. II, p. 24, n.

Church, nor entertained religious doubts. His retreats, his private chapel and chaplain at Heron's Ghyll, his pilgrimage to Lourdes, his enrolling as a Franciscan Tertiary, in the habit of which order he was buried, his building of the church of St. Mary, Star of the Sea—all this and more shows that he was more than ordinarily zealous in his religious practice. Yet he was distinctly less Ultramontane than his second wife, and he looked on Irish Catholics and their clergy with considerable disdain. His attitude towards the visible Church was very different from that of his more strait-laced Catholic contemporaries. He did not particularly care for secular priests, drawing a distinction between the dignity of the office and the deficiencies of its holders; he was opposed to 'petty parochial or diocesan tyranny' and he discriminated carefully between the doctrines of the Church and the casual utterances of the Pope, which he described to Champneys as the 'merely personal opinions of an amiable old gentleman, by which I am in no degree bound'.[1] He jested about some of the pious beliefs of his fellow-Catholics, saying, 'No one is thoroughly convinced of the truth of his religion who is afraid to joke about it, just as no man can tease a woman with such impunity as he who is convinced of her love.'[2] The doctrine of 'No salvation outside the Church' he interpreted in the strictly orthodox Catholic way, so as to embrace in the concept of 'the Church' all men of sincere good will, and in good faith. As love is above the sacraments, in his view it was possible to deduce religion from love.

What specific virtue, then, did Patmore see in the Catholic Church? 'To such a question', Champneys writes, 'he would answer that no other seemed to him to teach or produce so complete a surrender to the Divine Will, nor, for that very reason, to give equal aid to spiritual development.'[3] In addition, it is clear that he accepted the Church as the guardian of Revelation, and as that Teacher who confirmed the intuitions of the spirit. For Patmore, it was impossible for the authentic voice of God in the soul and the voice of the Church to disagree. His first loyalty, then, was to revealed truth as embodied in Catholic doctrine. But, as Newman looked forward to developments of Christian doctrine as men saw newer and richer significances in the original 'deposit of faith', so Patmore could write: 'The Visible Church is like the larva of the caddis-fly, from which the winged truth shall finally emerge, perfect and beautiful, but which at present inhabits a house of singular

---

[1] Champneys, *Memoirs*, Vol. II, p. 36.   [2] Gosse, *Coventry Patmore*, p. 210.
[3] *Memoirs*, Vol. II, p. 21.

grotesqueness.'[1] His attitude towards his religion was that expressed by St. Augustine: 'In essential things, unity; in inessentials, liberty; in all things, charity.'

Nevertheless, the picture which both Gosse and Champneys give, of Patmore as a naturally Catholic spirit, instinctively aware of the fullness of Catholic dogma before his conversion and, after it, happily browsing in the fields of Catholic theology, is too pat for so complex a personality. The burning of *Sponsa Dei*,[2] and of *The Angel in the House*, indicate his scrupulosity that he should not offend against what he imagined at the time to be orthodox doctrine. The burning of *The Angel* can be reconciled with Patmore's statement in his 'autobiography', that he did not have to alter one word to bring it into harmony with Catholic truth and feeling, only if a period of doubt and revaluation is allowed. The effort it cost him to make the following statement is hardly appreciated by those who regard him as an illuminated soul simply selecting whatever aspects of Catholic dogma happened to fit in with his presuppositions:

'When once God "has made known to us the Incarnation of His Son Jesus Christ by the message of an Angel", that is to say, when once it has become, not an article of abstract faith, but a fact discerned in our own bodies and souls, we are made sharers of the Church's infallibility; for our reasoning is thence forward from discerned reality to discerned reality, and not from and to those poor and always partially fallacious and misleading signs of realities, thoughts which can be formulated in words. Though he may express himself erroneously, no man, so taught, can be otherwise than substantially orthodox, and he is always willing and glad to submit his expressions to the sole assessor of verbal truth, whose judgments have never been convicted of inconsistency, even by the most hostile and malevolent criticism.'[3]

Was Patmore, then, a 'mystic', as he has been called by the greater number of his critics? To W. K. Fleming he is 'a prince of mystics',[4] while Caroline Spurgeon claims that he 'was so entirely a mystic that it seems to be the first and the last and the only thing to say about him.'[5] To label Patmore thus easily a mystic is to use the word in its broadest and least precise sense. If a genuine mystic is one who has personally felt the movement of God in his innermost soul, and who has passed through the mystical stages of

---

[1] *Rod, Root and Flower*, 'Magna Moralia', XXXVII, p. 184.
[2] The most accurate account of this much-discussed episode and of Hopkins's part in it, which was exaggerated by Gosse, Burdett and others, is given in Abbott's introduction to *Further Letters of Hopkins*, pp. xxxii–xxxvii.
[3] *Rod, Root and Flower*, 'Knowledge and Science', X, p. 71.
[4] 'Coventry Patmore', *Life and Letters*, Vol. IV, No. 1, Jan. 1930, p. 34.
[5] *Mysticism in English Literature* (Cambridge University Press, 1913), p. 47.

contemplation to experience a foretaste of Divine union, Patmore expressly disclaimed any such privilege in the preface to *The Rod, the Root and the Flower*, already quoted. The word 'mysticism' itself seldom occurs in his essays, and, when it does, it is almost always carefully defined. He refers to 'the study of true psychology, vulgarly called "mysticism" and "transcendentalism"',[1] and elsewhere writes:

> 'The "science of love" is indeed "mysticism" to the many who fancy its experiences . . . to be those of idiosyncratical enthusiasm or infatuation; but among "mystics" themselves, the terms of this science are common property.'[2]

What, in fact, is a mystic? As applied to Patmore, the term probably means little more than it does in Caroline Spurgeon's definition, one who has as his goal 'an attitude of mind founded upon an intuitive or experienced conviction of unity, of oneness, of alikeness in all things',[3] a definition which embraces Shelley, Wordsworth, Browning and Blake. In much the same way, Mary Ewer finds the unity running through all mystical manifestations as the fact that the mystic in some way or another 'takes up such a relationship of personal response towards some unity which he regards as in the highest degree greater than himself.'[4] In both of these senses, Patmore is clearly a mystic. Yet if we give the term a stricter connotation, that which he himself appears to have attached to it, namely, one who seeks through contemplation and self-surrender to obtain union with God, he must be excluded.

He is, in relation to Christian mysticism, a 'speculative mystic'. *The Unknown Eros* is the product of religious experience and of poetic vision stimulated by mystical reading, but hardly the product of direct mystical experience of the kind recorded, for example, by St. John of the Cross. Yet, as a speculative mystic, Patmore shows an understanding of the nature of the 'science of love' that can only be called expert. He understood the exact nature of the analogies between physical processes and spiritual processes which the mystics employ. He saw that mysticism was 'the science of ultimates . . . the science of self-evident Reality which cannot be "reasoned about" because it is the object of pure reason or perception.'[5] He knew that the mystic vision is, in Evelyn Underhill's words, that 'of a spiritual universe held tight within the bonds of

---

1 'A Spanish Novelette', *Principle in Art*, p. 196.
2 'Christianity and Experimental Science', *Religio Poetae*, p. 40.
3 *Mysticism in English Literature*, p. 3.
4 *A Survey of Mystical Symbolism* (London: S.P.C.K., 1933), p. 16.
5 *Rod, Root and Flower*, 'Aurea Dicta', CXXVIII, p. 50.

love; and of the free and restless human soul, having within it the spark of divine desire, the "tendency to the Absolute", only finding satisfaction and true life when united with this Life of God.'[1] As all mystics do, he saw Love as the centre of the mystical experience, and hence recognized that men who were not of his faith could know the presence of God in mystical union.

He recognized the element of gaiety and joy as a part of the mystical experience. And he began from the position that mystical insight is part of the faculty which every man possesses, that there is a continuity of spiritual with ordinary apprehensions, that, as a later writer put it, 'the mystical apprehension is the highest rung of a ladder that reaches from common sense to ecstasy'.[2] It is not a special faculty, a particular mystical sense; it is really the turning of man's will and love completely towards their source and goal. Patmore did not postulate, as some writers on mysticism have done, a special gift of the spirit distinct from the ordinary faculties as the 'mystical sense'. For him, it is a part of the 'light that lighteth every man who cometh into this world'. The normal means of reason and perception are in fact the very ways whereby man is intended to apprehend God. In holding to this concept of mystical experience, Patmore showed a sure instinct for the most fundamental point in mystical theology. Man is constituted for God and he is inalienably attached to Him. Consequently the mystic is not the man or woman who commands some special mysterious power which inflames the emotions and spurs on the will. He is the one who 'believes the evidence of his eyes', who focuses his emotions, his will and his reason on the chief end for which they are designed, namely, to bring his total personality into contact with God. Patmore knew, too, the difficulties which beset the way of the true mystic—the temptation to impatience, the rendering of an imperfect obedience, the mistaking of visions for the possession of the Divine Reality, all of which he describes in *The Rod, the Root and the Flower*. But he also knew of the rewards which await the pure and steadfast heart, and in his treatment of the mystical marriage, he passed behind the erotic detail to the simple truth of human love as a sacrament of that great mystery which is the 'burning heart' of the Universe. His attitude towards the visible Church is much the same as that of the great traditional mystics, who were not content merely to accept dogmas, but who used them as signposts down the paths of mystical exploration. Dogmas are for him not bonds, but wings.

[1] *Mysticism* (Methuen & Co. Ltd., 1912), p. 160.
[2] *The Meaning and Value of Mysticism*, by E. Herman (London: James Clarke & Co., 1916), p. 32.

Patmore had such a profound understanding of the essential character of mystical experience that many writers on the subject, Evelyn Underhill, Herman, Bremond and Martin D'Arcy among them, use his writings as a source of lively illustrations in describing the nature of the mystical life. Yet it is impossible to put him in the same class as Richard of St. Victor, St. John of the Cross, Jan Van Ruysbroeck and George Herbert. There are in his personality too many elements which prevent his being accepted as a mystic in the sense in which these men were. His conviction of man's superiority over women, however we may qualify it, his hauteur, his particular kind of waggishness, his political prejudices, his particular devotion to poetry as such—all these qualities prevented his becoming more than a 'mere reporter'. His later complete faith, as well as his pre-Catholic cast of mind, meant that he did not have to undergo that terrific struggle for reintegration which gives Donne's poetry some of its wider appeal and deeper poetic significance. Although, as we have seen, some of his best poetry was written out of a tension between his personality and his religious convictions, Patmore was never faced with the kind of intellectual or emotional problems which shake man to the very centre and which, in the solving, purge the spirit and refine the personality. Patmore's marked temperamental qualities suggest that, however much he may have yearned to put the world behind him, it was, until his last years at least, still much with him.

His case appears to illustrate exceptionally well the differences and the similarities which Henri Bremond found between the poet and the mystic.[1] Poetic experience and mystical experience, says Bremond, belong by their psychological mechanism to the same order of knowledge, unitive, not immediately conceptual. However, poetic activity is a profane, natural kind of preliminary sketch of mystical activity, 'so that the poet in the last resort is but an evanescent mystic whose mysticism breaks down'.[2] In fact, Bremond argues that the more a poet realizes the idea of the poet as such, the farther he is from the idea of the mystic as such, for the more of a poet he is, the more he feels the urge to communicate his experience, and the easier he finds the words by means of which his experience will be passed on to the reader. But the more of a mystic a man is, the less does he feel this need of self-communication, and the more such communication appears to him to be impossible of achievement. 'Poetic experience', he writes, 'does not permit the union of love

[1] *Prayer and Poetry*, by Henri Bremond (Burns Oates & Washbourne, London, 1927), Chap. XVIII, 'The Poet and the Mystic'.
[2] *Ibid.*, pp. 188–189.

which follows every normal mystic experience to take place. The poet *qua* poet only unites himself to the real in order to separate himself immediately from it.'[1]

For the greater part of his life, Patmore submitted himself to the kind of poetic experience which Bremond describes. But the evidence of his later life and writings seems to indicate that he moved, or was moving, in his last years towards the more directly mystical experience. His pilgrimage to Lourdes in 1877 was followed by a deepening of his religious faith. As he told Harriet, in 1878, during a second visit, he felt that he got there what he prayed for. And in his 'autobiography' he records that the visits to Lourdes gave him a gift 'which has never been for a single hour withdrawn'.[2] As he became more and more absorbed in religion itself, he gradually gave up poetry and retreated deeper and deeper into silence. The more he meditated upon the proposed poem to the Blessed Virgin, the less did he feel that poetry was capable of expressing all that was in his heart. The spiritual cold he told his son he experienced in his last years was certainly one result of his surrender to a life of contemplation. Above all, the evidence of *The Rod, the Root and the Flower*, with its profound insights, its note of humility, and its sometimes cryptic expressions of moments of vision, suggests that he had begun to pass through the veil of words to the reality behind.

His last words to his wife, 'I love you, dear, but the Lord is my Life and my Light', indicate that such remarks in *The Rod, the Root and the Flower* as, '"God leads us by our own desires" after we have once offered the sacrifice of them with full sincerity',[1] are the product, not of mere speculative mysticism, but of the consciousness of a closer relationship with God. There is no evidence to suggest that Patmore, during any part of his life, practised the heroic sanctity which is expected of the saints. But his intensified devoutness, his abandonment of poetry, his later utterances, which sometimes read like the joyful stammerings of one who has seen a great light, give grounds for believing that his years of speculative mysticism were beginning to bear fruit in a purgation of his spirit and in a surrender of himself to God beyond what he had once thought possible. In his last couple of years, he seems indeed to have felt the 'breeze of sudden wings' fanning his face.

Patmore is as much and as little typical of his age as are nearly all its important writers. Yet he stands in opposition to its most clearly-marked tendencies. His rejection of the contemporary notion of progress, his Catholicism, his political conservatism, his

---

[1] *Ibid.*, p. 193.   [2] Champneys, *Memoirs*, Vol. II, p. 56.
[3] *Rod, Root and Flower*, 'Magna Moralia', XLV, p. 193.

lack of concern with contemporary social movements, no less than the esoteric subject-matter of his later poetry, put him at odds with his times. He is characteristically middle-class Victorian in his awareness of moral values, his sense of the didactic dimension of poetry, his inability, at times, to distinguish between beauty and prettiness, his celebration of home, wife, domesticity, and his concepts of propriety. But he transcends these limitations by his broad-mindedness, his refusal to conform to conventions of thought and attitude, and above all by the drive and energy of his personality. He is the product of his age in so far as all men are such to a greater or a lesser degree, yet he sees his age, as very few of his fellow-writers did, *sub specie aeternitatis*. He does not, in fact, fit into any tidy little category. To one modern critic he is 'a combination of Catholic mystic and Colonel Blimp',[1] to another 'the greatest religious poet in English literature since the seventeenth century'.[2]

Careless of fashion and never deviating from his high conception of the nature of poetry, Patmore pursued his highly individual way. In an age which produced much great poetry and a much vaster quantity of very bad poetry, little was written that was more refined in character, more impassioned in religious feeling, and more austere in tone than Patmore's. It adds piquancy to his poetry to realize that the writer of the 'Psyche' poems was no Huysmans-like reclaimed decadent, nor a 'Bohemian' figure of the order of Thompson and Dowson, but a Catholic squire, three times married, a Tory in politics, and living a life of blameless respectability.

Patmore's intellectual interests were many and varied, as we have seen. He cannot be tied down to an obsession with the idea of married love, unless this concept is so widened as to embrace the whole of reality. And to everything he touched, architecture, politics, literary criticism, poetry, he brought his own characteristic and refreshingly individual point of view. It is not hard to find lapses of taste in his writings, nor to point to defects in his sensibility. Yet a reader who is prepared to read his work as a whole rather than in extracts, and who is not so hostile to his religious and his political premises that he is unwilling to look at man, society and Nature through Patmore's eyes, will find not only that he is in fact sharing in a genuinely poetic experience of a high order, but that he is prepared to accept idiosyncrasies, sentimentalities and occasional sinkings as inevitable elements in the special vision he is accorded. Few readers of Patmore would have him other than he is.

[1] F. L. Lucas, *Ten Victorian Poets* (Cambridge University Press, 1940), p. 81.   [2] Desmond McCarthy, *Criticism*, p. 75.

If, because of his limited output, his comparatively narrow range when compared with Tennyson or Browning, the absence of virtuosity in his poetry, and the touches of perverse temper in some of his work, he cannot be ranked in the first flight of Victorian poets, he is surely at the top of the second class. He is more dynamic and a richer poet than Christina Rossetti; he has more to say than Clough; he is more profound and more imaginative than Elizabeth Barrett Browning; he is more consistent and passionate than Barnes. His poetry may well be an acquired taste; yet it is possible to feel of it, as it is of the work of few of these others, that there is still much more to be learnt of it, and felt of it, that it contains a world of insight and experience whose significance is likely to increase rather than diminish as the generations pass.

APPENDIX

Patmore's Annotations on Swedenborg's Works

PATMORE'S OWN COPIES of Swedenborg's *Arcana Coelestia* and *The True Christian Religion* form part of the Patmore collection in the Francis Thompson room of the Boston College Library. Both works contain marginal notes in Patmore's handwriting, some of which have been reproduced in the chapter 'Patmore and Swedenborg'. While several annotations are to be found in the early volumes of the *Arcana Coelestia*, some of the later ones are unmarked, and the pages of other volumes remain uncut. However, many notes and dates, as already indicated, are written in the 'Index' of this work, and several of the sentences are underlined.

On the title-page of the first volume of the 'Index' (A to M) Patmore has written: 'This "Index" is a vast magazine of truths studied from new points of view—so as to have all the impressiveness of discoveries. They are preserved, indeed, in the esoteric teaching of the Catholic Religion, but popular Catholicism is opposed to them, and would crucify Our Lord again, if he were among us.' The words 'and official' have been added above the line between 'popular' and 'Catholicism'. Many of Patmore's pencilled comments show, among other things, his knowledge of the Bible, his wide reading, and his measure of agreement and disagreement with Swedenborg as a religious teacher. Here and there he has written in Biblical quotations which seemed to him relevant to particular statements of Swedenborg; for instance, beside the philosopher's 'Corn . . . denotes natural good, and new wine . . . natural truth', he has written, '"I will not drink of this wine again until I drink it with you again in my kingdom." Knowledge of natural conjunction—liable to profanations, hence withheld from the laity in the Eucharist.'

He also finds parallels with his other reading. On page 16 of Volume I, beside the article *Affection*, is pencilled 'Newman, Grammar of Assent'; on page 58, '"The flesh of Christ is the Head of Man." St. Augustine'; on page 493, 'See W. Barnes' Preface on Language'; on page 237, beside Swedenborg's 'The Spiritual food proper to man is to know', he has written, 'Note: "The Beatific vision is a substance which we suck as from a nipple." St. Bernard.' Other annotations show that Patmore found ample confirmation of his poetic theories and his ideas of marriage in the writings of the philosopher. For instance: 'Science is true, but poetry is the truth' (I, p. 390); 'Every true Poet is a "man of the celestial church", and his sins are far more sinful than those of others' (II, p. 995); and 'Charity desires the good of another; Love desires union' (I, p. 205, beside Swedenborg's 'Charity, which is the offspring of love').

His conviction that the greater part of Swedenborg's teaching is Catholic, even if 'esoteric' Catholic, doctrine comes out in other pencilled notes. On Swedenborg's 'Hence the church would be one if all had charity, notwithstanding their difference as to worship and doctrinals' (I, p. 133), he comments: 'This is pure R. Catholic teaching'; on another passage in which Swedenborg treats of the two essentials of the church as belief in the divinity of Christ, and love for the Lord with charity towards the neighbour, Patmore notes: 'This is strictly Catholic truth, like nearly, if not all, that S. writes' (I, p. 174); and he writes beside the section headed *Proprium*: 'This article is a profound and thorough exposition of the Christian doctrine of "nature" and "grace". C.P. April, 1863' (II, p. 935).

However, from the point of view of strict Catholic orthodoxy, he has several criticisms to make of Swedenborg's speculations. He seems to have been concerned mainly with Swedenborg's handling of the doctrine of the Trinity. On page 175 of the first volume of the 'Index', he has written: 'S. would have been a Catholic but for his ignorance of what Catholics mean by the Trinity. S. thought that they meant Being by Person.' On page 686 of the same volume are the words: 'S.'s ignorance of the doctrine of the Trinity makes all he writes into dead nonsense. If "Good" and "Truth" are persons all becomes alive and clear.' And on page 676 of Volume II: 'Swedenborg's ignorance of the Trinity makes all his account of marriage obscure and dead instead of living and clear to the spirit.

Marriage between Persons is a reality; between "Good" and "Truth" nothing.'

Various other notes show how Swedenborg's doctrines helped to influence the subjects and the temper of Patmore's later poetry. On page 61 of Volume I of the 'Index' the poet has underlined parts of a sentence as follows: 'There is a doctrinal of charity and a doctrinal of faith, and the former is at this day obliterated', and written in the margin: 'Motto for new Poem.' The back page of the same volume is filled with suggestions for the subjects of new poems. For instance: '*Subj*. Hell. Its depths where positive evil and pains are ultimate goods. Its heights and beatific regrets', which is almost certainly an early note for the ode 'Pain'. Similarly, the note: '*Subj*. The Holy War. The besetting sin to be attacked. Despairs the immediate forerunner of victory. Victory over this is victory over all. The besetting sin is that which threatens the peculiar love. S. and "Combat Spirituel"', contains germs of ideas which are expressed in the two odes, 'Victory in Defeat' and 'The Standards'. Likewise, the note: '*Subj*. "Vastations". See Arc. Vol. I, 7. The revival of the innocence of life at the end of great distresses, humiliations, illnesses', appears to look forward to the ode 'Auras of Delight'.

Perhaps the most interesting thing, however, which Patmore's annotations reveal is that at one time he planned to write a study of Swedenborg's philosophy, or, rather, a commentary on it. On the title-page of *The True Christian Religion* appears this note: 'Mem: Make epitome of the truths in S.'s writings, but not in S.'s language. A most useful book.' And, inside the back leaf of Volume II of the 'Index' to the *Arcana Coelestia*, a more explicit statement reads:

> 'The form of the work should be much like that of "Aids to Reflection".
>
> 'The Latin text, with translation, of S.'s chief doctrines, should be given, under a series of principal headings, as "Science", "Remains", "Perception", with remarks and additional extracts in explanation. None of the views should be formally adopted but the professed purpose of the work should be simply to place S.'s ideas—to some small extent—before the general Reader, freed from the sectarian associations which prejudice them.'

Over the page is an additional comment, listing eight of the articles in the 'Index', under the heading 'The most important articles.' In addition, on page 763 of Volume II of the 'Index', alongside Swedenborg's statement: 'Concerning a Gentile who said that from good he knew all truth; his surprise that Christians should reason about truths', Patmore has written: 'Motto for work on S.'

SELECT BIBLIOGRAPHY

IN THIS BIBLIOGRAPHY, I have confined myself to Patmore's own works and to books and articles written about him and his family. Some of the more important of the other books I have consulted, including those dealing with his times and his contemporaries, with mysticism and metrics, are listed in the notes. I do not claim that the list of books and articles on Patmore's work is complete, but it is as complete as I have been able to make it. In the case of Patmore's own writings, I have named the first edition of each book, omitting later editions, save for the most recent and accessible. Throughout the book itself, I have quoted, unless otherwise indicated, from the Oxford University Press edition of the poems, edited by Frederick Page (1949).

I. *Manuscripts*

Two collections of Patmore documents have been examined, one at Princeton University Library, the other at Boston College Library. Many of the letters in both places have been published, as a whole or in part, by Basil Champneys and Derek Patmore; among the most interesting of those unpublished are some twenty letters written by Patmore to the Suttons, in addition to those reproduced by Champneys, and twenty-nine letters from Thomas Woolner, R.A.

(a) *Princeton University Library*

1. *Letters from Patmore*: Forty-eight to Mr. and Mrs. H. S. Sutton (1848–1886); thirty-two to St. Clair Baddeley (1890–1894); and six single letters to various correspondents.

2. *Letters to Patmore*: Twenty-nine from Thomas Woolner to Emily and Coventry (1860–1890); twenty from Aubrey de Vere (1855–1893); seventeen from Edmund Gosse (1883–1893); nine from Robert Bridges (1883–1894); seven each from Sir Henry Taylor and W. Empson (Editor of *Edinburgh Review*); five from Thomas Carlyle (1855–1860); and letters from twenty-nine others, including G. M. Hopkins (August 21, 1885).

3. *Letters to and from other members of Patmore's family*: These include fifteen from Harriet Patmore and eight from Bertha Patmore to Mrs. H. S. Sutton.

4. *Miscellaneous papers*: A collection of notes in Patmore's hand, including working drafts of various articles, lists of proposed subjects, and several small

slips of paper with single sentences, some marked 'Body' and 'Aurea Dicta', indicating that they are unused portions of *The Rod, the Root and the Flower*. Also the manuscript of a posthumous appreciation of Patmore by Aubrey de Vere.

(b) *Boston College Library*

1. *Letters from Patmore*: Eleven to Edmund Gosse (1881–1896); five to Frank Harris (1888–1892); ten to Tennyson Patmore (1865–1895); and letters to eighteen other correspondents, including Alfred Tennyson, Ruskin and Havelock Ellis. Also carbon copies of fifty-two letters to Edmund Gosse (1886–1894).

2. *Letters to Patmore:* One from Alfred Tennyson.

3. *Letters to and from other members of Patmore's family*: Five from Emily to Tennyson Patmore; one from Alfred Tennyson to Emily; two from Harriet to friends; and two from P. G. Patmore to friends.

4. *Miscellaneous papers*: Manuscript of Patmore's 'Autobiography' (sixty-eight pages of grey 8vo paper); of the ode 'St. Valentine's Day', of an unpublished quatrain, of the first fifteen paragraphs of 'Dieu et ma Dame', and of a letter on Modern Volunteers (Champneys, Vol. I, pp. 72–73). An undated list in Patmore's handwriting, on British Museum paper, of twenty of his periodical articles written between 1852 and 1860. A notebook, with fifty-five pages detailing scientific experiments; with, on the cover, 'Poetry together with Original Notes on Scientific Subjects by C.P.'

6. *Other material*: Photostats of the British Museum manuscript of *The Unknown Eros* and of the Nottingham University manuscript of *The Rod, the Root and the Flower*. Sir Shane Leslie's unpublished manuscript of a variorum edition of *The Angel in the House*, incorporating the only existing manuscript of the poem, presented to Alice Meynell on her birthday, October 11, 1893, which is in the Grantham Library in Sussex. Manuscript of a poem by Henry Patmore, 'Algaia'.

II. *Patmore's Poetry*

In this list, and elsewhere throughout the bibliography, the place of publication is London, unless otherwise stated.

Poems (Edmund Moxon), 1844.
Tamerton Church-Tower (William Pickering), 1853.
Tamerton Church-Tower and Other Poems (J. W. Parker & Son), 1854.
The Betrothal (J. W. Parker & Son), 1854.
The Angel in the House: Book II. The Espousals (J. W. Parker & Son), 1856.
The Angel in the House: Books I and II (J. W. Parker), 1858.
Faithful For Ever (J. W. Parker), 1860.
The Victories of Love (Boston: T. O. P. H. Burnham), 1862.
The Victories of Love (Macmillan & Co.), 1863.
Odes. Privately printed, April 17, 1868.
Nine Odes. Privately printed, May 1870.
The Unknown Eros and other Odes I–XXI (George Bell), 1877.
Amelia. Privately printed edition of twenty copies, 1878.
Amelia (with two illuminated pages in vellum). Privately printed, 1878.
Amelia, Tamerton Church-Tower, etc. with a Prefatory Study of English Metrical Law (George Bell), 1878.
The Unknown Eros I–XLVI (George Bell), 1878.
Poems by Coventry Patmore, Collective Edition (George Bell & Sons), 1879.

The Poetry of Pathos and Delight, from the works of Coventry Patmore. Passages selected by Alice Meynell (Heinemann), 1896.

Poèmes, translated by Paul Claudel, with an essay by Valéry Larbaud (Paris: Marcel Rivière & Cie), 1912.

Poems by Coventry Patmore, edited, with an introduction, by Basil Champneys (George Bell & Sons), 1906.

Seven Unpublished Poems by Coventry Patmore to Alice Meynell. Fifty copies privately printed at Christmas 1922 at the Pelican Press by Francis Meynell.

The *Poems of Coventry Patmore*, edited, with an introduction, by Frederick Page (Oxford University Press), 1949.

The Children's Garland, an anthology selected and arranged by Coventry Patmore (Macmillan and Co.), 1862.

III. *Patmore's Prose*

(a) *Volumes*

Bryan Waller Procter (Barry Cornwall), an Autobiographical Fragment and Biographical Notes (Boston: Roberts Brothers), 1877.

St. Bernard on the Love of God (with Marianne Caroline Patmore) (C. Kegan Paul & Co.), 1881.

How I Managed and Improved My Estate (George Bell & Sons), 1886.

Hastings, Lewes, Rye and the Sussex Marshes (George Bell & Sons), 1887.

Principle in Art (George Bell & Sons), 1889.

Principle in Art, second edition (George Bell & Sons), 1890.

Religio Poetae (George Bell & Sons), 1893.

Religio Poetae, etc., new edition (George Bell & Sons), 1898.

Principle in Art and *Religio Poetae*, one volume (Duckworth & Co.), 1913.

The Rod, the Root and the Flower (George Bell & Sons), 1895.

The Rod, the Root and the Flower, edited, with an introduction, by Derek Patmore (The Grey Walls Press), 1950.

Courage in Politics and other Essays, 1885–1896. 'Now first collected by Frederick Page.' With a bibliography of Patmore's prose-writings, 'for the most part anonymous and unreprinted' (Humphrey Milford, Oxford University Press), 1921.

(b) *Contributions to Periodicals*

Two volumes of essays by Patmore, *Principle in Art* and *Religio Poetae*, were published during his lifetime. For the most part, these consisted of articles which had already been printed in various periodicals. Frederick Page's *Courage in Politics* reprinted a further thirty-nine articles. His Appendix II to this volume gives a list of all Patmore's periodical articles he has been able to identify. Most of these were printed anonymously, and Page's identification has been based partly upon references in Patmore's notes and correspondence, and partly upon internal evidence. I have checked these articles, and accept Page's attribution in all save one case, which is noted below.

The list of articles in Patmore's handwriting in the Boston College Library includes two not listed by Page, and five included by him on the basis of internal evidence only. In addition, I believe three other articles, one in the *Edinburgh Review*, and two in the *North British Review*, to be by Patmore.

The following list is based upon Page's. It includes the articles reprinted in the collected volumes, those listed by Patmore himself, and the new articles I believe to be written by him. I have rearranged Page's list, which is under various headings, into a closer chronological order. Unless otherwise indicated, the articles occur on Page's list or are named, in passing, in his *Patmore—A Study in*

Bibliography

Poetry. *P.A.* and *R.P.* indicate that the pieces were reprinted in the first edition of either *Principle in Art* or *Religio Poetae*; and *C. in P.* denotes those collected in *Courage in Politics*.

Douglas Jerrold's Shilling Magazine

1845

January. 'Leigh Hunt's "Imagination and Fancy".'
February. '"Essays: Second Series" by R. W. Emerson.'
June. 'Life of Jean Paul Richter.' 'The Morbidness of the Age.'
July. 'The Misanthrope.'
September. 'A Few Words Connected with Optimism.' 'The Philosophical and Aesthetic Letters and Essays of Schiller.' '"Rhymes and Recollections of a Hand-Loom Weaver" by William Thorn; "Poems" by Eliza Cook.'
November. 'The Man and his Age.'

Lowe's Edinburgh Magazine

1846

January. 'Jean Paul.'
February. 'Emerson.' 'Donne.'
March. 'George Herbert.'
April. 'Herrick.'
May. 'Arthur and his Knights of the Round Table.' 'Hood's Poems.'
June. 'Sir Tristam and Sir Galahad.' 'Countess Hahn-Hahn's Novels.' 'The New Timon.'

February 18, 19. 'Carlyle's "Cromwell"', *The Daily News.*
March 9. 'The New Timon', *The Daily News.*
July. 'Modern Painters: Vol. II', *Douglas Jerrold's Shilling Magazine.*

1847

March. 'Lord Lindsay's "Sketches of Christian Art"', *The Critic.*
May. 'Popular Serial Literature', *North British Review.*
August. 'German Lady Novelists', *North British Review.*

1848

May. 'Schelling's Philosophy of Art', *The Critic.* 'Tennyson's "Poems"— "The Princess"', *North British Review.* 'Sir Kenelme Digby, His Character and Writings', Part I, *The Gentleman's Magazine.*
June. 'Sir Kenelme Digby, His Character and Writings', Part II, *The Gentleman's Magazine.*
November. 'R. M. Milnes' "Life of Keats"', *North British Review.*

1849

August. 'The Aesthetics of Gothic Architecture', *British Quarterly Review.*
November. 'The Ethics of Art', *British Quarterly Review.* 'Shakespeare', *North British Review.*

1850

February. 'Ruskin's "Seven Lamps of Architecture"', *North British Review.*
March. 'Macbeth', *The Germ*, No. 3 (Reprinted in *The Germ*, the first four issues edited by Thomas B. Mosher. Portland, Maine; Thomas B. Mosher, 1898.)

Bibliography

1850

August. 'In Memoriam', *North British Review*.

October. 'British Museum Commission', *Edinburgh Review*. (In 'Library of the British Museum', *Edinburgh Review*, January 1859, Patmore writes (p. 217): 'We have yet to call attention to ... the 977 volumes of the New Catalogue, the whole of which made their appearance in the Reading Room since we had occasion, some seven years ago, to discuss the general principles on which it was resolved to execute this unparalleled literary undertaking.') [Despite the difference of two years in date, this article is the only one which could be referred to, and, unless the 'we' is a strictly editorial 'we', Patmore most likely wrote the earlier piece.]

November. 'William Allingham's Poems', *The Palladium*.

1851

February. 'The Social Position of Women', *North British Review*.

May. 'Ruskin's "Stones of Venice"', *British Quarterly Review*.

August. 'Character in Architecture', *North British Review*.

October. 'Sources of Expression in Architecture', *Edinburgh Review*.

1852

January. 'Letter on Rifle Corps', *The Times*.

August. 'American Poetry', *North British Review* (Patmore's list). 'Margaret Fuller Ossoli', *British Quarterly Review*.

December. 'Architects and Architecture', *Fraser's Magazine*.

1853

May. 'Glimpses of Poetry', *North British Review*. (In 'Poems by Matthew Arnold', *North British Review*, August 1854, *q.v.*, Patmore begins: 'It is not long since two volumes of poetry by "A", "The Strayed Reveller" and "Empedocles on Aetna", passed under our review.' These volumes are the subject of this review.)

November. 'American Novels', *North British Review* (Patmore's list).

1854

April 1. 'Allingham's "Day and Night Songs"', *The Critic*.

May. 'Ruskin and Architecture', *North British Review* (Patmore's list).

June. 'Ruskin's Lectures on Architecture and Painting', *The Critic*.

August. 'Poems by Matthew Arnold', *North British Review*. [In 'The Modern English Drama', *North British Review*, August 1858, Patmore writes: 'Mr. Matthew Arnold has been so fully and recently noted by us (Note: *North British Review*, Vol. XXI, p. 493) and what we said about his addiction to ancient forms of art is so exactly applicable to "Merope" that we need say little more about it. ...']

1855

October. 'Tennyson's "Maud" and "In Memoriam"', *Edinburgh Review* (Patmore's List).

November. 'Fielding and Thackeray', *North British Review*.

1856

October. 'New Poets', *Edinburgh Review* (Patmore's list). 'Victor Cousin on Madame de Hautefort and Her Contemporaries' (Patmore's list), reprinted in part in *Merry England*, August 1893. Also *R.P.*

1856

October 25. '"Craigcrook Castle", by Gerald Massey', *Literary Gazette*.

1857

February. 'Emmanuel Swedenborg', *Fraser's Magazine*. 'Mrs. Browning's
"Poems" and "Aurora Leigh"', *North British Review* (Patmore's list,
where the date is incorrectly given as November 1856).

July. 'London Street Architecture', *The National Review*.

July 4. 'A Pre-Raphaelite Exhibition', *Saturday Review*.

August. 'English Metrical Critics', *North British Review*. [Reprinted as
'Prefatory Study of English Metrical Law' in *Amelia, etc.*, 1878, and as an
appendix to Volume II of the collected poems.] (Patmore's list.)

August 15. 'Read's Rural Poems', *Saturday Review*.

October 17. 'Mr. Alexander Smith's "City Poems"', *Saturday Review*.

December 26. 'Walls and Wall-Paintings at Oxford', *Saturday Review*
(Patmore's list).

1858

January 9. '"Remarks on Secular and Domestic Architecture", by George
Gilbert Scott', *Literary Gazette*.

January. 'Hashish', *The National Review* (Patmore's list).

February. 'Poetry—The Spasmodists', *North British Review* (Patmore's list;
not noted by Page).

February 20. 'A Polyglot of Foreign Proverbs', *Literary Gazette*.

March 20. 'Recent Ultramontane Poetry', *Saturday Review*. (Page gives the
date of this article as March 3rd, but no such article appears in this issue.
A disparaging reference to Dante makes it doubtful, to my mind, whether
Patmore is in fact the author.)

March 20. 'Kingsley's "Andromeda, etc."', *Literary Gazette*. '"On Beauty:
Three Discourses" by John Stuart Blackie', *Literary Gazette*.

March 27. 'Primula: a Book of Lyrics', *Literary Gazette*.

April 10. 'Anastasia', *Literary Gazette*. 'Swedenborgiana', *National Review*
(Patmore's list).

May. 'Gothic Architecture—Present and Future', *North British Review*.

July. 'The Troubadours', *National Review*.

August. 'The Modern British Drama', *North British Review* (Patmore's list).

October. 'Guy Livingstone', *Edinburgh Review* (Patmore's list; not noted by
Page).

November. 'The Decay of Modern Satire', *North British Review* (Patmore's
list).

November 27. 'Mediocre Poetry', *Saturday Review*.

December 11. 'M. Michelet on Poetical Physiology', *Saturday Review*.

1859

January. 'Library of the British Museum', *Edinburgh Review* (Patmore's list).
'Dramatic Treasure-Trove', *Fraser's Magazine*.

February 5. '"Legends and Lyrics" (Adelaide Ann Procter)', *Saturday
Review*.

March 5. 'Massey's Poems', *Saturday Review* (date incorrectly shown by
Page as March 15).

May. '"Legends and Lyrics" and "The Wanderer"', *North British Review*
(Patmore's list).

July. 'Tennyson's "Idylls of the King"', *Edinburgh Review* (Patmore's list).

August. 'Idylls of the King', *North British Review* (Patmore's list).

November. 'New Poems', *North British Review*.

Bibliography

1860
July. 'De Biran's Pensées', *National Review* (Patmore's list).
August. 'Recent Poetry', *North British Review* (Patmore's list).

1862
June. 'William Barnes, the Dorsetshire Poet', *Macmillan's Magazine*.

1866
January. 'Mrs. Cameron's Photographs', *Macmillan's Magazine*.

1872
March 14. 'The Gothic Revival', *Pall Mall Gazette*.

St. James's Gazette

1885
March 9. 'Robert Bridges's "Prometheus the Fire Giver"' (*C. in P.*).
December 12. 'What about King Theebaw's Rubies?'
December 23. 'Pleasures of Property.'
December 26. 'Manifest Destiny' (*C. in P.*).
December 29. 'How to govern Ladylike Races' (a letter).
December 31. 'Robert Bridges's "Eros and Psyche"' (*C. in P.*).

1886
January 2. 'Cheerfulness in Life and Art' (*P.A.*).
January 6. 'Concerning an Ancient and Pernicious Delusion.'
January 22. 'Comparing Small things with Great' (*C. in P.*).
January 29 and February 6. 'Seers, Thinkers and Talkers' (*R.P.*).
March 1. 'Sonnets.'
March 5. 'The Point of Rest in Art' (*P.A.*).
March 6. 'To English Catholics' (a letter).
March 8. 'Walt Whitman.'
March 13. 'Great Talkers: Coleridge' (*C. in P.*).
March 20. 'Great Talkers: Goethe' (*C. in P.*).
March 22. 'Hegel' (*C. in P.*).
March 23. 'A Letter on Bishop Bagshawe.'
March 30. 'Great Talkers: Luther' (*C. in P.*).
April 1. 'Sir Thomas Browne' (*C. in P.*).
April 6. 'A Book of Hunting Songs' (*C. in P.*).
April 16. 'Swedenborg' (*C. in P.*).
April 17. 'Woolner's "Tiresias"' (*C. in P.*).
April 21. 'Minding One's Own Business' (*C. in P.*).
April 27. 'Calling a Spade a Spade' (*C. in P.*).
April 30. 'Architecture and Architectural Criticism' (*C. in P.*).
May 20, 21, 25, 27, 31; June 3, 5, 9. *How I Managed and Improved my Estate* (published in book form, 1886).
July 6, 12, 16, 20. 'In the Sussex Marshes' (included in *Hastings, Lewes, Rye and the Sussex Marshes*, 1887).
July 18. 'A Psychical Romance.'
July 29, 31; August 3. 'Investing in Precious Stones.'

Bibliography

1886

August 11, 14. 'Old Hastings' (included in *Hastings, Lewes, etc.*).
August 27. 'Mayfield' (included in *Hastings, Lewes, etc.*).
September 1. 'The Poetry of Negation' (*P.A.*).
October 4. 'Utilization of our Great Libraries' (a letter).
October 5. 'Old Coach Roads' (*C. in P.*).
October 6. 'Lord Randolph Churchill's "Dartford Speech"' (a letter).
October 7. 'Proverbs and Bon-Mots' (*C. in P.*).
October 9. 'William Barnes' (*C. in P.*).
October 12. 'Old English Architecture, Ancient and Modern' (*P.A.*).
October 16. 'Ideal and Material Greatness in Architecture' (*P.A.*).
October 30. 'Expression in Architecture' (*C. in P.*).
November 12. 'Shall Smith Have a Statue?' (*P.A.*).
November 13. 'The Morality of "Epipsychidion"' (*C. in P.*).
November 26; December 4, 9, 11 and 18. 'Architectural Styles' (*P.A.*).
December 2. 'What Shelley Was' (*P.A.*).
December 14. 'December in Garden and Field' (*C. in P.*).
December 31. 'Love and Poetry' (*R.P.*).

1887

January 7. 'The Weaker Vessel' (*R.P.*).
January 17. 'Pathos' (*P.A.*).
January 20. 'Rossetti as a poet' (*P.A.*).
January 25–27, February 4. 'Butchers' Prices.'
February 16. 'Crabbe and Shelley' (*P.A.*).
February 26. 'Unnatural Literature' (*C. in P.*).
March 3. 'Liverpool Cathedral' (*C. in P.*).
March 10. 'Churches and Preaching Halls', a letter (*C. in P.*).
March 16. 'Coleridge' (*C. in P.*).
March 23. 'How is it to End?' (*C. in P.*).
March 31. 'Blake' (*P.A.*).
April 2. 'Thomas Hardy' (*C. in P.*).
April 12. 'Poetical Coups-Manqués' (*C. in P.*).
April 13. 'Japanese Houses' (*C. in P.*).
May 7. 'Dreams' (*C. in P.*).
May 21. 'The Limitations of Genius' (*R.P.*).
May 28. 'John Marston' (*C. in P.*).
May 31. 'Poetical Integrity' (*P.A.*).
June 13. 'Prof. Brandl on Coleridge' (*C. in P.*).
June 23. 'Swinburne's "Selections."'
June 28. 'Keats' (*P.A.*).
July 9. 'Out-of-Doors Poetry' (*C. in P.*).
July 16. 'Aubrey de Vere's Poems' (*C. in P.*).
July 20. 'Principle in Art' (*P.A.*).
August 27. 'A Safe Charity' (*C. in P.*).
September 29. 'Why Women are Dissatisfied' (printed as second half of 'The Weaker Vessel', *R.P.*).
November 1. 'Lunacy and Punning.'
November 10. 'Emerson' (*P.A.*).
December 6. 'Memorials of Coleorton' (*C. in P.*).
December 19. 'Life of William Barnes' (*C. in P.*).
December 20. 'The Future of Poetry' (a letter).

22—C.P. 337

1888
January 16. 'Goldsmith' (*C. in P.*).
January 20. 'Real Apprehension' (*R.P.*).
February 18. 'Imagination' (*R.P.*).
March 12. 'The Revanche: Sedan or Waterloo?' (a letter).
March 14. 'Possibilities and Performances' (*R.P.*).
March 19. 'Courage in Politics' (*C. in P.*).
August 10. 'Arthur Hugh Clough' (*P.A.*).

Other Later Articles

1886
November. 'An English Classic: William Barnes', *Fortnightly Review* (*P.A.*).

1887
August. 'Thoughts on Knowledge, Opinion and Inequality', *Fortnightly Review* (*R.P.*).

1890
June. 'Distinction', *Fortnightly Review* (*P.A.*).

1891
January 31. 'Impressionist Art', *Anti-Jacobin* (reprinted as 'Emotional Art', *P.A.*).
February 7. 'Bad Morality is Bad Art', *Anti-Jacobin* (*P.A.*).
February 14. 'Conscience', *Anti-Jacobin* (*R.P.*).
April 18. 'Simplicity', *Anti-Jacobin* (*R.P.*).
September 26. 'Mrs. Walford's Novels', *Anti-Jacobin* (*C. in P.*).

1892
January 9. 'Builders' and Home-Decorators' Prices' (a letter), *Anti-Jacobin*.
July. 'Three Essayettes: Christianity and Progress; A "Pessimist" Outlook; A Spanish Novelette', *Fortnightly Review* (the first two reprinted in *R.P.*; the third in *P.A.*).
September. 'Peace in Life and Art' *Merry England* (*P.A.*).
November. 'Attention', *Merry England* (*R.P.*).
December. 'On Obscure Books', *Merry England* (*P.A.*).
December. 'Mrs. Meynell's Poetry and Essays', *Fortnightly Review* (*P.A.*).

1893
April. 'The Language of Religion', *Merry England* (*R.P.*).
August. 'Madame de Hautefort', *Merry England* (*P.A.*).

1894
January. 'A New Poet: Francis Thompson', *Fortnightly Review* (*C. in P.*).

1895
October 26. 'The Proposed Compliment to Journalism', a letter (*C. in P.*).

1896
June 13. 'Mrs. Meynell's New Essays', *Saturday Review* (*C. in P.*).

'*Aurea Dicta*—extracts from *The Rod, the Root and the Flower*', translated into French by Marthe Noguier, *Vigile*, Premier Cahier, 1930, pp. 121–132.

Bibliography

(c) Letters

Further Letters of Gerard Manley Hopkins, including his correspondence with Coventry Patmore, edited by Claude Colleer Abbott (Oxford University Press), 1938.

IV. *Books on Coventry Patmore*

Burdett, Osbert. *The Idea of Coventry Patmore* (Humphrey Milford: Oxford University Press), 1921.

Champneys, Basil. *Memoirs and Correspondence of Coventry Patmore*, two vols. (George Bell & Sons), 1900.

Gosse, Edmund. *Coventry Patmore* (Hodder & Stoughton), 1905.

Guido, Augusto. *Coventry Patmore* (Brescia: Edizioni Morcelliana), 1946.

Page, Frederick. *Patmore—A Study in Poetry* (Oxford University Press), 1933.

Patmore, Derek. *Portrait of My Family* (Constable & Co.), 1935.
   The Life and Times of Coventry Patmore (Constable), 1949.

V. *Books containing Essays on, or Extended Reference to, Coventry Patmore*

Alexander, Calvert, S.J. *The Catholic Literary Revival* (Bruce Publishing Co., Milwaukee), 1935: 'Coventry Patmore', pp. 54–70.

Beilby, Arthur Edgar. *Arthur Edgar Beilby His Book* (New-Church Press, Ltd.), 1936: XIII, 'Sex and Marriage, Here and Hereafter', pp. 112–120; XVII, 'An Appreciation of Coventry Patmore', pp. 140–148.

Bertocci, Angelo Philip. *Charles du Bos and English Literature* (New York, Columbia University), 1949.

Braybrooke, Patrick. *Some Victorian and Georgian Catholics: Their Art and Outlook* (Burns Oates & Washbourne), 1932: 'Coventry Patmore: Poet and Philosopher', pp. 3–31.

Brégy, Katherine. *The Poet's Chantry* (Simpkin, Marshall, Hamilton, Kent & Co. Ltd.), n.d.: 'Coventry Patmore', pp. 89–119.

Brimley, George. *Essays*, edited by William George Clark, third edition (Macmillan & Co.), 1882: 'The Angel in the House', pp. 204–238.

Burdett, Osbert. *Critical Essays* (New York: Henry Holt & Co.), 1926: Chap. VI, 'Two Footnotes on Coventry Patmore—I. Patmore and Divorce, pp. 82–86; II. A Daughter of Coventry Patmore (Sister Mary Christina)', pp. 86–90.

Claudel, Paul. *La Cantate à Trois Voix*, suivi de *Sous le Rempart d'Athènes* et de Traductions Diverses (Paris: Gallimard, eds. de La Nouvelle Revue Française), 1931. (Prose and verse translations of nine of Patmore's odes.)
   Positions et Propositions, Vol. II (Paris: Gallimard), 1934: 'Lettre sur Coventry Patmore', pp. 29–35.

Drinkwater, John. *The Muse in Council* (Sidgwick & Jackson), 1925.
   Victorian Poetry (Hodder & Stoughton, People's Library), n.d.

Du Bos, Charles. *Approximations* (Septième Série) (Paris: Editions R.-A. Corrêa), 1937: 'L'Amour selon Coventry Patmore', pp. 349–395.

Eaton, Vincent T. *The Works of Coventry Patmore* (unpublished thesis offered for M.A. degree, Columbia University, Dec. 1941).

Elton, Oliver. *A Survey of English Literature, 1830–1880* (two vols.) (Edward Arnold, 1920): Vol. II, 'Coventry Patmore', pp. 98–104.

Bibliography

Evans, B. Ifor. *English Poetry in the Later* 19*th Century* (Methuen & Co. Ltd.), 1933: Chapter VI, 'Coventry Patmore and Allied Poets: Coventry Patmore; Francis Thompson; Mrs. Alice Meynell', pp. 130–161.

Freeman, John. *The Moderns: Essays in Literary Criticism* (Robert Scott, Roxburghe House), 1916: 'Coventry Patmore and Francis Thompson', pp. 265–317.
    English Portraits and Essays (Hodder & Stoughton), 1924: 'Coventry Patmore', pp. 175–196.

Gosse, Edmund. *More Books on the Table* (William Heinemann Ltd.), 1923: 'The Laureate of Wedded Love', pp. 199–205.

Grierson, Herbert and Smith, J. C. *A Critical History of English Poetry* (Chatto & Windus), 1944.

Harris, Frank. *Contemporary Portraits* (Third Series) (published by the author, N.Y. City), 1920: 'Coventry Patmore', pp. 191–210.

Heath-Stubbs, John. *The Darkling Plain* (Eyre & Spottiswoode), 1950.

Hind, C. Lewis. *More Authors and I* (New York: Dodd, Mead & Co.), 1922: 'Coventry Patmore', pp. 240–246.

Johnson, Lionel. *Post Liminium: Essays and Critical Papers by Lionel Johnson*, edited by Thomas Whittemore (Elkin Mathews. Vigo St.), 1912, 2nd Impression: 'Coventry Patmore's Genius', pp. 238–245.

Larbaud, Valéry. *Ce Vice Impuni*—La Lecture, Domaine Anglais (Vol. III of *Œuvres Complètes de V.L.*) (Paris: Gallimard), 1951: 'Coventry Patmore (1823–1896)', pp. 58–106.

Leslie, Shane. *Studies in Sublime Failure* (Ernest Benn Ltd.), 1932: 'Coventry Patmore', pp. 113–178.

Long, Valentine, O.F.M. *They Have Seen His Star* (Paterson, St. Anthony Guild Press, N.J., U.S.A.), 1938: 'Coventry Patmore: Through Lover's Lane to God', pp. 20–36.

Lucas, F. L. *Ten Victorian Poets* (Cambridge: at the U.P.), 1948: 'Coventry Patmore', pp. 75–97.

MacCarthy, Desmond. *Criticism* (Putnam, London and New York), 1932: 'Coventry Patmore', pp. 74–80.

Maynard, Theodore. *Pillars of the Church* (New York: Longmans, Green & Co.), 1945: 'Coventry Patmore', pp. 246–273.

Meynell, Alice. *The Rhythm of Life, and other Essays* (London: John Lane; Boston: Copeland and Day), 1896: 'Mr. Coventry Patmore's Odes'.
    Introductory Note to *A Catalogue of the Library of Coventry Patmore* (Everard Meynell: The Serendipity Shop), 1921).
    The Second Person Singular and other Essays (Humphrey Milford, Oxford University Press), 1922, 2nd Impression: 'Coventry Patmore', pp. 94–109; 'A Hundred Years Ago', pp. 68–74.

Musser, Benjamin Francis. *Franciscan Poets* (New York: The Macmillan Co.), 1933: 'The Laureate of Wedded Love', pp. 157–172.

Neenan, Sister Mary Pius, M.A. *Some Evidences of Mysticism in English Poetry of the Nineteenth Century* (Washington, D.C.: Catholic University of America), June 1916: Chapter VI, 'Patmore: God Sought through Human Love', pp. 44–58.

Osmond, Percy H. *The Mystical Poets of the English Church* (Society for Promoting Christian Knowledge), 1919.

Powell, Thomas. *The Living Authors of England* (New York: D. Appleton & Co., 200 Broadway), 1849: 'Coventry Patmore', pp. 105–114.

Bibliography

Praz, Mario. *La Crisi Dell 'Eroe Nel Romanzo Vittoriano* (Firenze: G. C. Sansoni), 1952: 'L'Angelo Nella Casa' di Coventry Patmore, Appendix 1, pp. 387–413.

Quiller-Couch, Sir Arthur. *Studies in Literature* (Third Series) (New York: G. P. Putnam's Sons), 1930: 'Coventry Patmore', pp. 122–142.

Read, Herbert. *The Great Victorians*, edited by H. J. and Hugh Massingham (Pelican Books), 1938: Vol. II, 'Coventry Patmore, 1823–1896', pp. 388–402.

Collected Essays on Literary Criticism (Faber & Faber), 1938: 'Coventry Patmore', pp. 315–330.

The True Voice of Feeling (Faber & Faber), 1953.

Rhys, Ernest. *Lyric Poetry* (J. M. Dent & Sons Ltd.), 1913.

Shuster, George N. *The Catholic Spirit in Modern English Literature* (New York: The Macmillan Co.), 1922: Chap. VII, 'Poetry and Three Poets (De Vere, Patmore and Hopkins)', Patmore, pp. 108–115.

Symons, Arthur. *Studies in Two Literatures* (Leonard Smithers), 1897: 'Coventry Patmore', pp. 158–168 (reprinted in *North American Review*, 1920).

Figures of Several Centuries (Constable & Co. Ltd.), 1917: 'Coventry Patmore', pp. 351–375.

Thompson, Francis. *Literary Criticisms by Francis Thompson*. Newly discovered and collected by Rev. Terence L. Connolly, S.J., Ph.D. (New York: Dutton & Co. Inc.), 1948: 'A Poet's Religion', pp. 203–211: 'Patmore's Philosophy' (*Academy*, November 24, 1900), pp. 212–218; 'St. Bernard on the Love of God' (review of M. and C. Patmore's translation), pp. 556–559.

Tovey, Rev. Duncan C. *Reviews and Essays in English Literature* (George Bell & Sons), 1897: 'Coventry Patmore', pp. 156–168.

Weygandt, Cornelius. *The Time of Tennyson* (New York: D. Appleton–Century Co.), 1936: Chap. XIV, 'Coventry Patmore', pp. 259–266.

VI. *Periodical Articles and Reviews dealing with Patmore and his Work*

Anonymous. 'Poems by Coventry Patmore' (review of Patmore's first volume), *Blackwood's Edinburgh Magazine*, Vol. LVI, No. CCCLXVII, September 1844, pp. 331–342 (attributed doubtfully to John Wilson, 'Christopher North').

'Poems by Coventry Patmore', *North British Review*, Vol. XXVIII, No. LVI, May 1858, pp. 521–545.

'Faithful for Ever', *British Quarterly Review*, Vol. XXXIII, No. LVX, January 1861, pp. 142–150.

'The State of English Poetry', *Quarterly Review*, Vol. CXXXV, No. CCLXIX, July 1873, pp. 12–25.

'The Unknown Eros', *The Catholic World*, Vol. XXV, No. 149, August 1877, pp. 702–713.

'Mr. Patmore's Poems' (review of 2nd Collective Edition), *The Spectator*, No. 3028, July 10, 1886, pp. 934–935 (possibly by Richard Garnett; reference to a *Spectator* review by Garnett in Champneys, II, p. 225).

'The Unknown Eros', *The Spectator*, No. 3224, April 12, 1890, pp. 512–515.

'The Unknown Eros', *The Athenaeum*, No. 3291, November 22, 1890, pp. 693–694.

'Proposed Laureates': II. Mr. Coventry Patmore', *Daily Chronicle*, November 14, 1892.

'Mr. Patmore's Essays' (review of *Religio Poetae*), *The Spectator*, No. 3395, July 22, 1893, pp. 116–117.

'The Poet as Theologian' (review of *The Rod, the Root and the Flower*), *The Saturday Review*, Vol. 79, No. 2067, June 8, 1895, pp. 762–763.

'The Rod, the Root and the Flower', *The Athenaeum*, No. 3556, Dec. 21, 1895, pp. 862–863.

'Coventry Patmore—an Obituary' (followed by Francis Thompson's A Captain of Song), *The Athenaeum*, No. 3606, Saturday, December 5, 1896, pp. 797–798.

'Obituary Notice on Coventry Patmore', *The Spectator*, No. 3570, November 28, 1896, p. 751.

'Coventry Patmore—an Obituary', *The Dial*, Vol. XXI, No. 252, December 12, 1896, pp. 369–371.

'Coventry Patmore Dead' (Obituary Notice), *The Catholic World*, Vol. LXIV, No. 383, February 1897, pp. 693–696.

'Coventry Patmore' (article—review of Champneys' *Memoirs*), *The Nation*, Vol. 72, No. 1856, January 24, 1901, pp. 71–72.

'Coventry Patmore' (article—review of Gosse's *Life*), *The Nation*, Vol. 80, No. 2081, May 18, 1905, pp. 399–400.

'Coventry Patmore', *The Catholic World*, Vol. LXXXII, No. 487, October 1905, pp. 140–143.

(a) Review of 'The Figure of Beatrice' by Charles Williams, *Notes and Queries*, September 11, 1943, p. 179.

(b) 'Patmore and Dante', *Notes and Queries*, October 9, 1943, pp. 225–226. (The first unsigned, the second signed 'Reviewer'. Both by same hand. Almost certainly by Frederick Page.)

Note on 200 Patmore items, including his correspondence with H. S. Sutton, *Princeton University Library Chronicle*, Vol. XIV, No. 1, Autumn 1952, pp. 47–49.

'A.M.' 'The Rod, the Root and the Flower' (review), *The Bookman*, Vol. VIII, No. 46, July 1895, pp. 110–111. (Internal evidence makes it certain that this is *not* by Alice Meynell.)

Anselm, Father, O.S.F.C. 'The Late Mr. Coventry Patmore', *The Annals*, January 1897.

Barnes, William. 'Coventry Patmore's Poetry' (review of *The Angel in the House*), *Fraser's Magazine*, July 1863.

Baum, Paull Franklin. 'Coventry Patmore's Literary Criticism', *University of California Chronicle*, Vol. XXV, 1923, pp. 244–260.

Blunden, Edmund. 'Coventry Patmore 1823–1896', *The Saturday Book, Sixth Year*, edited by Leonard Russell (Hutchinson, 1946), pp. 128–134.

Bradley, Rev. Francis H. 'Coventry Patmore', *Revue de l'Université d'Ottawa*, Vol. VI, No. 3, Juillet–Septembre 1936, pp. 305–319.

Brégy, Katherine. 'Coventry Patmore': Part I, *The Catholic World*, Vol. XC, No. 540, March 1910, pp. 796–806; Part II, *The Catholic World*, Vol. XCI, No. 541, April 1910, pp. 14–27 (subsequently printed as a chapter of *The Poet's Chantry*, *q.v.*).

Burdett, Osbert. 'Coventry Patmore', *The Dublin Review*, Vol. 165, No. 331, October, November, December, 1919, pp. 245–260.

'Coventry Patmore (1823–96)', *The London Mercury*, Vol. VIII, No. 45, July 1923, pp. 279–291.

Bibliography

Chapman, Paul M. D., F.R.C.P. 'A Reminiscence of Coventry Patmore', *The Nineteenth Century and After*, Vol. LVI, No. CCCXXXII, October 1904, pp. 668–674.

Christmas, F. E. 'The Loves of Coventry Patmore', *John O'London's Weekly*, Vol. LVIII, No. 1361, April 29, 1949, p. 271.

Cohen, J. M. 'Prophet Without Responsibility: A Study in Coventry Patmore's Poetry', *Essays in Criticism*, Vol. I, No. 3, July 1951 (Basil Blackwell), pp. 283–297.

Connolly, Terence L. Review of Oxford University Press Edition of *Coventry Patmore's Poems*, 1951, and of Derek Patmore's *Life and Times of Coventry Patmore*. *Thought*, Vol. XXVI, No. 101, Summer 1951, pp. 317–319.

Cotterell, George. 'The Unknown Eros', *The Academy*, No. 964, October 25, 1890, pp. 358–359.

Crawford, Virginia M. 'Coventry Patmore', *The Fortnightly Review*, Vol. LXXV, No. CCCCX, February 1, 1901, pp. 304–311.

De Vere, Aubrey. 'The Angel in the House', *The Edinburgh Review*, Vol. CVII, No. 217, January 1858, pp. 121–133 (unsigned).

Downing, Eleanor A. 'Patmore's Philosophy of Love': (1) 'The Unknown Eros', *Thought*, Fordham University Quarterly, Voi. VIII, No. 4, March 1934, pp. 627–641; (2) 'The Unknown Eros', *Thought*, Vol. IX, No. 1, June 1934, pp. 62–77.

Dowden, Edward. 'The Unknown Eros and other Odes: Odes I–XXXI', *The Academy*, Saturday, April 28, 1877, No. 260, New Series, pp. 359–360.

Egan, Maurice F. 'The Ode Structure of Coventry Patmore', *Catholic University Bulletin*, Vol. V, No. 1, January 1899 (Catholic University of America, Washington, D.C.), pp. 3–21.

E.G.J. 'Coventry Patmore, His Relatives and Friends', *The Dial*, Vol. XXX, No. 350, January 16, 1901, pp. 37–39.

Fleming, W. K. 'Coventry Patmore', *Life and Letters*, Vol. IV, No. 1, January 1930, pp. 27–40.

Freeman, John. 'The Ideas of Coventry Patmore', *The Academy*, No. 1884, June 13, 1908, pp. 879–880.

'The Poetry of Coventry Patmore', *The Academy*, No. 1887, July 4, 1908, pp. 37–39.

'Coventry Patmore', *The Bookman*, Vol. LXIV, No. 382, July 1923, pp. 175–177.

'Coventry Patmore', *The Quarterly Review*, Vol. 240, No. 476, July 1923, pp. 123–135.

Gardner, W. H. 'The Achievement of Coventry Patmore': (1) 'The Early Poems', *The Month*, Vol. 7, No. 2, February 1952, pp. 89–98: (2) 'The Prose and Later Poems', *The Month*, Vol. 7, No. 4, pp. 220–230, April 1952.

Garnett, Richard. 'Poetry, Prose and Mr. Patmore' (review of *Faithful For Ever*), *Macmillan's Magazine*, Vol. III, December 1860, pp. 121–130.

'Mr. Coventry Patmore' ('Living Critics', No. V), *The Bookman*, Vol. IX, No. 54, March 1896, pp. 180–182.

'Recollections of Coventry Patmore', *The Saturday Review*, Vol. 82, No. 2145, December 5, 1896, pp. 582–583.

'Coventry Patmore', *Dictionary of National Biography* (Oxford University Press), Supplement, Volume XXII, 1901, pp. 1121–1124.

Garvin, Louis. 'Coventry Patmore: The Praise of the Odes', *The Fortnightly Review*, Vol. LXI, New Series, No. CCCLXII, February 1, 1897, pp. 207–217.

Gosse, Edmund. 'Poems by Coventry Patmore' (a review of the 1886 Collective Edition), *The Athenaeum*, No. 3059, June 12, 1886, pp. 771–772.

'Mr. Patmore's Poems' (review of the 1886 Collective Edition), *The Saturday Review*, Vol. 61, No. 1599, June 19, 1886, pp. 863–864.

'Coventry Patmore: A Portrait', *The Contemporary Review*, Vol. LXXI, February 1897, pp. 184–204.

'The History of a Poem', *The North American Review*, No. CCCLXXX-IV, March 1897, pp. 283–293.

Greenhalgh, Norman. 'Coventry Patmore—A Mid-Victorian Minor (1823–96)', *The London Quarterly and Holborn Review*, Vol. CLXXII, No. 1, January 1947, pp. 51–55.

Greenwood, Frederick. 'Coventry Patmore', *Blackwood's Edinburgh Magazine*, Vol. CLXXVII, No. MLXXVI, June 1905, pp. 812–823.

'G-Y'. 'Religio Poetae', *The Bookman*, Vol. IV, No. 22, July 1893, pp. 117–118.

Haddow, G. C. 'A Neglected Poet', *Queen's Quarterly*, Queen's University, Kingston, Vol. XXI, No. 3, January–March 1924, pp. 289–297.

Harper, A. E. 'Coventry Patmore, Poet and Realist', *Holborn Review*, April 1929, pp. 145–154.

Heinrich, G. 'Coventry Patmore: der Dichter der ehelichen Liebe', *Hochland*, Vol. XXIX, No. 8, 1931–1932, pp. 149–167.

Léger, Augustin. 'Le Poète de l'Amour—Coventry Patmore', *Le Correspondant*, Vol. 203; N. S. Vol. 167, No. 2, April 25, 1901, pp. 287–306.

'The Looker-On'. *Blackwood's Edinburgh Magazine*, Vol. CLXIII, No. DCCCCLXXXIV, March 1898, pp. 436–437.

Lubbock, Percy. 'Coventry Patmore', *The Quarterly Review*, Vol. 208, No. 415, April 1908, pp. 356–376.

MacColl, D. S. 'Patmore and Hopkins: Sense and Nonsense in English Prosody', *The London Mercury*, Vol. XXXVIII, No. 225, July 1938, pp. 217–224.

Maynard, Theodore. 'Coventry Patmore (1823–1896)', *The Freeman*, N.Y., Vol. VIII, No. 184, September 19, 1923, pp. 32–34.

'Coventry Patmore's Doctrine of Love', *Thought*, Fordham University Quarterly, Vol. XX, No. 78, September 1945, pp. 499–518.

Meynell, Alice. ''Twixt Anacreon and Plato', *Merry England*, December 1885, pp. 69–80.

'Coventry Patmore', *Catholic Encyclopedia* (Robert Appleton Co., N.Y.), Vol. XI, 1911, pp. 546–547.

Meynell, Wilfred (?). 'Coventry Patmore', *The Academy*, No. 1283, December 5, 1896, pp. 496–497 (signed 'W.M.').

Morse, James Herbert. 'Coventry Patmore', *The Critic*, New York, Vol. XXVI, No. 772, December 5, 1896, pp. 365–366.

O'Keeffe, Rev. Henry E., C.S.P. 'Coventry Patmore', *The Catholic World*, Vol. LXIX, No. 413, August 1899, pp. 646–662.

O'Rourke, Rev. James. 'Coventry Patmore', *Irish Ecclesiastical Record*, Vol. XXXVII, No. 4, April 1931, pp. 379–390.

Page, Frederick.—'A Neglected Great Poem—Patmore's "Tamerton Church-Tower"', *The Catholic World*, Vol. XCV, No. 568, July 1912, pp. 508–515.

'Coventry Patmore's "Unknown Eros"', *The Catholic World*, Vol. CV, No. 630, September 1917, pp. 775–785.

'Coventry Patmore—Points of View', *The Catholic World*, Vol. CXIII, No. 675, June 1921, pp. 380–388.

'The Centenary of Coventry Patmore', *The Dublin Review*, Vol. 173, No. 346, July 1923, pp. 24–37.

Patmore, Derek. 'The Poetry of Coventry Patmore' (report of an address), *Carmina*, a Monthly Review devoted to poetry, No. 9, 1931.

'Coventry Patmore' (review of Page's *Patmore—A Study in Poetry*), *The Bookman*, Vol. LXXXV, No. 509, February 1934, pp. 450–451.

'Coventry Patmore and Robert Bridges—Some Letters', *The Fortnightly*, No. 975, New Series, March 1948, p. 198.

'Three Poets Discuss New Verse Forms', *The Month*, Vol. CXCII, No. 1008, August 1951, pp. 69–78.

Patmore, Francis J. 'Coventry Patmore: A Son's Recollections', *English Review*, Vol. LIV, February 1932, pp. 135–141.

Patmore, J. Deighton. 'Some Childish Recollections of Coventry Patmore', *The Bookman*, Vol. LXXXII, No. 487, April 1932, pp. 57–58.

'Price, Frances' (Frederick Page). 'Patmore and the Oxymoron', *Notes and Queries*, August 29, 1942, pp. 124–125.

'Osbert Burdett and Patmore', *Notes and Queries*, January 30, 1943, p. 76.

'The Novelists' Material', *Notes and Queries*, February 13, 1943, pp. 105–106.

'The Prose of Coventry Patmore', *Notes and Queries*, July 17, 1943, pp. 40–41; August 14, 1943, pp. 105–106.

'Patmore: an Unreprinted Sonnet', *Notes and Queries*, November 6, 1943, p. 289.

'A Topographical Poem', *Notes and Queries*, February 26, 1944, p. 114.

'Patmore, Stevenson, and Cordelia', *Notes and Queries*, July 1, 1944, p. 15.

Quennell, Peter. 'Coventry Patmore' (review of Derek Patmore's *Life and Times of Coventry Patmore*), *New Statesman and Nation*, Vol. XXXVII, No. 947, April 30, 1949, pp. 445–446.

Shuster, George N. 'Patmore: A Revaluation', *Commonweal*, Vol. XXIV, No. 26, October 23, 1936, pp. 604–606.

Stoddard, R. H. 'Coventry Patmore—A Note', *The Book-Buyer*, New York, Vol. XIII, No. 12, January 1897, pp. 970–971.

Symons, Arthur. 'Religio Poetae', *The Athenaeum*, No. 3453, December 30, 1893, pp. 902–903 (unsigned, authorship indicated by letter from Coventry Patmore quoted by Symons in *Figures of Several Centuries*, p. 364).

'Coventry Patmore', *North American Review*, Vol. CCXI, No. 1, February 1920, pp. 266–272 (this essay reprinted from *Studies in Two Literatures*).

Thompson, Francis. 'Coventry Patmore' (review of B. Champneys' *Memoirs*, unsigned), *The Academy*, No. 1487, November 3, 1900, pp. 399–400.

'Coventry Patmore by Edmund Gosse', *The Athenaeum*, No. 4048, April 1, 1905, pp. 389–90 (unsigned).

'The Early Patmore', *The Academy*, No. 1635, September 5, 1903, pp. 214–215 (unsigned, authorship by internal evidence: repetition of phrases in *Athenaeum* article of April 1, 1905).

Times Literary Supplement. Correspondence on Coventry Patmore, May and June, 1932. May 12: Clifford Bax on Patmore and Ford. May 19: John Eglinton on Coventry Patmore's house and grave. May 26: Osbert Burdett on dramatic qualities of Coventry Patmore's verse. May 26 : W. K. Lowther Clarke on Coventry Patmore's house. June 2 : St. Clair Baddeley on Coventry Patmore's house; Basil Champneys on Coventry Patmore's house. June 9 : Basil Champneys on Coventry Patmore's house. June 23 : Derek Patmore on 'neglect' of Patmore.

Trobridge, George. 'Coventry Patmore and Swedenborg', *The Westminster Review*, Vol. CLXV, No. 1, January 1906, pp. 76–90.

Turner, Paul. 'Aurora versus The Angel', *Review of English Studies*, Vol. XXIV, No. 93, January 1948, pp. 227–235.

Ubald, P., and Claudel, Paul. 'Coventry Patmore, T. O. (1823–1896)', *Etudes Franciscaines*, Librairie Saint-Francais, Paris, Tome XXXI, No. 182, Février 1914 (includes Claudel's 'Lettre sur Coventry Patmore', *q.v.*).

Warren, C. Henry. 'A Most Eminent Victorian' (review of *Selected Poems of Coventry Patmore*, edited by Derek Patmore), *The Bookman*, Vol. LXXX, No. 476, May 1931, p. 111.

Waugh, Arthur. 'London Letter' (an obituary of Coventry Patmore), *The Critic*, Vol. XXVI, No. 773, December 12, 1896, p. 391.

Wheaton, L. 'Psyche and the Prophet', *The Catholic World*, Vol. CXVIII, No. 705, December 1925, pp. 355–366.

VII. *Patmore's Family*

Anonymous. 'The Angel in the House—Emily Augusta Patmore', *The Bookman*, Vol. III, No. 13, October 1892, pp. 12–14.

Eaton, Vincent T. 'The First Mrs. Patmore', *The Catholic World*, Vol. 164, October 1946, pp. 53–56.

Nicholl, W. Robertson, and Wise, Thomas J. (editors). *Literary Anecdotes of the Nineteenth Century* (New York: Dodd, Mead & Co.), 1896: 'The Angel in the House: Emily Augusta Patmore', pp. 377–384.

Gwynn, Aubrey. 'A Daughter of Coventry Patmore', *Studies*, An Irish Quarterly Review, Vol. XIII, No. 51, September 1924, pp. 443–456.

A Religious of the Society of the Holy Child Jesus. *A Daughter of Coventry Patmore: Sister Mary Christina, S.H.C.J.* (with a foreword by Rt. Rev. Dom Anscar Vonier, O.S.B.) (Longmans, Green & Co.), 1924.

Wheaton, L. 'Emily Honoria Patmore', *Dublin Review*, Vol. 163, No. 327, October–December 1918, pp. 207–233.

Patmore, Henry. *Poems*, Oxford, 1884.

Patmore, Peter George. *Chatsworth, or, The Romance of a Week* (Henry Colburn), 1844.

Index

347

Index

Index of References to, and Quotations from, Patmore's Works

POETRY

355

PROSE